RICHARD E. NORMAN AND RACE FILMMAKING

RICHARD E. NORMAN
AND
RACE FILMMAKING

Barbara Tepa Lupack

Foreword by Michael T. Martin

INDIANA UNIVERSITY PRESS   *Bloomington & Indianapolis*

This book is a publication of

INDIANA UNIVERSITY PRESS
Office of Scholarly Publishing
Herman B Wells Library 350
1320 East 10th Street
Bloomington, Indiana 47405 USA

iupress.indiana.edu

Telephone orders   800-842-6796
Fax orders   812-855-7931

© 2014 by Barbara Tepa Lupack

⊖ The paper used in this publication
meets the minimum requirements of
the American National Standard for
Information Sciences—Permanence of
Paper for Printed Library Materials,
ANSI Z39.48-1992.

*Manufactured in the
United States of America*

*Cataloging information is available
from the Library of Congress.*

ISBN 978-0-253-01064-3 (paper)
ISBN 978-0-253-01056-8 (cloth)
ISBN 978-0-253-01072-8 (e-book)

1 2 3 4 5   18 17 16 15 14

In loving memory of my parents,
George and Jane Tepa

and,
as always,
for Al
"an ever-fixed mark,
that looks on tempests and is never shaken"

CONTENTS

FOREWORD

BY MICHAEL T. MARTIN

THE TURN OF the nineteenth century into the twentieth marked a period of political upheaval and indeterminacy in the United States and world. Correspondingly, it gave rise to artistic and cultural renewal and invention, and it was the formative cinematic moment in the long history and struggle for black representation. Prefigured by defining cultural precedents of racial disparagement, reductive and demeaning archetypes were first evinced in literature, popular lore, minstrels, encyclopedic entries endorsed by the scientific community, illustrations in venerated national digests, and the ramblings and rants that passed for raced discourses of the day. These memorialized artifacts of popularized beliefs in the cultural marketplace of the early twentieth century framed debates about the "Negro problem" during the era of mass entertainment and "public amusements" and endure to this day in the national psyche; however many presumptions of a post-racial America suggest otherwise.[1]

In counterpoint, consider that from 1909 to 1948 more than 150 independent companies endeavored to make, distribute, and exhibit race movies—that distinctive aggregate of films crossing all manner of genres and that, oriented to and shown largely in segregated movie theaters, featured all-black casts.[2] Ironically a palliative to Jim Crow and an implicit challenge to black disenfranchisement, such movies engaged with the spectrum of African American life and experience and constitute the first counter-historical readings in American cinema.[3] Moreover, and arguably, as they comprised a range of visual and narrative styles, artisanal modes of production, and a fluid division of labor, these early productions bore traces of what would later become an African American cinematic tradition.

Among the few successful companies in the "race film business" were the Lincoln Motion Picture Company and the Micheaux Picture ["Film"] Corporation. However, in the archive of "race" companies too little is said for the Norman Film Manufacturing Company and, even less so, its founder, entrepreneur, producer, distributor, and exhibitor Richard E. Norman. Perhaps this motive suffices for a renewed consideration and revaluation of Norman's contribution to race filmmaking.[4]

A seasoned scholar, at ease and adept with historical methods, Barbara Tepa Lupack in her engaging study, *Richard E. Norman and Race Filmmaking*, renders an original and compelling case for this unique figure and his foundational contribution to race filmmaking, as she economically sets out and explicates in the opening chapters the terrain and defining events of early twentieth-century America. And, while a corrective to the lacuna extant in the literature, Lupack's interventions illuminate race filmmaking as a distinctive, although fraught, biracial enterprise that reflexively challenged totalizing narratives of race in popular culture and society.

I should say that I am not without prejudice regarding the address of this book, notwithstanding that it merits further and more critical deliberation, as well as consideration by the public. I anticipate that its publication and favorable review will cause considerably more attention to the Norman Collection housed in the Black Film Center/Archive and Lilly Library at Indiana University and, in doing so, enhance the collection's utility.

Among the book's virtues, salience, and robust claims consider this: Unpacking the racial and historical circumstance of race filmmaking, Lupack maps Norman's ascent (and descent) in the film business, his entrepreneurial acumen, ingenuity, and design for diverse black viewing audiences.

Her detailed back story accounts of the production of Norman's feature films in the order they were made suggests as much, as they reveal race movies' social value for black audiences.

No less important, Lupack's claims are largely in agreement with the essential argument in Jacqueline Stewart's seminal study that race movies performed a "crucial role in the process of modernization and urbanization of blacks."[5] While no doubt the case, it must be said that the African American encounter with modernity and urban life was neither unproblematic in the material world nor in the evolution of race movies, as it would later become in the 1970s. A case in point is Spencer Williams's film, *The Blood of Jesus* (1941), where the underbelly of modernity and black urban communities are depicted as sites of corruption and spiritual decay. And later still, in her masterwork, *Daughters of the Dust* (1991), Julie Dash anticipates rural African Americans' encounter with modernity and urbanization by the crossing of the Peazant family to the mainland—an exodus fraught with dangers that will test the fortunes and fate of the family as it presumably will fragment and disperse in towns and cities that await to rob them of their identities, along with their spirituality and folklore traditions.

We can add to the profile and public record, Norman's apparent rejection of—and his however unsuccessful—challenge to Hollywood's major studios and their complicity in American racism. Like Micheaux—with which some comparisons pertain—and in contradistinction to those demeaning portrayals of the day, Norman endowed protagonists with agency from subject positions black audiences could identify with and believe in.

In this very important regard, Norman's films deploy what David Wall and I refer to as class 2 *cine-memories* that contest dominant discourses, recuperate and critique accounts of the past, or that reconstitute the narratives of marginalized communities. Such films work in the service of a project of recovery and renewal to change the way history and human experience is read by audiences. And for race movies, their historical task and contribution we can argue was to represent the "New Negro" as a protagonist in history.[6]

I conclude with this: while certainly not a "movement" formalized by manifestoes and programmatic declarations, race movies pioneered a tradition of oppositional cinema that would decades later favor African Americans' screen images and portrayals in the long and continuing struggle for black representation.

And with Lupack's account, Richard E. Norman's place in that history of early race filmmaking is now assured.

ACKNOWLEDGMENTS

I AM DEEPLY indebted to a host of people in the research and writing of *Richard E. Norman and Race Filmmaking*.

The book would not have been possible without the generous assistance of the Norman family. Captain Richard E. Norman, son of Richard E. Norman, allowed me access to—and granted me permission to quote from and reprint a number of—his father's papers at the Lilly Library and the Black Film Center/Archive at Indiana University in Bloomington. A virtual treasure trove of information for scholars and film enthusiasts, those papers shed much new light on a vital and exciting era of filmmaking. Captain Norman also graciously shared his recollections and steered me to some outstanding resources, especially the Norman Studios Silent Film Museum, of which he is an active and founding member.

Mrs. Katherine Norman Hiett, daughter of Kenneth Bruce Norman, generously made available to me a number of family photographs and shared with me personal recollections, correspondence, and a very helpful genealogy.

I am also grateful to the Lilly Library at Indiana University in Bloomington, where—as Everett Helm Visiting Fellow in late spring 2011—I was able to conduct research on-site in the Richard E. Norman Collection.

Dr. Breon Mitchell, Director, and the entire administration and staff made me feel welcome and helped me to negotiate the Lilly's holdings. Especially generous with their time and their expertise were Dave Frasier and Zach Downey, who shared my enthusiasm for the project and who assisted me not only while I was in Bloomington but also afterward, when I requested additional materials that allowed me to complete the manuscript.

At the Black Film Center/Archive at Indiana University in Bloomington, I was also fortunate to have access to the Richard E. Norman Special Collection. Mary K. Huelsbeck, who was then Archivist and Head of Public and Technology Services at the BFC/A (and who is currently Assistant Director of the Wisconsin Center for Film and Theater Research), offered me invaluable assistance while I was at the BFC/A and in the months since then. She was, quite simply, a force of nature; I could not have accomplished as much as I did on-site without her help.

Dr. Michael T. Martin, Director of the Black Film Center/Archive, was immensely supportive of the project from its inception and has continued to offer encouragement throughout. Dr. Martin's suggestions were crucial to me in sharpening my approach to race films and in completing revisions of the manuscript. Also, BFC/A Graduate Assistants Gabriel Gardner and Stacey Doyle lent much assistance. Stacey scanned some of the images that appear in the volume and responded to numerous questions about the manuscript materials.

The Norman Studios Silent Film Museum in Jacksonville, Florida, performs an essential service in preserving and celebrating early film culture. From the outset, the NSSFM has promoted and encouraged my study of Norman and provided valuable materials and information. I am especially grateful to Devan Stuart, Chair of the Board of Directors and Director of Media and Publicity, who replied to my many inquiries with grace and good humor, shared with me some of the museum's unique resources, provided images, and generally offered me tremendous support. Rita Reagan, Historian and Director of Community and Education Outreach, also offered assistance and encouragement, as did Anthony Hodge, Board Co-Chair.

At the Autry National Center in Los Angeles, Marva R. Felchlin, Director of the Autry Library and Archives at the Autry Institute, answered my numerous questions and made available to me some scarce early Norman materials. Conducting research off-site can be an almost insurmountable challenge, but she made the process feel virtually seamless, for which I am particularly grateful. Also at the Autry, Marilyn Kim, Coordinator of Rights and Reproduction, graciously facilitated permissions and reprint rights, which allowed me to include some unique and valuable materials in the book.

John Kisch, founder and Director of Separate Cinema, co-author of *A Separate Cinema: 50 Years of Black Cast Posters*, and a pioneer in preserving black film culture, kindly offered to share with me some of the many rare and interesting images in his collection. He has long been supportive of my work, and for that too I thank him.

Once again, the University of Rochester's Rush Rhees Library afforded me access to necessary reference material. At the Cummer Museum of Art and Gardens in Jacksonville, Florida, Kristen Zimmerman, Registrar, provided information about Norman items in the museum's collections. I am grateful to the friends and colleagues who read portions of the manuscript or offered suggestions for its improvement. I am also grateful to the University of Rochester Press, publisher of my *Literary Adaptations in Black American Cinema: From Micheaux to Morrison* (2002; revised and expanded 2010); some of the ideas in the first chapter of this volume were first explored, in a different form, in that study.

As always, my greatest debt is to my husband, Al. His editorial judgments are sensitive and sound; and, more importantly, his support is boundless.

My own ideas about race films and filmmaking were shaped and influenced by the work of numerous film scholars and critics, to whom I am much indebted. Foremost among them are the pioneers of black film studies: Thomas Cripps, whose prolific work on race film (including *Slow Fade to Black* and *Making Movies Black*) has informed generations of scholars and film enthusiasts; Henry T. Sampson, whose *Blacks in Black and White* remains a comprehensive source and invaluable resource; Phyllis R. Klotman, whose extensive filmographies, especially *Frame by Frame*, provide vital information for researchers; Daniel J. Leab, whose study *From Sambo to Superspade* is certainly a classic; and Donald Bogle, whose *Toms, Coons,*

Mulattoes, Mammies & Bucks is required reading, as are his more recent studies.

For their influential work, both past and current, I am grateful as well to a number of other black film and culture critics: Peter Noble, Jim Pines, James P. Murray, Edward Mapp, Lindsay Patterson, V. J. Jerome, James Snead, Toni Cade Bambera, Clyde Taylor, Manthia Diawara, Gladstone Yearwood, bell hooks, Mark Reid, Ed Guerrero, Valerie Smith, Michele Wallace, Gerald R. Butters Jr., Davarian L. Baldwin, Anna Everett, and Jacqueline Najuma Stewart.

Among scholars of Micheaux and of other silent and early black film-makers, groundbreaking work has been published by Charles Musser, J. Ronald Green, Charlene Regester, Jane Gaines, Pearl Bowser, Louise Spence, and Patrick McGilligan. Articles by Phyllis Klotman, Matthew Bernstein, Dana F. White, and Gloria Gibson-Hudson have stirred interest in Norman and his work and offered me an excellent starting point.

Since so few early race films—and even fewer firsthand accounts of that era—survive, the oral record of George P. Johnson, brother of Noble Johnson and co-founder of the Lincoln Motion Picture Company, is especially significant. A special collection in the Young Research Library at the University of California–Los Angeles, the Johnson papers and recordings are an extraordinary resource for scholars, researchers, and film buffs alike.

Last but certainly not least, I am grateful to everyone at Indiana University Press, especially Bob Sloan, Raina Polivka, Jenna Whittaker, Angela Burton, and Candace McNulty.

AUTHOR'S NOTE

In the primary materials cited in this book—including Richard E. Norman's personal and professional correspondence, notes, distribution records, scripts, heralds, press sheets, pressbooks, mailers, promotional materials, and advertising—the original wording, spelling, and punctuation have been deliberately preserved, even when they are inconsistent or incorrect. Except in a few cases, quotations from the correspondence and citations from the scripts and other primary materials appear without [*sic*] and without correction.

ABBREVIATIONS

LIBRARIES/ARCHIVES

LL Lilly Library, Indiana University, Bloomington, Indiana

BFC Black Film Center/Archive, Indiana University, Bloomington, Indiana

OR Oral Record, George P. Johnson Collection, Department of Special Collections, Charles E. Young Research Library, University of California–Los Angeles

Autry Autry National Center, Los Angeles, California

BOOKS/ARTICLES

"African-American Press" Charlene Regester, "The African-American Press and Race Movies, 1909–1929." In *Oscar Micheaux and His Circle*. Ed. Pearl Bowser, Jane Gaines, and Charles Musser. Bloomington: Indiana University Press, 2001.

BBW Henry T. Sampson, *Blacks in Black and White: A Source Book on Black Films,* 2nd edition. Lanham, Maryland: Scarecrow Press, 1995.

BF Jim Pines, *Blacks in Films: A Survey of Racial Themes and Images in the American Film.* London: Studio Vista/Cassell & Collier Macmillan, 1975.

BFG Thomas Cripps, *Black Film as Genre.* Bloomington: Indiana University Press, 1977.

BMSS Gerald R. Butters Jr., *Black Manhood on the Silent Screen.* Lawrence: University Press of Kansas, 2002.

CNN Davarian L. Baldwin, *Chicago's New Negroes: Modernity, The Great Migration, and Black Urban Life.* Chapel Hill: University of North Carolina Press, 2007.

FAMPI Richard Alan Nelson, *Florida and the American Motion Picture Industry, 1898–1980.* Two volumes. New York: Garland, 1983.

FD Jane Gaines, *Fire and Desire: Mixed-Race Movies in the Silent Era.* Chicago: University of Chicago Press, 2001.

FH Shawn C. Bean, *The First Hollywood: Florida and the Golden Age of Silent Filmmaking.* Gainesville: University Press of Florida, 2008.

FSS Daniel J. Leab, *From Sambo to Superspade: The Black Experience in Motion Pictures.* Boston: Houghton Mifflin, 1975.

"Making" Thomas Cripps, "The Making of *The Birth of a Race:* The Emerging Politics of Identity in Silent Movies." In *The Birth of Whiteness: Race and the Emergence of U. S. Cinema.* Ed. Daniel Bernardi. New Brunswick: Rutgers University Press, 1996.

MM   Jacqueline Najuma Stewart, *Migrating to the Movies: Cinema and Black Urban Modernity.* Berkeley: University of California Press, 2005.

MMB   Thomas Cripps, *Making Movies Black: The Hollywood Message Movie from World War II to the Civil Rights Era.* New York: Oxford University Press, 1993.

"Planes"   Phyllis R. Klotman, "Planes, Trains, and Automobiles: *The Flying Ace,* the Norman Company, and the Micheaux Connection." In *Oscar Micheaux and His Circle: African-American Filmmaking and Race Cinema of the Silent Era.* Ed. Pearl Bowser, Jane Gaines, and Charles Musser. Bloomington: University of Indiana Press, 2001.

"Race Movies"   Thomas Cripps, "'Race Movies' as Voices of the Black Bourgeoisie: *The Scar of Shame.*" In Valerie Smith, *Representing Blackness: Issues in Film and Video.* New Brunswick: Rutgers University Press, 1997.

PRC   Linda Williams, *Playing the Race Card: Melodramas of Black and White from Uncle Tom to O. J. Simpson.* Princeton: Princeton University Press, 2001.

RBF   Mark A. Reid, *Redefining Black Film.* Berkeley: University of California Press, 1993.

RG   Anna Everett, *Returning the Gaze: A Genealogy of Black Film Criticism, 1909–1949.* Durham: Duke University Press, 2001.

"Scratching"   Matthew Bernstein and Dana F. White, "'Scratching Around' in a 'Fit of Insanity': The Norman Film Manufacturing Company and the Race Film Business in the 1920s," *Griffithiana* 21: 62–63 (May 1998): 81–127.

SFB   Thomas Cripps, *Slow Fade to Black:*
The Negro in American Film, 1900–1942.
New York: Oxford University Press, 1977.

TCMMB   Donald Bogle, *Toms, Coons, Mulattoes,*
Mammies, & Blacks: An Interpretive History
of Blacks in American Films. New 3rd edition.
New York: Continuum, 1994.

WHH   Pearl Bowser and Louise Spence, *Writing*
Himself into History: Oscar Micheaux,
His Silent Films, and His Audiences. New
Brunswick: Rutgers University Press, 2001.

WSBI   James Snead, *White Screens, Black Images:*
Hollywood from the Dark Side. New York:
Routledge, 1994.

RICHARD E. NORMAN AND RACE FILMMAKING

 Introduction: New Visions
of Opportunity

A UNIQUE AND important figure in the movie industry,
Richard E. Norman (1891–1960) is best remembered for the popular black-
cast, black-oriented feature films he produced between 1919 and 1928. To
appreciate fully Norman's landmark contribution to American cinema
culture and history, however, is to understand the social and racial environment in which he worked and which, in turn, shaped his cinematic vision.

The early decades of the twentieth century were, André Gaudreault
writes, an era in which "America joined the rush for imperial spheres of
control," when recent immigration "seemed to change the nature and appearance of American society, and when the industrial might of the United
States established the nation's position as the upcoming if not the dominant
economic power in the world."[1] For black Americans in particular, it was a
time of great hope, great change, and great challenge. The return of white
supremacy and the steady disenfranchisement of black voters through
grandfather clauses, poll taxes, literacy tests, residency requirements, and
other restrictive practices around the turn of the century crushed blacks'
hopes for political change at the ballot box, while the reemergence of the
Ku Klux Klan reinforced their sense of helplessness in the face of brutal racial injustice. Originally formed during Reconstruction to suppress Radi-

cal Republicans, the Klan had virtually disbanded after Southern whites regained ascendancy and drove blacks off the voting rolls.[2] But it was reestablished in 1915 by Atlantan William J. Simmons, its fires of hatred fanned by D. W. Griffith's venomously racist film *The Birth of a Nation* released that same year (and reputed to be the new Klan's most effective recruiting tool). The KKK soon evolved into a national organization that claimed a membership, by the mid-1920s, of four to five million.

Lynching, a way of exercising social control by reasserting white dominance, became the Klan's most public and sensational method of terror. It was, as Amy Louise Wood demonstrates, deliberately performative and ritualized, "through displays of lynched bodies and souvenirs, as well as through representations of the violence that circulated long after the lynchings themselves were over: photographs and other visual imagery, ballads and songs, news accounts and lurid narratives."[3] By one report, lynch mobs murdered 1,985 blacks between 1882 and 1903; and according to Tuskegee Institute records, an average of sixty-six lynchings occurred annually between 1900 and 1925. Throughout the South and even in states as far west as Nebraska and California and as far north as Indiana and Illinois, innocent black men, women, and even children were hanged, tortured, or burned alive; black homes and businesses were destroyed; and thousands without legal protection or recourse were driven out of town.

Even the Supreme Court contributed to the racial division. With its *Plessy v. Ferguson* decision of 1896, the Court upheld the constitutionality of state laws that provided "separate but equal" accommodations for blacks, a precedent that aided the spread of segregation in public places and on public transportation throughout the nation and encouraged other legislation that codified racial discrimination. The Jim Crow laws—named for a racist nineteenth-century minstrel song written and performed in blackface by white actor Thomas Dartmouth "Daddy" Rice—ensured that the separation of races was observed in restaurants, hotels, railroad stations, schools, parks, beaches, cemeteries, even brothels. Courts, in fact, used different Bibles to swear in whites and people of color.[4]

Recognizing the need to pursue political remedies both locally and nationally, blacks began to seek leadership roles in their own communities and, by the late 1920s, in Congress as well. They founded and published newspapers, including the influential *Chicago Defender* and the *New York Age*, and formed vital and enduring civic and protest organizations that championed black causes and mobilized dissent. The National Negro Business League (1900), for instance, was founded by Booker T. Washington to advance "the financial and commercial development of the Negro"; the National Association for the Advancement of Colored People (1909), which grew out of W. E. B. Du Bois's earlier Niagara Movement for the recognition of the principles of "human brotherhood," promoted racial justice through its campaigns for equality and universal suffrage; and the National Urban League (1910) maintained job and housing registries and offered other vital services to needy Southern migrants.

Even as blacks protested their humiliating and inequitable treatment, they readily demonstrated their patriotism. *"First* your country, *then* your rights," Du Bois urged in the *Crisis,* the NAACP's periodical.[5] Heeding his directive to "close ranks" in support of the war effort, black families bought millions of dollars in Liberty Bonds; and young black men—who were prohibited from serving alongside white soldiers in the army, afforded only the most menial positions in the navy, and excluded entirely from the marines—nonetheless volunteered for military service. Although some politicians expressed concern about placing firearms in their hands, ultimately 380,000 blacks were drafted, and some 200,000 served in France, 42,000 as combatants. Notably, the black 369th Infantry Regiment (the Harlem Hellfighters), assigned to the French army, saw more days in combat than any other U.S. unit and was the first Allied unit to reach the Rhine. For their extraordinary bravery, the Hellfighters were awarded the prestigious *Croix de Guerre*—the only U.S. soldiers to receive that honor. But the democracy that they and other black troops fought for overseas was denied them once they returned home: in 1919, soldiers still in uniform were among the victims of lynching by whites who wanted to restore the prewar social order of race subservience.[6]

To escape the threat of mob violence and to avail themselves of wartime employment, better wages, and improved educational opportunities, hundreds of thousands of blacks left their traditional homes in the South for the promise of a better life in the big cities of the North. The Great Migration, which began in the 1890s and continued until the Depression of 1930 stemmed its tide, reached a climax during World War I. The largest internal migration since the exodus of blacks from the South to the Western territories after Reconstruction, it dramatically changed American culture and gave rise to a black middle class in search of what Alain Locke called "a new vision of opportunity." In Chicago, the black population rose from 44,000 in 1910 to almost 110,000 in 1920. That same decade, the number of black residents soared from 92,000 to 152,000 in New York and from 6,000 to 41,000 in Detroit. But the sudden mass influx of blacks (more than 500,000 between 1916 and 1919 alone)—compounded by the recent waves of eastern and southern Europeans who had emigrated under the prewar "open door" policy—only intensified prejudice, increased racial and economic pressure, and created other social and cultural problems. Blacks typically found themselves ghettoized in areas like Chicago's South Side and New York's Harlem. Often at the mercy of white landlords, they were forced to endure overcrowding and unsanitary conditions in tenements formerly occupied by immigrants.[7]

Geographic segregation, however, did not prevent backlash and violence against the new arrivals. Race riots frequently ensued, though none more bloody than those initiated by whites in more than two dozen cities, from Illinois and New York to Georgia and Texas, during the summer and autumn of 1919. Resentment over the advancement of blacks, who had left behind the Southern cotton fields to assume positions in rapidly expanding industries such as railroads, steel mills, and auto plants and who were beginning to compete for other jobs traditionally held by white workers, combined with fear that black efforts to achieve racial equality might lead to a Bolshevik-like overthrow of the government. That fear was exacerbated not only by the press but also by President Woodrow Wilson himself, who asserted that returning "American Negro" soldiers might in fact be conveyers of that very bolshevism. Racial tensions exploded. During the six months of the "Red Summer" (so named by black activist and writer James Weldon Johnson), more than forty blacks were lynched, hundreds more were killed, thousands were injured in the attacks; and innumerable black families were left homeless.[8]

Much of the popular literature of the day attempted to mask the disturbing social realities with depictions of blacks as simple folk nostalgic for the "old ways" of the genteel South, as in the stories of Thomas Nelson Page. Alternatively, some blacks—as in the divisive and provocative novels of Thomas Dixon, later adapted to film by D. W. Griffith as *The Birth of a Nation*—were portrayed as vicious and misguided brutes who threatened an edenic land of mosses and magnolias and whose behavior demanded the restoration of the "natural" order. Other popular entertainments, such as the ubiquitous minstrel shows and Tom plays, operas, and parades that grossly distorted Harriet Beecher Stowe's abolitionist novel for comic effect, further glorified the plantation tradition as a model for the subjugation of blacks and reinforced the racist codes.

In fact, blacks were making enormous strides in education (at such prestigious institutions as Tuskegee, Hampton, and Howard); in science (through the groundbreaking work of women and men such as heart surgeon Dr. Daniel Hale Williams, botanist/inventor George Washington Carver, and surgeon and blood preservation pioneer Dr. Charles Drew, who went on to become the first director of the American Red Cross Blood Bank); and in the arts (in literature, through the poetry of Paul Laurence Dunbar and Langston Hughes, the novels of Charles Chesnutt and Jessie Fauset, and the folkloric tales of Zora Neale Hurston; in music, with such blues and jazz greats as Louis Armstrong, Duke Ellington, Fats Waller, and W. C. Handy; and in professional musical theater, with incomparable performers such as Ethel Waters, Bill "Bojangles" Robinson, and Eubie Blake). And the flourishing of a black renaissance that originated in Harlem gave rise to a new black aesthetic and to a vision of the "New Negro" as an outspoken advocate for race pride and equality, unwilling to tolerate Jim Crow discrimination.

Forging a strong black voice in the new medium of cinema, the most accessible and popular form of mass entertainment in the early twentieth century, proved considerably more complicated. "Most early filmmakers were white," Robert Jackson observed, "and simply participated in the life of their culture, absorbing and reflecting the racism—casual or vitriolic, conscious or intellectualized—of the era."[9] Consequently, although black characters had appeared on film almost from the beginnings of cinema in the 1890s, racial representation remained static and retrogressive. Typed in outrageous and demeaning caricatures that marginalized them, burlesqued their everyday lives, and emphasized their servile behavior, blacks appeared on screen as self-sacrificing Uncle Toms (such as the ubiquitous eponymous Tom in the numerous silent film versions of Stowe's novel produced between 1903 and 1927, or as the faithful house servant willing to give up his own freedom for his master in Griffith's numerous Civil War melodramas), dowdy devoted Mammies (often played by such fine but under-utilized actresses as Ethel Waters, Louise Beavers, and Hattie McDaniel, who virtually defined the role in *Gone with the Wind*), sexually aggressive "bucks" (like the depraved Gus, Griffith's "renegade Negro" and defiler of white Southern womanhood in *The Birth of a Nation*), exotic seductive temptresses (like Chick in *Hallelujah!*, Georgia Brown in *Cabin in the Sky*, and Carmen in *Carmen Jones*), doltish "coons" and "Sambos" (like the highly popular Stepin Fetchit and Willie "Sleep 'n Eat" Best), and mischievous "pickaninnies" (like *Our Gang*'s "Little Rascals" Buckwheat and Sunshine Sammy).[10]

The presence of black characters in many of the earliest pictures, moreover, constituted a form of black absence: in keeping with the old stage traditions, black roles were often performed by whites in outlandish costumes and heavy burnt cork make-up rather than by actual black actors—a practice that respected the sensibilities of white movie audiences, who insisted that even "reel" blacks observe the racial code. Using race and class division to exert control and domination, the white male in blackface served "the psychological function of reducing audience anxieties that might occur if real Negroes were used, especially in scenes of overt or covert sexual nature or when the Negro gets the upper hand over the white man." Playing on cross-racial desires, white moviegoers could therefore experience a perverse delight in watching a white actor perform transgressions associated with black behavior. Even on those occasions when blacks portrayed themselves in minstrel shows, vaudeville, and silent film, they usually had to don the exaggerated blackface make-up that marked them as clowns and buffoons since, as Daniel J. Leab explained, the filmmakers of the time, "a crude and pragmatic lot on the whole, accepted the prevailing beliefs about the limited abilities of the black and proceeded accordingly."[11] Early productions of a work such as *Othello*, in fact, typically featured white actors in the part of the Moor.

The degrading roles, by their very nature, relegated black performers to the background and contributed further to the sense of black erasure in cinema. In some cases, that erasure was literal: in parts of the South, for example, entire production numbers featuring black performers would be cut from films in order to placate white audiences who did not want to see black entertainers showcased in prominent roles. Similarly, the printed programs and publicity booklets distributed by the studios to promote their releases often excluded photographs of black actors, who might not even be listed in the production credits.[12]

Black absence also extended to the theaters where mainstream white films were shown. Since segregation practices ensured that most movie houses accommodated only white patrons, blacks were restricted to occasional off-hour movie screenings called "midnight rambles"; to the "Colored Only" sections of select theaters, which they entered and exited through separate doors away from the view of whites; or to black theaters, sometimes called race or ghetto theaters, which opened to accommodate the new black audiences but struggled financially to survive.[13] In fact, as late as 1929, when *Hallelujah!*, one of Hollywood's first all-black-cast musicals, was released in New York City, it premiered simultaneously at two very different venues: the downtown Embassy on Broadway for white filmgoers and the uptown Lafayette Theater in Harlem for blacks. The dual premiere allowed white audiences the comfort of watching scenes of black song, dance, and revivalist religion at a safe remove—that is, without having to engage with actual blacks. Discrimination was also evident in the disproportionately low salaries that many black actors were paid by the major studios and in the humiliating treatment they received, both on location, where they would be forced to seek substandard segregated accommodations, and on the lots, where they were consigned to special areas for their breaks and rarely allowed to socialize with their white co-stars.[14]

Early movies underscored the racial and social divide and reinforced the racist characterizations in other ways as well. Through their "repeatability," James Snead observed, movies "offprinted false racial models from celluloid onto mass consciousness again and again; real viewers came to expect unreal blacks on the screen and in the real world."[15] Not only in small communities throughout the United States where residents had never personally encountered blacks but also in countries throughout the world where American films were shown, the racially polarizing film imagery fixed in people's imagination the impressions of blacks as ludicrous figures "prone to frenzied dancing, shiftlessness, garish dress, gin tippling, dice shooting, torturing the language, and, inevitably, addicted to watermelon and chicken, usually stolen,"[16] who required the indulgence and the intervention of their white intellectual superiors. Unfortunately, lack of a strong visual past made it difficult for blacks to counter the gross distortions. It is little wonder, therefore, that black moviegoers found such early depictions offensive or that they sought out films that would speak to their particular cultural experiences and offer effective visual models of race ambition and uplift.

Those models would come in the new genre of pictures created in the 1910s and 1920s by independent race producers, who committed themselves to addressing the concerns of the neglected but steadily increasing black market. Curiously, perhaps, among the earliest and the best of those producers was a Southern-born white filmmaker: Richard E. Norman.

CHAPTER ONE

Race Matters: The Evolution of Race Filmmaking

[Instead of] a lot of slapstick, chicken-eating, watermelon Negro pictures like they had been making, . . . we made something that had never been made before . . . We were pioneers . . .

—George Johnson

EARLY RACE FILMMAKING is unquestionably the story of pioneers—pioneers like William D. Foster, the "Dean of Negro Motion Pictures," who foresaw a dynamic future for blacks in the film industry; Emmett J. Scott, a Tuskegee Institute official who struggled valiantly to produce a film in response to D. W. Griffith's vitriolic *The Birth of a Nation*; Noble and George Johnson, brothers and co-founders of the distinguished Lincoln Motion Picture Company, who produced high-quality pictures that promoted the ideology of race uplift; Robert Levy, the white founder of Reol Productions and the sponsor of the prestigious Lafayette Players, from whom many race filmmakers drew their casts; and Oscar Micheaux, the first black film *auteur* and the most prolific race producer of his day.[1]

Early race filmmaking is also the story of another pioneer, Richard E. Norman, who—though less well-known today than many of his contemporaries—was no less accomplished. An innovative white filmmaker who began his career as a traveling producer of white-cast "home talent" pictures in the Midwest, Norman moved his operation to Florida, then the country's moviemaking capital, in the late 1910s and began producing pictures for the underserved market of black filmgoers. The first and ultimately only independent race producer to own and operate his own studio, Norman released seven popular and successful feature films before the advent of sound pictures in the late 1920s forced him to curtail production. Those films were memorable not just for their thrilling plots and interesting locales but also for their casting of black actors in prominent, positive, and nonrestrictive roles.

Rather than just perpetuating crude and retrogressive representations, Norman and his fellow filmmakers determined to present realistic depictions of black Americans by creating an alternate set of cultural referents and establishing new black character types and situations, particularly those that reflected postwar social changes.[2] As George Johnson observed, unlike white moviegoers, who had long "based their idea of a Negro on the Stepin Fetchit [character,] the Negro himself was tired of seeing that type of picture. He wanted to see himself as he really was."[3]

Race films afforded that opportunity. An expression of group consciousness, they served as a source of pride for black viewers, who recognized them as products that were created by and for their community. By employing race consciousness and identification as cohesive and binding forces, those movies became "an articulation of self that challenged the dominant culture's ordering of reality."[4] Of particular significance was the way in which they would be "counterhegemonic without symmetrically 'countering' white culture on every point; for their oppositionality, if it could be called that, was in the circumvention, in the way they produced images that didn't go *through* white culture. Seen by blacks, largely unseen by whites, race movies featured an all-black world, a utopian vision of 'all-black everything.'"[5] And that is precisely why they were successful.

At first glance, the black-cast, black-oriented movies seemed to borrow the familiar genres of Hollywood films, from mysteries to Westerns. But, as film scholar Jane Gaines writes, race films in fact "emptied" those genres and "filled [them] with different issues and outcomes," so that while they appeared to be turned inward in their consideration of black community problems and black aspiration, they were simultaneously running commentaries on the white world that remained off-screen.[6] And even though race films did not, by any means, shatter the racial clichés or halt the negative imagery that dominated American film, they offered an alternative to those troubling depictions and challenged other movie producers to strive for more balanced racial and ethnic portrayals in their pictures—a clear response to the "call to duty" that publisher Lester Walton issued in the *New York Age* (September 18, 1920): "to present the Negro in a complimentary light, . . . to gladden our hearts and inspire us by presenting characters typifying the better element of Negroes."[7]

Race pictures also served a significant social and cultural function by helping to define black identity in the transition to modern urban life. As Jacqueline Najuma Stewart notes in her definitive study *Migrating to the Movies,* the Great Migration of hundreds of thousands of blacks from the South not only increased social and economic opportunities in Northern cities before, during, and after World War I; it also influenced the development of cinema as a major institution, particularly in terms of "its representational strategies and its practices as a social sphere," and allowed movies to play a crucial role in the process of modernization and urbanization of blacks. Whereas cinema's early racial politics was evident in the racist portrayals on screen, segregation in theaters, and exclusion of blacks from the dominant sphere of production, the new films being produced for black audiences provided a major site in which black subjects could be seen in modern ways and in which "Black public spheres were constructed and interpreted, empowered and suppressed."[8]

Yet even with the opening of movie houses in New York, Chicago, and throughout the North to accommodate the influx of migrating Southern blacks, the number of actual theaters where race films could be screened was small. Film pioneer William Foster reported that there were only "112 'colored' theaters in the United States in 1909, with those outside major cities being mostly 'five and ten cent theaters, vaudeville and moving pictures,'" and 214 serving a black clientele in 1913.[9] Black filmmaker and Afro-American Film Company founder Hunter Haynes, in an article for the *Indianapolis Freeman* (March 14, 1914), pegged the number at "238 colored houses in the United States [catering exclusively to black patrons] as against 32,000 white houses" in 1914.[10] Even in 1921–1922, peak years for race filmmakers, Richard E. Norman wrote that "scattered over twenty-eight states," there were just 354 "Negro theatres" (only 121 of which he considered to be outlets for his films); and he noted that, by the end of 1922, some of those theaters had already closed.[11] Moreover, those same black theaters typically showed more Hollywood films than independent ones, while white theaters, which had a much wider market, rarely booked independent race films at all.

The early race film producers had imagined that they could work toward racial uplift while turning a profit for themselves in a lucrative new industry. But they learned very quickly that they were at a significant disadvantage in terms of both financing and experience.[12] Some discovered that, despite their good intentions, they would be unable to compete with the major studios and never even moved into production with their story ideas. Others made only a single film before they too folded their operations. Still others sought backing from white investors simply to survive.

Most independent race filmmakers operated under other handicaps as well. Unlike the better-funded studio producers, who employed distribution agencies to circulate their films and who therefore were able to keep their studios open and working on new productions, they had to distribute their films themselves, usually by roadshowing them from town to town. "We had to make a picture," one early filmmaker recalled, "and then we had to close down everything and take the same man [actor] we made the picture with and go out and spend money traveling all over the United States, trying to get money enough to make another picture. But we were out of business all that time."[13]

In addition to the scarce resources at their disposal and the tough competition from the dominant film industry, race filmmakers also had to struggle to satisfy their various constituencies. In particular, they had to address and accommodate the preferences of black filmgoers, especially urban filmgoers "with disposable income and race-conscious views," by managing the contradictions that shaped the emerging black film culture, including "the politics of race stereotypy, the cinema's high and low appeals to largely working-class audiences, and Black moviegoers' increasingly sophisticated and diverse reconstructive viewing practices." Yet by adapting or reworking mainstream conventions to emphasize racial achievement—by "inhabiting" and incorporating white genres rather than merely "imitating" white forms, to borrow Jane Gaines's important distinction—those filmmakers were able to produce "city comedies, migration melodramas, and military newsreels that reflected and renewed assertions of American identity on the part of Black audiences."[14] Thus, despite the fact that virtually all early race films were underfinanced, poorly distributed, and technically inferior to the Hollywood product, they were, in themselves, remarkable social and cinematic achievements.

The first race filmmaker was William D. Foster, who recognized quite early the economic promise that the developing motion picture industry had to offer. While working in New York City for horseman Jack McDonald, he became interested in show business and took on the role of publicist for Bob Cole and Billy Johnson's A Trip to Coontown Company and later for the landmark musical shows *In Dahomey* and *Abyssinia,* starring the legendary black comedy team of Bert Williams and George Walker.[15] Attracted by the opening of Robert T. Mott's Pekin Theatre, a black-managed and operated playhouse, in 1906, Foster moved to Chicago, where he became the Pekin's business representative, a position that allowed him to view and book numerous black vaudeville acts. Under the pen name of Juli Jones, Foster also began writing articles on black show business for various race weeklies, including the *Chicago Defender;* and around 1910, he decided to enter the movie profession himself. After scraping together enough money to found the Foster Photoplay Company, he produced his first short, a two-reel comedy called *The Railroad Porter* (1912), now recognized as the first black-directed film, which had a strong opening in Chicago and was later shown in a few theaters in the East.

"One of the best informed men in theatricals hereabouts," Foster predicted phenomenal success for race men with the "bravery and foresight" to wrestle with the problems of movie production and presentation.[16] After all, "in a moving picture the Negro would off-set so many insults of the race—could tell their side of the birth of this great race."[17] To demonstrate his own bravery and foresight, Foster began investigating ways to establish himself in the industry. At one point he even headed to Florida, where Lubin, Pathé, Kalem, and other licensed film manufacturers were making movies, to evaluate the feasibility of building a studio there. But when he realized that rental and distribution companies were reluctant to book his releases into white theaters, his optimism turned to frustration. This "de facto economic boycott of the first black film producers," according to Henry T. Sampson, "gave birth to a separate black film industry in the United States," which "during the next forty years produced over 500 films featuring blacks which were shown in theaters catering to blacks with little distribution anywhere else."[18] Yet Foster would not share in that success. Although he went on to produce a few more shorts, he quit the business in 1917 to become circulation manager of the *Chicago Defender,* which he helped to make one of the most widely distributed black newspapers.

In 1928, hoping to resurrect his film career, Foster moved to Los Angeles, where he directed for the Pathé Studios a series of musical shorts featuring such legendary black performers as Clarence Muse, Stepin Fetchit, and Buck and Bubbles. He also began selling stock subscriptions to revive his Foster Photoplay Company and struggled bitterly "trying to get somewhere in this Business as a Producer," because he realized that "if a colored producing co don't make the Grade now it will be useless later on after all the Big Co.s get merged up—they will set about controlling the Equipment then the door wil be closed."[19] His assessment was ultimately correct, and his company released no new films.

Foster's early shorts were amusing if unsophisticated efforts that followed the generic formulas of the day. But while they poked fun at "dishonest and vain black urban types," his comedies also "reflected the vibrant culture African Americans were developing in cities" and featured a range of "New Negro" characters, such as the well-traveled Pullman porters who served as conduits of vital news and information about the cities that they visited on their routes and who were often treated as culture heroes within the black community.[20] *The Railroad Porter* (1912), for instance, which was the first racial comedy and which "inaugurated the 'chase' idea later copied by [the] Lubin Company, Keystone Cops and others," told the story of a young wife.[21] Thinking her husband is out on his run, she invites to dinner a finely dressed man who turns out to be a waiter. After the husband returns home, he pulls out his gun; the waiter, according to the *New York Age* (September 25, 1913), "gets his revolver and returns the compliment

... no one is hurt ... and all ends happily."[22] And in *The Barber* (1912), a barber posing as a Spanish music teacher engages in a series of comedic chases as he tries to evade an angry husband, the local police, and even an old woman whose boat he overturns when he jumps in a lake to avoid capture. Yet, though well received by audiences and favorably reviewed in local Chicago papers, Foster's shorts (none of which is extant) were rarely shown outside the Midwest; and his players, despite their strengths as stage actors, failed to attract national recognition as film stars, even in the black press.

Still, Foster's efforts marked an important beginning and a significant break "with the 'coon' tradition established by Thomas Alva Edison's *Ten Pickaninnies* (1904) and *The Wooing and Wedding of a Coon* (1905) as well as Seigmund Lubin's Sambo and Rastus series (1909, 1910, and 1911)" that were so popular in the early years of motion pictures.[23] Defying some of the early racial stereotypes in that "men are employed, marriages do take place, businesses are owned and operated by blacks, and violence does not conclude" every film, Foster's progressive, realistic, and culturally specific comedies were consistent with the ideology of racial uplift.[24] Moreover, Davarian L. Baldwin observed, by portraying black porters, barbers, and butlers as "hardworking heroes," those comedies combined "sensational entertainment with moral instruction to make the behaviors of laziness, indecency, and immodesty the subject of laughter" and promoted "cinema [as] a respectable enterprise and entertainment."[25] Thus Foster remains a seminal figure in cinema history.

Around the time Foster began producing his shorts, Emmett J. Scott, the personal secretary to black leader and Tuskegee Institute president Booker T. Washington, determined to make a major black film that would counter the racist portrayals in D. W. Griffith's *The Birth of a Nation* (1915), which had inflamed white fears and reinforced most of the pejorative typing that had been developing on stage since the mid-nineteenth century and in early motion pictures since the 1890s.[26] The NAACP, formed only a few years earlier in 1909, was already planning a film in response to Griffith's sanctimony and had even started negotiating with Carl Laemmle, the founder of Universal Pictures. Within the NAACP, however, there was division over the direction that film should take. As Thomas Cripps wrote in "The Making of *The Birth of a Race*," some members wanted to engage white attention through a film to be called *Lincoln's Dream*, which would laud black aspiration and celebrate black progress; others argued for a tale of "'black sufferings and strivings' that would meet with favor from conservative and radical alike." Still others supported W. E. B. Du Bois, the NAACP's ranking black intellectual and editor of its in-house publication the *Crisis*, in his desire to film his own works and a "pageant of Negro history."[27] When Laemmle insisted that the NAACP raise $50,000 toward the production costs to offset Universal's investment, the organization tried to come up with the funds but finally dropped the project, choosing instead to fight the Griffith picture through the courts and the picket lines.

At that point, Scott stepped in. Unable to revive the NAACP's interest or to salvage the film, he shifted his attention to a new project: the filming of Washington's autobiographical *Up from Slavery*. With Washington's death in November 1915, though, that project came to a halt, and Scott hastily signed a new contract to produce a different film, *The Birth of a Race*. According to its prospectus, that film—"the true story of the Negro—his life in Africa, his transportation to America, his enslavement, his freedom, his achievements, together with his past, present and future relations to his white neighbor and to the world in which both live and labor"—would draw on black talent and be an inspirational plea for mutual respect between the races. But financial mismanagement (including the fraudulent promotion and sale of stocks) and confused leadership created numerous and ultimately insurmountable problems. William Selig, the original producer, and his associates pulled out halfway through production, and Daniel Frohman, a New York veteran vaudeville producer, took over. Frohman, however, had a different concept of the film, and he immediately began shooting vast amounts of biblical footage in Florida, where he had located a public park with mock Egyptian architecture—footage that had no relation to what the Selig Company had already shot. After Frohman dropped out, the picture passed through the hands of several other white independent filmmakers before being completed at the Rothacker Film Manufacturing Company plant in Chicago. Scott and the other blacks involved saw themselves losing virtually all control of the venture.[28]

In 1918, almost three years after it was first conceived, *The Birth of a Race* finally premiered at Chicago's Blackstone Theater. Promoted as "The Greatest and Most Daring of Photoplays . . . A Master Picture Conceived in the Spirit of Truth and Dedicated to All of the Races of the World," the film was actually a flop.[29] As released, it moved from the creation of the world to other scenes from sacred history, all of which were re-created employing mammoth sets. But instead of hailing black achievement within the context of the development of civilization, it emphasized such decidedly anti-black images as the victimization of the Jews by the black army of the Pharaoh and the invasion of a white tribe by a black one, an incident that leads Noah to suggest that the "prejudice" that results from "living apart" is somehow tied to black failings; and instead of synthesizing the Gospels, the film promoted the notion of racial separation in the person of a very white Jesus before cutting abruptly to the voyage of Columbus, the ride of Paul Revere, and the proclamation of emancipation by Lincoln (curiously skirting any visual depiction of slavery itself).[30] Finally, according to *Moving Picture World* (May 10, 1919), in keeping with contemporary anti-German propaganda, a disconnected story about Oscar and George Schmidt, two German-American brothers with opposing views on the war, was thrown in for good measure. Meant to rouse patriotic fervor and celebrate America's entry into World War I, instead it rendered the film both formless and essentially structureless and made it "a striking example of what a photoplay should not be."[31] As George Johnson observed, the "change in treatment has so converted it into a war propaganda film that the original idea of moulding public sentiment in contradistinction to that of the Griffith production has been entirely lost."[32]

A few critics, like Genevieve Harris in the *Chicago Evening Post*, hailed the film as "a truly great photoplay." But most of the reviews were overwhelmingly negative. One Chicago reviewer decried the garbled plot and called the film "the most grotesque cinematic chimera in the history of the picture business," while *Billboard* observed that "the picture is perhaps the worst conglomeration of mixed purposes and attempts ever thrown together."[33] Disillusioned by the whole experience, Emmett J. Scott left filmmaking—although he continued to be prominent in the black community as the Army's Assistant Secretary for Negro Affairs, a position in which he was able to help other filmmakers, and in various other leadership roles.[34]

The bungled *Birth of a Race* marked a lost opportunity for achievement in race filmmaking. Yet even before that film had been completed, the noted black actor Noble Johnson, with the support of his brother, former real estate and newspaper man George Johnson, founded the Lincoln Motion Picture Company in 1916. Based in Los Angeles, the company was dedicated "to display[ing] the Negro as *he is in his every day life,* a human being, with human inclinations."[35] Having already demonstrated his box office appeal in various roles for Seigmund Lubin (who discovered him in Colorado in 1914) and for Universal Pictures, Noble planned to star in Lincoln's productions and also to contribute to their financing—and to the company's proposed expansion through the purchase of a print lab and studio and the establishing of a movie magazine—from the salary he earned from his studio film appearances.

Lincoln's first release was *The Realization of a Negro's Ambition* (1916), a two-reel black recasting of the Horatio Alger story. George Johnson described it as a "drama of love and adventure, pictured with a good moral, a vein of clean comedy and beautiful settings . . . minus all burlesque and humiliating comedy."[36] In the film, James Burton, a young black civil engineering graduate of Tuskegee Institute, leaves his parents' farm and his sweetheart Mary to seek his fortune in the West. After being rejected for a job at an oil field in California because of his race, he rescues the owner's daughter and is offered employment as the head of an exploration team. Realizing that the same kind of geological conditions he is studying exist on his father's farm, he returns home, strikes oil, becomes rich, and proposes to Mary. Together they realize all of their ambitions: family, friends, and home. Significantly, given the means and opportunity, James goes "directly back to his 'own people,' a recurring narrative device in race movies, which restrict action to an all-black world within which everything is won or lost—a circumscribed miniature of the white world."[37]

Well received everywhere that it was shown, *The Realization of a Negro's Ambition* set the standard for future race films. A contemporary black reviewer described it as a reflection of "the business and social life of the Negro as it really is and not as our jealous contemporaries would have us appear."[38] In Chicago, Teenan Jones, owner of the Star Theater, reported that the film delighted audiences and broke house records, while George Paul, manager of the States Theater, applauded the "clean-cut well-acted drama" for opening the eyes "of many who have associated all colored pictures with the lowest of the low comedy."[39]

New Lincoln features followed. *Trooper of Troop K* (1916), a fictional story about the massacre of the Negro troops of the famous fighting Tenth Cavalry during the battle of Carrizal in Mexico, starred Noble Johnson as Shiftless Joe, a goodhearted but careless fellow who eventually proves his heroism. The three-reeler, which "attempted to code true 'patriotism' as racially inclusive" by highlighting black military service, was another powerful story of racial uplift: through girlfriend Clara's faith in him, Joe improves himself and becomes a good race man.[40] In fact, the implication is that every Shiftless Joe can be reformed and can better himself personally and socially, particularly if he adopts the values of the black middle class.[41] The film played to capacity houses from Chicago to the West Coast as well as in schools and churches; and it confirmed, as George Johnson stated, "the remarkable ability of the Lincoln management to adapt itself to the news events of the day."[42] In 1917, after both Lincoln films were shown at the Tuskegee Institute, the *Tuskegee Student* raved that "such pictures as these are not only elevating and inspiring in themselves, but they are also calculated to instill principles of race pride and loyalty in the minds of colored people."[43]

The Law of Nature (1917), starring Noble Johnson, was released the same year. In that three-reel "social drama of the East and West, a virile production full of human interest and realistic western atmosphere," a woman leaves her home and her rancher husband to revisit the glamorous East of her former days.[44] But, realizing her folly, she returns to the West to rejoin her family. Like the company's earlier productions (none of which survives), *The Law of Nature*—a reverse of the standard tale of male desertion—proved to be "a fine story" and a "good box-office attraction," unusual for its depiction of a father lovingly caring for his son in his wife's absence.[45] As Gerald R. Butters Jr. observed, since black love and marriage were almost nonexistent in studio films, Lincoln "deliberately presented the wholeness of African-American family life, complete with romantic love and tenderness toward children."[46] An ad for the Omaha run described the picture as "classy" and uplifting with "a wholesome moral."[47] The manager of the Palace, a black-owned, black-run theater in Louisville, Kentucky, wrote to George Johnson that *The Law of Nature* "took on like wildfire," while the white-owned, white-managed Alamo Theater in Washington, D.C., listed the film as the "biggest drawing card" of all of Lincoln's productions.[48]

Lincoln's fortunes changed, however, after the Universal Picture Company of Hollywood exerted pressure on Noble Johnson, who was one of their feature players. As a condition of Johnson's contract with them, Universal insisted that he sever his ties with the company he founded and that Lincoln be prohibited from using his name or likeness in new advertising. Universal's repressive and cutthroat demand was no doubt precipitated by Johnson's success at the box office: the multi-talented actor, who had appeared in thirty-four films between 1915 and 1918, was such an attraction in the black community that black moviegoers readily turned out for the white studio pictures in which he was cast.

Ironically, it was his immense popularity in mainstream movies that spelled doom for Noble Johnson's fledgling black company.[49] As George Johnson described:

> Theaters all over the United States owned by both whites and blacks but catering to Negro trade were all showing the Universal serial, and other films, . . . in many cases because [Noble] Johnson was in them, as an actor but not as a star. When the Lincoln films came out with Johnson as a star the same theaters would place the large colored lithograph posters in front of their theaters. In many cities there were two theaters side by side or in the same block. So the theaters that did not show the Lincoln films, with Johnson, did not get any business. Naturally these theater owners complained to the Universal Film Company. . . . The result was that Johnson was called on the carpet and advised that if he wanted to continue as a Universal actor he must stop allowing himself to be shown in Negro films. Naturally Johnson had no choice but to resign from Lincoln, [and] to stop appearing in Lincoln films.[50]

The studio's ultimatum to Johnson, as Paula J. Massood observed, was typical of practices in Hollywood, which "seemed reluctant to bestow stardom on a black dramatic actor" yet used the contract system to limit his outside options.[51]

After Noble Johnson's departure, the company turned for leadership to George Johnson, who accepted the position of general booking manager but still retained his job at the post office in Omaha, Nebraska, where he was the first black clerk. A tireless worker, George opened several branch offices for Lincoln; employed advance men to promote its race features at smaller theaters; and forged a number of strong alliances, most notably with Tony Langston, the influential theater editor of the *Chicago Defender,* and Romeo Dougherty, an editor at the *New York Amsterdam News* (both of whom served as agents for the company). Most importantly, though, Johnson established the first black-operated national booking organization to facilitate distribution of Lincoln's films.[52] He also actively solicited investors through letters and pamphlets such as "The Secret of Getting Rich!" and "Three Strong Reasons Why You Should Buy Lincoln Motion Picture Co. Shares" that encouraged readers to support a black-owned business while getting in on the ground floor of a booming new enterprise.[53]

During George Johnson's tenure, the company released two more features. *A Man's Duty* (1919), with Clarence Brooks in the lead role originally meant to be Noble Johnson's, treated a man's moral obligation and his newfound happiness. *By Right of Birth* (1921), a six-reel photoplay whose screenplay was written by George himself, was another picture of race achievement in which slavery is reversed and negated by a legacy of wealth for succeeding generations. "A powerful drama of modern life and incidents," it was racial in appeal yet free from racial propaganda.[54]

Plans for a new production, *The Heart of a Negro,* were announced in 1923, but the film was never completed. Shortly afterward, Lincoln discontinued operation. Despite the quality of its features and the serious treatments of middle-class black life for which it was renowned, the company—beset by financial concerns—apparently felt unable to compete in the developing market of longer feature films. "We were too early," George Johnson would later observe.[55] Yet even after the demise of Lincoln, George continued his interest in the movie industry through a new venture, the National News Service, which he operated part-time out of the garage of his Los Angeles home. And "until the end of his life he made a business and eventually a hobby of collecting and disseminating information about the status and progress of African Americans in the entertainment industry" and chronicling his brother's career.[56]

Noble Johnson achieved even greater success. Hailed by the early black press as one of the screen's first true black American stars, he proved himself a reliable and versatile character actor. By the time he retired from the industry in 1950, he had performed in more than 150 pictures. Interestingly, though, few of his roles were as a black character: since Johnson's light skin was "often unreadable as 'black' in the visual ideology of the day," he was cast instead in a variety of brown-skinned roles, including Native Americans, Asians, Pacific Islanders, and other exotic characters.[57]

A contemporary of the Johnson brothers was Oscar Micheaux, founder of the Micheaux Film Corporation, the most successful of all of the race film production companies. Micheaux, one of the most flamboyant characters in the history of American cinema, was also a shrewd businessman and self-promoter. Fellow filmmaker Richard E. Norman hailed him as a "genius," and even George Johnson, despite claiming that Micheaux's "record [was] none too savory," called him the "world's greatest producer of all Negro Film productions."[58]

It was, in fact, only after corresponding with Johnson that Micheaux became interested in filmmaking. Johnson had invited Micheaux to Lincoln's regional office in Omaha, Nebraska, in May of 1918 to discuss the purchase of rights to his semi-autobiographical first novel, *The Conquest* (1913), to be filmed under the title of *The Homesteader*. Friendly negotiations occurred and contracts were drawn up. But, according to Johnson, at the last moment, Micheaux insisted on additional terms—including a doubling of the length of the proposed film (Micheaux wanted six or eight reels, rather than the three-reel version to which he had earlier agreed) and a guarantee that he be paid to travel to Los Angeles to oversee the filming himself—that ultimately proved unacceptable to Lincoln.[59] Although the two men exchanged several more cordial letters, Johnson recalled that "As he knew nothing of film production, had no Los Angeles connections or any money either, we could not come to any agreement," so the original deal fell through. Johnson, though, suspected that the real reason was that Micheaux had already caught "the film bug" and "decided that he didn't need Lincoln" after all.[60]

After terminating negotiations with Johnson, Micheaux embarked on an ambitious campaign to underwrite his own production of *The Homesteader*. With the same efficiency he had shown in soliciting orders for his novels, he prepared a stock prospectus for the picture (in which he boasted that the film, following the model of *The Birth of a Nation*, would play in the "largest theatres" in the "largest cities," and that "twelve million people will have their first opportunity to see their race in stellar role"), and began casting.[61] After writing the screenplay himself, he secured the necessary permits and kept production costs down by shooting some of the scenes in and around Sioux City, where he lived at the time, and in Gregory, South Dakota, near the site of the homestead he had purchased (and lost) when he was a young man. Less than a year later, when the film opened in Chicago in 1919 to large and enthusiastic crowds, Micheaux was well on his way to making his mark, both as a producer and as a showman. Over the next thirty years, in fact, he would make more than forty films, including a reworking of *The Homesteader* titled *The Exile* (1931), now recognized as the first black-produced talking motion picture.

Micheaux's films, however, were not technically brilliant—hardly a surprise, given Micheaux's lack of formal training; and reviewers were often less than generous in their assessments of his work. The *Baltimore Afro-American*, for example, criticized Micheaux's "jumbly-fumbly manner of directing," while Theophilus Lewis, in the *New York Amsterdam News*, called one of Micheaux's last silent films "thoroughly bad from every point of analysis, from the continuity, which is unintelligible, to the caption writing, which is a crime."[62] According to Lorenzo Tucker, who starred in several of Micheaux's pictures, one reason the movies might have been considered "technically poor" is that Micheaux realized his market would not support a bigger investment.[63] But it is also likely that, especially in his silent films, Micheaux was more concerned with their political, racial, and social message than with their style.[64]

Working on a very tight budget, Micheaux would shoot whenever and wherever he could, from empty and outdated studios in Chicago, Fort Lee, and the Bronx to the houses and offices of his acquaintances. And, like his contemporary Richard E. Norman, he would compile pieces of unused film for future use. Actress Shingzie Howard recalled that one morning, when no one was home, Micheaux took her to a white neighborhood and photographed her in front of an elegant residence; another time, when a woman in a fur coat arrived for an appointment, Micheaux escorted her to an interior office and then quickly returned to shoot Howard wearing the woman's fur.[65]

Micheaux's sets, of necessity, were usually small in scale; many of the important scenes in *God's Step Children* (1938), a film about the perils of race denial, for example, take place at the foot of a staircase in a friend's home, a spot that provided the best lighting angles. Micheaux would often rent equipment by the day. Retakes were a luxury he could not afford, and editing was minimal. Crews were usually comprised of cameramen who had been left behind as the dominant white film industry moved to Hollywood; Micheaux's casts, which tended to be uneven in their talent, ranged from fine veteran actresses such as his second wife Alice B. Russell to family friends and local citizens, whom he drafted in lieu of professional actors to minimize his costs.

Like fellow filmmaker and competitor Norman, Micheaux was in charge of virtually all aspects of the production of his films, from the writing of the scenarios to the handling of the books. Charles Fontenot notes that Micheaux's early pictures "took an average of ten days to shoot and usually cost ten to twelve thousand dollars"; even his later films rarely ran more than $20,000 in production costs—a fraction of the cost of white-produced studio films.[66] (By comparison, D. W. Griffith produced *The Birth of a Nation* [1915] for $100,000; and Carl Laemmle's major studio production of *Uncle Tom's Cabin* [1927], directed by Harry A. Pollard, was budgeted at $2,000,000.) Nevertheless, the Micheaux feature was almost always superior to those of most independent race filmmakers; and, although technically inferior to the Hollywood product, in other respects it "resembled the best B movies of the time."[67]

What particularly distinguished Micheaux's work, however, was its angle: just as the race newspapers and magazines took the major stories of the day and reported on them from a black perspective, Micheaux took the familiar Hollywood script and gave it a distinctly racial slant. But while "genre and characterizations may have been borrowed from white movies," Gerald R. Butters Jr. notes, Micheaux's films "were often set in a milieu with a black sensibility that changed the dynamics of the film's receptive structure."[68] Even as he "translated standard Western, gangster, and melodrama fare to a black context," Micheaux always added "something unique, if only in the form of his rough-hewn, self-taught technique."[69] And in his challenge of conventional portrayals and his addressing of black concerns from a black perspective, Micheaux originated a form of the protest film upon which later filmmakers would build.

Micheaux also understood the art of self-promotion. To finance his productions, he would personally call upon theater managers to offer them first rights to his works; often he would bring along several cast members to act out scenes that he was planning to shoot. Once a film was completed, Micheaux would carry stills to the theaters where his features were scheduled to play and try to get advance bookings for his next film. To boost the box office, he arranged promotional junkets and encouraged his stars to make personal appearances in the cities where his films were opening—a gimmick that many of the actors appreciated, since the extra publicity enhanced the stage careers that constituted their principal livelihood. And the provocative, teasing one-sheet lithographs and theater lobby cards that Micheaux designed himself were among the most colorful and artistic in the business.[70]

Like most race filmmakers, Micheaux's movie corporation was perpetually underfinanced, and it was by the sheer force of Micheaux's personality and his tireless self-promotion that he was able to survive through three decades of filmmaking. Although he experienced a variety of financial setbacks and reorganizations, most notably a voluntary bankruptcy in early 1928 precipitated by the mismanagement of the company by his brother Swan (an event he used as the basis of one of his silent films, *Wages of Sin* [1929]), Micheaux endured long after most of his fellow race filmmakers had ceased production. Even in the 1930s, when he was increasingly forced to seek backing from white financiers (sometimes called "angels") like Frank Schiffman and Jack Goldberg, he continued to exercise strict control over his projects.[71]

Above all, Micheaux seemed to understand his audience. Believing that moviegoers were more interested in good story lines than in blatant racial propaganda, Micheaux offered his viewers engaging characters with whom they could identify and popular plots that incorporated elements generally ignored by other filmmakers, from lynching and race purity to prostitution and underworld crime.[72] Intertwined in—and underlying—all of Micheaux's films, especially his early silents, was a definite racial, even politically activist, theme, usually drawn from topical and often controversial events. In *The Symbol of the Unconquered* (1920), for instance, one of several pictures that Micheaux produced as a black response to Griffith's *Birth of a Nation,* members of the Klan, at the instigation of white racist ex-Southerner Tom Cutschawl and Jefferson Driscoll, a light-skinned black man who hates his own race and is passing for white, attack black rancher Hugh Van Allen and attempt, unsuccessfully, to drive him off his oil-rich property. And in *Within Our Gates* (1920), in which the traitorous Eph spreads lies about hardworking black sharecropper Jasper Landry in order to curry favor with wealthy white planter Philip Girdlestone, Micheaux made another powerful statement about vigilante justice by including graphically violent scenes of the lynching of Eph and the burning of Landry and his wife. As the Omaha *Nebraska Daily* reviewer observed, the "radical" production was "the biggest protest against race prejudice, lynching and 'concubinage' that was ever filmed or written."[73]

While Micheaux, who released at least one film a year from 1918 to 1940, was the most prolific and successful of the early race filmmakers, he certainly did not have a monopoly in the field. In fact, by the 1920s, with the proliferation of movie theaters catering to black moviegoers, race film companies had begun springing up throughout the country, producing newsreels and full-length features that they plugged into those theaters and the black vaudeville circuits, as well as into white houses for special matinees or midnight rambles.[74] Among those black independents were the Unique Film Company of Chicago, the Seminole Film Producing Company of New York, the Bookertee Investment Company of Los Angeles, the Maurice Film Company of Detroit, and the Rosebud Film Corporation of Hollywood. As Thomas Cripps writes, most of these emerging black companies "floated on a wave of good intentions, but only a few struggled into production," while others survived long enough to release only one or two pictures. Their ambition often outstripped their capacity and their potential, so that in the end "they did not fail so much as they were over-whelmed by the impossible."[75]

In addition to battling problems of underfinancing, production quality, and unheralded releases, black independents also had to compete with white and white-backed independent filmmakers, who had begun to recognize the potential for profit in race films. An early black producer recalled that once the films gained popularity, white film companies started "[going] like hotcakes. . . . they figured we were making a mint of dollars. . . . the whites, most of them were capitalizing on the deal and a good many of them were nothing but a stock scheme."[76]

To be sure, the efforts of those white companies had decidedly mixed results. Many persisted in re-creating old formulas like the "funny Negro picture," which Dr. A. W. Smith, the founder of the Frederick Douglass Film Company, described dismissively as "Negroes in some hen roost, shooting craps, eating watermelons or [engaging in] razor fights."[77] The white-run Ebony Film Corporation of Chicago, for example, which employed its own company of black actors and included a single black staff member, relied on racist caricatures and stereotyped plot lines. Ebony made more than twenty one- and two-reel comedies such as *The Busted Romance* (1917), about "a stray 'coon' living by his wits, a town gambler, and a parson whose conscience can be made retroactive when money is shown"; *Spying the Spy* (1918), which featured "Sambo Sam," who tries to uncover a nest of German spies but finds only the initiation paraphernalia used by members of a black lodge; and *A Black Sherlock Holmes* (1918), a vulgar parody of Arthur Conan Doyle's detective that featured characters named "I Wanta Sneeze" and "Reuma Tism."[78] Ebony also rereleased under its name a series of racist shorts originally produced around 1915 by Historical Feature Films, such as *Money Talks in Darktown,* in which the uncultured, dark-skinned Sam tries to win Flossie's affection by lightening the color of his skin before realizing that her only concern is the color of his money. But after black moviegoers became offended by the degrading comedies, black theaters stopped booking Ebony's films, which led to the company's demise in 1919.[79]

Other filmmakers, however, continued to produce comparably low cinematic fare. In 1921, for instance, the Harris Dickson Film Company released *The Custard Nine,* based on Dickson's series of "Colored stories" from *The Saturday Evening Post* in which Virgil Custard leads Vicksburg's black baseball team through various farcical adventures. Notable only for the debut of actor Clarence Muse, *The Custard Nine* offered naive and negative portrayals of black life, to which black audiences reacted with great disdain. Lester Walton wrote in the *New York Age* (October 29, 1921) that Dickson's stories, which sought to ridicule both "the plantation and the professional Negro," were the very reason that he stopped reading the *Post.* While Dickson had "never heard colored physicians use the language of the illiterate and uneducated," wrote Walton, "he does not hesitate to poke fun at them with the same vigor and consistency as he does at lower types."[80] Similarly, in the mid- to late-1920s, Octavus Roy Cohen teamed with Al Christie on a series of "all-colored shorts," based on Cohen's stories for *The Saturday Evening Post.* Although they featured such fine actors as Evelyn Preer, Spencer Williams, Edward Thompson, Lawrence Criner, and Sam McDaniel (who were often forced to work in blackface), the shorts incorporated many of the stereotypes of "coon" dialect, dress, and demeanor that some whites found so amusing and that most blacks considered utterly degrading.[81] They were, George Johnson recalled, "cheap Negro pictures" full of the worst kind of caricatures.[82]

A handful of white or white-backed race filmmakers, however, managed to produce some outstanding work. Among that select group, Richard E. Norman was unquestionably the most prominent and one of the most prolific. His Norman Film Manufacturing Company turned out high-quality black-cast, black-oriented pictures like *The Green-Eyed Monster* (1920), *Regeneration* (1923), *The Flying Ace* (1926), and *Black Gold* (1928), which were free of derogatory stereotypes (and which are discussed at length in the following chapters). In the seven feature films that Norman wrote, produced, edited, financed, and distributed himself, he eschewed demeaning racial depictions and portrayed characters who were largely professionals: bank presidents, superintendents, advertising directors, engineers, doctors, captains, detectives, pilots, ranchers, lawmen. Ambitious and enterprising, they rode broncos, drilled for oil in the West, sailed the high seas, took to the skies, mastered the rails—and thrilled black audiences (and sometimes white ones, too) with their exciting adventures.

Another distinguished white-run race film company—and a strong competitor of Norman's—was Reol Productions of New York City, which emerged soon after World War I. Its founder, Robert Levy, was formerly the manager of the Quality Amusement Company, which sponsored the Lafayette Players, the respected Harlem-based dramatic stock company that provided acting talent for many of the early filmmakers. As head of Reol, Levy aggressively marketed his company's performers to black audiences—for example, he billed Edna Morton as "the colored Mary Pickford"—and established large circuits of theaters throughout many sections of the South and in a number of Northern cities for the distribution of its films. He also recognized the culture of the market by producing films such as *The Sport of the Gods* (1921) and *The Call of His People* (1922) that were adapted from classic black literature. According to Pearl Bowser and Louise Spence, Reol "promoted its films to theaters by emphasizing that they were based on the stories and plays of Negro authors" and even announced to the press that it was seeking talented black writers on college campuses to provide material for its pictures.[83]

Although Reol occasionally made comedies, the company specialized in good dramatic features such as *The Burden of Race* (1921), a film about the risks of interracial romance, and *The Secret Sorrow* (1921), about the two Morgan brothers—Arthur, an assistant district attorney in New York City, and Joe, the henchman for a corrupt politician—who take very different paths in life but are ultimately reconciled. The ten or more feature films that Reol produced before going out of business in 1924, in fact, were significant both for their quality and for the lack of stereotyping of their black characters, who were usually educated people in a wide variety of professions.[84] Yet, despite the fact that black theaters regularly booked Reol's films, Levy was disappointed that he did not get more support from the black community—a regret shared by many race filmmakers. An article in the *Baltimore Afro-American* (May 2, 1924) quoted Levy as saying: "Negro amusement buyers are fickle and possessed of a peculiar psychic complex, and they prefer to patronize the galleries of white theatres" over their own. Levy's sentiments seemed only to confirm William Foster's earlier fears that race filmmakers would not be able to capitalize on that "rich commercial plum from what should be one of our own particular trees of desirable profit."[85]

Another white-run company, the Colored Players Film Corporation of Philadelphia—founded in 1926 by white theater owner David Starkman—also released some memorable pictures. Among them was *Ten Nights in a Barroom* (1926), a black version of a familiar temperance novel in which, after his daughter's accidental death, Joe Morgan reforms his wicked ways, reconciles with his wife, and is elected mayor of his town. According to Thomas Cripps, *Ten Nights* made "a special plea to urban blacks, warning them against urban vices in a manner reminiscent of Micheaux"; and even churches acclaimed the picture.[86]

An even more notable film written by Starkman and produced by the Colored Players was *The Scar of Shame* (1926), which not only presented black audiences "with sharply etched messages of advocacy, aspiration, group unity, and slogans against racism" but also "laid the blame for black misfortune at the door of poor environment."[87] The story of an ill-fated marriage between promising black composer Alvin Hillyard and former washwoman Louise Howard, the film revealed the caste divisions that existed among dark-skinned and light-skinned and among middle- and working-class blacks. Alvin marries Louise to protect her from her abusive stepfather and her racketeer boyfriend Eddie, who wants to make her the star attraction at his nightclub. But Louise, "a child of environment" who lacks "the higher aims, the higher hopes," is swayed by the promises of stardom and rips up her marriage license, thereby destroying her marriage by her own hand.[88] After Louise is wounded during a confrontation, she falsely accuses Alvin, who is convicted of the crime. Years later, when he again encounters Louise, she still wants him and threatens to expose his past if he rejects her. But, writes Cripps, while Alvin has already "won the game of life by wanting it badly, Louise has lost because she sold herself cheaply."[89] After admitting that it was actually Eddie who shot her, Louise —burdened by her shame—kills herself, leaving Alvin free to marry Alice, a woman of his own class. The message of the film is synthesized in the final titles, as Alice's father, a corrupt lawyer, ironically observes that "our people have much to learn," particularly about the kind of class strife that is behind the picture's various tragedies.

The Scar of Shame, which made a powerful statement on race relations, remains one of the best independent race productions of the silent era.

Unfortunately, Starkman's career as a producer was short-lived: having exhausted his savings on his pictures, he found himself heavily in debt with little prospect of recovering his investment because of the limited distribution of his films.[90] In an effort to keep his company solvent, Starkman merged with black former vaudevillean Sherman H. Dudley; but they completed no new films together. By 1927, the Colored Players folded and Starkman was out of the business.

As cinema became mass entertainment for the lower as well as middle classes in the early decades of the twentieth century, the black movie audience grew rapidly, spurred in large part by the mass postwar migrations of Southern blacks to Northern cities and towns.[91] But the burgeoning race film industry, which had enjoyed a kind of golden age in the early 1920s with the support of the black press and the availability of fine theatrically trained black actors, was soon halted by a number of unfortunate events. A flu epidemic in 1923, occurring so soon after the pandemic of 1918, had an immediate and devastating effect by forcing the closing of many black and black-oriented theaters and amplifying the problem of distribution. White businesses, meanwhile, began buying up black theaters or building new ones in black neighborhoods; and by the late 1920s, they became increasingly unwilling to pay the costs of booking race films. As D. Ireland Thomas observed in a column in the *Chicago Defender* in early 1925, white theater owners "want it as cheap as a regular production of a white corporation and they know that this is impossible, as the producer of Race pictures is forced to get his profit out of a few Race theaters, while the white productions encircle the globe. Mary Pickford is just as popular in China as she is in America, etc. All Race movies make money regardless of their merit, yet the manager of a theater will try to tell you that his patrons do not like Race pictures."[92]

Even the black press started turning its attention away from the achievements of race filmmakers and toward the gains being made in Hollywood and in mainstream theater. Perhaps, as Pearl Bowser and Louise Spence write, black filmmakers received less coverage in the black weeklies because they invested less in advertising; "or perhaps the press was deserting Race pictures for the more costly, better-made Hollywood films where Blacks were beginning to find roles."[93] Whatever the reason, the same papers that had proclaimed that "no picture draws like a good Race production" and had urged theater managers to "all start booking colored pictures" and black patrons "to bear with men like Oscar Micheaux and other pioneers" by seeing their pictures even "if it hurts" became more direct in their criticism of race movies.[94] The intention of the black press, Charlene Regester suggests, may have been to encourage race filmmakers to strive for higher quality productions; but the timing proved to be especially inopportune, since "African-American filmmakers were engaged in a desperate struggle for survival." And although that press "never really abandoned its role of attacking white racism and encouraging the promotion of racial self-determination, its harsh words for African-American filmmakers may have unwittingly harmed this dimension of the industry, at least to the extent that press reviews affected the box office."[95]

Black audiences were also becoming more selective. Even though they craved black images on screen, they increasingly patronized only the highest quality race pictures, which often were not those being produced by the perpetually underfunded independents. Furthermore, the release in 1929 of the major studio productions *Hearts in Dixie* and *Hallelujah!*, the first of a number of popular black-oriented musicals, spelled disaster for most of the remaining small race companies, who lacked the capital to keep up production and to acquire the sound equipment that the new era of talkies demanded. By the end of the decade, the Depression had finished off all but the sturdiest.[96] The Johnson brothers, Robert Levy, and David Starkman had long ceased production; Richard E. Norman had turned to the development and marketing of nonsynchronous sound systems as a way of staying involved in the industry; and even Oscar Micheaux, who survived the transition from silent to sound films, found it increasingly difficult to compete with Hollywood's studio productions.

The role of the race filmmaker, as Micheaux had observed early in his career, was to make photoplays that were truthful to "the colored heart from close range" and that raised members of the race "to greater heights" by presenting them "in the light and background of their true state." Clearly, he was not alone in that ambition: Norman, the Johnson brothers, and other early race filmmakers also strove in their productions to provide "a miniature replica of [black] life."[97] They removed black characters from the proverbial hen roosts and away from the stereotypical watermelon contests and razor fights; and they placed those characters instead in middle-class living rooms and offices and on frontier ranches that signaled the unlimited opportunities within the reach of aspiring blacks—the "New Negroes"— who were willing to work hard to achieve their ambitions. And in that, and in many other ways, they created a new cinema, a separate cinema, that challenged prevailing racist notions and proved that race indeed matters.[98]

The close examination of the life and career of Richard E. Norman that follows—and that is based in large part on his personal and professional correspondence and on numerous other documents that he preserved—illustrates the travails that Norman and his fellow race producers endured and the triumphs that they achieved against seemingly insurmountable odds. A glimpse at a remarkable man and at his equally remarkable age, the study sheds new light on early race filmmaking and confirms the significance of Norman's cinematic legacy.

CHAPTER TWO

"Have You Talent?": Norman's Early Career

RICHARD EDWARD NORMAN JR. was born on July 13, 1891, in Middleburg, Florida, a small rural town outside of Jacksonville. The oldest child of Richard Edward Norman Sr. (1855–1942), a pharmacist who owned his own store, and Katherine (Kate) Kennedy Bruce Norman (1861–1939), he had two brothers—Earl Redding Norman, who volunteered and served with the Royal Canadian Forces during World War I and who later drowned at a Florida beach, and Kenneth Bruce Norman, who became a partner with Richard in the film production business before leaving to pursue other interests.[1] After high school, Richard attended Massey Business School in Jacksonville, where he honed a number of the skills that would serve him well throughout his career.

According to his family, Richard was an industrious young man. As a teenager he began working at a local Jacksonville theater, where he often entertained audiences by playing the piano, possibly providing musical accompaniment to some of the early silent pictures screened there. After his parents separated in 1910, Richard and his brothers moved with their mother to Kansas City, Kansas, to be closer to her relatives. In Kansas City and later in Chicago (where he met and married his first wife, Ethel), Richard found employment with several film companies and also pursued some of his own entrepreneurial ambitions.

One of Norman's first business ventures was the development of a cola-based drink that he called "Passi-Kola" (sometimes spelled "Pasi-Kola" or "PassiKola") and touted as an ideal beverage that possessed remarkable life-giving power. With the pharmaceutical expertise and technical support of his druggist father, Norman concocted a formula—a concentrated extract of the passion flower kola nut combined with tonics of other fruits and extracts, including lemon, orange, banana, pineapple, grape, and vanilla—for what he claimed was the finest and most salable soda-fountain or bottled beverage ever produced.[2]

An early advertising card designed by Norman outlined some of the product's physiological and medicinal benefits: "It exhilarates and invigorates, but does not intoxicate. It cures headache promptly and relieves exhaustion and that tired feeling at once. Restores exhausted nerves. Nourishes the brain. A drink for old and young. Creates appetite, promotes digestion and tones the system. It surpasses all others in taste and effect, and is the most refreshing and delightful beverage ever lifted to human lips." And since Passi-Kola added vigor and strength to the body, it was highly recommended for athletes and bicyclists.[3] Potential buyers could be assured that it was "one of the finest Morning Bracers, or Revivers and Nerve Foods, against which the most skeptical Physician can not have the least objection." (The bracing effect may have been the result of the alcohol content—as much as twelve percent, according to Norman's son, Captain Richard E. Norman—which gave the drink a "real 'kick.'"[4]) Another advertising card that Norman designed explained exactly how the product could be adapted for personal consumption or commercial sale.[5]

Whether Passi-Kola was indeed the best carbonated beverage is arguable. But it was certainly not the best-known or best-selling: that distinction belonged to Coca-Cola, the iconic American soft drink developed in the 1880s and first sold as a patent medicine at pharmacies and soda fountains. Initially, Norman strove to differentiate his drink from his rival in both taste and color. But as he reworked the formula according to his father's recommendations, he eliminated a number of the original ingredients, from the costly grape juice to the signature passion flower extract; and he added caffeine as well as burnt sugar, both staples of Coca-Cola, to give Passi-Kola the familiar dark brown color that buyers seemed to want.[6]

Once the formula was finalized, Norman began investigating the process of trademarking it. Valid for thirty years and renewable for another thirty, trademarks could be registered only if they had been used in commerce with a foreign nation or Indian tribe. But that provision, as Norman's father noted in a letter, could be satisfied "by sending samples to a dealer in Mexico or Canada. Or to an Indian Agent."[7] Since the actual trademark could consist of any single word, compound word, sign, symbol, picture, figure, autograph, or monogram, alone or in combination, Norman settled on Passi-Kola. Spelled out in a flowing script similar to that of Coca-Cola, that logo would appear on all of the labels.

Norman also determined to find a catchy slogan to use in promoting his drink. Among those he invented (all of which used an earlier spelling of the product) were "Uneeda Pasi Kola For that Tired Feeling"; "Drink Pasi Kola, It's a Whizzer!"; "Drink Pasi Kola, Your Nose Knows"; and "Drink Pasi Kola, A Breath from the Orient." And he composed a list of "10 Reasons Why You Should Drink Pasi Kola," the most convincing of which was "CONTAINS NO COCAINE."[8]

As late as spring 1915, Norman was still tinkering with—and trying to perfect—his beverage. In a letter written from his home in Little River, Florida, Norman's "loving father" offered further suggestions for producing and marketing Passi-Kola to make it more competitive with Coca-Cola. Since the Passi-Kola syrup contained no preservative, it could be sold "to Druggists same as Coca Cola-Cheri Cola.... It could also be sold to bottlers ready made and so [we] could get a profit on the sugar." The elder Norman, who dispensed the drink at the soda fountain counter of his pharmacy, added that he was continuing to investigate Coca-Cola's marketing strategies—that is, to discover whether the company paid a lump sum for the sole privilege in a town or whether it contracted gallon and delivery prices outright. In a postscript, he advised Norman to add shaved ice to improve the flavor of his drink before presenting it to potential buyers.[9]

At least one major business, the Des Moines Brewing Company, took notice. In a letter of June 1, 1915, the company's treasurer wrote Norman that "we would be willing to talk matters over at any time you want to suggest a meeting for a conference" to assess the drink's prospects. Whether the two parties actually met cannot be confirmed; but no deal was ever struck.[10] Local Florida businessmen also expressed interest both in Passi-Kola and in a variant of the formula that Norman at one point considered marketing under another name. According to a letter from the elder Norman dated June 21, 1915, one Miami bottler had recently sampled the kola syrup and "wants it[,] but he is a jackleg."[11]

Despite Norman's hopes for its success, Passi-Kola proved to be a bad investment. But even before abandoning plans to produce the drink, Norman had already set his mind on a more ambitious career—filmmaking, a field that he entered around 1912, soon after he moved with his mother and brothers to the Midwest.[12] Precisely what stirred his interest in the industry is unknown. Perhaps it was an inventor's curiosity about the emerging film technology. Perhaps it was a businessman's sense of the profits to be made. Or perhaps it was simply a fascination with prominent film producers such as Kalem, Thanhouser, Lubin, World, Gaumont, and Biograph, who had gravitated from the North to the more hospitable climate of Norman's home state of Florida to establish studios and create "the First Hollywood."[13]

Like his contemporary Oscar Micheaux, Norman probably learned the craft of filmmaking on his own. He began as a film developer and later became a cameraman and a producer.[14] Over the next few years, he was associated with a number of different film companies, some of which he used merely as a mailing or regional address, others of which he founded and owned. Business cards, contract forms, and stationery from the period show that from the mid- to late-1910s Norman conducted business under various names, including the Magic Slide Manufacturing Company and the International Publicity Company of Kansas City, Missouri; the Superior Film Manufacturing Company and the Capital City Film Manufacturing Company of Des Moines, Iowa; and the Norman Film Manufacturing Company, "Guaranteed Technically Excellent Photoplays, Industrial, Advertising and Special Event Motion Pictures," of Chicago, Illinois.

As his son Captain Richard E. Norman observed, the enterprising Norman was among the first motion picture producers to recognize the commercial possibilities of contracting with cities to make "movies of municipal progress."[15] Norman's first films were fairly straightforward industrial advertising shorts for local businesses and promotional pictures for civic and fraternal organizations such as the Ancient Order of United Workmen, a Masonic benefits society in Little Rock, Arkansas, and the Brotherhood of American Yeomen of Des Moines, whose "Homecoming" he recorded.[16] Norman also filmed a wide variety of local sporting and social events, including field meets and Fourth of July celebrations.[17] According to surviving documents from those early years, Norman would be paid a set amount for each foot of film that he shot "depicting scenes, buildings and streets... and such other subjects as may be selected and determined." A down payment was required at the time of contract and the balance was due upon delivery of the developed film, which Norman processed himself at a laboratory that he established in Des Moines.[18]

As "home talent" motion pictures—short films with local people in the cast—became the latest stunt nationwide, Norman began promoting himself as a traveling film producer.[19] Using as an introduction a business card that read "R. E. Norman, Director and Photographer of Successful Photoplays Featuring Home Talent, Des Moines, Iowa," he would scout out promising towns in the Midwest and invite their citizens—especially those who were most prominent or distinguished—to act out little skits, which he then filmed and showed for a set price at area theaters. Captain Norman recalled his father's methods:

> He would film, develop and edit the picture at cost in his Iowa lab headquarters and return to the city with the completed version. After expenses, Dad would split the profits on a 60–40 basis with the city and the local theatre showing the picture. (Sixty percent for him, forty percent divided between the city and theatre owner.) After the initial showings ended, the city would retain ownership of the film and they could use it later for promotional efforts. Nearly everybody involved would come and bring their friends to the screenings at ten or fifteen cents admission. Many saw the picture time and again and the local theatre manager would run it, run it, and run it. As a result, the profits were very good.[20]

To publicize his home talent pictures, Norman advertised as widely as his budget would allow. In an illustrated ad he purchased in the Chicago-based *Photoplay Magazine,* for example, he offered readers the opportunity to "ACT IN A PHOTOPLAY" and "Give Your Talent the Acid Test of the Screen." His Norman Film Manufacturing Company (with a South Park

Avenue, Chicago address), he noted, could guide and assist amateur actors: "You don't have to go outside of your city to act in a real photoplay that will give you a chance for screen expression in a scenario best suited to bring out original facial or gestural play."[21]

Norman also created and published "Have You Talent?," a sixteen-page booklet "free for the asking" that explained how ordinary people could make their screen debuts and even embark on a film career. The booklet encouraged aspiring actors to explore "A NEW DEPARTURE IN FILM-LAND" by forming a photoplayers' club, which Norman would then direct, photograph, and cast in appropriate productions. The Norman Film Manufacturing Company, he underscored, was "the only organization to recognize the local photoplay" and to afford players experience before the camera—experience that might ensure their employment with a major film company such as Essanay, which two of Norman's players had already secured. Testimonials from theater managers affirmed the "quality and drawing power" of Norman's pictures and assured that his claims of success were valid. "Maybe," the booklet concluded, "you have a special scenario you wish produced, a big local idea filmed, a pageant or other big local occurrence that a story can be woven around. Let us hear from you."[22]

While some of Norman's earliest traveling movies consisted largely of scenes of local interest that showcased community landmarks and towns-people, others were actually rather clever and original productions. *The Wrecker,* for example, a "successful railroad photo-drama" and "powerful, thrilling, gripping melodrama," featured "A Sensational Head-On Collision, Train Wreck, Automobile Collision, Thrilling Mail Race, Stirring Fight between Hero and Villian and Pistol Battle." Using stock footage of a major railroad wreck—footage he may have purchased or filmed when he was affiliated with the International Publicity Company, which specialized in "Making Animated Pictures of Resorts, Cities, Railways and Manufacturing Plants"—Norman wrote a short script "of LOVE, HATE AND JEALOUSY" around the climactic event. As Norman's promotional materials declared, *The Wrecker* was "not an advertising film, but a clean, consistent photoplay that would appeal to all from an amusement standpoint, with the added attraction of local characters and settings."[23]

The plot of *The Wrecker,* summarized on the programs that were distributed at each of the local showings and in the press information that Norman provided to the local newspapers, involved the proverbial love triangle. Jim Hilton, an engineer on the M. N. & Q. Railroad, is in love with Helen Powers, the beautiful daughter of Railroad Superintendent Bernard Powers. One day, after Helen's car is struck by a truck that is en route to a fire, she is rescued by Jack Manning, another railroad engineer, who pulls her from the wreck; and the two fall instantly in love. Naturally, Helen's jilted suitor is angered by this turn of events. Jim's jealousy only increases when Powers selects Jack to man the Mail Special in a race to earn the government's fast mail contract to Chicago. The race has special meaning for Jack as well: if he is successful, he will secure promotion to assistant superintendent and win Powers's consent to marry Helen.

As the race nears, Jim is tempted by Satan himself to commit an act of sabotage. Yielding to the temptation, Jim throws a switch that wrecks the north- and southbound mail trains that are due to pass the double track just before Jack's train pulls out of the station. The two trains crash in a terrible head-on collision (which, as Norman noted, is a scene of "an actual wreck[,] and at the time the pictures [of it] were taken, the fireman of one of the engines lies buried beneath his engine").[24] Although the wreck delays Jack's train, he nonetheless presses on and, against all odds, wins the race—and Helen's hand. The film ends with the marriage of the happy young couple.

The photoplay usually ran about one thousand feet—that is, two reels, or approximately twenty minutes. It required as few as two days to shoot, since only fifty to two hundred feet of original film were filmed on-site. The local footage would then be intercut with existing stock at Norman's laboratory in Des Moines.[25] Although the plot of each version of *The Wrecker* was essentially the same, Norman tailored some of the details to accommodate local interests or concerns. If, for example, a town had multiple merchants, Norman might showcase their businesses by having Jack and Helen wander down the main street looking into the store windows as they shopped for her wedding gown and trousseau. ("The shopowners would thus get all involved," Captain Norman recalled, "and eventually it became a whole city operation and was advertised as such.")[26] Or, if a large number of townspeople came forward to volunteer their talents, Norman created roles for them as extras—in some cases, as members of the bridal party, as railroad yard workers, or as fellow inmates at the jail where Hilton is incarcerated after admitting his crime. And in at least one version, Norman added a comic, if stereotypically racial, twist: as Hilton attempts to escape the jail through a hole in the wall, the "fat negro convict" ahead of him becomes stuck and must be removed "with the assistance of an iron bar and a good board." Ultimately, Hilton is pursued and killed; the other inmate is captured; and a happy ending is ensured.[27]

Not only did Norman appreciate the value of an exciting story line; he also understood the need for vigorous promotion of his photoplays once they were produced—a skill he honed over the years and put to especially good use with the elaborate "ballyhos" (that is, the sensational advertising and publicity schemes) for his later feature-length films. In order to create interest in *The Wrecker* before it premiered, for example, he prepared "teaser" copy that he distributed to local newspapers. One typical teaser was a provocative headline alluding to the marriage of the two actors who played the roles of Helen and Jack. The story that followed would describe their union, which invariably came as a great surprise to readers; list the name of the local minister (or the actor who played him) and the church at which the ceremony was performed; and note that the wedding was not an elopement since it had the full approval of the bride's father. The story would conclude with the statement that "the announcement of this wedding, however, should not be taken too literally, as it is possible to be married quite frequently in the movies." Then, having piqued the curiosity of local moviegoers, the paper would print the dates and times that *The Wrecker* would be shown. Alternatively, Norman suggested to the theater managers that they plant an attention-grabbing headline announcing that the star of *The Wrecker* had been "Seriously Injured in Automobile Collision." The follow-up article would reveal that the "injury" was actually staged as part of the collision scene in Norman's railroad drama—as audiences could witness for themselves when they came to view the picture.[28]

While Norman drew his all-amateur cast from ordinary citizens, he typically chose the most prominent or influential among them for his leads. From a marketing perspective, the strategy was effective: the best known names invariably drew the largest crowds to the picture. By offering the role of Railroad Superintendent Bernard Powers to the town's mayor, commissioner, or other high-ranking official, for example, Norman knew that he could count on filling the theater—often with that person's family, friends, and political cronies alone. Similarly, Norman filmed many of the important scenes in and around the houses of the most affluent townsfolk, who clamored to see themselves on screen. Manager W. M. Savage confirmed that when the Alton, Illinois version of *The Wrecker* was shown in his theater, it attracted "the best society, even the exclusive set as well as the top gallery," all of whom left feeling very pleased to have appeared in the picture.[29] W. F. Tilford, manager of the Tilford Theatre in Murphysboro, Illinois, had a similar recollection. "The select class were our biggest boosters," he stated. Now "everyone in town wants to be a movie actor. . . . they want another picture produced right away."[30]

A romance-thriller that showcased the latest technology by incorporating automobiles and modern high-speed trains, *The Wrecker* appealed to both male and female viewers; and, according to the reviews preserved in Norman's personal scrapbooks, it was enthusiastically received wherever it was performed. In Belleville, Illinois, for instance, the paper lavished praise upon the first-ever local photoplay, staged over two days at the Illinois Central railroad station and in the public square and starring the town's Mayor R. E. Duvall. "Any time Mayor Duvall gets tired of mayoring," the article observed, "he has a job waiting for him with Essanay, Selig, Vitagraph, World Film or any of the hundred other companies that can the actors for future consumption." Residents packed the Lyric Theater in January 1916, to see Duvall and the rest of Belleville's talent "indulge in a few steps in the histrionic art. Those who got in were well repaid." The reviewer offered a rather colorful and detailed account of what the audience saw:

> A flash and a flicker and there was Mayor Duvall sitting in a big chair on the lawn of his home. Up comes Miss Melba Hoerner, supposed to be the daughter of the superintendent of the railroad. She kisses the mayor on the cheek and the audience calls for the censor board. Along comes Alfred E. Kern, who is going to be a villian, only you don't know it yet. They hop into an automobile and so far not one of them has looked in the camera. Flash!

Who is this cigar laden piece of dapperness strolling down Main [S]treet? None other than Jack Manning, the hero of our little tale. Manning is played by Charles Meyer with a vigor and verve that are inspiring. Well it all goes along with precision and point. To tell the harrowing plot would spoil it. . . . There's the devil of jealousy depicted, but the image of jealousy doesn't do it as well as Alfred Kern [who ends up "languishing in the City Bastille"]. And there is a wedding of the hero and heroine by Rev. Highfield [the real-life pastor of the First Presbyterian Church, who performs the marriage "moviecally"].[31]

Afterward, Lyric's manager, John G. Frederick, took great pleasure in recommending Norman's work to other photoplayers, since "his proposition far exceeded my expectations." During its initial three-day run, Frederick confirmed, *The Wrecker* played at ten- and twenty-cent admissions to a standing-room-only crowd of 1,700.[32]

In Kankakee, Illinois, where a local version of *The Wrecker* enjoyed a three-day run at the Court Theatre in May 1916, the home talent movie earned similar acclaim from the audience and the local press. Reviewers noted that the film, undoubtedly the biggest hit ever staged in Kankakee, was "as clear as a crystal all the way thru. . . . The little plot running thru the film is good and the local people taking part proved themselves clever amateurs," while Mayor Ben Alpiner deserved special praise as "a star [who] took to the camera posing like a regular Francis Bushman." D. H. Bestor, manager of the Court Theater, agreed: "Mr. Norman absolutely means and knows film making business," he wrote. "If you give Mr. Norman a little of your assistance, select a popular cast and stage a local photoplay along his advanced lines you will give the people of your city something that will live a long time in their memory as one of the biggest successes ever staged in your city."[33] In Murphysboro, Illinois, Norman's two-reel railroad photoplay showed to a full house for three days, both matinees and nights, at advanced admission, and patrons "went crazy over the film."[34] In Carbondale, Illinois, A. W. Barth, manager of the Amusu Theatre, called *The Wrecker* the strongest drawing card of the season and marveled that Norman managed to incorporate into the cast over a thousand students and faculty at Southern Illinois State Normal University as well as a large group of Illinois State Dairymen who were meeting at the school.[35]

The accolades were echoed by theater owners and managers throughout the region. Chas. H. Carey, manager of the Grand Opera House in Oshkosh, Wisconsin, recalled that *The Wrecker* was a "big hit" that received unanimous acclaim from his patrons during its four-day run, while Frank McCarthy, manager of the Rex and Strand Theatres in Beloit, Wisconsin, declared that Norman's "magnificent community play," which played to capacity business at top prices for its entire run, was "as fine as any exchange or producer ever sent out."[36] From St. Louis to Little Rock, from Tulsa to Des Moines, from Lorain to Fort Dodge, *The Wrecker* attracted large crowds that happily paid to watch and to celebrate their local talent on the screen.

Perhaps the best testament to *The Wrecker*'s popularity was its longevity. Norman's records show that local versions of the photoplay were filmed and shown, mostly in the Midwest, for more than four years. J. B. Price, manager of the Star Theatre, Hannibal, Missouri, provided the first surviving review in 1915: he stated that, in his long history as a showman, he had seen no production that pleased people more than *The Wrecker* or offered such universal satisfaction.[37] The picture was still satisfying audiences as late as December 1919 in Oklahoma City, where *The Theatre Bulletin* announced that *The Wrecker*, a "Real Photoplay Enacted by Home Folk," was playing for four days at the New Folly Theatre.[38]

Another of Norman's popular home talent moving pictures was *Sleepy Sam, The Sleuth*, a one-reel detective farce that, like *The Wrecker*, intercut local scenes with stock footage, used a prepared script, and required only a handful of props—two dark slouch caps, one checkered cap, one auto duster and goggles, a gunny sack, and a local newspaper—to stage.[39] "A Real Reel Scream," *Sleepy Sam* was advertised as "A Local Photo Play made in your city. 1,000 laughs in 1,000 feet. Acted by your friends. Replete with comical surprises. Be sure and see the funny photo players of this city and their comic capers."[40]

In the picture, the eponymous Sam learns from the newspaper (whose name was changed, in each version, to correspond to the town in which the picture was being filmed) that chicken thieves have been busy at Silas Brown's farm. After he falls asleep, Sam dreams that Farmer Brown has hired him as a detective to "apprehend the fowl criminals." That night, while on guard near the hen house, he surprises two thieves and gives chase in his automobile. But the thieves steal a bomb from some bearded Italian anarchists and blow up Sam's vehicle. The accident causes a temporary delay, but soon Sam sets off again in pursuit of the criminals. As Sam gains on them, they loose another bomb that assumes a tremendous size, rolls over him, and mashes him flat. Fortunately, Professor Buggsy, who is nearby collecting beetles, discovers Sam's plight and resuscitates him with a "pulmotor." Once again, Sam resumes the pursuit. But after many such adventures, Sam awakens to find it has all been a dream.

The "delightful" and "mirthful little skit" enacted by local players was enhanced by interesting cinematic techniques such as bridging and iris shots.[41] The sixty-four short scenes not only incorporated "car chases, foot chases, characters who are flattened into cardboard-thin pancakes, and balloon-size bombs that are tossed back and forth like hot coals" but also featured "an Inspector-Clouseau-like detective who bumbles his way through the investigation and pursuit of justice."[42] Usually screened as part of a double bill with another comedy, *Sleepy Sam* was apparently just what audiences had been craving.[43] Like *The Wrecker*, it played for three-day runs in Maquoketa, Iowa, and other cities in the Midwest to sold-out crowds for admissions of fifteen to twenty cents.

Pro Patria (1916), another of Norman's home talent movies, used its local players in a different and distinctive way.[44] According to the promotional material, the "first and only real college play ever written and filmed by University talent" was "staged in the Twin Cities [of Urbana and Champaign], in and around the Campus, showing the beautiful University of Illinois buildings, fraternity and sorority houses and some wonderful interior scenes, taken in the Chemistry Building, the largest instructional Chemical Laboratory in the world."[45]

The plot of the picture combined collegiate love and foreign intrigue. After his father experiences a severe business loss, serious-minded university junior Dale Gordon is rejected by his social-climbing fiancée Inez and forced to leave his fraternity in order to work his way through school. At the chemistry department, where he secures a position, he succeeds in developing a powerful and valuable explosive. Meanwhile, wealthy Mexican Eduardo Salazar, a fellow student of Dale's, is attracted to Inez's sorority sister, pretty coed Betty Gibson, whom he fascinates with tales of his beautiful home beyond the Rio Grande and whom he tries to win with the gift of an expensive pearl necklace. But when Betty returns the gift and turns him down for Dale's good-natured but irresponsible young frat brother Happy Harding, a despondent Eduardo decides to steal Dale's formula and give it to the powerful Mexican faction with whom he is connected. At first, Eduardo is assisted by another student, James Blake, whom he blackmails and threatens to expose. Blake, however, reveals Eduardo's criminal intent to Dale, who locks the formula in a drawer. When Eduardo, now working alone, breaks into the building to steal the formula, Dale catches him in the act. During the ensuing fight, Eduardo destroys much of the laboratory equipment before he escapes; but, in his haste, he falls down the stairs and is killed. The picture ends at the fraternity formal, where Betty accepts Hap's pin and the newly wealthy Dale proposes to Helen Carmen, the young woman who—unlike Inez—realized Dale's true worth and stood by him in his darkest times.

The four-reel film, which was filmed in ten days "of thrills, excitement and hard work," was based on a scenario by Vivian Woodcock Kay, the wife of Professor Kay of the State Geological Survey; Mrs. Kay also played the lead role of Betty, the adorable winsome freshman.[46] Reviews of the picture in the *Chicago Herald, Champaign Daily News,* and *Champaign Daily Gazette* were overwhelmingly positive. In the University's *Illini* newspaper, reviewer "F. L." observed that *Pro Patria* "held the interest of the audience through out, not only because it had a local interest but because it was a cleverly acted, thrilling story"; and, as a whole, the finished play seemed well produced and entirely professional.[47] In another edition of *Illini,* "The Critic" concurred, calling the movie "beyond expectation," with "everything above average: every picture and every closeup is extremely clear due to the excellent work of Mr. R. E. Norman who photographed the production." The exciting plot, full of Illinois loyalty and spirit as well as national pride and interest, was matched by the excellence of the acting, from local stage celebrities and members of "Mask and Bauble" Heinie Sellards (as Dale) and Richardine Woolman (as Helen) to Arthur Metzler (as Happy), one of the Illini Photoplayers.[48] Interest in the picture was so strong, in fact, that a Champaign theater manager pledged to bring *Pro Patria* back for a three-day return engagement that fall.

The home talent photoplays occasionally reaped other unexpected rewards for Norman as well. In Marinette, Wisconsin, for instance, where he was contracted to film a local version of *The Wrecker*, Norman met Gloria Des Jardins, one of two sisters who played supporting roles as bridesmaids in the picture. He later cast Gloria in the starring role of another local talent film, *Marinette Adopts a Baby*; and eventually—after the local bishop granted her a religious dispensation to marry a divorced man—they wed.[49] In a 1975 Jacksonville *Times-Union and Journal* interview with Lyn Lazarus, Gloria Norman recalled the circumstances of their first meeting: "I am sure you know the line," she said. "He asked me if I'd like to be in the movies, and I said sure!"[50]

Norman's early pictures, however, were not limited to railroad adventures, hen house comedies, and collegiate capers. He also filmed a number of short historical films. One such film, *Buried Alive*, subtitled "Historical Indian Production of John Stink, Osage Indian Outcast," recounted a tale of love, hate, and intense rivalry in an Osage Indian village in the 1870s.[51] Swift Fox, son of Chief White Hairs, is in love with Laughing Water. But Grey Wolf, who wants Laughing Water all to himself, conspires to get rid of his rival. As Swift Fox falls ill, the Medicine Man is called upon to dispel the Evil Spirits that have sickened him. Instead, he puts the young brave into a trance and pronounces him dead. When Swift Fox is "BURIED ALIVE" on a hilltop, a sentry is posted to keep watch overnight and to keep away the spirits until his soul can safely reach the Happy Hunting Ground. But when the brave awakens from his trance, the sentry sends out an alarm that alerts the villagers, who are convinced that the resurrected Swift Fox is a ghost. Weak and starved from his harrowing ordeal and crazed by the sight of his beloved in the arms of Grey Wolf, he drags himself to the cabin of white settler James Owen, who feeds and clothes him. In the final scene, the viewer is told that Swift Fox is now Owen's guardian: "To-day [Swift Fox] roams the streets of Pawhuska, OK/ and is called an evil spirit by the Indians who have named him JOHN STINK. He sleeps outside his Guardians Hardware Store and refuses to have anything to do with anyone else but him."

Produced around the same time, *Real Facts About the North Field Minnesota Bank Robbery, or The Younger Brother in Minnesota* had a similar Western orientation.[52] After a Missouri farmer is killed by a Union soldier during the Civil War, his sons—Cole, Jim, Bob, and John Younger—vow revenge and "become Guerillas [who] let no chance escape to pilfer the Yankees and Federal troops." When the brothers learn that their mother has been hounded to death and their family home devastated, their desire for revenge grows even more intense, and they join one of the most savage fighting units in the Confederacy. After the war, they move to Texas, where John is forced into a quarrel and "wantonly murdered"; and, with the influx of Yankees and Carpetbaggers, Cole, Jim, Bob, and their friends are persecuted for their wartime activities. Deciding "to adopt desperate measures to make a living as their professions are all usurped," they form an outlaw band. During a heist at the Northfield Bank, several members of the Younger Gang are wounded; the rest are pursued and—after a shootout and a siege in a swamp—captured by the sheriff's posse. Bob dies from consumption contracted in the swamp; Cole and Jim are sentenced to life in prison but are soon pardoned. "Dejected," Jim commits suicide; but Cole takes up residence in Missouri. In the final scene he is pictured "in his Home to-day at Lee['s] Summit."

Another of Norman's short historic pictures, made around 1915 or 1916, told the story of an even more notorious American outlaw: Belle Starr, the "Bandit Queen." Renowned for her crack shooting skills, her stylish wardrobe, her Indian husband, and her colorful male companions, including Jesse James and Cole Younger (who was rumored to have fathered her child), Starr was killed in an ambush in 1889, just days before her forty-first birthday, and immediately became part of popular legend. Norman's *Bell* [*sic*] *Starr, A Female Desperado*, filmed in Oklahoma and Kansas, begins with the escape of Belle, "a born guerilla," from the federal troops who have captured her, and it ends as she "DIES WITH HER BOOTS ON."[53] Also dramatized in the film's eighty scenes are some of the most climactic events in Starr's life: her marriage to Jim, who is killed by the posse that is hotly pursuing the pair; her organizing of an outlaw gang, who assist her in exacting frontier vengeance; her "depredations" (some of which, like the theft of a Jewish peddler's outfit, are—according to the script—scenes with "lots of comedy"); her feigned interest in a bachelor bank cashier whose courtship she encourages and whom she later robs of $30,000; and her love for her young daughter Pearl, who learns of Belle's death when she sees her mother's horse return, riderless and bloodied, to their cabin.

Describing one of the scenes in the film to a local reporter, Norman explained Belle's popular appeal:

> I was portrayng a historic incident about a member of Belle Starr's gang, Blue Duck, who borrowed $2,000 from her and lost it in a card game in Fort Dodge. Belle Star, on learning of the loss of her money, single handed returned and held up the gamblers, and instead of getting $2,000, as a historic fact, she got $7,000. An backing out of the gambling hall, she said, "Gentlemen, there is a little change due you. If you want it, come down in the territory"; and with this she fired a shot and galloped away on her horse. They never came down in the territory for the change.[54]

It was another outlaw, however, Belle's nephew Henry Starr, the "Bandit King," who would play an even more eventful role in Norman's film career. A notorious criminal, Starr became the leader of a gang of robbers who preyed on banks throughout the state of Oklahoma beginning around the turn of the century. In March of 1915, the gang decided to pull an especially daring job by simultaneously robbing two banks in the small town of Stroud. But a local boy, seventeen-year-old Paul Curry, discovered the plan, foiled the robbery, and shot Starr, who was later captured and incarcerated for several years. Upon release, Starr not only declared himself a changed man ("I'm off crookedness for life," he swore); he also decided to document his redemption by filming a feature-length movie about the bungled robbery, in which he planned to assume the starring role.[55] After attracting a group of investors to underwrite the project, he returned to Stroud to shoot the picture. For further authenticity, he engaged the services of Paul Curry and some of the actual tellers he had robbed to play themselves in supporting roles.

Produced by the Pan American Motion Picture Corporation and originally distributed by Peacock Pictures, *A Debtor to the Law* premiered in 1919. Yet, while the film made money, Starr did not: reportedly he was cheated out of his share by his business partners and soon returned to his old profession.[56] Only two years later, he was shot to death in Arkansas while trying to rob a bank.

Although *A Debtor to the Law* has long been attributed to Norman and included among his race films in several filmographies, it was neither a Norman production nor a race movie. (The film, in fact, was entirely white-cast.) The misattribution may be due to the fact that, for a time, *Debtor* appeared on a sidebar listing of Norman's films on the company's stationery (a common practice of film producers and distributors, who used their correspondence to announce and promote recent releases), in advertising materials, and even on the preprinted attendance and record forms that Norman used to track the distribution and gross of his pictures.[57] Yet, while Norman did not actually produce *Debtor*, he played a crucial role in promoting it.

Both as a filmmaker and as a businessman, Norman was always on the lookout for interesting opportunities. He recognized that producing films was just one facet of the movie business; distribution and marketing was another. Consequently, in addition to his own pictures, Norman sought to acquire rights to the films of other filmmakers, which he could then distribute—either as independent features or as part of a double bill with his own productions—within the territories he covered. He was especially interested in material that overlapped with his own films and interests, which included stories with Western or criminal themes.

In early 1922, Norman exchanged several letters with M. K. Fink, President of Peacock Productions, Inc., in Kansas City, Missouri, who offered him State Rights to show *Debtor* in parts of the Southeast. While a "bandit picture" was not a masterpiece of the picture-making art, Fink wrote that *Debtor* had proven to be a strong box office attraction that earned "a considerable sum of money" from distribution in his territory of Texas, Oklahoma, Arkansas, Kansas, Missouri, Southern Illinois, Iowa, and Nebraska.[58]

Norman responded almost immediately.[59] Noting that he had already produced several outlaw pictures, including the successful Scout Younger films, Norman claimed that, years earlier, he had come close to taking over the production of *Debtor*. At the time, though, the situation with the promoters was so chaotic that he decided against tackling it. But since his film company already had three roadshows out, he felt he could give *Debtor* the "special lobby display" it needed and was therefore willing to "get together on a percentage proposition" to handle the film in his territory.

Norman was soon in contact again, this time with M. R. Lubin of Tulsa, Oklahoma, to finalize distribution rights. After receiving a print, however, Norman found the quality of *Debtor* to be poor, with missing parts and titles, and the film itself simply not up to his standard. Nonetheless, he believed that—by reediting and updating it in light of Starr's ignoble death the year before and by presenting the picture to moviegoers as a kind of modern morality tale—he could salvage it. The reediting and repackaging could be accomplished expeditiously by eliminating some of the sameness in the film, especially the repetitious robbery scenes, and by interposing several titles "of a moral nature . . . [to] help the picture over." Norman added that making a steady print without streaks—something he asserted his company could accomplish at the cost of three-and-a-half cents a foot—would improve the photography of the picture by at least fifty percent. Assuming he could get an extension on rights for the states of Florida and Georgia, he concluded that he would be happy to negotiate for even more territory.[60]

Lubin replied to Norman, urging him to make the necessary improvements and to prevent laboratory delays by reassembling the print himself.[61] That is precisely what Norman did; and by the spring of 1923, he was handling distribution and promotion of the reedited film. In addition to the existing paper (heralds, handbills, one-sheet posters, three-sheet posters, etc.), photos, slides, and cuts that he purchased from Peacock Productions, Norman also developed some new advertising, including a series of Western-style ads. One of the most effective of those ads was fashioned after an actual wanted poster. "WANTED!" it read, over a photo of a fashionably dressed Starr. "Henry Starr, Last of the Great Western Outlaws, wants every man who dreamed when he was a boy of becoming a bandit—and every woman who knows such a man—to know what an outlaw's life is really like and what it leads to. See 'A Debtor to the Law' and more thrills than you've ever had packed into one evening will be your REWARD!" Another ad, which announced that "He 'Fined' the World One Million Dollars—and He Collected!," featured a prominent image of Starr's gang, fully armed and "waiting" for the viewer. Other "Stunts" and "Stimulators" that Norman proposed to theater owners to "Pack 'Em In!" included the hiring of a man dressed as a cowpuncher to ride, masked, through the streets of the town:

> In the afternoon put a sign on his back which reads:
> "My Name's Rattle-Snake Pete.
> I'm Going to Join
> HENRY STARR
> The Famous Oklahoma Outlaw
> at the ____ Theatre Tomorrow."
> When you open *A Debtor to the Law* hitch the same horse at the curb
> outside your house. Have signs on either side of him that say:
> "My Pal HENRY STARR
> Last of the Western Bandits
> IS INSIDE
> Go In and See What Happened at Other Places Where He Left Me Waiting."

Still other promotions were targeted to specific groups, such as preachers (whose pulpit could "GIVE BOOST TO 'DEBTOR'"), teachers (who could use the "educational value and strong moral" of the film to educate their pupils), and prisoners (who "might derive good from seeing it"). Most of the advance flyers had a common theme: the film, promoted as "An Authentic Page From the Most Virile Chapter in American History" and a "Real Heart Stopping Drama of Life in the Raw When the West Was 'Wild,'" was undeniably "ONE OF THE GREATEST MORAL LESSONS EVER SCREENED."[62] And in fact, in Norman's hands, *Debtor* found a new audience and continued to draw moviegoers for the next decade.[63]

Norman clearly brought both his entrepreneurial spirit and his business acumen to his early work as a local talent filmmaker; and he achieved a modicum of success with short pictures such as *The Wrecker, Sleepy Sam,* and *Pro Patria,* which he filmed on-site in various cities and localities and then developed in his own laboratory in Des Moines. But it was neither his own white-cast pictures from the 1910s nor the white-oriented films like *A Debtor to the Law* which he handled and distributed that secured Norman's place in the industry. Rather, it was his feature-length race films, which he began producing in the 1920s, that established Norman's reputation and through which he made his most enduring contribution to American cinema.

Richard E. Norman with his family. From left to right: Earl Redding Norman (brother), Katherine Kennedy Bruce Norman (mother), Richard Edward Norman Jr., and Kenneth Bruce Norman Sr. (brother). (*Courtesy of Mrs. Katherine Norman Hiett*)

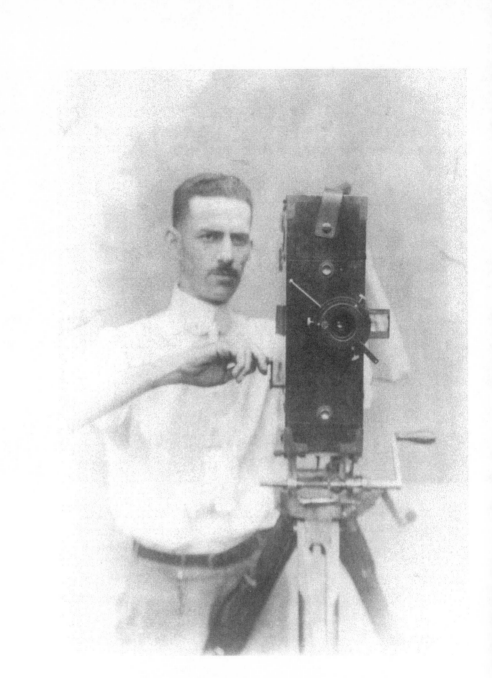

During Richard E. Norman's early years in the industry, his brother and business partner Bruce Norman (pictured here) roadshowed the Norman Film Manufacturing Company pictures—and sometimes operated the camera during production. (*Courtesy of Mrs. Katherine Norman Hiett*)

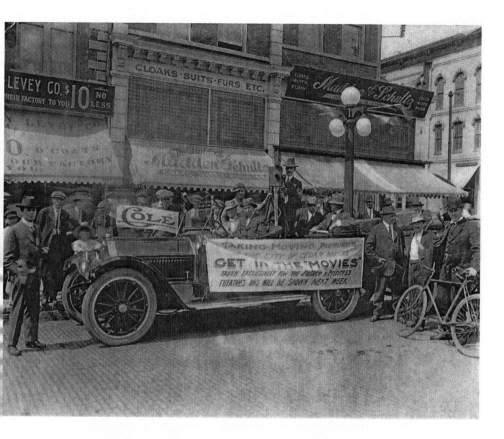

For his "home talent" pictures in the 1910s, Richard E. Norman traveled throughout the Midwest and offered citizens the opportunity to perform in a prescripted photoplay set in their town. After developing the film and combining it with stock footage at his plant in Des Moines, he would return to the town to exhibit the picture. (*Courtesy of the Lilly Library, Indiana University, Bloomington, Indiana*)

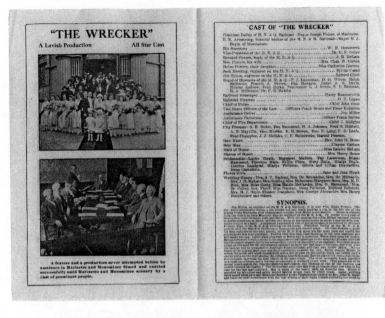

Don't Miss This

BELL STARR

The old Indian Territory

Female Bandit

3100

Feet

3100

Feet

A Thrilling Historical Melodrama showing the life and final tragic death of America's most Famous Female Bandit.

A Great Moral Lesson in Three Reels of superb motion pictures.

NABOB THEATRE
Wednesday, October 16th only

A handbill for *Bell Starr,* one of Norman's early historical Western shorts. Starr, a legendary female bandit who associated with infamous outlaws Cole Younger and Jesse James, was the leader of a notorious outlaw gang that operated in the Oklahoma territory. (*Courtesy of the Lilly Library, Indiana University, Bloomington, Indiana*)

Facing, top. The Wrecker, "a thrilling railroad photo drama," was Norman's most popular white-cast local-talent picture. This version, filmed in Marinette, Wisconsin, featured Gloria Des Jardins (Norman's future wife) as one of the bridesmaids. (*Courtesy of the Lilly Library, Indiana University, Bloomington, Indiana*)

Facing, bottom. Pro Patria, another of Norman's local photoplays, was a story of collegiate love and espionage. Filmed at the University of Illinois, it was acted by the Illini Photoplayers. (*Courtesy of the Lilly Library, Indiana University, Bloomington, Indiana*)

Left. Promotional materials for the Henry Starr picture *A Debtor to the Law,* which Norman did not produce but which he reedited after Starr's death and distributed for almost a decade. A relative of Belle Starr, Henry Starr was a notorious horse thief and train robber. (*Courtesy of the Richard E. Norman Collection, Special Collection REN, Black Film Center/ Archive, Indiana University, Bloomington, Indiana*)

Facing, top. A rental agreement for *The Green-Eyed Monster* and *The Love Bug.* Norman's contracts typically outlined the terms of the rental, the amount of heralds and other advertising paper that the exhibitor ordered, the seating capacity of the theater, even the population of the city in which the picture was being played. (*Courtesy of the Richard E. Norman Collection, Special Collection REN, Black Film Center/Archive, Indiana University, Bloomington, Indiana*)

Facing, bottom. An advertisement for the original eight-reel version of *The Green-Eyed Monster* (1919), Norman's first black-cast feature film, which had a dual plot: a serious dramatic story of racial uplift and ambition and a comedic subplot full of chases and farcical misadventures. (*Courtesy of the Lilly Library, Indiana University, Bloomington, Indiana*)

A six-week tally of percentages and rentals for *The Green-Eyed Monster*, detailing the dates and places where the film was shown as well as the daily box-office and advertising receipts. As the figures indicate, *The Green-Eyed Monster* was a huge success. (*Courtesy of the Lilly Library, Indiana University, Bloomington, Indiana*)

The poster for the reedited five-reel version of *The Green-Eyed Monster* (1920), which included footage of an actual train wreck. Billed as "the greatest picture of its kind," *The Green-Eyed Monster* proved to be one of the most popular race films of the decade. (*Courtesy of the Lilly Library, Indiana University, Bloomington, Indiana*)

From *The Green-Eyed Monster:* As he embarks on the great mail race, engineer
Jack Manning (Earl Cumbo) gets a kiss for good luck from Helen Powers
(Louise Dunbar). Helen's father, Railroad Superintendent Powers, stands
nearby. (*Courtesy of the Richard E. Norman Collection, Special Collection REN,
Black Film Center/Archive, Indiana University, Bloomington, Indiana*)

From *The Green-Eyed Monster:* A tramp (played by Norman's favorite actor, Steve "Peg" Reynolds) reveals to detectives the identity of Manning's rival, Jim Hilton (Jack "Buddy" Austin), who threw the switch to derail the north- and southbound trains and caused the big wreck. *(Courtesy of the Richard E. Norman Collection, Special Collection REN, Black Film Center/Archive, Indiana University, Bloomington, Indiana)*

From *The Love Bug* (1920): While shooting craps with fellow players (Mustard Prophet, Hogface, Pink Eye, and Cinnamon), String Bean Oldfield suffers a streak of bad luck. He hopes to reverse that streak with the purchase of Cinnamon's lucky goat, Lily; but she literally eats up his profits. (*Courtesy of the Richard E. Norman Collection, Special Collection REN, Black Film Center/Archive, Indiana University, Bloomington, Indiana*)

From *The Love Bug:* Romantic rivals twice-widowed Mrs. Margerine Scrubb (Maud Johnson) and never-married Miss Cuspidora Lee (Maud Frisbie) are prepared to fight for the affections of bachelor Quintus Weefalls (Robert Stewart). (*Courtesy of the Richard E. Norman Collection, Special Collection REN, Black Film Center/Archive, Indiana University, Bloomington, Indiana*)

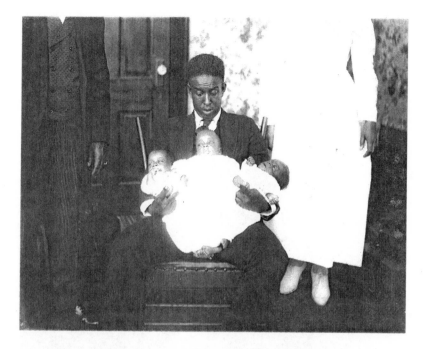

From *The Love Bug:* Marriage to Dazzle Zeanor holds many surprises for Quintus—in particular, his newborns (played by "Real Colored Triplets"). (*Courtesy of the Richard E. Norman Collection, Special Collection REN, Black Film Center/Archive, Indiana University, Bloomington, Indiana*)

Before they could be exhibited, Norman's films had to be vetted by state—and sometimes also by city—censors, who often required the excising of certain scenes and titles. (*Courtesy of the Lilly Library, Indiana University, Bloomington, Indiana*)

Richard E. Norman in Oklahoma in the early 1920s, during the filming of his all-black-cast Westerns, *The Bull-Dogger* and *The Crimson Skull*. (*Courtesy of Mrs. Katherine Norman Hiett*)

As the advertisement boldly announced, *The Bull-Dogger* (1922) was an exciting Round-Up Western that showcased the rodeo skills of champion bulldogger Bill Pickett and other black cowboys. (*Courtesy of the Lilly Library, Indiana University, Bloomington, Indiana*)

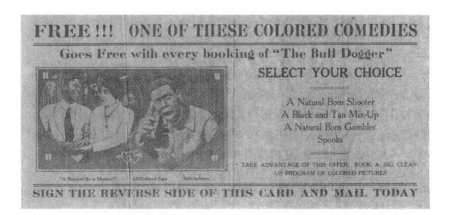

Norman employed various promotions to induce theaters to book his pictures. One such promotion was this mailer, which offered a free short comedy with each booking. On the back of the mailer was a return reply postcard for the exhibitor's convenience. (*Courtesy of the Lilly Library, Indiana University, Bloomington, Indiana*)

CHAPTER THREE

"Not a White Man in the Cast": Norman's Early Race Films

BY THE END of the 1910s, Richard E. Norman had not only demonstrated his entrepreneurial skills but also gained a reputation as an independent producer of home talent moving pictures. Traveling throughout the Midwest, he created scores of short films that intercut stock footage with images of local scenes and ordinary people. But Norman had grown anxious to move beyond local talent, industrial, advertising, and historical shorts into the burgeoning business of feature films. At the same time, he decided to establish a base for his new operation by relocating to his hometown of Jacksonville, Florida.

Jacksonville proved to be an ideal location for Norman. In the decade between 1910 and 1920, Florida had become a mecca of modern filmmaking.[1] As Richard Alan Nelson noted in *Florida and the American Motion Picture Industry, 1898–1980,* Florida offered a number of distinct advantages. The sunny climate and especially the mild winters, "well suited to the slow orthochromatic film stocks of the silent era," allowed producers to maintain shooting schedules year-round. Transportation links to the city were well established, with good "rail, steamship, and roadway connections to the population and industry centers in the Northeast and Midwest." (A trip from New York to Florida, for example, could be completed overnight, whereas travel to the West Coast typically required five days.) Production costs were reasonable. And because of the historically depressed state of Florida's economy, land costs remained low, at least until the boom in the mid-1920s. So did labor costs, since local laborers generally received wages below the prevailing national standard—"a potentially significant factor for big pictures requiring thousands of extras." Moreover, once trained, the cadres of support and technical workers provided a continuing presence and a resource for other producers. And civic leaders, local chambers of commerce, and newspapers, all of whom recognized the financial benefit that film production brought to the state, largely supported the interests of the industry.[2]

The Florida Times Union (May 6, 1914) described how Florida had evolved into a center of silent filmmaking:

> Florida, to many a few years ago, was a veritable forest of mystery, full of every imaginable wild beast, pitfall, swamp and tangled thicket. Those who had not come and seen for themselves shied at the very mention of the name of the fair peninsula. So well can the first expeditionary forces of the motion picture artists be remembered. They came hurriedly for the color of the wild, and went away convinced that the state . . . offered a far wider range of advantages to photo-playing than any other section of America. The result has been that Florida scenes are now figuring more largely and more prominently in photo-playing than any other known section.[3]

While the prospect of year-round location sites attracted many Northern-based filmmakers to cities from Miami to Tampa–St. Petersburg, it was Jacksonville—then one of the principal financial, manufacturing, distributing, and transportation centers in the Southeast—that quickly emerged as the heart of Florida's motion picture industry.[4] From 1912 to 1914, in fact, there were more movie units working there than in Los Angeles; and, as Terry Ramsaye noted in his early history of the motion picture industry *A Million and One Nights*, Jacksonville continued for some years to overshadow Los Angeles as the winter studio capital.[5]

The first of the major filmmakers to capitalize on Jacksonville's resources was Kalem, a New York City–based company founded in 1907 by George Kleine, Samuel Long, and Frank J. Marion. During the 1908–1909 winter season, Kalem established the first location studio in the United

States—that is, according to Shawn C. Bean in *The First Hollywood*, "the first permanent filmmaking location that wasn't in the Northeast and the first to prove that a temperate climate was essential to filmmaking."[6] In its first season alone, Kalem produced a total of eighteen films (including the classic mixed-race story *The Octoroon* [1909]), almost all of which utilized Florida's authentic natural backgrounds. The profits that Kalem earned from these pictures kept the company returning to Jacksonville for many winters to come and even motivated it, for a time, to produce its features there throughout the year.

Other filmmakers soon followed. The Motograph Company of America, an independent Baltimore-based company, arrived in 1910, with promises (ultimately unfulfilled) to create a real sensation among the picture men of the day.[7] After taking over Motograph's studio space in Jacksonville's Dixieland Park, the next year William Selig and his Selig Polyscope Company imported their exotic menagerie of lions, camels, and elephants and began turning out a series of successful animal pictures, sometimes called "dramas of the jungle." Also at Dixieland Park, Essanay—the company's name a merging of the initials of its Chicago founders George K. Spoor and Gilbert M. Anderson—filmed several of its trademark Broncho Billy Westerns; and both Lubin and the Vim Comedy Company later used that location as well. In fact, it was in his Jacksonville-based comedy *Outwitting Dad* (1914) that Lubin first cast a visiting theater manager–turned-actor (credited as O. N. Hardy) as a fat boy who pretends to be a bad man in order to scare his brother's future father-in-law. That actor would subsequently be featured (as "Babe" Hardy) in eleven Vim comedies shot in Jacksonville before winning real fame in Hollywood as half of the classic Laurel and Hardy comedy team.[8]

Jacksonville was also the place where Adolph Zukor's Artcraft Picture Corporation shot its first picture, *Broadway Jones* (1917), starring the noted actor, playwright, and composer George M. Cohan—and the place where such distinguished producers as Gaumont, Thanhouser, and Vitagraph filmed scores of their pictures.[9] And it was the place where a few filmmakers established more permanent roots. The Eagle Film Company, for example, built a large studio with both indoor and outdoor stages and a film processing laboratory on a multi-acre site in the Jacksonville suburb of Arlington.[10] Eagle occupied the premises from 1915 to 1917 and rented space to the Gates City Picture Company and other producers. And the Klutho Studios, built and largely self-financed by prominent Jacksonville architect Henry J. Klutho in 1916–1917, was a state-of-the-art facility that incorporated innovations such as a unique system of sunshields that could be moved by a series of pulleys to correct for changes in light. Klutho made a few films, including the "Sunbeam Comedies," starring actor Hilliard "Fatty" Karr, under its own name; and it also leased facilities to other companies—Yorke-Metro, Paramount, Florida Funny Film Corporation, and Briggs Pictures—before selling to Berg Productions.[11] Ultimately more than thirty production companies "set up camp in town, helping the city earn the nickname of 'World's Winter Film Capital.'" And between 1909 and 1926, approximately three hundred films were produced in Jacksonville alone.[12] But a variety of factors—from the political controversy over the efforts of newly elected Mayor J. E. T. Bowden to attract increased investment in the film business to the failure of local banks to support financing of the venture; from America's entry into World War I to the deadly outbreak of influenza in 1918, which claimed hundreds of thousands of lives—eventually brought the expansion to a halt. And Jacksonville's once-vital place in the motion picture industry was soon usurped by Hollywood.

The Jacksonville to which Richard E. Norman returned around 1920, however, was still very much a place of promise and possibilities. Inspired by the small and independent filmmakers who were engaged in making pictures that sometimes rivaled those of the major studios, Norman decided to expand his own business by moving into feature films. And the particular type of feature film he wanted to produce was the race picture, which employed a black cast and was created for black audiences and usually shown only in black theaters.

Although Norman never commented specifically on what attracted him to race filmmaking, he no doubt observed the crowds of enthusiastic black filmgoers at the midnight rambles and special "colored showings" in the towns and cities through which he traveled as a home talent producer. And, like film distributor H. G. Till, who believed that "the making of motion pictures with all-negro casts is a money making branch of this industry that has been too long neglected," he recognized the financial potential in producing and distributing pictures for such a broad but underrepresented market.[13] "There is," Norman wrote a colleague, "no better angle of the motion picture business you can get into for quick returns and sure profit than the distribution of Negro Pictures."[14] Yet, Captain Richard E. Norman insisted, his father's motives were not just monetary:

> My Dad, of course, was a businessman. But an underlined thought in his mind was the desire to do something constructive to better race relations. Through his films he was committed to helping the black players live up to their potential and show what they were capable of as performers and human beings.[15]

For his first race feature, Norman revisited a subject that he had successfully explored in scores of earlier home talent motion pictures. *The Green-Eyed Monster* was a black-cast remake of Norman's familiar railroad story *The Wrecker* (occasionally shown under alternate titles, including *The Green-Eyed Monster*). The white-cast home talent versions of *The Wrecker* were two-reelers, approximately a thousand feet long, the bulk of which consisted of stock footage of a train wreck that Norman intercut with local scenes and actors. For his feature-length film of *The Green-Eyed Monster*, however, Norman realized that he would have to rework the material significantly: he added characters, developed the relationships between them, and extended the action by incorporating chase scenes and other plot elements typical of contemporary popular serials. At the same time, he determined to give the story a fresh twist by introducing a comic subplot.

The main plot of *The Green-Eyed Monster* essentially re-created the events of *The Wrecker;* and like its predecessor, it capitalized, in Phyllis R. Klotman's words, "on the audience interest in men, machines, and movement."[16] At the same time, it also reflected the postwar employment opportunities for blacks who had migrated north in new and emerging industries, including railways, steel, and transportation. Although the film is not extant, it can be reconstructed from the promotional stills and other materials archived in the Richard E. Norman Collection at Indiana University, especially the rare original shooting script annotated in Norman's hand (printed in full in the appendix of this volume), which for the first time makes available the entire plotline. The initial subtitle card of the script set the scene: "This story occurs before the nation had assumed chaperonage over the arteries of travel and transportation, when railroads were on a competitive basis for the Government Fast Rail Contract."

The film opens with a shot of E. N. Armstrong (played by S. D. Mc-Gill), "financial banker of the rich and renowned, the proud and the powerful, the famous and farflung M. N. & Q. Railroad," seated at his desk examining some plans. Behind him, significantly, hangs a framed photograph of "Negro Presidents of the Republic." Traffic manager Henry High (J. A. Simms), "who had outwitted rivals on other lines," enters Armstrong's office and observes that because traffic has reached such magnitude, a double track is needed on the Chicago branch. Advertising director J. Frank Keeley (Ira P. Davis) joins his colleagues and, in another subtitle, informs them that in spite of all his "tall advertising assertions," the railroad has suffered since it lost the government fast mail contract to a competitor. The three men agree that implementing double trackage is essential to regaining the contract.

The scene shifts to the railroad yards, where Superintendent Bernard Powers (played by Dr. R. L. Brown Jr.), dubbed "Old Faithful" for his "loyalty and unflagging devotion in his unparal[l]eled career of service and fidelity," is issuing instructions to the railroad men. Among those men is Jim Hilton (Jacksonville native Jack "Buddy" Austin), a railroad contractor who is smitten with Powers's daughter, Helen. Meanwhile, in another part of town, Helen (Louise Dunbar) is seen getting into her car and being driven away by her chauffeur.

As Helen arrives at the railroad yard and greets her father, Jack Manning (Earl Cumbo), the "crack engineer on the Cannon Ball Limited," descends the steps of his engine cab and doffs his hat. While Powers and Hilton review the construction plans, Helen steals glances at Manning. But when he catches her looking at him, she snubs him; and he is left "standing in foolish attitude with oil can in his hand unconsciously pouring oil in his other hand." Quietly amused by this incident, Helen continues to watch Manning until her father concludes his business. "Work must commence immediately," Powers announces, "and the track rushed through in time for the Mail Race."

After Helen and Hilton leave the railyard, her car breaks down on a country road. While the chauffeur repairs the problem, Helen gets out to admire the scenery. Hilton follows; and, as they seat themselves on a fallen log, he proposes to her. In a subtitle that reads "No Jim—I don't love you," she demurs. Once the chauffeur completes the repair, they resume the ride.

"In the loom of destiny, woven by fate," however, even bigger troubles await: their car is struck by a "Speed Maniac" and bursts into flames. Fortunately, Manning, who has been standing on a nearby corner, rushes in to save Helen. As he places her on a cot in the ambulance, she regains consciousness long enough to recognize him as her rescuer. Angry that he has been bested again by Manning, Hilton stalks off. The next scene is a quick fade in/fade out shot of Satan, who plants the seeds of jealousy and revenge.

Over the next few days, Manning visits Helen, who is convalescing at home. Hilton, too, comes to call on her; but after he finds the pair lost in intimate conversation, he leaves, more jealous of them than ever. Back at the railroad yard, where work continues on the double track, Hilton confronts Manning and warns him that the next time he catches him "lamping" around Helen, he will trim his lights. "A fast and furious fight" ensues; but even after he loses, Hilton tries, in a most ungentlemanly fashion, to brain Manning with a big lump of coal and threatens to "get" him. In the next scene, Satan reappears, laughing at the hatred that has been stirred up.

Hiding in the bushes, Hilton watches as Manning approaches Powers and haltingly asks for Helen's hand. Powers, though, expresses doubt that the young man can properly support her. As Manning makes his case, Helen nestles her head on her father's shoulder to win his approval. Suddenly, Powers glimpses an article in the paper he has been reading and gets an idea. "Your engine will pull the mail special," he tells Manning. "If you win the mail race I will appoint you my assistant, then you can marry Helen."

But Hilton has different plans. After learning that construction of the double track is complete, he yields to temptation by Satan and pledges to keep Manning from winning the race by throwing the switch that will wreck the north- and southbound trains now speeding down the new track. What follows is a scene simply titled "The Wrecker."

Back at the railroad yard, as Manning prepares to board the cab of his engine, a messenger runs in with a telegram informing him of the terrible accident ahead. But Manning will not be deterred. Assuming that the tracks will be clear by the time he reaches the accident site, he departs at ninety miles an hour.

At the scene of the wreck, police detectives question a tramp (played by Norman's favorite actor, one-legged Steve "Peg" Reynolds), who reveals the identity of the real criminal. Hilton is detained; and when he tries to escape custody, he is shot, recaptured, and incarcerated. At the Powers home, however, the news is happier: Helen is handed a telegram that reads "Manning wins mail race. Mail contract ours."

A few weeks later, Helen and Manning are joyfully reunited; and, as the subtitle confirms, "The new assistant superintendent receives his reward." A series of fade in/fade out shots intercut Helen and Manning's marriage ceremony with images of Hilton peering out from behind the bars of a prison. The film ends with the newlyweds being pelted with rice as they enter a waiting limousine and start to kiss. Jack "pulls down the shades—fade."

The story of middle-class black life was exciting, well crafted, and consistent with the aims of racial uplift. By placing his characters in professional positions of authority and dignity—as engineers, railroad superintendents, surveyors, traffic managers, policemen, detectives, and advertising directors—rather than in stereotypically degrading scenarios, Norman highlighted the opportunities within reach of those aspiring blacks who were willing to work hard to achieve their ambitions—opportunities increasingly available to blacks in postwar American society. He also very carefully and deliberately emphasized the symbols of success that such opportunities afforded: the elegant home of the Powers, with its flowering gardens and goldfish-filled fountains; the spacious and comfortable office of the superintendent; the refined and professional attire of the principal characters; the chauffeured car at Helen's disposal; and the big wedding celebration, complete with a limousine that takes the happy couple away. Since blacks in most studio motion pictures of the day were typed by their tattered and exaggerated garb and restricted to roles as chauffeurs and servants, race audiences could take special pride in such anti-typing.

The Love Bug, Norman's second film, was billed as a sequel to *The Green-Eyed Monster*.[17] But it was, in fact, a reworking of the subplot of the original eight-reel version. In contrast to the main plot, which treated its middle-class characters with appropriate decorum, the subplot was a formulaic and derivative low comedy. Typical of early white-produced films, it depicted a wholly different class of black characters, from scheming gamblers to razor-toting Mammies, all of whom were engaged in a series of Keystone Cop–like adventures. Norman probably intended that comedy to complement the main plot; and, at the most rudimentary level, it did. Like Helen, who is courted by two suitors, the hero of the comic subplot, Quintus Weefalls, is the object of two women's attentions. But whereas the courtship of Helen and Jack is treated in a serious and realistic fashion, the pursuit of Quintus is portrayed as a succession of farcical misadventures and humorous deceptions reminiscent of William Foster's shorts.

Interwoven throughout the original film, the subplot begins in scene 19 of the script with the brief appearance of Quintus (played by Robert Stewart), a railroad fireman who is clumsy at everything but handling the shovel on the Cannon Ball Limited that Manning engineers. He reappears in scene 32, where he is pouring sand into the dome of an engine boiler. Looking up, he sees Helen Powers, who has come to visit her father at the railroad yard. Quintus—who, according to the subtitle card, has a strong back but a timid heart when it comes to the fair sex—is distracted by Helen's beauty. "My! She sho am purty," he remarks in an exaggerated dialect, as he absently pours the balance of the sand on Manning instead of into the dome—an error that causes Manning to "sputter" and strike Quintus with an oil can as Quintus beats a hasty retreat.

The comedy continues in scenes 46 through 93, in which String Bean Oldfield, a "Speed Maniac" who drives a cut-down racer, is stopped by a police officer for speeding. Getting off with a warning after he promises to be good, String Bean hurries away to a dilapidated building to shoot craps. But, in his hands, the dice prove to be cold—because, as his friend Cinnamon (Slim Jones) implies, he lacks a good luck charm like Lily, Cinnamon's pet goat. "How much you take to divorce yo'self from Lily," String Bean asks, "an' marrify me to Lady Luck?"

Two dollars later, with Lily now at his side, String Bean goes on a winning streak and cleans out his fellow players Mustard Prophet, Hogface, and Pink Eye. But before he has a chance to gloat over his good fortune, he discovers that Lily has, literally, eaten all of his profits. Aiming "to give dis goat exercise to digest dat spondulix [money]," he ties her to the back of his racer and drives away, speeding so madly down the road that the rope breaks, Lily goes flying, and his racer runs head-on into the car in which Helen and Hilton are riding. This time, String Bean, dazed and gracefully draped over a fence when the police officer arrives, is dragged away. "Wuz hard luck a dewdrop," he exclaims, "I mus' be a lake."

The comedy picks up again in scene 100, where Skeeter Butts (played by Billy Mills), "matrimonial adjuster in courtship, marriage, and divorce," is sitting outside his establishment, the Shin Bone Eating House (in the film, the sign actually reads "Skinny Bone Eatin Hous"), and reading a newspaper upside down, to suggest his illiteracy. Quintus sits down next to him and confides his desire to "mahry and sottle down." Skeeter, it turns out, knows of two eligible women, "hard to chose betwix." When Quintus replies that he "ain't goin' to commit bigatry" by pursuing them simultaneously, Skeeter recommends writing a letter to each, putting the two letters in a hat, and then drawing one at random. Quintus composes his missive: "de rose am red and de vilet am blu / sugar am sweet an so am you / Ah sees you by de Shoo Fly Chuch under / de chinabury tre Satiddy nite. / yos for matrimoney."

Thinking it would be a good joke, Skeeter mails both letters. When Miss Cuspidora Lee (played by Maud Frisbie), "an old maid not at all adverse to matrimony," receives hers, she rejoices: "Oh! Lawdy mussy! A man at las'!" The other recipient, Mrs. Margerine Scrubb (played by 425-pound Maud Johnson), a widow who "had already outlived her second husband and was looking for a third," is similarly thrilled: "Come great deliverer! He am my man." Her joy is so great that, still clutching her letter, she begins dancing and falls into a steaming washtub.

In scenes 150 through 185, both women arrive at the appointed spot under the chinaberry tree. Taking notice of each other, they discover they have been duped and resolve to give Quintus a greeting he will never forget. But seeing Margerine reach into her sock for her razor and Cuspidora pull out a revolver, Quintus resorts to flight. Just as the women catch up to him—one insisting "Ah teach yo' to triflicate wif a poo' widow's affections," the other proclaiming "Ma heart am injured an' demands justis"—they witness something moving in the graveyard. Assuming it is a ghost, they scatter. But the ghost is actually a white-suited Skeeter, who has come to apologize to Quintus and to get him help "in cotin' [courting]." Skeeter sends him to Dazzle Zeanor, an actress and woman of Ethiopian beauty. For two dollars, Dazzle agrees to teach Quintus the art of seduction.

In scene 292, Quintus again encounters Margerine and Cuspidora, both of whom continue to seek his affection and are now prepared to fight each other for it. Running to Dazzle, he asks, "What's I gwine to do when deys hot for me?" Dazzle responds, "Ah' fix dat cause dis is leap year and I want's you fo' myself." Her plan is for Quintus to fake serious illness: she paints white spots on his face and places him in the back of a black-covered "Pest House" wagon pulled by a "near dead bony old horse." In a sad and comical procession down the street, the wagon passes Margerine, who locks herself inside her house, fearing "Small poxes! An' I bets Ah gots it!" The scene is repeated at Cuspidora's house: she, too, quickly retreats indoors. The procession, however, as well as the comic subplot, soon ends—not in a funeral but with the wedding of Quintus to Dazzle.

When the original double-plotted, eight-reel version of *The Green-Eyed Monster* was released in late 1919 or early 1920, the reaction to it was mixed. Black audiences responded quite favorably to the story of racial uplift and achievement and to the attractive cast of black professional characters. But that story seemed undercut, even mocked, by the frenetic subplot and the exaggerated caricatures that harked back to the racial comedies many black moviegoers found so offensive. Norman himself eventually admitted that the two plotlines—one "of ambition," the other of "low comedy with ambitionless characters"—were so different as to be at odds with each other. As early as the premiere, in fact, "we found that the comedy hurt the drama."[18]

So Norman made what proved to be a very wise decision: he split the film into two pictures, a love story/thriller and a comic farce, which he then reworked and released separately. (Since it was common practice to pair a feature film with a short comedy "scream," however, they were occasionally shown on the same bill.) As Norman later observed in a letter to the manager of the Auditorium Theatre in Atlanta, Georgia, the new *Green-Eyed Monster* "is now in 5 reels and has been re-titled and is a hundred per-cent better than it was with the comedy,"[19] while the comedy, on its own, was proving to be a success as well.

Unfortunately, no copy of that five-reel version of *The Green-Eyed Monster*, released in 1920, survives. But the publicity materials suggest that there were many "startling scenes"—"Horrible Train Wreck. Rescue from a Burning Automobile. Bloody Fist Fight in the Railroad Yards. Pistol Duel Between Detectives and the Villain. Thrilling and Startling Mail Race. Hair-Raising Abduction of the Heroine and Her Rescue by the Hero After a Thrilling Chase on a Steel Monster."—all of which made the "STUPENDOUS ALL-STAR NEGRO MOTION PICTURE, A BIG SPECTACULAR PRODUCTION TEEMING WITH THRILLS! ACTION! PUNCH!" clearly "worth going miles to see." Yet while most of those scenes had appeared in the original eight-reel version, several of the fights were extended; and another scene—of Helen being taken hostage—was added when Norman edited and expanded the film for separate release.[20] It was that new scene that raised the ire of the Chicago censor, who insisted that the "rejected suitor's revenge" be eliminated before the film was approved for play.[21] Censors in other states, though, passed the film without requiring any cuts or deletions.

The pressbook and the poster for *The Green-Eyed Monster* claimed that $1,000,000 worth of railroad equipment was used in the filming of the production and that the climactic train wreck alone cost $80,000 to produce. But much of the actual footage was not even new to the film, and the inflated production costs were merely hype to attract a broader audience.[22] What is true, however, is the fact that "the characterizations were enacted by colored people chosen from many different walks of life," including "The Lawyer, Doctor, Banker and Finished Actor and Actress [who] portray this strong appeal to the highest ideals of nature and lesson of the lowness and result of jealousy, The Green Eyed Monster."

Norman was quick to point out both in his promotional materials and in his correspondence with theater owners and managers that "THERE IS NOT A WHITE MAN IN THE CAST, nor is there depicted in the entire picture anything of the usual mimicry of the Negro" (a phrase that he repeated often in describing his black-cast productions). That all-black casting was no doubt the reason the photoplay was "endorsed by the most prominent colored people of America" as well as by Norman's fellow producers. Distributor True Thompson, for instance, hailed *The Green-Eyed Monster* as the

best colored picture yet made and congratulated Norman on his achievement.[23] Even George Johnson, co-founder and manager of the Lincoln Motion Picture Company, who—as Matthew Bernstein and Dana F. White
noted, was never one to lavish praise on his competitors—described the
film as "one of the biggest drawing cards ever played to negro houses. . . . By
no means a comparison to Micheaux pictures in class or acting or direction;
nevertheless because of its thrills and action went over big."[24]

In large cities as well as in small towns, the picture broke attendance
records, especially when one of the stars appeared in person to advertise
it.[25] M. Wax, of the Royal and Keystone Theaters in Philadelphia, Pennsylvania, happily reported that *The Green-Eyed Monster* had proven to be
a wonderful attraction that did excellent business and pleased all of his
patrons. W. C. Kennedy of Knoxville, Tennessee, affirmed that "it broke
house records in our 1,200-seat Gem Theater." R. H. Murray, manager of
the Dunbar, Hiawatha, and Forsaker Theaters in Washington, D.C., said
it was "the best colored picture we have played in our houses. It made real
money for us." E. Silberman of the Douglas Theater in New York City
found *The Green-Eyed Monster* to be such a "knock-out . . . that we turned
them away daily" throughout the week-long run.[26] F. C. Dillon, manager
of the Lincoln Theatre in Louisville, Kentucky, called it a good picture that
earned a good profit: "Crowded houses every night. Perfectly satisfied, for
the public was well pleased."[27] At the Pike Theatre in Mobile, Alabama, the
film "grossed $551.88 business." Paul E. Thompson, of the Palace Theatre
in Dallas, Texas, agreed: "Very few, if any colored pictures are equal to the
Green Eyed Monster."[28]

Paul Barraco of the Washington Theater in Houston, Texas, went even
further: he noted that *The Green-Eyed Monster* was one of the few pictures
that did strong repeat business—a fact that was proven in theaters such as
the Aldridge in Oklahoma City, Oklahoma, where attendance, second run,
surpassed first runs on other race company's features.[29] Even in the white
theaters where it was played during midnight performances, *The Green-
Eyed Monster* "did a big business."[30] Norman's colleague S. H. Henderson
witnessed one such showing, in Shreveport, Louisiana:

> Several nights since, a friend and myself were standing in a vacant doorway
> on Texas street, this city, watching a motley throng pack the Grand Opra

House directly across from us. It was midnight. Gay posters informed those who cared to look that the doors would open, presently, upon a midnight frolic—negro cast. It looked like a thoroughly cosmopolitan crowd. It was. They came from every walk of life. The oil king rubbed elbows with the lesser lights from "the bottoms" and the American with the Jap, the chink, and the Greek. Negroes were barred. We went. And behold! We saw THE GREEN EYED MONSTER. I wonder if you know that they are showing that picture in white houses. . . . I can readily see, though, where you are cleaning up with it. Man, you never saw such a mob as packed that house. And it was midnight.[31]

The appeal of *The Green-Eyed Monster*—not only to black but also to white viewers—was due in part to its clever incorporation of the modern high-speed train and automobile technologies, which surprised and delighted audiences. As Phyllis R. Klotman has suggested, more than most of his contemporaries, Norman had a real ability "to use the new technology to good purpose."[32] But the film was sensational in other respects as well, such as its human interest, dramatic suspense, and thrilling situations, all of which the *Chicago Defender* lauded in its review.[33] Above all, as Norman wrote to a theater manager in Charleston, West Virginia, who was booking the picture, it satisfied the black moviegoers for whom it was intended: "A colored audience want a lot of fighting, shooting, train wrecks. That's what The Green-Eyed Monster has."[34] (Notably, though, one exhibitor was reluctant to book the picture "as it hasn't enough loving in it."[35])

The strongest promotional ballyho for the film was the appearance of Steve "Peg" Reynolds, the one-legged actor who performed a few vaudeville skits before each screening. Yet exhibitors also found other interesting ways to publicize the picture. The manager of the Grand Opera House in Meridian, Michigan, for instance, wrote Norman to tell him about an especially effective stunt he used in promoting *The Green-Eyed Monster*. "I taken one whole sheet beaver board had the local sign painter make a chinese dragon on same used small green light globes for eyes and used red light behind shade to show the rest of the dragon up used this in dark lobby with the wording on the beaver board 'THE GREEN EYED MONSTER' and had the date painted on same and I went over the top with this picture."[36]

Norman's second film, *The Love Bug,* advertised as a sequel to the *The Green-Eyed Monster,* was edited down to two reels and released separately in 1920. Although only a fragment of it survives, publicity materials and press sheets for the comedy indicate that it retained all of the original scenes of Quintus's courtship by the widowed Mrs. Margerine Scrubb and the never-married Miss Cuspidora Lee as well as the clever ruse that he employs to escape their attentions and to win the hand of Dazzle Zeanor. But a new ending was added. In a final scene, the now-married Quintus— stunned and obviously overwhelmed—cradles in his arms the latest addition to his family: three adorable babies (played by "real Colored Triplets"). By transforming the hapless Quintus into a good family man, a role rarely afforded black characters in white studio productions, Norman gave the familiar story a twist that differentiated it from the more generic formulaic comedies of its day and added an element of "comic uplift."[37] The picture was further distinguished by its cast, most of whom were members of the Billy Mills Company, a team of highly regarded black actors, rather than white actors in blackface—or, for that matter, black actors in blackface. With their excellent physical comedy, Mills and his fellow castmates offered an unconventional take on the conventional material.

Almost immediately after completing production of the two films, Norman began roadshowing them, sometimes playing *The Green-Eyed Monster* alone, sometimes screening it in tandem with *The Love Bug.* The road work was often tedious: typically, Norman would drive a slow route from town to small town hand-carrying prints of the pictures and delivering them personally to his exhibitors. But the roadshows were generally quite profitable. *The Green-Eyed Monster* proved to be a particular favorite with audiences. On a single six-week tour through the South in February and March 1921, the picture grossed $3,770.06.

With its action-packed scenes of high-speed train races, colliding locomotives, automobile chases and crashes, dramatic kidnappings, and happy endings, Norman's first all-black-cast feature *The Green-Eyed Monster* excited moviegoers and demonstrated Norman's skill at writing, producing, developing, editing, and distributing films for the race market. It would, moreover, go on to become one of the most popular race films of the 1920s and continued to be shown well into the 1930s, years after the advent of talking pictures. Even more significantly perhaps, together with its comic sequel *The Love Bug*, *The Green-Eyed Monster* gave Norman credibility as a successful and serious producer of "colored motion pictures" and, in turn, allowed him to explore other innovative themes and approaches in his subsequent film projects.

CHAPTER FOUR

"Taking Two Hides from the Ox":
The Bull-Dogger and *The Crimson Skull*

THE SUCCESS OF *The Green-Eyed Monster,* his first race feature, and its comic sequel *The Love Bug* greatly encouraged Norman. And
so, as Matthew Bernstein and Dana F. White observed, he "continued filmmaking in this vein, combining his staged story scenes with found footage
or actualities he shot himself to create gripping five or six reelers."[1] His next
venture, Norman determined, would be a black-cast Western—actually,
a series of Westerns—to be shot on location in Oklahoma, a territory he
had visited often during his years as a traveling home talent film producer
in the 1910s.

Norman knew that the Western, full of action and adventure, was a
uniquely American genre that audiences had long enjoyed. Some of the
earliest cinematic shorts, in fact, were performances by Annie Oakley and
William "Buffalo Bill" Cody at Buffalo Bill's Wild West Show and Sioux
ghost dances filmed in the late 1890s by William K. L. Dickson's Kinetoscope for Edison's "Black Maria" Studios.[2] And among the most popular
films of Norman's day were the Broncho Billy pictures—several of them
produced in Norman's hometown of Jacksonville—starring Broncho Billy
Anderson (the stage name of Gilbert Maxwell Aronson), America's first

cowboy movie star, and Universal's Western serials, which included *The Bull's Eye* (1917) and *In the Days of Buffalo Bill* (1922).[3]

While working as a traveling filmmaker, Norman had produced a number of short Western-themed pictures, including one about Cole Younger and another about the notorious Belle Starr; and later he successfully distributed another outlaw film, *A Debtor to the Law,* which he reedited after Henry Starr's death. The subject of his new feature film, however, was not Oklahoma's infamous white bank robbers but rather its black cowboys, heirs to the original black and mixed-race cowpunchers who helped settle the American West.[4] Some of those cowboys likely were descendants of plantation slaves from Georgia and South Carolina who had run away to the Seminole Indian Nation in southern Florida and who later moved westward, with the Seminoles, to the Oklahoma territories, or of the "Exodusters" who migrated west during Reconstruction to seek new opportunities.[5]

The West itself had other important connotations for filmmakers, especially for Norman and his fellow race producers, who saw it as a metaphor for black individualism and opportunity—literally, one of America's last frontiers. Founders of the influential Lincoln Motion Picture Company Noble and George Johnson, who had been born in Colorado and raised in Oklahoma, used a Western setting for several of their films. In Lincoln's first release, *The Realization of a Negro's Ambition* (1916), engineer James Burton travels west to the oil fields of California to seek his fortune and returns to his parents' farm with newfound skills and knowledge that allow him to achieve success; and in a later Lincoln film, *The Law of Nature* (1917), a woman leaves her home for the glamour of the East before realizing her error in judgment and returning to the security of the ranch and the family she abandoned. For Oscar Micheaux, another of Norman's contemporaries, the West symbolized the values of honesty, hard work, and right-thinking, in contrast to the hypocrisy and corruption of the city.[6] Micheaux's films *The Homesteader* (1919) and *The Exile* (1931)—the first all-black-cast talkie (and a picture that Norman later distributed)—were based on Micheaux's own experiences as a black homesteader near the Rosebud Reservation in South Dakota and depicted the adventures of a humble black pioneer who finds happiness and attains financial success on the prairie.

Like the Johnsons and Micheaux, Norman recognized both the novelty and the symbolic value of Western themes and characters. Using the
"All-Colored-Town" of Boley, Oklahoma, as his primary location, he hoped
to gather sufficient footage to produce three films, which he outlined early
on in a letter to his brother and then–business partner Bruce. The first film
would consist of "some good Round-Up stuff and bucking scenes, Bulldogging contests," with a short story line built around the cowboy action; the
second would be a more traditionally plotted outlaw picture to be called
"The Crimson Skull"; and the third would be a picture titled "The Fairy
Tale." Although making all three films would require more "coin" than
Norman currently had, he assured Bruce that "we will do the best we can.
We may be able to put 'em on—and some way scratch around and get the
Paper." He also promised that, if successful, he would give Bruce half inter-
est on two of the films, so they both could make some money.[7] (According
to Bruce Norman's daughter Katherine Norman Hiett, Bruce had already
acquired experience behind the camera, as a photographer for the Klutho
Studios, owned by local Jacksonville architect and moviemaker Henry J.
Klutho.)[8]

The site that Norman selected for much of his filming was the Miller
Brothers' 101 Ranch, a 150,000-acre property founded in 1893 by Confed-
erate veteran Colonel George Washington Miller, in Bliss, Oklahoma.
Owned and operated by brothers Bill, George, and Zach Miller (the Colonel's sons), the 101 was not only a working cattle ranch; it was also the home
of the popular 101 Ranch Wild West Show, which at one time featured such
top performers as Tom Mix, Will Rogers, Bessie Herberg, Buck Jones,
and even an ailing and elderly Buffalo Bill Cody, who appeared briefly in
a World War I recruitment show called the "Military Pageant Prepared-
ness." Originally a local attraction, the Millers' Wild West Show went
on the road in 1907 and eventually became a national and international
sensation.

In the summer of 1921, the ranch employed about one hundred cowboys, ten of whom were black. The most renowned was Bill Pickett, a legendary black rodeo and trick rider with a wide following. After observing
trained bulldogs corral stray steers by gripping the most sensitive areas
of their faces, Pickett created his most famous stunt: he would jump from

a moving horse onto a steer, which he wrestled to the ground and then immobilized with a strong bite to its lip. The signature move, a favorite among rodeo audiences, earned Pickett the nickname "The Bulldogger." Norman later boasted of him: "Bill Pickett is the colored man who invented bull-dogging. The late Theodore Roosevelt who saw him perform said: 'Bill Pickett's name will go down in Western history as being one of the best trained ropers and riders the West has produced.' Bill Pickett appeared before the King and Queen of England. He was then featured as the headliner attraction with a famous Wild West Show. He has toured South America and outstunted cowboys in Brazil and Argentina. He outstunted the Mexicans at bull fighting 15 years ago in the Bull Ring in Mexico City, and his record still stands."[9]

In preparation for his film shoot, Norman contacted Boley Sheriff John Owens to enlist his service as a supporting actor and to determine precisely what equipment and extras might be available on-site—riders, mounts, rifles, "chaps, boots, six-gun, and caliber of same"—so that he would know which props to transport from Florida. "We must have the assurance of the co-operation of the Boley citizens," Norman emphasized, adding "WE DO NOT ASK FOR ANY FINANCIAL assistance," just the usual cooperation and privileges accorded any moving picture company in California and Florida. The film, he assured Owens, would be seen by thousands of people, and although it would not be "a civic picture" (that is, a home talent–type picture), the publicity would bring tremendous value to his city by showcasing its development and progress.[10]

Norman had already visited Bliss, where he signed up Bill Pickett at a salary of $50 per week, with an assurance of an extra $25 pay for each week that Pickett spent on the road promoting the films after they were completed. To bind the bargain, Norman advanced Pickett a check for his first week's salary. In a letter to his brother Bruce, Norman wrote that he found Pickett to be a fascinating character: although illiterate and not particularly handsome, he had more friends in the country than any other black man around.[11] In another letter to Bruce, Norman elaborated on his description: "Pickett is a good negro and knows his place. Is 55 years old. Originated 'Bulldogging' and is the undisputed champion and has been for 38 years."[12] But because most of his upper teeth were missing, he "would not do for a lead, villain or Father part. I will have to use him in a cowboy part where he has more action than acting." Nonetheless, Norman concluded that "I can depend on Pickett"—a belief he would soon have reason to question.[13]

Once he had signed Pickett, Norman set out to secure rodeo and other action footage that he could film or purchase (and possibly reserve) for later use, as he had done with the footage of the train wreck that he intercut with the scripted scenes in *The Green-Eyed Monster.* Learning that a Championship Cowboy Contest, with competitors from all over the country, was being held on August 24–27 at the Western League Ball Park in Oklahoma City, Norman brought a proposal to the organizers, the Rainbow Division Veterans, Oklahoma Chapter, of Oklahoma City, Oklahoma: he would edit a short home talent–style picture that they could show locally in exchange for rights to incorporate the footage later in his own feature film.[14] The contract, dated August 20, 1921, outlined the terms of the agreement. For the sum of one dollar, Norman would be awarded "exclusive rights and privileges for the making of moving pictures and the exhibition of same." In consideration of those rights, Norman and the Veterans would split, equally, "[all] receipts secured from a local Oklahoma City, Oklahoma exhibition" of the film, after which Norman would be granted permission "to change the name and cut up and dissemble the aforesaid moving picture and use it in story form in conjunction with other characters."[15]

Norman filmed other area contests and rodeos as well. At the end of August, he spent two days at the Okmulgee Round-Up making "some good pictures" and picking up a few Indian curios for a reasonable price; at the Wellington Round-Up in Kansas, he shot additional footage, including more "Indian stuff."[16] He also contacted K. L. Williams, who was in charge of the 101's moving picture interests, to negotiate rights to film a big rodeo that the 101 Ranch was staging in early September. That event was expected to attract sixty cowboys who would be competing for $3,000 in prizes; and "many Indians would be there too."[17] But when Norman arrived at the rodeo to shoot Pickett, the organizers were so busy that they would not let him film the contest while it was on. Instead, he had to stage his scenes later, but he ultimately got better pictures as a result. In one of those pictures,

Pickett threw the steer when he jumped on him from his horse and they rolled over togeather and Pickett cut a perfect cart wheel in the air and landed on his neck. It only sprained his leg a little and the steer buried his horn up to his head in the earth and it took two men to pull it out. I have him in scenes throwing the steer with his teeth. Also I have pictures of a thousand head of cattle near a water hole on the ranch and hired 6 cowboys to drive most of them away for a Rustler scene. Also Charlie Smith of Ft. Worth, Texas in roping scenes of a steer and tying him. He is a negro cowboy who was entered in the 101 Rodeo and is a fine roper. He wants to go on the road for us. I also have scenes of Pickett riding a steer without a saddle and a few other catchy things.[18]

At times, though, the filming proved to be a challenge. Norman later recalled, "I had to get out in the sun and shoot pictures when I was chasing bulls around the field or being chased by them."[19] But in just a few weeks he managed to accumulate several thousand feet of interesting material. At the Oklahoma City contest alone, he shot "good stuff" that included "bucking and bulldogging scenes, steer riding, steer roping, etc.," and even a picture of Red Ward, one of the contestants, being thrown and killed by his horse. To that footage, Norman planned to add several staged scenes of Pickett bulldogging, which could then be intercut to make it appear "as if [Pickett] was in this contest and have him win." With a story that Norman wrote as a framework, that picture—eventually titled *The Bull-Dogger*—would "not be so hard to make." Norman also knew he could make excellent use of the leftover rodeo footage by combining it with other staged scenes of Pickett performing some fake rope spinning, shooting, and a little riding, along with "views of Sheriffs at Boley pulling off some fake crack shot stuff." That footage would be incorporated into a second film, *The Crimson Skull*.[20]

Yet even as he was plotting his current films, Norman was already thinking ahead to different movie ideas and fresh ways to expand his film business. As he wrote Bruce, since finances made it difficult for him to film the three race Westerns he originally planned, he had another scheme under his hat: to take the story of *The Bull-Dogger* and remake it with a white cast, changing the name and using Ruth Roach, Champion Woman Trick Rider of the World, as his leading lady. (Roach appears briefly, stunt-riding, in *The Bull-Dogger*.) "I have quite a few pictures of her in the Okmulgee and Oklahoma City Round-Up," he observed, "and by using Pickett as one of the cowpunchers on her dads ranch—they both go to compete in the Round-Up—she wins horsewoman honors and he the Bulldogging." Norman added that he could get white actor Carl Hackett of Tulsa, the leading man in twenty-four Westerns produced the previous year in Oklahoma, to perform the lead; that way, with a second round-up film, he could be assured an even wider circulation. It was certainly an intriguing notion: filming a white (actually, a mixed-race) version of his race picture, just as—with *The Green-Eyed Monster*—he had filmed a race version of one of his early white-cast pictures. But the notion passed quickly. By the time he finished *The Crimson Skull,* he had other projects in mind; and he never revisited the Roach picture idea.[21]

While he was shooting the stunts around which he would fashion his black-cast Westerns, Norman began lining up his other lead actors. He placed ads in the *Indianapolis Freeman* and the *Chicago Defender* that read:

WANTED!
Colored Talent

To act in Western moving pictures in Oklahoma. Must have stage experience and good photographic qualities. Leading lady for cowgirl part. Leading man for cowboy part. Character man for Mexican part. Prefer riders, but if you can't ride, we will teach you. Send photo, height, weight, experience and lowest salary you will work for. Photo will be returned. State whether bright or dark skin.[22]

The ads apparently generated quite a few replies. But apart from "one Negro in Denver [who looked] good from his photo" and who owned his own chaps, Mexican outfit, and saddle, the candidates were not particularly promising.[23]

At the same time that he was advertising in the trade papers, Norman was also pursuing other players like Anita Bush, "The Mother of Colored Drama," more directly and with considerably more success. A distinguished stage performer, Bush had begun acting as a young girl and later toured overseas in the landmark American musical comedy *In Dahomey* with legendary dance-and-comedy team Bert Williams and George Walker.[24] When Walker's illness forced the company to disband, she returned to the United States and formed her own acting troupes, first the vaudeville company called the Hula-Hula Dancers and then the Anita

Bush Players, who eventually became the Lafayette Players Dramatic Stock Company (sponsored by Robert Levy, of the Quality Amusement Company and later of Reol Pictures), based at the Lafayette Theatre in Harlem, New York.

Realizing that Bush's name alone would lend distinction to his picture, Norman contacted her in June 1921 to gauge her interest in the Western project and to inquire about her availability. Bush replied promptly, saying that although she was playing vaudeville, she would consider canceling the rest of her time if Norman's proposition was worthwhile. "I have had experience in all classes of Dramatic Shows also Comedies," she declared. "But if you want an experienced rider, I can't say that I am one. But I have lots of nerve and learn anything quickly. I can row, drive, ride a wheel, sail a boat, dance, and do most anything required in pictures."[25] She added that she could also help to assemble a first-class cast that would film well together because she knew "all the good ones."[26]

Norman followed up, giving Bush the particulars: in late August or early September, he would be producing two Western pictures with an all-black cast in Oklahoma—two pictures rather than the three he originally intended, "on account of the condition of the colored theatres," which could not support increased "colored production . . . at present." *The Green-Eyed Monster*, Norman believed, had set a precedent with a story that had a good moral and was free of race problems yet also full of action. *The Crimson Skull*, one of the two Westerns he had in mind, would be equally authentic in its portrait of actual black cowboys and real Western life. But to guarantee that the production had merit, he needed characters who would look the parts and who could ride and act, so he asked Bush for her suggestions for a strong leading man as well as a villain. The picture, he assured her, would require only two weeks of her attention: "If you could arrange to lay off your act for that time, it would be a change for you, and a vacation too as the work will not be hard on your part."[27]

Bush's demand for salary, however, posed some concern. Asserting that her reputation would be a drawing card for Norman's picture, she requested $200 pay a week plus transportation; and she also asked Norman to find a role for her vaudeville partner, because curtailing their act for the duration of the filming would leave him without any income. "He is a dancer and it wouldn't be fair to him for me to take two weeks off when we have booking."[28]

In her next letter just a few days later, Bush included photographs of her partner, who could act but not ride; and she provided information about other actors who might serve either as leading men or as heavies, since they "make up for any character splendidly." Two of those men were "nice looking" and light-skinned (with the "high yellow" complexions that race producers seemed to prefer); two were brown-skinned but would "also film well." All were box-office attractions, yet none was a skilled horseman because, as Bush reminded Norman, riding was not a skill required for the stage.[29]

One of those actors—whom Norman ultimately chose to star in *The Crimson Skull*—was Lawrence Chenault, a longtime leading man in black silent film. Before joining Bush in her eponymous dramatic company and in the Lafayette Players Dramatic Stock Company, he had worked in some of the most famous shows of the day, including Williams and Walker's *Abyssinia,* and with several of the most distinguished acting companies, including the Pekin Stock Company of Chicago; and he would go on to perform in more silent pictures than any other race actor. To appear in Norman's Western, Chenault wrote, he would need $125 a week in salary plus travel expenses.

As the end of August neared, Norman still had not reached agreement with his dramatic leads on the matter of money. Citing once again the limited market for race films, he explained to Bush that he simply could not afford the steep salaries that she and Chenault wanted. But if they could come to more reasonable terms, he promised to make her stay in Boley both pleasant and profitable.

> You probably are aware of the fact that production cost is one of the most vital problems of the Negro photo-play, and as our picture will be produced for colored theatres only, it will have a possible distribution in about 120 theatres; 85 per cent of which have an average seating capacity of but 250. These figures are no comparison with the 22,000 white theatres in which our product will find no market. White and Colored theatres are closing [all] over the country and only running part time; manufacturers are forced to curtail production and production cost and laying off many white stars who are glad to work for $100. a week in California.

He concluded that he was not trying to beat her down but merely impressing on her that it would be impossible to support her salary and other expenses. Even Pickett, an undisputed national champion, was earning only a quarter of what Bush had requested. And "his name alone will draw more than any other member of the cast."[30] As for Chenault: privately, to Bruce, Norman confided that while he could get an amateur in Boley to play his part, Chenault would attract moviegoers and earn back his salary by his adaptability and quick work.[31]

By the middle of September, just two weeks before shooting was set to begin, Norman laid out his final offer: a salary of $125 per week for Bush and $80 per week for Chenault (plus transportation costs between New York and Boley for both actors), with an extra allowance of $25 a week to be paid to Bush's partner, whom it would be impractical to bring to Oklahoma for a small role for the duration of her employment. The contract, Norman claimed, made Bush's expense "the highest of any colored performer." Although he could not guarantee her more than two weeks' work, he reassured her that if rainy weather did not delay production, he would try to use her in an extra picture and thus make her stay even more lucrative.[32] But, in a postscript to a letter to Bruce in which he reported on the salary discussions, he noted, "Another thing—I think after I finish 'The Bulldogger'—and while they [Bush and Chenault] are here—they will work for less in 'The Crimson Skull.'"[33] (Using the same actors in simultaneous or successive films was a strategy that other race filmmakers employed as well. As George Johnson later recalled, "you can use the same cast, the same time and the same studio and everything, and make three or four of them [a series of pictures] far cheaper than you can make one.")[34]

With his lead actors lined up at last, Norman turned to details such as wardrobe and props. Bush, he suggested, should bring with her a few of her best looking small hats, because one of the opening scenes he was planning would show her arriving on the train in everyday clothes. She would also need shirtwaists that might go well with her cowgirl outfit: "In fact [bring] anything you have that you think will be of use."[35] He also informed her, quite diplomatically, that there would be several pairs of ladies boots available for her to try on when she got to Boley, since she had stated that her shoe size was a "3½" but her foot tracing indicated that her true fit was a full two sizes larger.[36] Norman wrote to Chenault, too, to advise him: "If you have anything in the way of shirts that you thik will do for a cowboy role, or Mexican, please bring them with you. Also trousers that will be good for a western character. We wish to use you as a cowboy in one of our pictures. We have several outfits you can select from, but the shirts and trousers may come in handy for you."[37]

Costumes for the extras also had to be located and paid for. "I can get plenty of riders," Norman noted in a letter to Bruce, "but will have to rent about 10 pairs of chaps and about 6 guns with holsters."[38] In total, he estimated that he would need to place a deposit of around $200 on costumes and about $100 on guns, with full rental costs amounting to at least $660 ($135 for costumes and $525 for chaps and Western gear).[39] As for other props, Norman appealed to Bruce to ask their mother for the loan of her Spanish monkey sculpture, which he wanted to use in a Mexican scene in which the villain appears: "I know she will howl—but I will get her another if we break it."[40] Since money was so tight, he also instructed Bruce to bring with him a neighbor's gun for use in one of the scenarios.

The money was tight partly because of the low budget that Norman needed to work within—a problem typical of most independent race filmmakers. Norman had originally set that budget at just under $3,000, which he believed would cover *The Bull-Dogger* and *The Crimson Skull* and possibly a third film as well. But when he started to calculate the actual expenses, he realized how difficult it would be to produce even a single picture for that amount. Yet, as he told Bruce, it would be a shame "while you have things going not to be able to put over another"—especially since, with the group of cowboys and actors already assembled, the second film could likely be produced for a fraction of the cost of the first. Everything, Norman concluded, would depend on the money he could scrape together and on the cooperation of the cast.[41] With his profits from *The Green-Eyed Monster* already invested in the Westerns, Norman planned to ask his mother for a $700 loan; and he urged Bruce to raise additional funds any way that he could, even by borrowing "a few hundred for a short time" in order to get the film negatives made and paid for. The prints and paper, he claimed, could be managed afterward by degrees.[42] He also congratulated Bruce on the good work he was doing from Jacksonville with rental on their earlier films, because "we certainly need the money now."[43]

Production costs, however, kept mounting. The costumes alone, Norman wrote Bruce, were giving him a devil of a time. "When I narrowed the order down to 4 costumes, consisting of 2 Mexican, 1 cowgirl and one skeleton, Harrelson of K. C. [Kansas City] refused to handle the order on a two weeks use and Chicago the same way. Evidently these movie companies have been treating 'em rough and they will only do business when you pay several times the value of the costume in rental." To get around the high fees, Norman decided to buy the chaps instead; and he found a local costumer to sew a Mexican costume for $16 and a cowgirl outfit for $8. He also purchased complete khaki outfits for $14, just a little over the Kansas City rental price of $13.50. Most impressively, he made the hoods for the outlaw "Terrors" himself and bought ten unionalls (one piece jumpers) for $1.70 each. "They are dark blue and with the hoods and bandana handkerchief around neck—and guns strapped at waist—they will be O.K." and certainly more affordable than the $16 per piece costume rental.[44]

Norman was also growing increasingly concerned about Pickett's acting ability. Although there was no question that the rodeo stunts Pickett performed were spectacular, Norman confessed to Bruce that he feared that Pickett would be unable to "put over" the part of the sheriff in *The Crimson Skull*. His looks were too homely, and he "photographs up real dark—besides[,] with his missing teeth, he might burlesque it. I might have to use Sheriff Owens for this part" instead.[45] At one point, Norman even considered abandoning production of *The Crimson Skull* altogether and focusing instead on *The Bull-Dogger* and a film compilation of similar stunts to be titled *A Rodeo Star*, which would highlight Pickett's strong cowboy skills rather than his weak acting. Norman even went so far as to prepare a script for that compilation, a two-reeler using some of the extra shots of Pickett and other black and white cowboys riding and performing rodeo stunts.[46] But, as he wrote Bruce, given the choice between producing *A Rodeo Star* or *The Crimson Skull*, "I would select 'The Crimson Skull.'" So he decided to rework the original scenario for *The Crimson Skull* by stealing a little comedy out of *The Bull-Dogger* and rewriting Pickett's part accordingly.[47]

Even bigger problems developed when Pickett refused to honor his contract. In a letter to Joe Miller, owner of the 101 Ranch, Norman explained that he desperately needed Miller's intervention with his cowboy star:

> I sent for Pickett the last week in September and he appeared in Oklahoma City in an intoxicated condition and so much under the influence of liquor that I had a hard time to keep him out of jail, (he got in an argument with a negro shoe repairer and the shoe repairer pulled an automatic on him when Pickett threatened to kill him and they were just about to call in the police when I was notified of this).

Pickett then demanded $150 in addition to the advance Norman had already given him. He claimed that the money was the balance owed him as back pay for the month of September, during which he was officially under contract but not actually working on the film. He also insisted on receiving an extra fifty dollars a week salary for any future work. Norman tried to get Pickett to go to a hotel and sober up so he could "talk sence" to him; and he paid his fare back to Boley. But he needed Miller to use his influence with Pickett, who was still in Miller's employ, "to have him do the right thing by me."[48]

Once the situation with Pickett was resolved, Norman began production on the scripted portion of *The Bull-Dogger*, which he described as a "Round-Up film . . . full of action" with "about two reels of story with Pickett in it."[49] Although the film itself does not survive, a fragment of an early version of the shooting script is extant (and is printed for the first time, along with a draft of the scenario, in the appendix to this volume). The handwritten outline that Norman had "all doped out" the first moment he saw Pickett perform his act suggests that he conceived a series of shots showing Pickett on the Bar L Ranch where he is employed as foreman, followed by round-up images of Pickett and champion roper Charlie Smith riding and roping steers, with subsequent scenes of Pickett and the other "Champions of the World" performing stunts and outwitting the cowpunchers who try to drive away his herd. (Notably, Norman would reuse the round-up footage in his next film as well, in a scene in which "1,000 cattle are shown being rounded up and 'Rustled' by Outlaws.")[50] To that rough scenario, Norman added a framing story, a romance between Pickett's daughter Anita (played by Anita Bush), a recent graduate of Linwood College, and Tom Stone, cattle boss at the Bar L. The reward that Tom wins for the capture of the Mexican desperado Manuel Vandalo becomes "a nice wedding present" for the young couple, who prepare to "tie the hitch."

Yet the plotting of the five-reel film, as even the promotional materials for *The Bull-Dogger* suggest, was secondary to the action.[51] "*The Bull-Dogger,*" read one ad, "Features Colored Cowboys. Bull Dogging and throwing the Wildest Steers from the Mexican Border. Riding and Tameing Man-Killing Bronks. Wild Horse Racing. Wild Steer Riding. Steer Roping, Calf Roping, Goat Roping. Fancy Roping, Trick Roping, Fighting and Throwing Wild and Enraged Steer with their Bare Hands And Many Other Surprises. Thrills! Thrills! Thrills! Laughs Too." Pictured prominently was Bill Pickett, "Champion Bull-Dogger of the World," throwing a bull with his teeth, along with "Colored Cowboy" Nate Williams riding Dynamite, a bucking bronco, and Pete Haddon performing some trick roping.[52]

The posters, heralds, and other paper that Norman designed and sold to theater managers also emphasized the film's action.[53] A window card announced: "Coming to Your Favorite Colored Theatre. *The Bull-Dogger* featuring Bill Pickett, Colored Hero of the Mexican Bull Ring[,] and the Greatest Array of World Champions Ever Assembled in a Motion Picture." Just above an attention-grabbing headline—"DID YOU EVER SEE REAL COLORED COWBOYS? HERE THEY ARE"—were images of Pickett along with Benny Turpin, George Larkin, Pete Haddon, Charlie Smith, Steve "Peg" Reynolds, Buck Lucas, numerous "Colored Punchers Branding on the Bar L Ranch," and "Champion Lady Riders of the World." In a direct appeal to black moviegoers, the window card underscored the fact that "THE 'BULL-DOGGER' IS YOUR PICTURE. SEE IT."[54] Another herald featured a large image of Reynolds as well as small headshots of Bennie Turpin and Anita Bush in costume and an inset of several characters, including Bush standing over an injured cowboy in the ring.[55]

Bush assumed an even larger role—and received top billing—in Norman's second Western, *The Crimson Skull,* a six-reel "baffling Western Mystery Photo-Play With a Brilliant Cast of Colored Artists" that was filmed the same month as *The Bull-Dogger*. In the pressbook for the new picture, Norman exhorted exhibitors to

> Make it your business to read every story and advertisement in this campaign book. This comes pretty close to being the showman's ideal of what a picture should be—THRILLS! ACTION! PUNCH! MYSTERY! And real STARS. This is Anita Bush's first [though, in fact, it was actually her second] appearance in Motion Pictures. She is known from Coast to Coast as "the Little Mother of Colored Drama." She proves that she is as versatile in Pictures as she is on the Stage.[56]

The enthusiastic reception of *The Green-Eyed Monster,* Norman observed in the pressbook, had convinced him "that the Colored theatre goer wanted stories that did not leave a bad taste in their mouth. Their ideals had been shaped by White Productions full of red blooded romance and thrilling feats of daring and skill." That is why, he explained, he had interwoven those basic elements into the plot of *The Crimson Skull,* which he felt was the equal of any white picture.

The pressbook also detailed Norman's challenges in planning and producing the film, from securing the services of "the Authorities and Colored Citizens of the All-Colored City of Boley," where Norman identified real black ranchers, cowboys, and United States Deputy Sheriffs for parts in the picture, to establishing a temporary studio, arranging the enormous expense of transporting the lead actors, and teaching them how to ride Western-style.[57] All of these efforts, however, guaranteed the authenticity of the story, so that there was nothing in *The Crimson Skull* that smacked of the amateur. "The photography is as clear as crystal and as steady as a rock and up to the technically excellent standard set in our past productions."

The plot of *The Crimson Skull* (whose original shooting script is printed for the first time in the appendix to this volume) was certainly full of adventure and suspense. The tranquility of the peace-loving little city of Boley has been destroyed by the Terrors, a band of hooded outlaws led by "The Skull." According to the pressbook, they

> have sown mortal fear into the hearts of the less intrepid of the Countryside, and they have the Sheriff in their power. The "Law and Order League" force his resignation and offer $5,000.00 for the capture of "The Skull," Dead or Alive. Lem Nelson, fearless Cattleman and owner of the Crown C Ranch, is persuaded to take the Sheriff's job. Bob Calem, his Ranch Foreman, is in love with Nelson's daughter, Anita, and he volunteers his aid to help capture "The Skull."

But in order to effect the capture, Bob must join the outlaws. Meanwhile, Anita and Peg (Steve Reynolds) are taken hostage. After Bob helps them escape, he is accused of being a traitor to the gang. To determine his guilt, he is tried by the test of "The Crimson Skull."[58] According to one of the film's title cards, after a "grim skull" is suspended over a tablecloth and lit by a torch placed below it, Bob is warned that a single drop of melted blood from the skull's jaw will spell his guilt or innocence and thus decide his fate. If the number of drops is uneven, he will be sentenced to death.[59] (Interestingly, according to family members, Richard and Bruce rehearsed the scene at their mother's kitchen table, using a real human skull and chocolate syrup for the blood.)[60] The test exonerates Bob, who ultimately outwits the outlaw band by baiting them with misinformation about a payroll at the Boley bank. After a big shoot-out, the Terrors are captured and their identities exposed. For his bravery, Bob wins both the $5,000 reward and the hand of his beloved Anita (a resolution virtually identical to that of *The Bull-Dogger*).

The film, an "epic of Wild Life and Smoking Revolvers" that "opens with a crash and ends with a kiss," contained some interesting twists: for instance, Sheriff Nelson's son Buck is revealed to be a member of the Terrors, and the mystery is resolved by an oddly designed snake emblem ring that he wears on his finger and the secret hand gestures with which he signals his fellow outlaws. But the melodrama was balanced by the "side splitting comedy" of Reynolds, who performed his usual variety of humorous stunts, often utilizing his wooden leg as a weapon. According to the pressbook, Reynolds, "the one legged marvel, pulled off more action than the average two legged white puncher in a White Western." With "nothing but his trusty wooden leg to defend him and the sheriff's daughter against 'The Skull' and his gang of 'Hooded Terrors' he fought their way to freedom and did a piece of wild riding that proved he is a marvel."[61] Just as remarkable was Lawrence Chenault, in a triple role that included hero and villain.[62] (What made Chenault's performance that much more remarkable, as Norman later recalled in correspondence with actress Shingzie Howard, is that Chenault was able to act at all, given the prodigious amounts of liquor that he consumed: "He won't stay sober on the job . . . [which] caused me the loss of a lot of time and money.")[63] And Bill Pickett, recast as one of the sheriff's deputies, reprised his familiar role as the Bull-Dogger when he twisted the neck of a desperate outlaw "as he would bull-dog a bull," thereby helping to save the sheriff and his deputies from the Skull.[64]

By November 1921, with the filming of both pictures completed, Norman assembled an early print of *The Bull-Dogger* that he planned to start showing locally in Oklahoma and Texas. Reporting on his progress to Bruce, he wrote:

> The picture [*The Bull-Dogger*] is really good. It is in 5 reels and about the length of the G. E. M. [*Green-Eyed Monster*]. Full of fast action and I have a wild steer fight in it that beats that one of Pickett that I bought [from K. L. Williams at the 101 Ranch]. I didn't realize what a good thing I had at the time until I had seen the fight on the screen that I had filmed when I made the scenes in Okmulgee. I used the wild Bill stuff and as you say—it wasn't much and would have been a knock to the Crimson Skull, but I trimmed it down and with the scenes in the saloon leading up to the steer fight with Pickett it gets by very nicely. The Crimson Skull is in 7 short reels now and without titles or this wild bill stuff, so we will have to do some trimming to it. I had an old cut out of Lum Nelson that was a rotten introduction of him in The Cimson Skull and also another cut out and extra scene of Pickett and Young in the branding scene and so I framed this up as Nelson owner of the ranch on which Pickett was Foreman and Nelson tells him that he can get leave to go to the Okmulgee Round-Up and in that way I saved the day and worked the thing up from scraps that we were going to throw away.[65]

Still determined to "grind out the dough" and raise capital with second-run showings of *The Green-Eyed Monster* and *The Love Bug,* Norman hoped to get a second print of *The Bull-Dogger* developed by early January 1922 so that Bruce could start playing it.[66] "I will make you the proposition of you taking one third of the profits," he wrote. "All you will be out is your time. I am standing the cost of the production and we will deduct the amount of ware and tare on the print I will send you—the cost of advertising etc and devide the remainder as suggested. I think if fair."[67] That way, he concluded, they could pull together enough money to complete the editing of *The Crimson Skull* in record time. In the meantime, he urged Bruce to keep the home fires burning, and added, "Mother said that you contemplated selling the Dodge—don't do it. It isn't necessary. We will get by some way. I think the pinch is about over and we will start the new year O.K."[68]

On Christmas Day, Norman wrote Bruce again with another progress report. Holiday attendance at local showings of *The Bull-Dogger* had proven disappointingly slow: in fact, "the junk that I have in the way of chaps, guns etc. has been getting the business, otherwise I would have done practically nothing. The theatres are doing eight to fifteen dollar business, and even poor[er] on other colored pictures." He was, however, picking up display items such as a stuffed "Armadilla" in order to have plenty of curios, which would be valuable in drawing whites as well as blacks to the roadshows that they would soon be running.[69]

Although the market was glutted with race pictures—and although he decided to wait until business conditions improved before officially releasing *The Crimson Skull*—Norman knew that his cowboy Westerns, especially if promoted properly, would appeal to black audiences.[70] So he urged his showmen and exhibitors to "advertise as if you meant it. . . . There's no use having goods like this if you don't let people know you have it. . . . Spend a few extra dollars and watch them come rolling back with a lot of little brothers." In addition to the lithographs, window cards, and heralds that would "pack 'em in," Norman also recommended that theater managers employ catch phrases and promotional stunts similar to those he used in connection with *A Debtor to the Law:*

> The day before you show "The Crimson Skull" rent a skeleton costume from the Costumers, and on the quiet dress up a man in it and put him on a horse with this sign on his back.
> $5.00 REWARD
> If You Can Guess My Name
> See Me In
> "THE CRIMSON SKULL"
> Have this rider parade the Colored Section and keep his mouth shut. When you open "The Crimson Skull" hitch the horse outside your theatre and hang on both sides of the saddle signs that read:
> My Pal
> "THE SKULL"
> Is Inside
> Go In And See What Happened At Other Places He Left Me Hitched
>
> ———
>
> Here's Another Sure Fire One! Dress up a one-legged Colored Man in a Cowboy Suit and have him parade with this card on his back:

See Me In
"The Crimson Skull"
Six Reel Colored Western at the Theatre To-Day[71]

Whereas advance promotions like these whetted people's interest, it was the ballyho for the pictures that really drew them in. In addition to the usual big Western lobby of guns, chaps, and animals, Norman advised exhibitors to hang on one of the revolvers a sign that read "This is the gun that Vandalo, the mysterious outlaw, used in 'The Crimson Skull.'"[72] Or, stretching the truth in the interest of good showmanship, he recommended posting a card on an ordinary pair of boots, stating that the "boots [were] worn by Bill Pickett, World's Champion Cowboy.'" But undoubtedly the biggest attraction of all continued to be Steve "Peg" Reynolds, who would make personal appearances in the towns where the feature was booked. In a letter to a theater manager in Indianapolis, Norman described Reynolds's appeal:

> Reynolds is the only one legged picture actor in existence and is in a class by himself. He does a 15 to 30 minute vaudeville act and knocks 'em cold, and besides this, he has been worth his salary on bally alone thru the colored section and at the theatres. He has several costumes which he changes from day to day, and his method on the bally is to go thru the colored sections, he sings several songs thru a big megaphone, gets the people out of their houses and then tells them about the picture when he has secured their attention, then he does a few funny tricks, and as a result, the theater is packed during the shwoing.[73]

As Norman had hoped, both Westerns opened strong. *The Bull-Dogger,* for example, drew interest from theaters like the Princess in Vicksburg, Mississippi, and the Dreamland in Monroe, Louisiana—theaters in which, as F. C. Holden, booking agent for the Southern Amusement Company, noted in a letter to Norman, "We have just about given up playing colored cast pictures."[74] Since it was a feature-length film, *The Bull-Dogger* was often shown with a second shorter picture. According to Norman's detailed distribution records, sometimes the double bill included *A Debtor to the Law,* the Henry Starr Western that Norman reedited and began successfully distributing after Starr's death. At other times, the second film was a short comedy such as *A Natural Born Shooter* (Historical Films/Ebony,

1917), *A Black and Tan Mix-Up* (Ebony, 1918), *A Natural Born Gambler* (Biograph, 1918), or *Spooks* (Ebony, 1918), which Norman usually offered free with every contract, so that exhibitors could "book a big clean-up program of colored pictures."[75] Those comedies—one-reelers that he picked up at small cost and that featured antic blackface performances and racist routines—were not consistent with the professed aims of Norman's own race films, which he proudly claimed did not demean "the colored man, [and would] please him 100%."[76] Yet the double features were lucrative and certainly helped to draw and entertain the crowds. By February 1922, in fact, Norman had two concurrent roadshows out on *The Bull-Dogger,* each with a full lobby of Western curios. As he wrote to Abraham Rosen, one of his distributors, "These shows are cleaning up and are playing to 4 times the business than the ordinary negro picture."[77]

Audience response to *The Crimson Skull* was even more enthusiastic than it was for *The Bull-Dogger.* Single-day box office receipts ran into the hundreds of dollars—$296.10, for example, at the Pekin Theatre in Montgomery, Alabama; $399.00 at the Belmont Theatre in Pensacola, Florida; $445.12 at the Maceo Theatre in Tampa, Florida. "Theatres are reporting excellent business on *The Crimson Skull,*" Norman wrote to O. E. Belles at the Main Theatre in Cleveland, Ohio. "This picture grossed over $941. last week in Grand Theatre, Memphis, Tenn. And we grossed over $800. here in Jacksonville on a two day run in the New Frolic Theatre. Gem of Knoxville, Grand of Chattanooga, Grand of Memphis, Douglas of Macon, Ga. did more business on this feature than they have on any other picture the last year and a half."[78] Due to capacity business, the film was held over in Kansas City for four extra days, "making a combined run in Kansas City Mo. and Kansas City Kansas of 16 strait days and breaking all records for continuous runs on a colored picture." At the Auditorium Theatre in Atlanta, Georgia, at the Lincoln Theatre, Nashville, Tennessee, and at the Plaza Theatre, Little Rock, Arkansas—all movie houses with over a thousand seating capacity—the film filled the seats and "please[d] the audience."[79] And in Birmingham, Alabama, "'THE CRIMSON SKULL' played to over SIX THOUSAND paid admissions in two days at Famous Theatre."[80] Still other theaters screened to standing room only and even turned patrons away from both afternoon and night showings.[81]

In his correspondence with theater owners and distributors, Norman noted that *The Crimson Skull* would cost them a little more than the regular race picture to rent because it "cost us 4 times as much as *The Green-Eyed Monster*" to make, and the production expenses are "62.9 greater per theater than a White Picture." But the exhibitor "will be justified in paying" for such a certain money-maker, which will "clean-up." *The Crimson Skull*, after all, "has proven the seasons greatest box-office attraction" and "has made more money than any two colored pictures."[82] The theater willing to mount a good advance display, Norman claimed, would hang up another record.[83] He assured one potential distributor that he figured on getting $2,000 out of New York City alone on the picture.[84]

Yet while audiences found Norman's Westerns thrilling, censors took issue with certain scenes or subjects. Norman's problems with censors, compared to those of his colleague Oscar Micheaux, whose controversial films were cut or banned in many states, were minor.[85] In fact, some censors like Maude Gandy, Special Film Representative to Kansas Censors, passed both *The Bull-Dogger* and *The Crimson Skull* exactly as Norman had submitted them.[86] But other censors demanded revisions or eliminations. Evalyn Frances Snow, the censor for the Ohio Department of Education, for instance, insisted on numerous changes to *The Bull-Dogger* (which had been submitted to her under an alternate title), including the deletion of virtually all of Pickett's signature bull-dogging scenes and a subtitle pertaining to the killing of one of the riders.[87] A frustrated Norman, who was completing the final editing of *The Crimson Skull* at the time, tried to find something positive in Snow's report. As he wrote Bruce, "I was going to put one scene in 'The C. S.' of Pickett bull-dogging, but now I have thought better of it and have left it out."[88]

In Pennsylvania, the State Board of Censors was even stricter: it disapproved *The Crimson Skull* entirely. Referring to "Section 6, Act of 1915," the censor cited the reason for disapproval as "Masked criminals, shooting and other violence of all kinds, robbery and successful defiance of authorities throughout."[89] (Notably, *The Birth of a Nation* [1915], whose plot centered around the violence committed by masked members of the Ku Klux Klan, did not receive similar censure and continued to be played for decades nationwide.) Knowing that the censor's report might impede bookings of *The Crimson Skull,* Norman warned Bruce not to discuss the matter with distributors or exhibitors until he had an opportunity to address it.

Since "that bank stuff and the grewsome skull stuff" seemed to be among the censors' greatest objections, Norman assembled his print so that both could be cut out without ruining the story.[90] He wrote Bruce with the specifics: "The Censors might cut out the allegation to robbing the bank, also details of the fake hold up of the pay roll. They may also cut out the trial skull scene. This all can be done—and not spoil the picture. The prisoners can escape—and Chenault never be acused of the trick and the story go right on. Also all allegations to robbing the bank can be eliminated and the title about a scheme to make some easy money etc put in—and when they show up in force to rob the bank—the inference is broad enough."[91] Yet apparently the cuts and revisions were not enough to satisfy the censor or to get the State of Pennsylvania's approval—although Norman's later films passed the same censor without any complications.[92]

Censors were not Norman's only worry. High production costs and distribution difficulties created even more pressing concerns—concerns that George Johnson and other contemporary race filmmakers shared. On March 1, 1922, in fact, only a month before the release of *The Crimson Skull,* Johnson contacted Norman about the possibility of collaborating on a national distribution exchange for race films. By then, the once successful Lincoln Motion Picture Company had fallen on hard times: a few years earlier, Noble Johnson had been forced by Universal Studios, for whom he was under contract, to terminate his affiliation with the company he had founded; and although Lincoln continued without him, it had not released a film since *By Right of Birth* in 1921.

According to George Johnson, the white studio producer made his picture for $10,000 or $15,000; then he "walk[s] across the street and turn[s] that over to a distribution company at so much [percent], and the distribution company advances him $10,000 on the next picture. That's all he has to do; he doesn't have to worry a bit about showing the picture." But since race producers "don't have any way of getting rid of their picture" except by roadshowing or booking it themselves, they needed to devise some viable alternatives.[93]

In his letter to Norman, Johnson proposed one such alternative: the formation of an organized system of production and distribution that could handle race pictures at cheaper costs and higher returns. Such an organization would be a real boon to financially strapped race independents. Not only could it "produce for them, making a production to order just as they desire, useing their own stories, ideas and basing same in proportion to the amount of money they wish to spend"; but it could also handle distribution once the production was complete. Those services would be vital because

> no producer of Negro pictures is doing sufficient business to justify a single handed production and distribution organization. Very few white organizations are able to do so. The older companies with their facilities, connections and reputations are generally the basic production companies, producing more pictures for other concerns than they do for themselves.[94]

Naturally, Johnson argued, since it was located in Los Angeles and enjoyed "a close connection with the large studios, laboratories, directors, actors, and business houses," his company had a distinct advantage over a new distribution organization. And he encouraged Norman to consider an alliance:

> If you have not obligated yourself on present release of your pictures and are in a position to shelve same for a few months, why not consider holding back your present release until fall and in the meantime get in touch with us and lets see if we cannot work out some combination, some cooperation that will be beneficial to both of us in the better times that are coming.

As Johnson noted, few companies were doing well in the current financial climate. Reol Productions' Booker T. Washington picture would likely be their last: "From what we gleaned while East their efforts have not been successful financially." The latest report on the Micheaux firm was also less than positive. The company's most recent release was still tied up, and Micheaux was in Florida selling stock and planning a Florida production. And another race producer, Bookertee Film Company, was idle. So, Johnson concluded, "all in all it looks like the Norman and the Lincoln are in a better position to really do something worthwhile in the future," especially by incorporating with each other.[95]

Norman's response to George Johnson was tepid at best. Calling the offer of combination interesting, he generally concurred with Johnson's observations regarding the production of race motion pictures. But he pointed out that his own dealings with black theaters on the white pictures he had produced earlier in his career convinced him that a $75,000 corporation of Lincoln's size (and financed by stock sales) could never realize a significant profit on its investment; nor could a firm like Micheaux's ever satisfy its stockholders. The fact that the Norman Company, with a very limited number of people in its employ, had not become a corporation ensured that it was in a better financial condition than most race producers. Norman attributed that situation to careful management and to "our abstainance from entangling alliances."

Moreover, Norman doubted that the organizing system of distribution Johnson proposed could actually be accomplished because the large outlay of capital would prevent decent returns on the investment. Therefore, he implied, he was much happier doing business independently, just as he had done for years. And while he supported the notion of a mutual understanding among race producers for their protection from unscrupulous exhibitors in the handling of films and the settlement of rightful claims, amalgamation, as Johnson had originally suggested, was out of the question for him.[96]

Norman also informed Johnson that, instead of amalgamation, he planned to State Right his pictures—that is, to sell the film rights to territorial distributors, who would be in charge of exploiting the picture in the territory that they controlled. Distributors would then keep the entire profit or bear the whole loss.[97] And that is exactly what he did with both *The Bull-Dogger* and *The Crimson Skull*. To Abraham Rosen of the American Colored Film Exchange of Baltimore, Maryland, with whom he formed a long and often nettlesome alliance, Norman sold New York, Pennsylvania, New Jersey, Delaware, Washington, D.C., Virginia, and West Virginia rights.[98] Rosen pronounced *The Crimson Skull* ten times better than *The Green-Eyed Monster,* and called it the best film ever produced with an all-black cast.

To distributor True Thompson, of the True Film Company, in Dallas, Texas, who would become a longtime colleague and ultimately a fellow filmmaker as well, Norman offered the Southwest, a top territory and one he had considered reserving for his own exploitation. But, as Norman explained, since the manufacture and the distribution of motion pictures were two separate branches of the industry, he had decided to State Right *The Crimson Skull* so he could devote himself to new productions. Norman assured Thompson that he could make a handsome profit exploiting the picture in his territory; in fact, Norman claimed that Thompson could net a 100 percent return on the investment in a period of about 90 days.[99] And indeed, after viewing a print that Norman had sent him to screen, Thompson contracted for the rights and praised the quality of the picture, singling out Steve Reynolds's part as being especially good.[100]

Norman followed up with a letter to Paul E. Thompson, with specific advice on roadshowing *The Crimson Skull* in Oklahoma's key cities: "we would suggest that one of the best advertising stunts you can pull off is to purchase a cheap skeleton costume similar to the one used in this production and dressing a local negro in each town in it and have him stand in front of the show, and walk through [the] negro section with window card or sign on his back. We are doing this and it is a bigger advertisement than our man Steve Reynolds who is out with my brother and costs much less. Man to wear this costume can be procured for a dollar and a half a day."[101] (Thompson eventually signed over rights to Texas and Oklahoma to another distributor, Alfred N. Sack, of San Antonio, Texas, but kept other key states for himself.)[102] And to M. Barney, of St. Petersburg, Florida, Norman offered State Rights to *The Crimson Skull* in North and South Carolina, Georgia, and Florida at a figure that he claimed was bound to make Barney money: "We furnish each purchaser with a list of theatres, prices secured in past releases and all dates. This eliminates all hazard." Especially with the exploitation accessories that were available, he assured Barney, *The Crimson Skull* "will book like wild-fire and it only remains for you to play it right to make a clean-up."[103]

State Righting, though, was not the sole method by which Norman distributed his films. He also contracted with individual theater managers and exhibitors, either for straight rentals or for percentages (though he preferred outright sales, since the percentage plan entailed too much bookkeeping and was, he claimed, unsatisfactory to both parties concerned).[104] Establishing the necessary business contacts and cultivating those relationships, however, usually involved extensive correspondence and travel to the various regions of the country where the films might ultimately be rented and shown. As Matthew Bernstein and Dana F. White observed, unlike Hollywood's distribution system, which allowed film circulation on a national scale through major-metropolitan exchange offices employing several hundred employees to coordinate and execute itineraries for the hundreds of prints in circulation at any given time, "the lone race film-maker . . . [had] no such infrastructure." As a result, his expense came from remarkable inefficiencies. Distributing his films alone, Bernstein and White wrote, meant that

> Norman coordinated and followed up on schedules from afar, and relied on the mail to communicate open dates, cancellations and rebookings with his customers, as well as print shipments. Such "long distance" distribution involved considerable pre-planning, and a minimum of six weeks and ideally two months to "get the dates you wish" to create efficient routes, ideally composed of a complete circuit beginning and ending in Florida.[105]

It also meant that Norman was dependent upon the punctuality of the train and mail systems and the good will—and the good word—of the exhibitors with whom he negotiated. In the early years of Norman's feature filmmaking, Norman's brother and business partner Bruce served as his road man—that is, he literally took to the road with prints of the company's films and met personally with theater managers and owners to arrange future bookings. The two brothers worked closely and collaboratively, developing a kind of literal and figurative shorthand in their various business dealings.

But Norman also traveled rather widely on his own, getting acquainted with potential exhibitors and exploring new business opportunities himself. A meticulous record-keeper, Norman maintained extensive paperwork on the theaters, owners, and managers that he visited. His tally sheets outlined the details of every screening of his films, broken down by individual theater; for some theaters, those records spanned a remarkable three decades, from the late 1910s through the early 1940s, and provided a virtual history-at-a-glance of Norman's film career. Similar tallies existed for each state in the territories that Norman covered—twenty-eight states in all, from the South to the Mid-Atlantic and the Midwest.

Norman's business files included hundreds of index cards that he used like a Rolodex and that typically listed the street address and seating capacity of the theater, the names of competing theaters, the quality of the projectors and other equipment in the house (a vital consideration, since poor machinery could ruin prints and add to Norman's costs), the professional experience of the projectionist, the admissions prices the theater charged for matinee and evening screenings, the proximity of the theater to black areas (such as the "Negro Mining Camps" in Birmingham), the interest in vaudeville, the availability of a local band, the race, religion, and ethnicity of the owner or manager, and other background material Norman considered relevant. The card on St. Louis, Missouri, for example, read:

St. Louis, Mo. 80,000 Col.
Venus Theatre, 4264 Finney Ave.
    Seats 485
E. F. Austin, Mgr. Colored.
    Suburban House. Wants first run.
15 cts. Adm.
Machines not extra. Speeds.

Jest-A-Mere Theatre, 4300 Page
    Street. Seats 600
Chas. Pittman, Mgr. Colored.
    Suburban
Opposition to Pendleton. Wants
    first run. 15 cts. Adm.

Star Theatre, 16 South Jefferson
    Street. Seats 600
Christ Efthim, Mgr. White. Down
    town
Theatre plays to 15 cts. Adm. White
    and Colored audience. One day
    stand.

Retina Theatre, Market Street.
    Seats 300
Down town theatre playing all
    short subjects. 10 cts. Adm.
    J. H. Gentner, Mgr.
White Manager. Very independent.

For each showing, Norman collected and recorded information such as the total gross, the cost of advertising, the number of complimentary passes versus paid adult or child admissions, the competing events ("county fair in town for two days"), and even the afternoon or evening weather or other conditions that might have affected attendance.

But perhaps the best portrait of the opportunities and the challenges Norman encountered, particularly with the frequent and usually unexpected closings of race theaters and with competitors willing to undercut his prices for rentals of race films, can be found in Norman's correspondence with his brother Bruce. In one such series of letters, Norman detailed a swing he took through the upper Midwest and the South in August and September of 1922.

> [I will] jump to Chicago to try to get The Bull-Dogger passed there [by the City of Chicago's censor] also The Crimson Skull and if you havent been able to close a deal with St. Louis—to jump there with the car and leave it there and go to Kansas City on the train as the roads are partly dirt to Kansas City but are concrete from Chicago to St. Louis and from St. Louis I can drive to Indianapolis over good roads and then to Cincinnati, Louisville etc. home. I might jump to Cleaveland from Cincinnati but don't know . . . as to whether I will come home by way of Nashville or Washington. . . . It takes gas to win 'em boy.[106]

In Chicago—where he noted that the Vendome Theatre had not run any race pictures over the past year because the high graft required to get them passed and the low price of rentals had removed all the profit—Norman actually lost money because he needed to replace his starter and to invest $25 more in a new tire. "That will mean three new tires so far on this trip. . . . Had the pleasant experience of having to change a tire on State Street to-night. Punctured on a piece of glass and my spare didnt have a pound of air in it. I have driven the old bus 3228 miles in the last 6 weeks."[107]

Leaving for Gary, Indiana, Norman wrote Bruce that "Chicago is a dead one [town] and I never worked so hard in my life to book our two pictures and had such little success."[108] Gary proved no better. "I might as well have not gone there. . . . They had tried a couple of Michauxs films to attract negros, so I could do no business." After driving to Indianapolis, Norman "talked to the manager of the Senate who also has the Indiana and with the Dunick—they are the only three houses running colored pictures. I made him our best proposition and he is thinking it over until I come back there for the car. I dropped off at Springfield, Ill. and found the Pekin there closed."[109]

With the financial picture so bleak, Norman was aware that he could not afford to turn down any reasonable offer: "Business is bad and these other birds [Reol and Micheaux] are selling their stuff—even if it is at a cheaper price. The exhibitors are discouraged and sing the blues overtime, but they are a little hopeful for Fall business if this hot weather and the Railroad strike will let up. About 5000 negros are out in S. Louis on account of it and it has put business bad there and the same here." But he decided to go on "to St. Joe, Omaha and circle back through Des Moines and line up as many of these birds as possible. They havent got anything booked—because they wont pay the price—or have lost heart and are not booking any negro stuff so I am going to load them up."[110] In another letter to Bruce, Norman noted that even Omaha was "on the bum." While in Nebraska, he had met Micheaux's brother Swan, who was playing *The Dungeon* on percent and not doing much business. Swan confirmed that things were looking bleak for the Micheaux Company, too.[111] And in Indianapolis, the picture situation "was on the hog." Norman noted once again that "Raeol [Norman's consistent misspelling of Reol] is selling their stuff for a song and it is not drawing. It is a case with us to get the best price possible, or sit on the curb and see the parade go by. So I have got into the parade for what little we can get out of it."[112]

The road work was also beginning to wreak havoc in other ways as well. After learning from his mother that his brother "had the Dengue" and guessing from the tone of her letter that she was suffering with it too, he confessed his concerns to Bruce. "I get worried when I am away for fear that she may get seriously sick and you can't reach me, but it is hard for you to keep in touch with me when I am jumping around like this."[113] And he begged Bruce to look after her and to pay her rent because he did not have a cent in the bank, only the little money that was left in his pocket.[114] Moreover, Norman was anxious to return to his new bride Gloria, whom he had met while making home talent films in Wisconsin, and to learn what Bruce and his mother thought of his "fine little pal."[115] Given the poor economic conditions at the race theaters, he was understandably feeling disappointed with the industry. "We might as well close out," he told Bruce, "as negro pictures have lost their novelty and pull. And as soon as I can book things out—I am going to look around for some white stuff" to distribute to make up the difference.[116] And, in fact, he did just that. As he wrote A. Schustek in early 1923, "This year, I have taken on the distribution of several white features and hope to do well with them."[117] (Although he concentrated on producing race pictures, Norman continued throughout his career to distribute white films as a way of supplementing his income.)

After Bruce left the business in early 1923 to pursue professional opportunities unrelated to the film industry, Norman had to hire other booking agents to roadshow his films and to arrange future bookings from theater managers and other potential exhibitors.[118] One of Norman's earliest outside road men was M. C. Maxwell, described by E. L. Cummings of the Managers and Performers Consolidated Circuit in Pensacola, Florida, as a good artist and an extra good salesman who was strictly honest and reliable in every way.[119] "I am starting out M. C. Maxwell on the road," Norman wrote to fellow film producer and distributor Alfred N. Sack, who replied: "I know Maxwell personally and believe he should make you a good man."[120]

An entertainer and skilled magician, Maxwell had spent many years performing on the vaudeville circuits and was familiar with the entertainment industry. But even his extensive experience did not obviate the hardships of being on the road or the difficulties at the distribution end of the business. Just as Norman's letters to Bruce had, Maxwell's correspondence with Norman documented some of those difficulties. In a letter from Valdosta, Georgia, for example, Maxwell wrote to express his frustration:

> We didn't do much last night, the fair is getting lots of them, and putting out special efforts for the night crowds at a reduced price, so I thot it best to charge 20 and 30 for the attractions, as money is very scarce here the town is about gone as far as colored people is conserned. I will try a matinee to day at 4:30, as school wont be out untill 4 oclock, I went to the schools this morning and announced it, will charge the school children 10¢, and adults 25[¢] for the matinee. You notice we had only 28 children last night, will try to get them to day, will let the teachers in free for matinee as the boosting they will do will be worth that. . . . I have the boys out in suits to day [performing the bally], carried them to the school this A M made quite an excitement, the teachers couldn't keep them quiet.[121]

Apparently, the efforts had minimal results. In a follow-up letter, Maxwell reported from Dothan, Georgia, "I plugged the town [Valdosta] good yesterday for two hours with the boys, one with skull suit and other one with chaps, but the fair had just closed and a colored minstrel tent had just played here, and it left the town in a financial strain, so much so that I couldn't book the 'Bull Dogger' for $25.00 . . . [The theater manager] just wont book anything for the present, the Reol people have been trying to book him a programe for Thanksgiving at $15.00 and he wont accept that, the exodus has hit this section hard and they are yet going." Maxwell concluded by saying that he had no "hopes for to night": "I can see now as I predicted that I wont make any money on this propersition, and am just losing good time at a time that I can less afford it." He only hoped to be able to "do something" at his next stop in Alabama.[122] Yet in Troy and then in Birmingham, the story was the same. "You need not book me any further than you have at present," Maxwell advised Norman. "I see no hopes of making anything on this job."[123]

Although Maxwell soon stopped serving as Norman's road man, later that year both he and his wife accepted roles in Norman's next race picture, *Regeneration;* and afterward, as part of the promotion, Maxwell would occasionally make personal appearances in the towns where the film was being shown. Over the years, the relationship between the two men remained cordial. Even as late as 1930, Maxwell wrote Norman to say that he was planning to "try Florida" and suggested that he might be available for future acting work.[124]

As of December 1922, *The Crimson Skull* was still drawing audiences. "Business has picked up this Fall," Norman wrote K. Lee Williams, the distributor of the Miller Brothers' 101 Ranch Feature Attractions, "and we have been roadshowing all territory on 'The Crimson Skull' that we did not dispose the State Rights on. Grossed over $800. here in Jacksonville in 2 days and over $900. in 3 days at Memphis. Had special lobby and ballyho." The real reason for Norman's letter, though, was to inquire if Williams had produced any new films that Norman's company might distribute.[125]

Earlier in the year, Williams had offered "Friend Norman" exclusive rights to Buffalo Bill's last performance, a short film that Norman agreed was worth giving a trial on a 50–50 split receipt basis. But Williams, who did not have a copy of the picture that was not already working, never acted on Norman's proposal. He explained that he had "practically" sold two prints of Buffalo Bill for South America; in order to send Norman a show, he would have to get a new print at a cost of $145, which he felt would not be worthwhile in the long run.[126]

To Norman's most recent inquiry, however, Williams replied that *The Crimson Skull* looked like a real attraction; and he added, "I made a new [non-race Western] picture this fall and have been doing fine with it since opening Nov. 3rd. Have special truck and carry big lobby and live elk. Have sold only one state right, which was an accident, but am going to start advertising next month." If Norman was interested, Williams could offer him a deal on a single print at $350 so they both could "make a few dimes."[127] The picture in question was *The Cherokee Strip*, "a true story of yesterday and today" based on actual historical events of early Oklahoma history and starring daredevil cowgirl Helen (Mrs. Hoot) Gibson.

Once again, though, no arrangement with Williams was reached. So Norman—who had already successfully negotiated rights to the Henry Starr picture, *A Debtor to the Law*—queried other distributors and film-makers about their features, comedies, and educational and travel subjects. "We distribute our product in 28 states," Norman claimed, "and are in a position to place meritorious subjects at fair rentals." He added that "We have a modern equipped exchange in Jacksonville and have men on the road at all times who are in a position of placing contracts that will net you a handsome profit."[128]

The replies Norman received varied. Some distributors responded that they handled only short subjects suitable for home and nontheatrical use or catered to nontheatrical business. Others would consider doing business only on outright sales. Still others were willing to sell the entire lot of their films in a single purchase at a special price for a cash deal. One distributor, Western Feature Films in Chicago, Illinois, offered the Lightning Bryce serial in perfect condition; but because it had already been broadly distributed, Norman decided against handling it (though he did order two of Western's comedies, along with various two-reelers from other distributors, including *Stanley in Darkest Africa* [part of the "Stanley the African Explorer" series], *The Jungle Outcasts*, *A Kaffir's Gratitude*, *A Siren of the Jungle*, and *The Rajahs Sacrifice*, all produced by the Centaur Film Company, and a Selig animal feature).

Norman's special interest, it seems, was in criminal and prison features, particularly films such as *The Pardon*, *The Finger of Justice*, *The Escaped Convict*, and *Who Shall Take My Life?*, all of which focused on the issue of capital punishment. The most appealing was clearly *Death in the Electric Chair*, the only picture ever produced, by the permission of the

Prison Board, "within the cold stone walls of Sing Sing Prison." Chas. Marks at Western assured Norman that, exploited properly, it could be a gold mine.[129] According to the flyer, *Death in the Electric Chair* showed the gruesome realism of the whipping post and the damp dungeons and the horrors of the death chamber. Moreover, Marks wrote, a full and complete line of advertising was available, along with "a Rogue's Gallery, containing photos of murderers, yeggs [burglars], confidence men, and criminals of all descriptions." One especially sensational accessory was a genuine electric chair. When placed in a department store window as an advertisement for the film, it required police to keep the sidewalks clear; and when placed in the theater lobby, it reportedly caused both men and women to faint from fright. Marks also noted that he had printed a book in connection with the film that netted as much as $400 a day in profit. Priced at 25¢ each, "This is not a pressbook, but contains stories and pictures of Prison Life and is sold in theatres during the run of the picture."[130]

Norman corresponded at length with Western to secure rights; but the picture, which had to be ordered directly from the laboratory, cost $800, a figure that Norman claimed was simply too high. After unsuccessfully attempting to negotiate the price, he decided to produce his own film, *The Soul Robber*, which he described to actor Clarence Brooks as a race picture with the electric chair that "will be a knock-out and have wonderful exploitation possibilities."[131] Almost immediately and certainly prematurely, Norman announced the production of the film in his company's press and promotional materials and even began investigating the possibility of renting or purchasing a replica of an electric chair that he could display in the theater lobbies as part of his ballyho.

While there is no evidence that Norman ever produced—or even began development of—*The Soul Robber*, he never totally abandoned the idea of making or distributing a good prison film. In the spring of 1924, he contacted John T. Glynn, the head of Glynn Detective Services in Leavenworth, Kansas, who had recently published an article in *Billboard* about an exhibit he was preparing on crime and prisons, to be shown at various upcoming fairs. Believing that Glynn was overlooking the great possibilities of moving pictures to aid him in his educational campaign, Norman proposed making a film that, when paired with Glynn's big ballyho, would pack any theater. Norman noted that he already had 356 theaters that would show such an attraction and could secure 2,000 more in the United States alone.[132]

After Glynn indicated interest and mentioned that he might be able to arrange to have footage shot inside and outside of Leavenworth's prisons, Norman followed up by submitting two propositions for his consideration.[133] Norman could either produce the picture, with Glynn supplying the exhibit and offering a short lecture on the picture, for which he could receive a percentage of the receipts or a stipulated guarantee. Or, alternatively, Glynn could produce the picture with Norman on an equal financial basis.[134] Ultimately, nothing came of either proposal: the prison drama turned out to be another promising yet unrealized project. But to the end of his career, Norman continued to seek out other unusual proposals as well as to secure films by other producers for distribution along with his own features.

It was, however, the production of his own films, which he wrote, cast, produced, edited, and marketed, that gave Norman the greatest personal and professional satisfaction. His two Western pictures, *The Bull-Dogger* and *The Crimson Skull,* which were enthusiastically received by black audiences (and some white moviegoers as well), solidified Norman's reputation as one of the leading race filmmakers of his day and encouraged him to move on to even more ambitious but risky movie projects.

CHAPTER FIVE

"A Risky Experiment":
Zircon and *Regeneration*

THE YEARS 1923 and 1924 were exciting ones for Norman. Not only did he continue to distribute and promote his two popular Westerns, *The Bull-Dogger* and *The Crimson Skull*, but he also defined a landmark black action serial, *Zircon*, to be filmed in fifteen episodes; wrote and produced a new film, *Regeneration*, a "Romance of the South Seas"; forged valuable alliances with Clarence Brooks and D. Ireland Thomas, seminal figures in race films; and moved his film operation into his own studio, the site of the former Eagle Studios in Arlington, Florida, a suburb of Jacksonville.

The black serial was a project that Norman conceived soon after he completed *The Crimson Skull*. From his experience distributing *The Green-Eyed Monster* and his other race pictures, Norman knew that black theaters were anxious to acquire first-run black-cast films; and he realized that, if offered an entire serial for a reasonable price, they would be likely to book it. Norman also believed that establishing and cultivating a "true black star" in his proposed "Star Series"—that is, an actor with visibility and name recognition—would not only benefit him but also bring increased attention to the race film industry.

Black characters had never before been prominently featured in a serial, much less one as thrilling, action-filled, and ambitious as Norman's promised to be. But they had occasionally appeared in recurring minor roles in early film series produced largely for white audiences. Those series, however, only reinforced contemporary comic stereotypes, particularly that of the "coon," a figure described by historian Stanley Elkins as "docile but irresponsible, loyal but lazy, humble but chronically given to lying and stealing," and characterized by Daniel J. Leab as "subhuman, simpleminded, superstitious, and submissive" to whites, frequently childlike in his dependence, with foolishly exaggerated qualities, including an apparently hereditary clumsiness and an addictive craving for fried chicken and watermelon.[1] The "coon" was best exemplified by the character of crazy Rastus, who became a generic name for black stooges on screen. Among the first of the slapstick comedies centering on the escapades of Rastus were Lubin's *How Rastus Got His Pork Chops* (1908) and Pathé's *How Rastus Got His Turkey* (1910), in which Rastus tries to steal Thanksgiving dinner for his wife Eliza and daughter and ends up carrying off a piece of the fence as well.[2] In *Rastus in Zululand* (1910), Rastus falls asleep in the sun (since, as the film suggests, a "darky" likes warmth) and dreams that he is shipwrecked in Zululand, where cannibals capture him and prepare to boil him for their dinner. Although the chief's large and ugly daughter intercedes on his behalf, Rastus prefers the pot to matrimony (a preference the chieftain, another black savage, nearly obliges); but he awakens from his dream just as the pot's water is about to boil. Rastus continued his chicken-thieving and antic behavior in other shorts, including *Rastus and Chicken, Pickaninnies and Watermelon,* and *Chicken Thief,* all released around 1910–1911.[3] In Vitagraph's "Sonny Jim" films, produced by Tefft Johnson, Jim and "his little colored friend Lilly" (as studio advertising described her character) have similar comic adventures. In *Cause for Thanksgiving,* for instance, Jim trades his turkey for Lilly's baby brother (also named Rastus) because Lilly's family has plenty of children but no food. And in *The White and Black Snowball* (1915), after rescuing Lilly from some young toughs who want to steal her mittens, Jim tries to rub her cheeks and forehead white with snow since he knows that his mother will not allow such a "dirty" face inside her home.

Similar characters were featured in the Hal Roach "Our Gang" comedy series, which premiered in 1922 and continued throughout the next decade and for many years beyond, in reruns and syndication. Yet, while the Little Rascals Sunshine Sammy, Pineapple, Farina, Stymie, and Buckwheat broke new cinematic ground in showing that black children could actually share adventures and misadventures with white children, the black Rascals rarely rose above caricature in their looks, dress, or speech patterns. Many of the shorts that followed merely reinforced that typing. In "The Cabin Kids" pictures produced by Al Christie in the 1930s, for example, the "clever little pickaninnies" sang and "cut capers" as they braved the Wild West (*Way Out West* [1935]), crashed the big top (*Pink Lemonade* [1936]), encountered frights on a stormy night in a deserted cabin (*Spooks* [1936]), and saved a maestro and his orchestra by performing their own brand of swing music (*Rhythm Saves the Day* [1937]).[4]

The serial that Norman had in mind, however, was a radical departure from such early cinematic series. His "Colored Serial Supreme"—originally titled *The Fighting Fool* but later renamed *Zircon* (though sometimes the titles were used interchangeably)—would comprise fifteen two-reel episodes "Teeming with Big Fights, Thrilling Situations, Suspense, Mystery, Adventure, Love."[5] Above all, though, it would showcase black characters in serious starring roles rather than in the low-comic supporting parts to which they were usually relegated.

By mid-1923, in promotional materials for another one of his films, Norman announced that his new serial *The Fighting Fool,* featuring an "ALL COLORED CAST," would be "COMING!" soon. An advance flyer that he developed especially for distributors, theater owners, and theater managers offered a fuller description of the episodes of *Zircon* (some of which, like the serial itself, had by then been retitled).

> Chapter 1. *The Spider's Web* [originally titled *Human Checkers*]. John Manning, a young chemist and mining engineer in the employ of the Egyptian Potash Company, discovers a new wonder substance, naming it "Zircon." A rival interest, The Potash Corporation, hires a criminal known as "The Spider" to steal the formula and the manufacturing process. Manning and his sweetheart, Helen, are enmeshed in "The Spider's Web," with apparent death staring them in the face because of their refusal to give up the secret.

Chapter 2. *The Wheel of Death.* "The Spider," after securing by force a sample of Zircon, leaves Manning to die on the spinning hub of one of the monstrous wheels of the potash pump.

Chapter 3. *The Poison Cloud.* "The Fox," in the employ of the Potash Trust, while analyzing the sample of Zircon, is surprised by Manning. "The Fox" releases a poison cloud in his laboratory and leaves Manning to die.

Chapter 4. *The Desert Trap.* On a journey into the desert to rescue Helen, Manning is trapped by The Spider's gang and left to die in a raging sandstorm.

Chapter 5. *The Living Tomb.* Helen and Manning seek shelter on an ancient tomb of "Cliff Dwellers" and are trapped there and left to die of suffocation.

Chapter 6. *The Crocodiles' Jaws.* Upon their rescue from the living tomb, Manning and Helen are attacked by an army of crocodiles, with no apparent escape from death in sight.

Chapter 7. *The Plane of Death* [originally titled *The Sky Demon*]. Manning and Helen escape from the crocodiles but they are captured again by The Spider's gang. They are bound in an airplane. One of The Spider's gang takes them aloft in the airplane, then he jumps out with the only parachute, leaving them to certain death in the pilotless plane.

Chapter 8. *The Ship Killer.* Falling into the ocean in the plane, Manning and Helen are rescued by a ship on which The Spider is fleeing to a foreign country with the Zircon formula, which he plans to sell to foreign interests and doublecross the Potash Trust. Manning regains the formula but The Spider traps him and Helen in the hold of the ship, then scuttles the ship. The water slowly rises in the hold, swirling higher and higher around Manning and Helen.

Chapter 9. *Flames of Fear.* Failing in his purpose, The Spider escapes the sinking ship in a lifeboat after having set fire to the ship, leaving Manning and Helen helpless to roast alive.

Chapter 10. *Tigers of the Sea.* Drifting on a raft at sea, Manning is forced to fight for his life with a monstrous tiger shark.

Chapter 11. *Jungle Death* [originally titled *Jungle Terror*]. Making land, The Spider is surprised to see that Manning and Helen have been cast upon the island. Manning and Helen are bound to trees to be devoured by a monstrous snake.

Chapter 12. *Sands of Death.* Managing to escape, Manning discovers the richest deposits of potash in the world on the island and the potash is rich in the mineral Zircon. The Spider, with the formula, leaves Manning at the mercy of the quicksands, taking Helen with him.

Chapter 13. *Trail of "The Spider."* Manning is rescued from the island and trails Helen, who is about to suffer dishonor at the hands of The Spider.

Chapter 14. *The Vanishing Prisoner.* Manning rescues Helen from The Spider's clutches and captures him. But The Spider vanishes with the aid of one of his confederates, who has a mysterious substance which makes him invisible. Manning is bound in a cabin by the invisible Spider and the cabin is blown up.

Chapter 15. *Millions.* Peg, a one-legged friend of Manning's, secures some of the invisible powder, and, making himself invisible, rescues Manning from the cabin just before it is blown up. The Spider is killed by a piece of rock debris from the explosion. The Spider's gang is rounded up and captured. Helen, who is the daughter of Manning's employer, is married to Manning and with the newly discovered rich deposits of potash and the secret formula of Zircon, the Potash Trust is forced out of business and Manning becomes a millionaire.[6]

Some of the details of the episodes were familiar: the names of the heroine Helen Desmond and the hero John Manning, for example, recalled those of Helen Powers and Jack Manning, the main characters in both the white-cast home talent and the black-cast feature film versions of *The Green-Eyed Monster.* And the basic plot point of the serial—the discovery of the wonder substance Zircon, which is stolen from Manning's laboratory by the Spider, who intends to sell it to foreign interests—recalled the intrigue at the heart of another of Norman's early pictures, the home talent film *Pro Patria,* in which university student Dale Gordon develops a powerful and valuable explosive that fellow student Eduardo Salazar tries to steal for the Mexican faction with whom he is connected. (That attempted theft likewise resulted in the destruction of a laboratory and a death.) But *Zircon* also exploited audience curiosity in other interesting and novel ways—that is, in its depictions of exciting but dangerous locales, like the tropical islands full of quicksand, crocodiles, monstrous snakes, and enormous man-eating sharks; of quasi-historical sites, such as the ancient tombs in which Manning and Helen are trapped; and of new technologies like airplanes, which figure prominently in two of the episodes.

Norman had financed his earlier films himself. Using his own money as well as money from his brother and then-business partner Bruce, Norman underwrote *The Green-Eyed Monster;* and with the profits from that first feature film, along with additional funds borrowed from his mother and short-term loans that Bruce secured, he produced *The Bull-Dogger* and *The Crimson Skull*.[7] Although it is not possible to confirm the actual costs of those two Westerns, the budget that Norman initially set for them—and for a proposed third Western, which was never made—was a bare-bones $3,000. By comparison, a single Micheaux film ran between $10,000 and $20,000—considerably more than Norman's pictures, yet still a pittance relative to most white studio features.[8]

But Norman realized that the production of a multi-part serial would be significantly more expensive than his earlier pictures, particularly since—as he claimed—each chapter would cost almost as much as a feature film to complete. Accordingly, the budget that he projected was around $10,700: $3,000 for himself as producer, writer, and editor; $2,500 for stars, actors, and extras; $1,500 for props and interiors; $500 for the cameraman; $1,200 for thirty thousand feet of raw stock; $300 for developing costs; and $1,700 for two positive prints. As part of his total expense, Norman also estimated spending in excess of $1,100 on advertising materials, including lobby cards, lithographs, press sheets, and slides, plus an additional $240 on reels and shipping cans.[9]

To meet those costs, Norman settled on a different method of capitalizing his project—a profit-sharing agreement—which he explained in a form letter to theater owners. Writing that he had decided to make a colored serial called *The Fighting Fool*, a picture unlike any other race production, Norman offered them the opportunity to buy into it. "Contract on the serial," he advised, "is secured by a Profit Sharing Rental Franchise which gives the exhibitor a chance at double revenues. First, from increased business in his theatre, and second, a participation in the net profits of the rental earnings of the serial, according to the pro rata amount of his rental." Thus, the exhibitor had twice the incentive to invest in the production.

The actual franchise terms and contract prices, which varied from city to city and even from theater to theater, were based on a ratings system that Norman created. The profit-sharing rental franchise signed on May 25, 1923, between the Dunbar Theatre of Savannah, Georgia, and the Norman Film Manufacturing Company, for example, stipulated that the episodes would be available to the theater immediately upon release at a rental of

$35 per print, for a total rental fee of $525, with "seventy dollars down June 1923 and seventy dollars down the month of July 1923 balance upon receipt of each episode."[10] The signed contract with the Hippodrome Theatre in Danville, Virginia, however, contained somewhat different terms: $20 per print, total rental fee of $300, with "six episodes in advance upon notification of release and balance upon receipt of each episode."[11] To John Mills at the Colonial Theatre, Portsmouth, Virginia, Norman quoted a price of $25 per episode; to J. A. Long at the Rapeed Theatre in Tyler, Texas, Norman wrote: "Price on 'The Fighting Fool' [the original name of the serial] our 15 chapter Colored Serial for your theatre is $22.50 per episode."[12] For the Elk Theatre Company, with small theaters in Italy and Waxahachie, Texas, the price was even lower: $10 an episode.[13] One "business-getter" mailing took a different approach entirely, urging exhibitors to "write us what your figures are and make us an offer" for the profit-sharing rental franchise on the serial, while still other theaters received a promotional coupon promising that, upon advance rental of fourteen episodes, the fifteenth and final episode would be provided free of charge.[14]

The one constant in Norman's booking negotiations, though, was his determination to collect sufficient advance funding to cover his production costs. In a letter of May 18, 1923, to P. A. Engler, of the Famous Theatre, "Birmingham's Theatre for Colored People," in Birmingham, Alabama, Norman explained:

> This serial will not be released until same is booked solid, as it will come to theatres on a circuit. Advertising will consist of ones, threes, sixes, twenty four sheets, banner, slides, trailer, heralds, window cards and photos. In fact, a complete assortment of advertising accessories to put this serial over to top money. It will cost us practically as much to make each episode of this serial, as it would to make a feature. But we have been able to reduce the cost to the exhibitor to a fraction of the cost of a colored feature AND GIVE THEM A NOVEL ATTRACTION THAT WILL DRAW FOR 15 SOLID WEEKS and to as much business as a colored feature.[15]

Engler's response was clearly heartening. He wrote Norman: "I believe that a *good* colored serial will go over and I believe it would be profitable, but remember, this guess is made on the assumption that it is good. You know if it did not measure up, you would suffer as well as the exhibitors, as they would gradually drop off and make it rather expense towards the last." That said, Engler assured Norman that he could count on him; and he added that Norman was right in making these fellows assert themselves before going ahead. "I know the old story after you have it made, they can tell you they didn't tell you to make it. I am accepting this from you where I might not from someone else, as I have confidence in you making what they want and in your ability to make one worth while."[16]

E. Wilson from the True Film Company offered similar accolades and concerns. "Sincerely hope," Wilson wrote, "that you have kept up the Norman standard and quality in your latest venture as a serial. It is just fifteen times more risky than a feature. We have never run a colored serial, in fact, this is the only one we have ever heard of. We give you credit for knowing your business, therefore, let's hope this is A-1."[17]

In letters to Abraham Rosen, the distributor who purchased State Rights to several of Norman's films, Norman once again justified his financing decision. "We are not going to hold the sack on a risky experiment as this is, as if the exhibitors are not going to co-operate with us to the fullest extent. So far, the response to our circular sent have been gratifying. We have received many wires and offers of booking."[18]

Norman was certainly not exaggerating. The requests for franchise pricing, schedule dates, and other booking information flooded in—from theaters as far south as the Lincoln in Miami and the Liberty in St. Petersburg, Florida, the Palace in Lake Charles and the Jefferson in Marrero, Louisiana, the Valdosta in Valdosta, Georgia, and the Grand Central in Dallas, Texas; as far north as the Circle Theatre in Detroit, Michigan; and as far west as the Apex in Topeka and the Dunbar in Kansas City, Kansas, the Progress Pictures Corporation in St. Louis, Missouri, and the Dixie in Tulsa, Oklahoma. Several theaters were willing to advance-book *Regeneration*, Norman's next feature film not yet in production, with the understanding that they would get the first offer on the serial.[19] Still other theaters wrote to say that, while first-run pricing was too steep for their houses, they would welcome quotes on second-run pricing or flat rental.

In response to the inquiries, Norman reiterated the benefit of the profit-sharing rental franchise, which allowed exhibitors to participate in the rental profits according to the pro rata amount of their own rental—

though he emphasized that he had only about 200 theaters for distribution, against a possible 15,000 on a white serial.[20] To one theater manager who had questioned the franchise fee, he explained: "We have had to base our rental price on production costs, with an added fair return on the investment, divided into a distribution of 260 theatres."[21] To his colleague E. Wilson at the True Film Company, Norman offered further details: "A Colored Serial has to be somewhat higher than a white serial. We have based our estimate per episode at one third the cost of a feature in the majority of cases. Giving the exhibitor three times the drawing power for the same money. . . . The serial will be good . . . [but] we must have the co-operation of the exhibitors."[22]

To make it good, however, Norman knew he needed skilled performers who would excite his audience and keep them coming back to the theater for each new chapter. Fortunately, D. Ireland Thomas, the manager of the Lincoln Theatre in Charleston, South Carolina, and a columnist for the important black newspaper the *Chicago Defender,* was willing to lend his assistance. Thomas had met earlier with Bruce Norman in Charleston to discuss the proposed *Zircon* serial; and on May 1, 1923, at Bruce's suggestion, Thomas wrote to Richard Norman, stating that he had contacted actor Clarence A. Brooks and urged him to pursue a role. "A fine fellow, a gentleman who do not drink or smoke, a hardworker and honest," Brooks, Thomas attested, "is very popular and is well liked and a good mixer[;] and I would like to see him featured in your serial."[23] Thomas also indicated that he knew people who might be willing to assist with financing and that he himself might wish to take a small part in *Zircon.* Even more significantly, Thomas offered to promote the serial by providing free publicity in his column. "Let me have the dope that I want and I will start them talking about it and it will not cost you one cent."[24]

Acting immediately on Thomas's suggestion, Norman wrote directly to Clarence Brooks and enclosed a circular giving him the working outline of the fifteen episode serial, whose cast would comprise the best talent of the race. Stating that the role of Manning would fit Brooks like a glove and add to his laurels, Norman added that the part of Helen Desmond, *Zircon's* leading lady, might be filled by Anita Thompson, Brooks's co-star in Lincoln's *By Right of Birth.*[25]

Clarence Brooks replied with a friendly letter, acknowledging that he was pleased to know that he had not been forgotten and noting that this was the second time he had been approached concerning an affiliation with Norman's firm.[26] The part of Manning, he agreed, would be ideal for him, and he had the utmost confidence that he could portray the character with due credit. Moreover, he confirmed that he had already approached Thompson and could make similar contacts with other prominent artists.[27] Since he was widely known by many film performers in the East, he would have no trouble securing their services for parts in the picture—though, of course, "the principle interest to such other talent would be the salary." As for himself, he wrote he was still connected to the Lincoln Theatre but had been a bit inactive in the distribution end of the business for some time because he was taking a much needed rest and also getting used to married life. Therefore he was not interested in booking completed attractions for Norman, only in producing the actual pictures. As for salary, he asked for an agreement of three months' work at a minimum wage of $100 per week plus round-trip transportation to Jacksonville, because any lesser terms would not allow him to break even.

Since Brooks was not only an accomplished actor but also a knowledgeable industry insider, Norman was gratified by his interest. "I don't believe that there is any colored screen performer who is more intimately familiar with the colored picture situation, both from a production and distribution standpoint than yourself," he replied. Recognizing that Brooks "entertain[ed] no illusions as to the future of the colored pictures," Norman went on to offer his own assessment of the state of the race film industry and to inquire if Brooks shared his conclusions. That assessment was actually quite perceptive. "The colored picture situation," he observed, "is in a chaotic condition."

> Raeol with its entry in the field of pictures and its feverish booking activity, has killed the novelty. It is history among the colored exhibitors that their production has ceased to draw to the extent that they have refused to pay reasonable prices for colored pictures. I have seen Raeol contracts that would surprise you for their prices—as low as $7.50 a feature. And we have refused to ship out a feature any less than $25. Michaux [Oscar Micheaux, whose name Norman consistently misspelled] has done what he can to hold up prices and production. But he has had to produce more pictures than

he would have, in order to offset Raeol. Ben Strasser had produced several features without a knowledge of the theatre situation and has sold these features as low as $25. in places like Chattanooga, where the rental should have been a hundred up. Now summing up the situation, I find that the colored theatre owner in an astonishing number of cases, refuses to pay more than a set price for a colored feature—no matter what the original cost of this production to the producers or its possible drawing power. This price has been largely dictated by him, because he was able to get colored features from someone at such and such a price. The whole condition can be summed up in the one word OVERPRODUCTION. As long as Lincoln, Michaux and Norman were the only ones in the field, they were doing their utmost to hold up prices, by personal exploitation and a minimum of productions.

The salvation of the colored picture, Norman repeated, lay in creating a colored star with tremendous box office drawing power and putting him in novel attractions. *Regeneration,* his next feature film, Norman emphasized, was "novel"; so was his serial.[28] To that end, he was willing to offer Brooks a permanent position with the Norman Company: twelve months, at a weekly salary to be augmented once Brooks was actually producing pictures, plus a commission on bookings and stock options, if the company were ever to incorporate.

Brooks responded that he agreed closely with Norman's observations; and he reiterated that although he had been inactive in the picture world for the past few months, he was positive that, apart from their good friend D. Ireland Thomas, there was no one more conversant with present production than he was.[29] As for the prospect of year-long employment, Brooks expressed appreciation but explained that he had originally volunteered his services for only three months, since "it was not possible to complete a serial in less time and produce it half way decent." While a longer tenure could be arranged, it would need to be negotiated after he was on-site. Factoring into Brooks's decision were his reluctance to relocate from California, which he professed to love, and his investment income properties, which required direct monitoring. But most importantly, Brooks claimed, a move to Florida might keep him from purchasing all of the assets of and productions from the Lincoln Motion Picture Company, on whose board he had served since its founding. "This proposition [of becoming sole owner of that firm] has been just recently offered me . . . at a ridiculously low price in proportion to its actual worth." Yet assuming that he and Norman could arrive at an appropriate salary and a method of securing an interest in Norman's productions, Brooks stated that he would consider making the purchase of the Lincoln Company's name and "stuff" to be a part of his "permanent connection" to Norman.[30]

Perhaps the most interesting part of Brooks's letter was an outline he attached of the report he delivered to the officers and directors of the Lincoln Motion Picture Company in Los Angeles in February 1922. In that report, much of which was as pertinent to Norman's company as to Lincoln's, Brooks discussed the "General Natural Conditions and Outlook for the Future" of "Colored Theatre Patrons and Colored Pictures." The past season had been very trying, he noted, and business was at a stand-still, partly because of a lack of personal interest and partly because so many people were out of work. Theaters were still booking race pictures, but the bad ones had left an "ill taste" in the public's mouth and greatly hurt exhibition of the good pictures.

"Colored patrons," Brooks continued, "are using discrimination in patronizing pictures same as exhibitor who is now buying them. Colored pictures are no more novelties—everybody having seen them—and 'All Colored Cast' has lost its pulling power." Consequently, he believed that companies had to take steps to maintain the public interest by establishing a movie hero for the entire race to look up to and by centralizing publicity to assure both the public and the exhibitor of the best possible product.[31]

Norman greeted Brooks's letter with much enthusiasm.[32] Brooks's topical outline to the Lincoln Motion Picture Company, he wrote, was correct in the main outline.

> Your prediction in 1922 that business would steadily get better has been borne out in some instances. Instances where real management prevailed in the colored theatre. When the boom was on, most any so called theatre manager was making money, but when the slump came, the real test of showmanship arrived, and I am sorry to say that the test found the majority of colored theatre managers woefully lacking in real business ability. Many theatres closed down, are still closed down and others to-day are barely existing.

Claiming to have personally interviewed every theater owner and played every theater catering to a black audience, Norman observed that it was no secret that some of his company's pictures held unbroken records for size of theater and size of population "due to personal exploitation." As proof, he cited a sampling of box-office figures from the previous fall: $635 for one day at Tulsa, Oklahoma; $685 for one day at the Gem in Knoxville, Tennessee; $508 for one day at Chattanooga; $967 for two days in Dallas, Texas; and over six thousand paid admissions in two days at Birmingham, Alabama. "This spring," he added, "we have jumped business in little towns from 14 paid admissions on a regular program to $72. net on the one day. This is not big business, but in proportion to regular business it is big." And considering "the ratio of business between white and colored features, Colored features are drawing as good, if not better to-day. But not to the extent where high prices can be procured."

While race pictures had to be produced as cheaply as possible to allow filmmakers to make any profit from them, Norman insisted that they also needed to be of a high caliber in order to draw moviegoers. A fifteen-part serial such as his proposed *Zircon,* with two reels per episode, was therefore "a risky experiment" since it meant making the equivalent of six five-reel features—"and there is also the distribution problem." But if Brooks came to Jacksonville and devoted his entire time to production and a program of education among the black theaters, Norman was convinced Brooks could ensure the serial's financial success and also personally cash in on it. Yet, he underscored, under no circumstances would he produce and release the serial until it was booked solid.

"If the colored theatre owner don't want a serial, we wont cram it down his throad," Norman insisted, "but he does want one." The majority, however, prefer to wait until the serial is made

and then due to a lack of competition, offer you $10. an episode when it should be $35. well knowing that you are almost sure to accept that rather than nothing. But we don't expect to be caught that way—they must show their good will by booking the serial before it is entirely produced. Therefore, we will produce a limited number of episodes, say one, two and number fifteen; having a complete 6 or 8 reel feature, which in emergency can be booked as such and if bookings on the serial justify it, we will make the balance of the episodes.

Since a number of contracts had already been secured from exhibitors who showed good faith, Norman concluded that the serial looked like a landslide. And to ensure that the serial would in fact *be* a landslide, Norman began announcing to theater owners and managers—likely without Brooks's knowledge and certainly without his consent—that Clarence Brooks had already been signed as the hero in the production.[33]

Brooks's response to Norman's letter was equally enthusiastic and detailed.[34] Agreeing that a black star would revive the public interest in race pictures by giving audiences what they were hungering for, he again supported the notion of a serial. Furthermore, he believed that, even if it was as lengthy as six five-reel features, the serial could be made for about 40 percent less and over its lifetime would play in 20 percent more houses. He based his "booking conclusions" on the fact that

> There are many first run theatres that will not book a feature behind the opposition house and many vaudeville theatres that cannot afford to book a feature even second run behind a straight picture house. In the case of a serial many of these houses would book behind the other just the same as they oft time book other serials. Second runs could be made to the other theatres that would justify them from the standpoint of both rental and patronage. Many vaudeville houses would be glad of such an opportunity.

Taking the venture "out of the experiment class" and putting it "into the investment class" would, however, require strong exploitation and distribution, which were the foundation of any film's success. Yet Brooks advised Norman not to worry about those exhibitors who might try to force him to accept a low rental after the serial is complete. He alluded to the strategy that D. Ireland Thomas often used, of showing still photos of his films directly to townspeople, who then pressed the management of their theaters to book the productions. That kind of local pressure, Brooks confirmed, "always made the exhibitor meet our terms before the dawn of a new day." So, as long as Norman had "the goods and a little strategy," he would not need to worry getting a fair rental price for his pictures.

But while the most efficient and profitable method of distribution was a circuit booking, Brooks questioned if Norman's method of traveling from city to city to investigate whether exhibitors wanted a serial and then apprising them of his program of financing and distribution was the best way to establish that circuit. He suggested that a better approach might be to produce the feature *Regeneration* with the cast that he intended to use in

Zircon along with the first episode of the serial, and then to make a trip to the major Southern cities in order to screen both. Brooks added that he and Thomas would be willing to make similar trips to the major cities of the Midwest and the East. That way, Norman could not only establish his distribution circuit for both his serial and his features simultaneously but also make his contracts and accept deposits "from the revenue derived from the new feature which will not be any more than would be required to road show the feature itself." Furthermore, by convincing the exhibitor that he had a star and a nationally known cast of good actors, Norman would muster enthusiasm for his serial and deflect skepticism, since the exhibitor "will not realize the serial will be completed with his deposit monies and therefore will not hold back in booking or making a deposit, like he is sure to do when you go to him empty handed to get both a contract on something 'to be' and also a deposit."[35] Finally, Brooks suggested that Norman share their correspondence with D. Ireland Thomas, who might determine any angles that they had overlooked. Concluding that he welcomed a definite proposition, Brooks signed his letter "Yours for the success of colored pictures."

In reply, Norman confirmed that he had already consulted Thomas, who reinforced their views about the future of race pictures and reiterated his desire to see Brooks featured in a series of Norman's films.[36] But from the tone of Norman's letter, it was clear to Brooks that something had changed. "Fall is almost here," Norman wrote, "and the outlook for Colored pictures is more or less uncertain." Then he offered a sobering analysis of the industry:

> Michaux is busy producing another picture and I can't imagine for what reason. He is not marketing his pictures. I do not know of a theatre in the South that has ran his last two pictures, *Deceit* and *Virgin of the Seminole*. He sold 7 North Eastern states to a man in Baltimore on these pictures to be marketed this Fall. Price paid was about half what a colored picture would bring through personal exploitation. Ben Strasser has announced that he has started on a serial. Same was done through a circular to Eastern exhibitors some two months ago. This is not reliable information as he is working on what capital he can interest that is not familiar with the possibilities of the Colored Picture. The last three pictures he produced were financed by three different groups of angels [outside white investors] and they practically made nothing on the venture. Raeol is selling what they have at a song and at the present time you can't tell what way they will jump.

Norman went on to explain his revised plans for his *Zircon* serial and his next feature—plans that seemed largely at odds with Brooks's earlier suggestions.[37] Norman still intended to produce a colored serial featuring Brooks, he announced, but "we have decided not to start production at the present time." Instead, "we are going ahead and producing 'Regeneration' using talent near at hand and some of which we are importing from New York City." It would not pay to bring Brooks or Anita Thompson, the actress whom Brooks had proposed (and with whom he had negotiated) for the lead in *Zircon*, from Los Angeles to perform in the picture; furthermore, he had decided that it was not a wise policy to invest capital in the partial production of a serial, as Brooks had recommended. Emphasizing that he had just expended considerable capital on the studio and laboratory equipment of the Klutho Studios, which was being dismantled, Norman believed that the investment would position him to make pictures more economically the next year, when he would know better where the market stood.

Norman also affirmed that "we have been careful not to embarrass ourselves or you by making any announcement of a connection between us in the production of forth coming pictures"—a reference, apparently, to Brooks's concern that a failure to reach an understanding would work to Norman's disadvantage.[38] "We are pretty well agreed," Norman emphasized, "[to await] the time when we feel that things are ripe to spring a Star Series [such as *Zircon*]," a time "when the mass of present pictures have had their run and the field is open for Colored Pictures at a fair price." Thanking Brooks for his interest, he trusted that they would keep in touch from time to time.

Brooks was no doubt surprised by the radical change in tone and in direction that Norman was proposing; and the letter appeared to bring the prospect of a collaboration between the two men to a rather abrupt conclusion. Moreover, the letter effectively marked an end to the landmark serial project as well. Although Norman kept hoping to return to *Zircon*—and although for years he continued to advertise, promote, and even accept contracts and bookings for it—he would never again come as close to the possibility of production.

At the same time that he began corresponding with Brooks, Norman also contacted J. Albert English, the manager of the Pekin Theatre in

Montgomery, Alabama, to inquire whether he would like to spend his summer vacation at nearby Mayport and Manhattan Beaches, where *Zircon* would be filmed. English, Norman wrote, was precisely the caliber of actor to play the Spider, a villainous character who "walks partly sideways, stooped in figure, glittering eyes set close together and eyebrows that slant up from the corners . . . [which] accents the position of the eyes. Yet, he is capable of defending himself and possessed of superhuman strength." The part of the Spider had real potential and required a performer with stage presence, and he felt that a man like English could acquit himself "with honors to the Serial and to the histronic ability of the colored race." Norman also offered English a big part in *Regeneration,* if English could spare the time.[39]

English seemed genuinely excited by the role that Norman described. "I must say," he replied in his elegant script, "that the side lines of the Serial are Great and will do all in my power to help make it so." After signing his name "The Spider," he added "Ha Ha" and, in a postscript, promised to try to make Lon Chaney take notice.[40] Norman, in turn, expressed gratitude to English for his cooperation but provided few particulars, either in terms of salary or of scheduling. He explained that since the undertaking of a serial involved much planning, all locations would have to be plotted and all props prepared in advance; and prerelease bookings would have to be secured. But Norman promised to keep English informed as to the progress and to allow him plenty of time to arrange to get away from his duties in Montgomery without imposing undue hardship on him or on the Pekin Theatre.[41] Although no formal agreement with English was ever signed, Norman began announcing to exhibitors that he had cast "Arthur [*sic*] English, former head-liner on Keith Vaudeville and the only man capable of playing a real character part," as the villain of *Zircon.*[42]

Soon other prominent black entertainers began contacting Norman directly, among them S. T. Whitney of "Whitney and Tutt," who noted that he and his brother had just completed their roles as male leads in Micheaux's *Birthright* and would be open to a limited engagement. "Years of experience have made us versatile enough to enact most any kind of roles that might be depicted in a Colored photo-play."[43] Edward G. Tatum, who had already been in touch with well-known actress Evelyn Preer, also approached Norman to say he was looking forward to meeting to discuss the serial.[44] And Mozel M. Perry (the stage name of Hazel Perry), who inquired about a role, sent a picture as well as a description of her physical attributes. She had been working of late, she wrote, but was currently resting and therefore would be available.[45] (Norman responded that he might place Perry in another one of his pictures; but ultimately he found her to be "too stout and a little too old.")[46]

Meanwhile, D. Ireland Thomas, who had introduced Norman to Brooks and who had advised Norman on ways to ensure the future of the race picture, continued to make good on his promise of free publicity with great write-ups in the *Chicago Defender*, on both the serial and the feature that Norman was planning. In a letter thanking Thomas for his support, Norman stated that Thomas's column was an enormous boon to the colored picture, and he reported that *Zircon* was coming together slowly but surely. Yet, hinting at the problems he was already facing, Norman acknowledged that "it is a new proposition to the colored theatres and will take much publicity and missionery work before it will be safe for us to produce it."[47]

By mid-summer, however, Norman had turned his attention away from the fifteen-part serial. Claiming that "sea pictures are all the rage now," he began planning a new feature film, *Regeneration*, set in the South Seas (an exotic locale similar to one of the settings in *Zircon*). Apparently, Norman had long been interested in a good sea story. As far back as 1921, he had considered "a big marine moving picture" that he could either produce or distribute; both he and his brother Bruce, in fact, had queried colleagues at various film exchanges in search of an available film showing undersea life with mermaids or a feature along the lines of the Jules Verne stories that might suit their purposes.[48] Norman even began tracking down appropriate exhibits and ultimately secured an "actual" mermaid in a glass case.[49] But before he could put her to good use in theater lobbies, he abandoned his marine movie for his Western pictures, *The Bull-Dogger* and *The Crimson Skull*.

Regeneration allowed Norman to return to the tropical island setting that he had earlier imagined. Norman's "Romance"—advertised as "A Colored Novelty Worth Booking. Gripping Story! Romantic Setting! All

Colored Cast!" and full of "Love! Thrills! Adventure!"—depicted "A Girl, a Man, Cast Upon an Uninhabited Island, a Garden of Eden. Then The Serpent—." Marking "an Epoch in Colored Picture Production," *Regeneration* had "A SMASHING THEME DONE IN A SMASHING WAY. THE FIRST COLORED PICTURE WITH A REAL STORY AND A SEX THEME. JUST THE PICTURE YOU HAVE BEEN WANTING TO PRESENT TO YOUR AUDIENCE, HUNGRY FOR REAL RED BLOODED ROMANCE. READY TO JAMB YOUR THEATRE THE MINUTE YOU HANG OUT A ONE SHEET."

"The story," J. A. Jackson wrote in *Billboard,* is "a strong one and filled with thrilling sea stuff."[50] Violet Daniels, the only child of a widowed sea captain, is left an orphan after her father's death. But he has bequeathed to her a strange legacy: a map showing the location of buried treasure on an island in the South Pacific. Jack Roper, owner of the fishing schooner Anna Belle, is in love with Violet, who enlists him in her quest to find the treasure island. But the villainous Knife Hurley (also known as "The Serpent"), a mate on Jack's ship, conspires with the crew and plots to seize the map in order to win the treasure for himself.

In the middle of the ocean, a fight ensues over possession of the map. During the fight, a lamp is overturned and sets the ship on fire. With the coveted map in hand, Hurley escapes with his cutthroat crew in the only lifeboat and leaves Jack and Violet behind to perish. Fortunately, using a raft that they have crafted, they manage to save themselves from certain death on the burning ship.

After drifting for days without food or water, the two are cast upon an uninhabited island, which they name Regeneration and on which they live a Robinson Crusoe–like existence for years. But eventually, through a bizarre twist of fate, Hurley and his crew land on the island, which turns out to be the mystical island pictured on the map. Together, though, Jack and Violet defeat Hurley, who is left to die on the island; and, in the climax of the film, they discover the buried treasure and are rescued.[51]

Although the film does not survive, the promotional materials that Norman developed offer important clues to the plotting. In a "business-getter" mailing that he sent to theater managers and exhibitors, Norman provided "A Few Side Lights on 'Regeneration'":

Cast up by a relentless sea—

He opened his aching eyes with the reflection of something vividly white half-blinding them. The white was the silvery sand of an uninhabited island that sloped away from him until it merged into the sea.

"I'm glad you opened your eyes. I began to fear that you were dead," said the girl.

Two mounds of earth and the skeleton in the deserted hut told their tale. He twisted his head in the direction of the mounds near the cabin.

"Ten years and never a sail!" He said hoarsely. "One life; that's all."

Her eyes were on his; there was a kindling light in them.

"A year—we'll wait a year. If we're still here then, Jack—"

"Violet, I'll give you my solemn word not to kiss you for a year."

He slept in a cave in the sands on the beach, she in the hut.

"I'll have to come up somewhere on the island to sleep, Violet; the autumn tides'll wash me out of my cave."

And the girl helped to make that second compartment in her cabin into a sleeping place for the man.

Nature had provided the girl with a secluded bathing pool. She sat on a rock, in the edge of the pool, combing her hair. The soft warm rays of a setting sun dried her wet skin. "The Serpent" discovered her.

A "Garden of Eden" shattered, there followed a conflict between the man, "The Serpent" and his cut-throat crew, ending when the island sank into the depths of the sea with "The Serpent" and his crew as the man and the girl sailed away in the rescue ship.

Norman's "Side Lights" suggest that *Regeneration* was in fact a reworking of portions of his unproduced serial *Zircon*, especially episodes nine through fourteen, in which the Spider, who wants the formula for the manufacture of Zircon all to himself, eventually traps John Manning and his sweetheart Helen in the hold of a ship, which he sets on fire. But *Zircon*'s lovers, instead of roasting alive, as the Spider had intended, survive on a raft. After drifting for a while at sea, they make land, only to discover that their nemesis is on the same island. Once again, they are forced to fight for their lives, in quicksand and against other elements; and Manning must save Helen from the clutches of the Spider, who wants to dishonor her. But eventually the Spider is killed by his own devices; his gang is rounded up and captured;

and the lovers are rescued and returned to civilization, where they cash in on the formula and are happily wed. *Regeneration,* however, transforms the villainous Spider into another evil archetype, the Serpent (Knife Hurley), who lusts after Violet and tempts, menaces, and ultimately tries to destroy the Adamic lovers on their Edenic island before being vanquished himself.

In casting for his new feature, Norman contacted a number of actors and actresses for possible roles. Among them were Irma Boardman, M. C. Maxwell's sister-in-law, whom he considered for the female lead; Earline Jackson, an inexperienced new actress he felt might be suitable for a supporting role; and Bobbie Smart, whose services would be required for only a few hours over a period of three or four days, depending upon weather conditions and location.[52] Norman also corresponded with Anita Bush, his female star from *The Crimson Skull,* before concluding that she was too old.[53] Another of his former actresses, "one of my old Green Eyed Monster girls," photographed "up fine in face, but [was] a little slender" and therefore was not suitable either.[54]

Ida Anderson and Edna Morton, two other established actresses, were also in touch with Norman about the female lead; but ultimately he rejected both of them because of their salary requirements. Writing to M. C. Maxwell, Norman noted, "These two young women are finished artists and much in demand on account of their talent. But their demands are absolutely unreasonable. $40 a day is alright to pay in New York where you can use them a few days, but to transport talent to Jacksonville and use them over a period of weeks at that figure is prohibitive."[55]

After Anderson insisted on the same $200 a week pay she received for performing in white pictures, Norman informed her that she was laboring under a delusion that producers of race pictures could match such a salary. And he reiterated—as he often did in such circumstances—the fact that "White Pictures have a possible distribution of 15,000 theatres, including all colored theatres," while "Colored Pictures have a distribution of a bare 100 theatres." (Notably, the number of colored theaters that Norman cited varied, according to the context.) The "greatest colored picture ever produced [his own *Green-Eyed Monster*] played in only 105 theatres in boom times," and since then, many of those theaters have closed and "revenues have decreased 50% in the last two years. Colored Pictures have ceased to be a novelty and have lost their original drawing power." He also told Anderson that he was in correspondence with two women, one of whom had starred in ten and the other in four race pictures, and that they demanded $75 a week, a salary they knew was not out of bounds. He cautioned Anderson that she lacked those actresses' experience and that he had made her a proposition only because she was a type that suited the picture he was producing.

In fact, Edna Morton—one of the two actresses to whom Norman had referred in his letter to Anderson—also made salary demands that Norman considered excessive. Morton, who had completed ten pictures in a year and a half for the Reol Company (pictures, Norman observed, that failed to draw big business), had originally quoted Norman a salary of $125 per week.[56] When he reminded her that present conditions in the field did not warrant high salaries, she dropped her request, to a salary of no less than $100 a week for a period of three weeks plus transportation expenses, and added: "All things considered, I am quite sure it would be a financial loss to me, as well as lowering the standard I have set for myself as an artiste of the screen justified by my past performances."[57] Responding dryly that "We have cut our eye teeth and we will absolutely not pay high salaries in the production of colored pictures because the small market will not justify it," Norman railed against her former employer Reol Films for bringing rentals "down to the extinction of profits" and made it clear to Morton (whose promotional photograph he returned) that he intended to keep looking for the right actress to serve as his lead.[58] Apparently regretting her hastiness, Morton sent Norman another letter in late August. But by then he had lost all interest in her. "She has come down off her high horse," Norman observed, "but she hasn't the looks for the part."[59]

Norman had earlier outlined his requirements for his lead actress in *Regeneration.* Since she was the only woman in the picture, she should be "good looking." And though she did not need to possess any great dramatic ability, she had to be willing to learn. "When Violet Daniels is cast on the Island of Regeneration, she becomes somewhat ragged through the lapse of time, which shows parts of her legs and neck, just enough to intrigue the fancy and I want the glimpses to be pleasing"; so "good figures . . . will add to the charm of the picture."[60] Above all, he was insistent upon a lead "with all the youth and charm of face and figure to create the proper romantic atmosphere . . . [and to] bring out the big theme," which was more overtly sexual than that of any of Norman's earlier pictures.⁶¹ He admitted, in fact, that he was endeavoring to work in several nude but artistic bathing scenes on the desert island that could be nicely removed, if required by censors. But he hoped those scenes, one of which featured the villain peering lustfully through the bushes at the terrified girl, would not have to be cut because they would draw audiences "like a mustard poultice."⁶²

The lead finally went to the light-skinned beauty Stella Mayo, wife of "The Great Mayo, Magician." Norman cast her alongside M. C. Maxwell, Norman's former distributor and road man, who had suggested the names of other possible actresses whom Norman had considered.⁶³ Although Maxwell was a professional magician and had performed widely on stage and in vaudeville, *Regeneration* was his first on-screen appearance. But Norman believed that Maxwell's physique was well suited to the part of Captain Jack Roper, "and if we cast convincingly, little dramatic ability will get bye with proper coaching."⁶⁴ His salary would be $40 a week plus transportation costs (though the salary was later raised to $50, to compensate for production delays).⁶⁵ Alfred Norcom was cast as the villain, the dark-skinned and menacing Knife Hurley. Dr. R. L. Brown, who had played Superintendent Powers, Helen Powers's father, in Norman's first race film, *The Green-Eyed Monster,* assumed the part of Violet Daniels's father. Steve "Peg" Reynolds, Norman's longtime favorite actor, played what he claimed was the greatest part of his career, while Charlie Gaines, Clarence Rucker, and Cary Brooks appeared in supporting roles.⁶⁶

The filming of *Regeneration,* however, was not without some complications. Set to begin in early to mid-August, the shooting—on the Mayport and Manhattan Beaches along the Florida coast where working conditions were favorable and the weather tolerable for making a picture during the hot summer—was delayed a month after one of the leads developed appendicitis.⁶⁷ Nonetheless, Norman still believed that the film could be completed in two to four weeks, in time for fall business.⁶⁸ Since there were few new race pictures currently playing, he realized that a good one, especially a high class thriller with so much "fast and furious" action, would go over big. Micheaux had just finished his latest picture in Roanoke, Virginia, but there was no telling when it would be released, so Norman knew that if he could get *Regeneration* out by fall, it would make him money.[69]

But it was not only the delays that kept production costs rising. The making of his "knock-out," Norman wrote to his distributor Abraham Rosen, required him to hire a schooner and take it to sea, where the deck was smeared and rigged with several hundred pounds of harmless but very expensive Newmanfyre for the fire scenes. And there were no fewer than eighty-seven interior scenes on nine different sets. In addition, the entire cast had to be boarded in Mayport at big expense. But Norman remained confident that the film could be rushed to release for a fall showing.[70]

In advance advertising for *Regeneration*, Norman—ever the good showman—not only hyped the film but also exaggerated some of the facts of the production:

> One year's time was consumed in searching for a Colored Cast true to type. The producers searched New York, Chicago and the entire United States for Virile Type Performers that would add the proper realism to "Regeneration." Result—a cast that is flawless. Five weeks were spent in constructing props and sets, many more weeks in production. The action of this smashing picture sweeps you out on the High Seas. A two Masted Schooner, 7 miles at sea, is burned before your eyes. No expense was spared to make "Regeneration" a credit to your theatre and to the colored performer. Matchless Photography and light effects never before accomplished in a Colored Picture. Sun Rises and Sun Sets furnish a background of beauty against which the smashing action of this picture sweeps. Fights in the Second, Third, Fourth and Sixth Reel that can't be surpassed for realism and punch.

As he did with his earlier films, Norman proceeded to develop a complete line of exploitation accessories that included "Brilliant Five Color Lithos, Two Style Window Cards, 11 x 14 Rotographs, Heralds, Slides, Trailer—In fact, everything you need to PUT IT OVER BIG." Among the window cards was an especially racy image of Violet (Stella Mayo, billed as the "Sensational Colored Screen Beauty"), in silhouette and behind reeds but clearly naked as she bathed in the ocean waters, and another of the Serpent (Alfred Norcom), leering at the half-clad woman, that would be sure to titillate filmgoers.

In the promotional materials, Norman also recommended several effective exploitation angles that theaters should use. One was to "Dress your

Lobby with Palms, Palmettos, Moss and have a load of White Sand scattered on floor of Lobby. Get a Small Boat and put in Lobby with this Sign on it: 'A Blazing Ship in the South Pacific—Two Souls Bound in Its Cabin, Left to Perish by a Cut-Throat Crew.' What was their REGENERATION? All Colored Cast Here Today." Another angle was to give that boat to some lucky child at a drawing on the last day of the showing. But perhaps the best tip of all to "Mr. Exhibitor" was to stimulate business by barring all children under sixteen (though Norman underscored that the theme was handled delicately enough even for younger viewers). As one later critic observed, Norman thus managed to establish himself "as both the Motion Picture Association of America and its violator."[71]

After several local showings, *Regeneration* was officially released on December 25, 1923.[72] The next month, Norman began roadshowing the picture, claiming that *Regeneration* was the sensation of the year and would bring business back to the 1920–1921 level. The roadshow included Steve "Peg" Reynolds, whose unique methods, Norman claimed, ensured standout success for the exhibitor.[73] In a letter to Guy Shriner, he described Reynolds's act and observed that "he is not only one of the stars [of *Regeneration*], but the greatest Colored Advertiser his race has produced. That is why I have had him all over the United States . . . I have had him in my employ for three years and if he wasn't bringing home 'the bacon' I wouldn't be taking him" on so many trips throughout the country.[74] At a few theaters, M. C. Maxwell also appeared—sometimes alone, just to boost *Regeneration*, sometimes alongside the popular Reynolds, to double the ballyho and increase local interest in the feature.[75]

The box-office profits proved as strong as Norman had predicted. *Regeneration*, the press information claimed, broke the attendance record of eight years standing at its premier showing in a Jacksonville theatre and was still breaking box-office records, playing to longer runs and more satisfied patrons than any race picture previously released.[76] To one exhibitor, Norman wrote: "Cutting out bunk and getting down to brass tacks; it is grossing more business than any colored picture released since boom times. We have just come in from a trip to Florida after topping the high water mark set by all our other productions, and even beating our Green-Eyed Monster record."[77] "Over 6,000 paid admissions Famous Theatre,

Birmingham, 2 days, seats 470," Norman boasted to another exhibitor, and it packed houses both "matinee and night."[78] In Houston and Port Arthur, Texas, "we broke records . . . and smashed box office."[79] In Dallas, "we were forced to hold the picture over a day to take care of the crowds on a 3 day run; the same was true in Waxahachie, Okmulgee and Houston."[80] In Kansas City, it played twenty straight days and had to be held over two extra days to handle the crowds.[81] In Richmond, Virginia, "we grossed $1138.40 in 2 days."[82] In Knoxville, Tennessee, "we had 1800 people in the Gem theatre for one show."[83] In Memphis, Tennessee, the film did $712 gross on a "two day stand and in very bad weather."[84] M. C. Maxwell, on a visit to New Orleans with his family, reported that *Regeneration* had turned away business four blocks long until 12:15 PM and was breaking all records at the Lyric Theatre, where it blockaded Burgundy Street, while *The Crimson Skull* had played a week earlier and did well too. (It was no coincidence, Maxwell suggested, that—given Norman's outstanding numbers—"Macheaux was here booking some of his last releases."[85])

Spring business was profitable as well. *Regeneration* was "going like wildfire"; all copies of the picture were advance-booked for the next few months.[86] In small theaters and small towns, *Regeneration* proved to be a real drawing card.[87] And in larger venues, exhibitors were "bust[ing] 'em wide open" by investing fifty cents and securing "25 gallon ash cans full of white or brown building sand . . . [to scatter] on the floor of the lobby leaving aisles around the ticket booth and exits," as Norman had advised, so that their patrons would "sit up and take notice."[88] In fact, wherever *Regeneration* was exploited properly, Norman observed to Maxwell, it turned away business; and both managers and audiences wanted more pictures like it.[89] He also noted that "Michaux and myself are about all who have any production plans and it looks like competition couldn't stand the decreased revenue and we have a clear field." Yet even Micheaux was having trouble financing his pictures, Norman claimed, and Micheaux's recent vigorous campaign was successful only because he was booking in the wake of Norman's films.[90]

By summer, *Regeneration* was still turning away one to two hundred people everywhere it had been strongly exploited on the road. So Norman embarked on a tour north through the Carolinas, with Steve "Peg" Reynolds along to advertise and ballyho.[91] That tour, on which Norman played a single copy of the film, netted $1,547.50 over thirty-one days. By fall, the picture was also doing considerable business on the East coast, playing to business as high as $1,571 in a single day and grossing from four hundred to eight hundred dollars a day in small and large theaters. The manager of the prestigious Plaza Theatre, on Fifty-ninth Street and Madison in New York City, admitted that *Regeneration* was "the best colored picture he had ever screened," a fact "borne out by 95 per cent of the colored theatres in the United States who have already booked and played this great attraction."[92] And Norman was already negotiating new dates in the Midwest. As he boasted in a letter to Thomas James of the Comet Theatre in St. Louis, Missouri, *Regeneration* was worth contracting for many reasons. "It ran for 17 strait days in Washington, D.C. opening at the big Republic Theatre, the finest type and catering to the highest class of colored people in the United States," and was setting records for first-run bookings in the East that even Micheaux could not match. So, Norman urged:

> Now, Mr. James, you have played colored pictures showing the lowest type of colored man and white man in the same picture. You have possibly played a so called colored picture, using the word "nigger" in the sub-titles, and in this event, we are safe in saying that your patrons are ripe for a Colored Picture free from all these things which are a detriment to a successful colored production. Regeneration is a picture that you will be proud to offer your patrons. It is to-day playing in the Roosevelt Theatre, catering to an audience composed of 40% white and 60% colored. How many of the so-called Colored Pictures you have played could do this without race friction in the audience?[93]

Even on second-run showings, *Regeneration* "hung up" records. Crowds at some theaters were so large that Norman wrote into certain of his sharing contracts (as with J. A. Dicharry, manager of the Lincoln Theatre in New Orleans) that his company would be responsible for paying the policeman who had to be hired to maintain order. And as late as summer of 1925, Norman started another roadshow west with the film, because he had had so many requests for a return of his "famous" *Regeneration*.[94]

Yet while Norman affirmed that the picture "is all the press sheet says of it [and is] doing top business," he confided to his friend and colleague

Guy Shriner, "Man to man, REGENERATION cost me a pretty penny"; and he added that since the market for race productions was shrinking, he had to do everything he could to exploit his pictures in order to earn decent profits.[95] Nonetheless, to those exhibitors who were complaining of poor business, Norman continued to tout *Regeneration* not only as a "101% attraction, the theme striking a popular chord due to the handling," but also as "the best we have so far released"; and he informed them that all copies of the picture were booked well ahead.[96]

Surprisingly, despite the frankness of the film's sexual themes, Norman encountered relatively few problems with state censors. In Virginia, no cuts whatsoever were required.[97] In Pennsylvania, though, the censor insisted upon four eliminations, all of them curiously related to acts of binding: in the second reel, "Elim. all views of man actually binding Violet's hands with rope"; in the third reel, "Reduce views where Jack's hands are shown bound with rope when lying on cot to two flashes of three feet each"; and in the fifth reel, "Elim. view of man actually binding girl with rope to tree" and "Elim. all close-up views of girl bound to tree."[98] And in New York, the censor demanded that, in the second reel, a scene of struggle between the crew and captain on the stern of the boat be shortened by half and the scene of Violet with a pistol holding up the crew be eliminated entirely.[99]

The success of *Regeneration* encouraged Norman to start planning his next pictures. Based on the "Coming Attractions in Production [with an] ALL COLORED CAST" that he listed in his promotional materials, there were many projects that he was already pursuing, among them:

A COLORED SHERLOCK HOLMES. Modern Detection of Crime.
THE SOUL ROBBER. A Prison Picture and the Electric Chair.
MIRACLE OF LOVE. Story of a Waif of the Streets.
BLACK EARTH. In it Lay the Secret of Untold Wealth.
TARNISHES. Is the Double Standard Right?
CREATURES OF SIN. Underworld Thriller.
TRANSMIGRATION. Life After Death.
THE DEHORNERS. Story of the Timber Thieves.
EACH TO HIS OWN. A Smashing Theme.
BULLET PROOF. Bluff in the Saddle.
BLACKBALLED. Full of Pathos and Humor.
THE VANISHING RAY. Detective Thriller.

DARK WATERS. Adventure in the South Seas.
PAYING HIS PRICE. Story of a Stage Struck Beauty.
THE JAIL BIRD. Could He Come Back?
HER GREAT ATONEMENT. Domestic Drama.
HELD BY HATE. A Western with a Different Twist.
THE SECRET BAR. Life's Legacy to One Woman.
BODY AND SOUL. Holding the Mirror to Nature.
FROM THE DARK. A Love that Death Couldn't Conquer.[100]

But even more significant than the coming attractions (none of which ever went into production, much less was completed or released) was another announcement that Norman made in that same promotional mailing. "The Norman Film Mfg. Co.," he wrote, "is the only Company Making Colored Pictures that Owns and Operates Its Own Studio and Laboratory." Norman repeated the claim in a letter to M. C. Maxwell: "I have a very fine plant," he wrote, "and every facility to make pictures now—across the river in Arlington and next year, I hope to produce on a more extended scale if the market will justify it."[101] In a subsequent letter to Maxwell, he reiterated: "We are the only Company making Colored Pictures owning and operating a completely equipped plant" and therefore able "to make pictures consistently and cheaper than any other company and produce at a profit . . . where others can't make a profit."[102]

Owning his own studio had long been a dream of Norman's. Beginning in the early 1920s, as the majority of Florida's film studios folded or began leaving the East for Hollywood, Norman and a few of the other producers who remained behind were able to purchase some of their inventory. Norman had already acquired studio and laboratory equipment from Klutho when that studio was dismantling in 1922. (Earlier that year, before the studio closed, Norman had been in discussions with Klutho about the possibility of "erecting a building [for Norman's use] adjoining his studio." But because of Klutho's heavy financial losses, that expansion never occurred; instead, Klutho sold the studio, which closed permanently soon afterward.)[103] With the sale of the former Eagle Studios in 1923, however, Norman was able to take over an entire studio facility and turn it into his own film plant, where he could write, shoot, produce, develop, and edit his own pictures.[104] (Contracts, however, reveal that the actual purchase of the studio was not finalized until the following year.)

Located on more than an acre of land on Arlington Road in Arlington, just across the St. John River from Jacksonville, the Norman Film Manufacturing Company Studio consisted of five buildings. As Shawn C. Bean writes, "The large production building housed a darkroom, a projection room, and a walk-in safe for film storage. There was also an actor's changing cottage, a prop storage garage, and a set building."[105] A swimming pool, with a pump connected to a huge generator, was positioned among the buildings and served as the set for sea and water scenes. Furthermore, at the time of purchase, Eagle's "staging, laboratories, klieg lighting system (used both for interiors and later afternoon exteriors), and on-site power plant were all in excellent working order."[106] Norman was convinced that the property would afford him access to more advanced equipment and facilities than he could rent or lease and therefore could position his company to produce features more economically within a year.[107]

Significantly, with the purchase of the former site of the Eagle Studios, Norman not only achieved his own dream; he also reached another milestone in the film business—he became the first (and ultimately the only) race producer to own his own studio. Neither the founders of the Lincoln Motion Picture Company, with their prestigious pedigree and popular star Noble Johnson, nor Oscar Micheaux, with his prolific film production, would ever match that feat. Norman's establishing of his Norman Studios in Arlington thus reconfirmed the entrepreneurial ambition that he had first revealed as a young businessman and distinguished him in yet another way from his peers in the race filmmaking industry.

A poster for Norman's *The Crimson Skull* (1922), an all-black Western that starred Anita Bush, "The Little Mother of Colored Drama." Lawrence Chenault, one of the most prominent leading men in silent films, played three different roles, as hero and villain, in the picture. (*Courtesy of the Lilly Library, Indiana University, Bloomington, Indiana*)

Promotional window card for *The Crimson Skull*, showing Anita Bush and Steve "Peg" Reynolds being held hostage by the Skull and his gang, who are terrorizing the peace-loving town of Boley. (*Courtesy of the Lilly Library, Indiana University, Bloomington, Indiana*)

Norman became the first and only race film producer to own and operate
his own studio. That studio, in the Jacksonville suburb of Arlington, Florida,
consisted of five buildings and a pool for shooting water scenes. (*Courtesy of
the Norman Studios Silent Film Museum*)

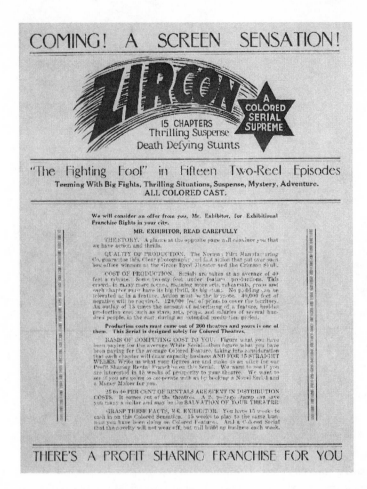

COMING! A SCREEN SENSATION!

ZIRCON

A COLORED SERIAL SUPREME

15 CHAPTERS
Thrilling Suspense
Death Defying Stunts

"The Fighting Fool" in Fifteen Two-Reel Episodes

Teeming With Big Fights, Thrilling Situations, Suspense, Mystery, Adventure.
ALL COLORED CAST.

We will consider an offer from you, Mr. Exhibitor, for Exhibitional Franchise Rights in your city.

MR. EXHIBITOR, READ CAREFULLY

THE STORY. A glance at the opposite page will convince you that we have action and thrills.

QUALITY OF PRODUCTION. The Norman Film Manufacturing Co. guarantee this Clear photography and fast action that put over such box office winners as the Green Eyed Monster and the Crimson Skull.

COST OF PRODUCTION. Serials are taken at an average of 40 feet a minute. Some twenty feet under feature productions. This crowds in many more scenes, meaning more sets, rehearsals, props and each chapter must have its big thrill, its big stunt. No padding can be tolerated as in a feature. Action must be the keynote. 40,000 feet of negative will be required. 129,000 feet of prints to cover the territory. An outlay of 15 times the amount of advertising of a feature, besides production cost such as stars, sets, props, and salaries of several hundred people, in the cast during an extended production period.

Production costs must come out of 200 theatres and yours is one of them. This Serial is designed solely for Colored Theatres.

BASIS OF COMPUTING COST TO YOU. Figure what you have been paying for the average White Serial—then figure what you have been paying for the average Colored Feature, taking into consideration that each chapter will draw capacity business AND FOR 15 STRAIGHT WEEKS. Write us what your figures are and make us an offer for our Profit Sharing Rental Franchise on this Serial. We want to see if you are interested in 15 weeks of prosperity to your theatre. We want to see if you are going to cooperate with us by booking a Novel Serial and a Money Maker for you.

25 to 40 PER CENT OF RENTALS ARE SPENT IN DISTRIBUTION COSTS. It comes out of the theatres. A 2c postage stamp can save you many a dollar and may be the SALVATION OF YOUR THEATRE.

GRASP THESE FACTS, MR. EXHIBITOR. You have 15 weeks to cash in on this Colored Sensation. 15 weeks to play to the same business you have been doing on Colored Features. And a Colored Serial that the novelty will not wear off, but will build up business each week.

THERE'S A PROFIT SHARING FRANCHISE FOR YOU

Receipt No.....................

PROFIT-SHARING RECEIPT COUPON

RECEIVED OF.. Theatre

.... City

.... State

$.................... in payment of Rental on Episode No...........
of the Serial "Zircon."

The holder of a sufficient amount of these coupons is entitled to participate in the net Rental Profits covered by his Profit-Sharing Rental Franchise and in event said amount of coupons totals 14 to receive free rental of Episode No. 15.

NORMAN FILM MANUFACTURING CO.
Jacksonville, Florida

By....................................

THIS IS EXACT REPRODUCTION OF WINDOW CARD

The Norman Film Mfg. Co. Presents the Super Feature Photoplay

Regeneration

SENSATION OF THE YEAR

"A Girl, A Man, Cast Upon an Uninhabited Island, a Garden of Eden, Then the Serpent"

ROMANCE IN SOUTHERN SEAS FEATURING

STELLA MAYO SENSATIONAL COLORED SCREEN BEAUTY

Supported by M. C. Maxwell, Alfred Norcom, Charlie Gaines, Clarence Rucker, Dr. R. L. Brown and Steve Reynolds

ALL COLORED CAST   SIX SMASHING REELS

As the window card suggests, Norman's "South Sea Romance" was more overtly sexual in its theme than any of his earlier films. Here, Violet Daniels (Stella Mayo, shown in silhouette) bathes naked in the ocean waters. (*Courtesy of the Richard E. Norman Collection, Special Collection REN, Black Film Center/ Archive, Indiana University, Bloomington, Indiana*)

Facing, above. Originally titled *The Fighting Fool,* the fifteen-episode black serial *Zircon* was an ambitious project. Although it was never produced, Norman used elements from its plot in his later films. (*Courtesy of the Richard E. Norman Collection, Special Collection REN, Black Film Center/ Archive, Indiana University, Bloomington, Indiana*)

Facing, below. Determined to finance his serial *Zircon* in full before he started production, Norman devised an innovative *Zircon* profit-sharing franchise by which exhibitors could quickly recoup their investment and increase their returns. (*Courtesy of the Lilly Library, Indiana University, Bloomington, Indiana*)

From *Regeneration* (1923): Violet holds at bay the crew that had earlier abandoned her and Jack Roper (M. C. Maxwell), the schooner's captain, and left them to die on board the burning boat. One censor insisted that this scene be deleted before the film could be exhibited. (*Courtesy of the Lilly Library, Indiana University, Bloomington, Indiana*)

D. IRELAND THOMAS
Presents

MISS BESSIE COLEMAN
The Only Colored Girl Aviator In The World.

IN PERSON

AND ON

THE SCREEN

SHOWING HER FLIGHTS IN EUROPE AND AMERICA.

Charleston,S.C.,
January,15,1926.

Mr.R.E.Norman,
Jacksonville,Fla.

Dear Sir;-

I am directing the tour of Bessie Coleman in person with two reels of
film showing her flights in Europe and America. She is a powerful drawing card.

She desires to have a production made of her self and I am thinking that
you might work out a plan to use her in a production with a story built
around her and her plane. She is now on the east coast Florida and will
be in Jacksonville within a week or so. If you are interested and will
let me know just how to reach you I will meet her in Jacksonville and we
can talk over the matter. Please let me hear from you and what you think
of this preposition. Of course I do not think that she would want to pay
you outright for the production and I thought that you could hire her to
feature a production for you as with her reputation I think it would be
a winner. Let me hear from you at once. Read the enclosed bill and
you will get an idea of just who she is and why she is such a strong puller

D.Ireland Thomas.

Address all correspondence to D. IRELAND THOMAS, LINCOLN THEATRE,
Charleston, S. C.

Managed by Norman's colleague D. Ireland Thomas, famous female
aviator Bessie Coleman was interested in making a picture with Norman.
But before they reached a formal agreement, she was thrown from
her plane and killed while practicing a stunt she planned to perform
the next day at an airshow in Norman's hometown of Jacksonville.
(*Courtesy of the Lilly Library, Indiana University, Bloomington, Indiana*)

In *The Flying Ace* (1926), a "smashing airplane detective mystery" that highlighted race patriotism, World War I veteran aviator Captain William Stokes (Lawrence Criner) must solve the mystery of a missing railroad payroll. (*Courtesy of the Lilly Library, Indiana University, Bloomington, Indiana*)

As he did with all of his feature films, Norman developed a wide variety of promotions and "exploitation accessories" for *The Flying Ace,* including lithographs, window cards, rotographs, heralds, and slides. (*Courtesy of the Richard E. Norman Collection, Special Collection REN, Black Film Center/Archive, Indiana University, Bloomington, Indiana*)

Facing, below. After Ruth Sawtelle (Kathryn Boyd) is kidnapped by a rejected suitor, Captain Stokes—pictured here with his sidekick and mechanic Peg (Steve Reynolds)—performs a daring airborne rescue in *The Flying Ace.* (*Courtesy of the Lilly Library, Indiana University, Bloomington, Indiana*)

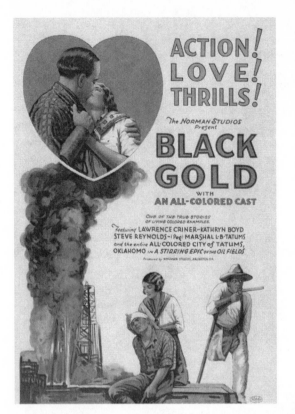

Advertised as a "True Story of Living Colored Examples," Norman's oil field adventure *Black Gold* (1928) was filmed in and around the all-black town of Tatums, Oklahoma. (*Courtesy of the Lilly Library, Indiana University, Bloomington, Indiana*)

From *Black Gold:* Bar Circle Ranch foreman Ace Brand (Lawrence Criner),
the film's hero—with assistance from cowhand Peg and Alice Anderson
(Kathryn Boyd), the bank president's daughter—exonerate Matt Ashton
and expose the conspiracy against him. (*Courtesy of the Lilly Library,
Indiana University, Bloomington, Indiana*)

Facing, below. From *Black Gold:* Driller Peter Barkley and bank cashier
Walter Worder conspire to implicate innocent rancher Matt Ashton
in a theft so they can claim the well on his oil-rich property. (*Courtesy
of the Lilly Library, Indiana University, Bloomington, Indiana*)

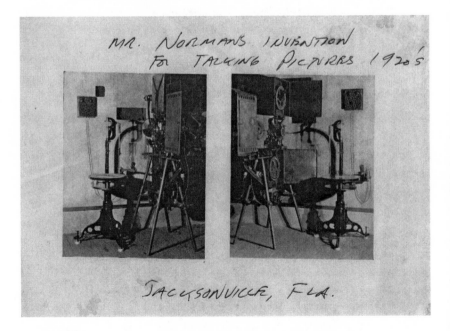

Although roadshows often involved extensive travel and complicated arrangements, they were, for Norman, a necessary way of distributing his race films. This record shows some of the cities that Norman visited, the films that he showed, and the profits that he earned. (*Courtesy of the Richard E. Norman Collection, Special Collection REN, Black Film Center/Archive, Indiana University, Bloomington, Indiana*)

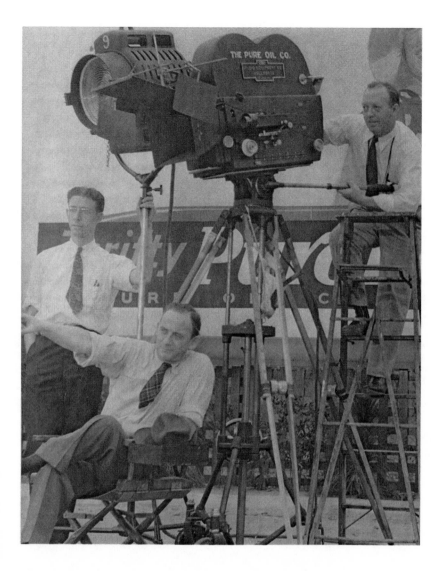

Above. In the 1930s, Norman returned to the production of industrial and advertising films. He is pictured here at his Jacksonville studio shooting an exterior scene for the Pure Oil Company. (*Courtesy of the Lilly Library, Indiana University, Bloomington, Indiana*)

Facing, below. As pictures moved from silents to talkies, Norman developed a nonsynchronous sound system that exhibitors could install in their theaters. But more efficient and sophisticated systems soon rendered Camera-Phone obsolete. Norman, who had invested heavily in his product, was virtually bankrupted as a result. (*Courtesy of the Lilly Library, Indiana University, Bloomington, Indiana*)

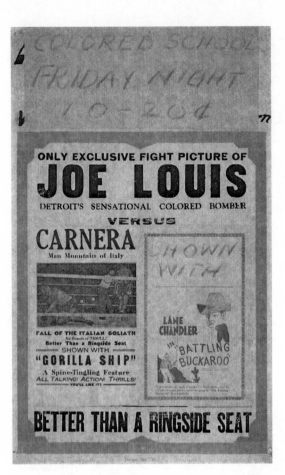

The fights of Joe Louis, the celebrated "Brown Bomber" and heavyweight champion, were rarely shown in white theaters. Norman quickly discovered that he could make a profit showing the fights, often in conjunction with feature films that he produced or distributed. (*Courtesy of the Richard E. Norman Collection, Special Collection REN, Black Film Center/Archive, Indiana University, Bloomington, Indiana*)

Facing, below. Throughout the 1930s and into the 1940s, Norman —often using his own portable movie projector—showed his feature films at schools and churches. He remarketed the pictures accordingly: the suggestive *Regeneration* became an "educational" modern Robinson Crusoe story. (*Courtesy of the Richard E. Norman Collection, Special Collection REN, Black Film Center/Archive, Indiana University, Bloomington, Indiana*)

By the late 1940s, Norman had purchased two movies theaters. After he and his wife Gloria refurbished "The Famous Theatre (for Colored)" in Winter Park, Florida, and renamed it the "New Famous Theatre," they announced its Grand Opening with a special program of shows. (*Courtesy of the Richard E. Norman Collection, Special Collection REN, Black Film Center/Archive, Indiana University, Bloomington, Indiana*)

CHAPTER SIX

"You Know We Have the Goods": *The Flying Ace* and *Black Gold*

THE NORMAN STUDIOS in the Jacksonville suburb of Arlington, Florida, was a source of great pride for Richard E. Norman.[1] Writing to an old friend in Des Moines, he bragged that he was "still in the movie business—bigger than ever. Haven't struck it rich, but am making fair progress. Now have the finest plant South of New York and the only one in Jacksonville or near Jacksonville."[2] A picture of the new studio was prominently displayed on the company's advertising materials and also on the letterhead of the stationery that Norman redesigned. "Above is a picture of our new plant located at Arlington, Florida," he indicated in a letter to fellow filmmaker and distributor Albert A. Fish. "In it, we have every device for making motion pictures, props, scenery and costumes which will save you many hundreds of dollars if you decide to come to Florida and make your next picture."[3]

With the new studio came new opportunities. One project that especially interested Norman was the possibility of a collaboration with Captain Edison C. McVey, the self-described King of Stunts. A skilled black flyer and one of the world's greatest aeronautic daredevils, McVey had recently formed the Afro-American Film Producers, a small Texas-based company organized for the production of motion pictures that would illustrate the ability of blacks behind the footlights and prove their worth "as shining constellations" in drama and comedy. One of the company's aims was to educate the public by bringing to the screen the teachings of the church, the school, and other institutions; another was to "open the avenue of producing within our race a Mary Pickford, Douglas Fairbanks or a Charlie Chaplin." Afro-American's greatest asset was, of course, McVey; and he promoted himself accordingly: the company's advertising brochure featured an image of him, in flight gear and goggles, superimposed upon an Ace of Spades playing card.[4]

The first picture that McVey planned to make through his new film company was *From the Clouds*, a six-reel aviation story based on his own adventures, with a projected cast of fifty black actors. The picture, he claimed to prospective investors, would be the last word in photoplays enacted by colored performers; and he insisted that of the "fourteen million Negroes in the United States at least one million will see the picture." At an admission of twenty cents per person, the gross receipts for the picture would amount to two hundred thousand dollars. So McVey urged investors to be wise and to get in on the project while they had the chance: "You have worked for your money, now let your money work for you."[5]

Norman first met McVey in San Antonio, where he was promoting his own films. Not long afterward, on May 20, 1924, he contacted McVey to offer him a role in an upcoming picture. The role would earn McVey "real money"—more than McVey "could [earn] with the scheme he was framing" when they last saw each other in Texas. Norman also promised that if McVey made good in the first film, he would consider financing him in a picture in which he would star. Everything, however, was contingent upon the status of *From the Clouds*. "This offer," Norman wrote, "will depend as to whether you have already filmed your picture and will show it, because I believe that if you do this that it will hurt your reputation to appear in anything that is not strictly professional."[6]

McVey responded that he had recently located his company "in a western town . . . just below San Antonio" and was "rehursing for the western scenes for same." Although he expected to start shooting as soon as the weather permitted, as yet there was no picture to exhibit. Therefore, if given a better financial or professional opportunity, he was willing to drop his own production plans and even to share the 1,800 to 2,000 feet of negative he had shot earlier as a sample of his stunt work. Those stunts included "changing from plane to plane, from top of train to plane, [and] catching an aeroplane on the ground from a flying start." In fact, McVey boasted, "there is no possible feats that I am afraid to undertake on Land, Sea or in the Air."[7]

While Norman was anxious to pursue an agreement, he reminded McVey (as he did with virtually all of his potential actors) that his salary would have to be reasonable because of the limited distribution of race films.[8] Norman's offer was fifty dollars a week.[9] Filming would take place at his new studio, "the largest plant in the South-East, fully equipped to make both comedy and dramatic subjects." But Norman would not be able to provide a plane for McVey because no pilot in Jacksonville was willing to let a stranger fly his machine without a guarantee of the full price in case of damage. Instead, Norman planned to stunt-double McVey's part in any actual flights, using the original pilot with his own plane for the air sequences. He doubted that the doubling would create a problem, since McVey's value lay in the fact of his reputation as a flyer rather than in his physical participation in every flight scene. Besides, Norman believed that he could incorporate into the film some of the sample stunt footage that McVey had already shot, in the same way that he had intercut the stock footage of train wrecks in *The Green-Eyed Monster* and Bill Pickett's rodeo adventures in *The Bull-Dogger* and *The Crimson Skull.*

Although McVey expected the term of his service to be at least twenty-five weeks, Norman quickly corrected him: no such length of time would be required to complete a single picture, and no series of pictures was being contemplated. But Norman reassured him that he had in mind an excellent detective thriller that involved some flying. If McVey, with his injured leg, "could get the proper action in it," they could negotiate an arrangement that would allow him to travel with the picture. Making personal appearances and giving short talks would keep McVey busy on the road—"about 2 weeks in Florida, . . . about 10 weeks thru Texas and the West, and about 12 weeks thru the Carolinas and North-East. Salary will depend on the drawing power of the picture and as to whether you make good." Norman also hinted at another "little idea" in conjunction with the picture that would add to McVey's income and that would be financed after the picture was made. But it was up to McVey to prove himself. If he succeeded, Norman promised, "your salary will be more than you are asking and your period of employment will be longer than you have suggested."[10]

McVey countered with two of his own "propersitions." The first was to resurrect and film his own story, now titled *Coming From the Clouds;* the second was to promote the picture by flying "in an aeroplane across the U.S.A. stoping in principle cities in rout across. Since other nations of the world is making such wide reputation in Aeronautical Scionce at present this give this field a wide and broad oppertunity to make good if it is handled properly."[11] Norman tactfully deflected both ideas. Telling McVey that a white-cast film by the name *Coming From the Clouds* had already been released, he proposed a different scenario, one that he knew he could manage with a man of McVey's limited stage experience. After it was produced, they could discuss plans for other pictures.[12] As for the transcontinental flight: while it had "possibilities," Norman doubted that McVey would receive the proper cooperation or permissions but stated that the idea might be worth revisiting at a later time.[13]

Unfortunately, before Norman and McVey produced even a single picture together, the partnership dissolved—in large part because of a miscommunication in their correspondence. In late summer, Norman wrote McVey that he had postponed the start date for the new picture until October 1. But since Norman was leaving on an extended month-long road tour, he told McVey it would not be "policy" for him to come to Jacksonville until his return.[14] When Norman was delayed even longer than anticipated, McVey—who had been at Norman's disposal since July—understandably became frustrated. Norman's failure to honor their original commitment, McVey claimed, had left him at a great disadvantage: he had turned down several lucrative lecture dates as well as an opportunity to produce a picture financed by people with ready cash in their hands. In light of such hardship, McVey hoped that Norman would reconsider his production plans and press forward immediately with the film that they had been discussing.[15]

Norman, who was still in the South roadshowing *Regeneration,* replied that he regretted "exceedingly" that his change of plans, over which he had no control, had put McVey in an embarrassing position; and he added, a bit disingenuously, "I understood from your letters that you were making plenty of money and more than busy with your lecture work, and as I didnt hear from you in such a long time, I gathered you were in no hurry to come to Jacksonville." Norman asserted that he had been ready to start work on a new picture on October 15. But "I had not definately decided which one of several stories I was going to produce as I was not absolutely sure that I could depend on you." He had since booked additional dates on his *Regeneration* roadshow and would not be back in Jacksonville until after Thanksgiving. "After I return there I will start getting props and talent ready for my next picture. This will take a few weeks. . . . Now at that time if you are open, I can use your services. But I dont want to stand in your way to make money." He assured McVey that there would be no hard feelings if he were no longer interested in the project because he could easily substitute Clarence Brooks, who had significantly more professional picture experience.[16] Whether or not it was his intention, with that letter Norman effectively terminated their relationship.

But while he never reached an agreement with McVey, the experience convinced Norman that he wanted to produce his own aviation story. By drawing on the plot devices he had planned to incorporate into the "Plane of Death" episode of his proposed serial *Zircon* and by basing details of his film's hero on ace flyer McVey, Norman determined to create his own version of the Black Ace. Over the next few months, he kept developing the story, investigating props, and considering potential actors. By late spring 1925 he was already corresponding with exhibitors to advise them—much too optimistically, it would appear, since he had not even begun production—that his new feature *The Black Ace* would be ready for release in the summer. (In that same mailing, he also claimed that the fifteen-episode serial *The Fighting Fool* [the alternate title of *Zircon*], which he had essentially abandoned months earlier, was in progress and would be released soon.)[17]

As he was moving forward on his aviation film, Norman was presented with another opportunity similar to the one that he had discussed with McVey. The *Chicago Defender* columnist and theater manager D. Ireland Thomas, who had promoted Norman's earlier films and offered valuable advice on the direction and casting of the *Zircon* serial, contacted Norman in early January 1926 to announce his latest business venture: a tour of Bessie Coleman that he was directing. "The Only Colored Girl Aviator in the World," Coleman was, according to Thomas's press sheet, a "Dashing and Daring Girl who Flirts with Death in Her Airplane." A graduate of an aviation school in Paris and the sole female holder of an international pilot's license, Coleman was reputedly the only woman able to handle a 22-horsepower German Benz plane. Through her remarkable aviation feats, including numerous barnstorming stunts, she had "blazed a new trail for the race." (By some accounts, Coleman was a trailblazer in other ways as well: it is reported that she rejected a contract on the Seminole Film Producing Company's picture *Shadow and Sunshine* because she believed her part was racially demeaning.)[18] On tour, Coleman spoke about her adventures and screened two reels of film showing her groundbreaking flights in Europe and America. She was, Thomas assured, a powerful drawing card, as the testimonials from James J. Thomas, mayor of Columbus, Ohio, and Vic Donahey, governor of Illinois, confirmed.

The reason for Thomas's letter was not just to promote Coleman but also to apprise Norman of her desire to make a film. "I am thinking," Thomas wrote, "that you might work out a plan to use her in a production with a story built around her and her plane."[19] He believed that, given Coleman's reputation, it would "be a winner."

The prospect of working with Coleman piqued Norman's curiosity. Yet while he agreed that a picture with her would be an excellent attraction, he was unwilling to assume the full costs of the project. "I wouldn't care to undertake the financing of [such] a picture," he told Thomas, "as I am up to my neck in production in my own interest."[20] But he suggested an alternative plan: if Thomas or Coleman found investors willing to advance four to five thousand dollars, Norman could make a "proper kind of picture" that would ensure big returns for everyone involved. An investment on that scale was imperative, Norman explained, because "Colored audiences," especially those in the North, were becoming increasingly critical, so filmmakers had to spend more "in production than here-to-fore" in order to earn their patronage. By using his own studio facilities in Jacksonville, however, Norman could complete a quality picture that would cost

Coleman double or triple that amount to make elsewhere.[21] And since he was just starting a new picture of his own with thrilling airplane stunts, he was already equipped to supply all the props that Coleman might require.

While Norman was corresponding with Thomas, Bessie Coleman contacted him directly. Her personal appearances in Chicago and other cities, she wrote, had been a success in every house she had played. As "the most known colored person (woman alive) other than the Jazz singers," she was certain that the photoplay she had in mind—*Yesterday, Today and Tomorrow,* based on her "life work"—could "go big"; and she proposed that they collaborate on it.[22]

What actual agreement, if any, the two reached is unclear because only a few weeks later, on April 30, 1926, Coleman was killed while practicing for an airshow to benefit the Negro Welfare League in Norman's hometown of Jacksonville. As she flew over the city with her manager William Wills to scout landing locations for a new parachute stunt that she would be attempting the next day, her newly purchased Curtiss JN-4 biplane went into a spinning dive.[23] The thirty-six-year-old Coleman, who was not wearing a seat belt at the time, was thrown from the plane and died instantly. Her untimely death shocked the public and made her the object of much fascination—a fascination that, in a macabre bit of showmanship, Norman later exploited to promote his own aviation film.

In casting *The Flying Ace* (originally, and alternatively, titled *The Black Ace*), Norman had contacted Shingzie Howard, an actress who starred in several of Oscar Micheaux's films and whose name had been suggested by a mutual friend. Impressed by how well she photographed, Norman believed that he might have a role that would reflect positively on her. As always, though, he insisted that her salary would have to be reasonable, since "Colored Pictures are traveling a rock road right now and profits are to the vanishing point." But he expressed his hope that she might be the breakout "box office star [of] the Race" he had long been trying to establish and that her repeated appearances in good pictures would create audience demand that would result in increased attendance and strong box-office receipts.[24]

Pleased by Norman's proposal, Howard agreed to work for $100 a week plus expenses. But since she had committed to performing in six pictures for the Colored Players Film Corporation, a recently founded company in Philadelphia "composed of wealthy Jewish people who are out to make colored pictures exclusively," she would not be available immediately; the first of those films, *A Prince of His Race*, a "delightful story without any race question," was already in progress. The Colored Players, Howard wrote, apparently had the same idea as Norman—to commercialize a single actress—and they were expecting her to bring them big returns. But as soon as the picture was completed, probably within three or four weeks, she would be at leisure to make Norman's picture.[25]

Norman, in fact, was glad that Howard was starring in *A Prince of His Race*; the success of that film would make her an even greater attraction in his own production. (A good businessman, he also suggested that she indicate to the Colored Players his desire to lease them his studio facilities and to distribute their picture, either for the entire United States or just for the South alone.) He described to Howard the lead roles he was looking to fill in his new film, "a detective mystery story with a railroad setting full of action and plenty of thrills."[26]

Hero—A young war-time aviator. Age about 25 years.
Villain—usual type, rather romantic. Is aviator also.
Railroad Station Master. Father of Heroine. He is rather a frail,
 timid man of 45–55 years of age.
Heroine, daughter of Station Master. (Yourself Probably.)
Constable, hick type about 45 years old.

Howard responded that since *A Prince of His Race*, despite a few problems with lighting, was ahead of schedule, she might be available sooner than she had anticipated. The Colored Players Film Corporation, she reported, was grateful for his kind offer of production facilities and distribution, but the company was looking into equipping its own studio; and the president, David Starkman, planned to tour the country himself selling his own product. As for Norman's film *The Flying Ace*, it sounded "immensely interesting and thrilling. The title, itself, should be a drawing card." Howard also suggested several possible actors whom Norman might employ as male leads. Lawrence Chenault, a good performer and "the usual villian type," had established quite a reputation as one of the finest black actors on the legitimate stage and in the ten films in which he had worked. Chenault would therefore prove "an asset to any picture made for our Race." And Andrew Bishop, the popular actor and matinee idol who was currently out on the road with his own stock company, would make an ideal hero.[27]

Norman had already worked once with Chenault, and the experience was not a positive one. "Chenault is a good actor," Norman told Howard, "but won't keep sober on the job. He caused me the loss of a lot of time and money [on *The Crimson Skull*], and this precludes me useing him again." Bishop, on the other hand, though admittedly an excellent and reliable performer, would not suit any of the types in the picture: he was too heavily built and, with his almost white features, too light-skinned.[28] Anxious to finalize the cast so he could start filming, Norman asked Howard for contact information for some of the other actors with whom she had performed, including Harry Henderson, William Clayton, and Howard Agusta.[29] *The Flying Ace*, he bragged, will be more advanced than anything produced by colored performers so far and will be a distinct novelty for a colored picture.[30]

While he communicated directly with a number of actors, Norman also corresponded with other colleagues about possible stars for his film.[31] In a letter to Albert A. Fish, he refined his description of the heroine, specifying that she should be eighteen to twenty-five years old, and wrote that he was considering Josephine Tally for the lead, to play opposite her former *Smiling Hate* co-star Harry Henderson. But Norman wanted assurance from Fish that Tally and Henderson were a reliable pair. "There is two things I want to steer clear of in making a negro picture," he emphasized; "one, temperement and the other, liquor. I don't want performers who will give trouble along either line."[32] Norman and Fish also discussed the new Colored Players Film Corporation, for whom—it later turned out—Henderson was under long-term contract. Fish suspected the company of trying to poach some of his black talent, from cast to directors and assistants, while Norman predicted (incorrectly) that the Colored Players' recent venture would terminate with the making of the one picture.[33]

Although the cast that Norman eventually hired did not include Howard, Chenault, Henderson, or Tally, it was nonetheless a strong one. The stars, a husband-and-wife acting team, were veterans of one of the best and most distinguished acting companies in New York; and among the supporting actors were some other familiar names. In press materials for the film, Norman described his performers in detail:

LAWRENCE CRINER. One of the Original Lafayette Players who played Svengali in Trilby, the Hunchback in the Hunchback of Notre Dame and The Frog in The Miracle Man, all great stage successes, adds to his fame in the role of Captain Billy Stokes in THE FLYING ACE. Mr. Criner is the virile type of athletic manhood necessary for motion picture leads. As "The Flying Ace" he chalks up another mark for the histronic ability of his race.

KATHRYN BOYD. Pretty, demure, yet possessed of the nerve of a female dare-devil. She plays the role of Ruth Sawtelle in The Flying Ace, a role calling for her to climb a slender rope ladder suspended from a plane a mile high in the air in order to escape from the burning plane in which she is in. Miss Boyd is late of the Lafayette Players and comes of a well known family. Her father is Rev. Allen Boyd, of Nashville, Tenn. She was a student of Fisk College at Nashville and also of Oberlin College at Oberlin, Ohio.

GEORGE COLVIN. More familiarly known as "Daddy Colvin." He is the 62-year-old wonder who has delighted audiences for the past 50 years. He started in show business at the age of 12 playing pickininy roles and is as spry today as many youngsters. He plays the role of Thomas Sawtelle, the Station Master in The Flying Ace.

BOISE DE LEGGE. Actor-Player-Manager, is well known for his versatility. He has staged successes on the stage for a number years and is well known to the theatre goers over the United States for his pleasing personality and ability as a real performer. He plays the role of Blair Kimball, the Paymaster in The Flying Ace.

LIONS DANIELS. One of the landmarks of the colored show business. Better known as "Skunkum Bowser" he has been bringing gladness and joy to the thousands for the past 20 years by his funny antics. He plays the role of Jed Splivins, a small town constable and deputy sheriff, in The Flying Ace.

SAM JORDAN of the team of Jordan and Jordan, Standard T.O.B.A. [Theater Owners Booking Association] Vaudeville Act, has played the T.O.B.A. Circuit from New York to Miami and has one of the best acts and personalities on the stage. He plays the role of Dr. Maynard, a crooked dentist in The Flying Ace.

STEVE REYNOLDS (Peg). PEG, of Green-Eyed Monster, Crimson Skull and Regeneration fame, is well known to the thousands of theatre patrons who have seen the Norman Films. He is the one legged wonder who does stunts that no two legged man can do. In The Flying Ace, he rides a bicycle and shoots through his hollow crutch, bringing grief to a gang of crooks. He again pulls off a barrel of laughs and thrills.

According to the contract that Lawrence Criner signed with Norman, film-ing of *The Flying Ace* would begin on June 21, 1926, and be completed within two weeks. For his services and for the services of his wife and of actors Samuel Jordan and Lions Daniels, Criner would be paid $550. If additional shooting days beyond the initial two weeks were required, Norman agreed to pay an extra $176, to cover three more days of Jordan and Daniels's work and a full week of Criner and Boyd's.[34]

"The Flying Ace," Norman promised, "Marks Another Epoch in Col-ored Picture Production." His promotional materials described it as "A Smashing Airplane Detective Mystery Done in a Smashing Way. The First Colored Picture with Real Flying in it, Real Stunts, Loops, Parachute Jumps, Changing Planes, Flying Upside Down, Fights on Land as Well as in the Air. Just the Picture You Have Been Wanting to Present to Your Audience, Hungry for Real Red Blooded Romance and Thrills, Ready to Jamb Your Theatre the Minute You Hand Out a One Sheet on 'The Flying Ace.'" In a letter to exhibitors, he declared: "You will find The Flying Ace the biggest money maker you can book. It has a real cast, and is a Novel Colored Picture, timely too, coming right on the heels of the death of Bes-sie Coleman, colored aviatrix. Tho, The Flying Ace, has stunts in it and thrills that she never attempted, or could do."[35] And to a theater manager in Lexington, Kentucky, Norman drew a further connection between his film's protagonist and one of America's most iconic figures: "You can see the possibility of a negro Lindenberg [sic]."[36]

In the picture, Captain William (Billy) Stokes, a hero of World War I and a "Flying Ace," must solve the most baffling case of his career. As head of the intelligence department of one of the big American railroads, he has been called upon to investigate the disappearance—as "in a puff of smoke"—of Paymaster Kimball along with the $25,000 payroll of the Eastern Division. All of the clues point to the guilt of Thomas Sawtelle, the aged stationmaster of the little railway station at Mayport. Ruth, the stationmaster's daughter, believes firmly in her father's innocence and in Captain Stokes's ability to clear his name. Finley Tucker, a fellow aviator who is in love with Ruth, tries to divert Stokes's attention and win Ruth's affection; but, after she rebuffs his repeated proposals of marriage, he drugs her and takes her hostage in his plane. Stokes follows Tucker, and in a daring airborne rescue, facilitates Ruth's escape from Tucker's burning plane by means of a rope ladder. After even more thrilling rescues and adventures, Stokes—with the aid of his one-legged sidekick and flight mechanic, Peg—resolves the mystery by revealing that both Sawtelle and Kimball were drugged, that Kimball was killed and his body hidden in a swamp, and that Sawtelle was framed for the crime by the villainous Dr. Maynard and Deputy Sheriff Jed Splivins, whom he exposes. "A tiny wisp of excelsior [wood shavings], a small vial, white stains on a man's hands, the smell of fresh paper money on another's hands," the press sheet hints, "aid Captain Stokes to save an innocent man from prison" and to earn Ruth's devotion.

In his promotional "Sidelights," Norman provided details about the making of the film, particularly the plane sequences:

> Over two years ago, the Norman Studios conceived the idea of producing an airplane picture with all-colored cast. Realizing the impossibility of securing competent colored players who could really fly, they set about constructing a special plane which could be operated by inexperienced flyers. The plane was constructed true to scale and patterned exactly after the famous Curtiss J.N.D 4's [the model of plane that Bessie Coleman was flying when she was killed]. It was powered with a Ford motor with electrical starter. Every detail was perfect in the dummy plane. The wings and fuselage were covered with painted oil cloth, the engine enclosed in a metal hood and real airplane engine parts were used on the outside. It took exactly six weeks to construct this plane and cost exactly twice as much as a real plane could have been rented for. But this plane was designed to throw both cockpits into one and be safe for the performers, and finally to be burnt up. A special automatic camera was used to produce the loop effect of the plane. Also a real plane was used for the actual flights in the air. . . . A cast of cool headed artists were secured, as they were dealing with "an engine of death" and some thrilling stunts were necessary entailing some risks and peril calling for cool heads. No company, making colored pictures have attempted and successfully made a picture like The Flying Ace. It even has situations in it which HAVEN'T BEEN SHOWN IN A WHITE PICTURE. Mr. Norman, who designed the working plane, has had a great deal of experience with the Curtiss Airplane Company and has made many pictures for them. This experience enabled him to "pull off" a real thriller. And best of all, it is full of good laughs and smashing fights, interspersed judiciously through the six reels.[37]

As Phyllis R. Klotman observed, the real star of *The Flying Ace* is the plane, prop though it was. "It is the symbol of Captain Stokes's heroism, his past triumphs, and his ability to use the new technology to good purpose." Yet the film as a whole was definitely more aspirational than factual. "The history of African Americans in the United States armed services, and especially in the air force," according to Klotman, "flies in the face of the storied 'reality' of *The Flying Ace,* even assuming the conventional latitude of the movie serial." Since blacks were allowed only menial and restricted wartime roles (and were prohibited even from fighting alongside white soldiers in combat overseas), "there is no way that the handsome hero could have flown missions in France for the U.S. Air Force during World War I." In fact, it was not until October of 1940 that the War Department allowed "Negroes . . . [to begin] training as pilots, mechanics, and technical specialists, and [announced] that Negro Aviation units would be organized as soon as the necessary personnel were trained." Despite the racist reality of his day, however, Norman "seems to have reached beyond the headlines and produced a hero his intended audience hungered to see and identify with."[38]

Just as Norman had filmed much of *The Bull-Dogger* and *The Crimson Skull* in the "All-Colored-City" of Boley, Oklahoma, he originally planned to produce portions of *The Flying Ace* in the "fast growing Development of Christenia, Florida, a City for Negros Only." In an agreement drawn up, but never signed, between Norman and the owner-developers of Christenia, the production would be set in that city, which would be credited in the opening subtitle (as Boley was in the earlier film) and "at proper intervals throughout the six reels of the picture THE BLACK ACE [the film's original title] as are necessary to the development of the story of said picture and which will not detract from the merits of the picture and make a flagrant advertisement." For the savvy bit of public relations, specifically for "the advertising value that Christenia will derive through its exhibition in Negro Theatres" and in heralds and playbills for the picture, Christenia agreed to pay the Norman Studios the sum of two thousand dollars, half of which was payable upon signing, the other half upon completion of the picture and "its premier exhibition in a theatre convenient for viewing by the party of the second part or at a private exhibition to them."[39] In the end, though, the agreement fell through, and it was not Christenia that was featured in the opening sequences. Rather it was Mayport, specifically the Mayport Station, which Norman had used before in his first race picture, *The Green-Eyed Monster.*[40] The rest of the film, including the dramatic plane sequences, was shot on-site at the Norman Studios in Arlington.

Captain Richard E. Norman, who grew up on the studio lot and who eventually became a commercial pilot, recalled some of the tricks that his father employed in filming those stunning aerial shots. "The scenes where the plane was supposed to be upside down were done by flipping the camera upside down. They made a mistake though. They should have set up fans. No one's hair ever moved."[41] Nonetheless, those scenes were as innovative as they were exciting, and, given the public's enormous fascination with flight, accounted for much of the film's popularity.

As with his other features, Norman developed a full line of advertising accessories, including "Brilliant Five Color Lithos, Window Cards, 11 × 14 Rotographs, Heralds, Slides, Trailer"—everything the exhibitor needed to "PUT IT OVER BIG." The posters, produced by Norman's longtime printer J. V. Ritchey of the Ritchey Litho Corporation, were particularly sensational, both in their composition and their vivid color; and Norman urged theater owners and managers to use plenty of them, along with heralds and flyers, to bring in the crowds.[42] Interestingly, though, there had been a serious problem with the first set of one- and three-sheet *Flying Ace* posters that the company printed. "If your name wasn't on them," Norman complained to Ritchey, "I wouldn't have recognized them as having been executed by you. The three sheet looks like white actors, and to further make matters worse, the wording 'With and [*sic*] all colored cast' is small and not displayed to overcome the defect of the white looking actors." Norman was fearful that owners and managers of black theaters would be critical of the paper, since the three-sheet did not stand out from any of the white posters they would be displaying. So he urged Ritchey to run a deeper color on the actors' faces to match the sketch he had originally been sent. "The negros down south," he explained, "can't read and they know it's colored when they see high-brown faces. Those up north, don't want their faces too black, so the high-brown colors soots all." Without a correction of the colors, the theater managers "will use these posters as one of the things to beat me down on my picture."

Another inducement to moviegoers that Norman recommended theaters use was the highly entertaining ballyho by Steve "Peg" Reynolds, who performed some amazing stunts in *The Flying Ace,* including riding a bicycle and shooting villains through his wooden leg. As Norman noted to one of his exhibitors, Reynolds "does a vaudeville skit now and in addition to his bally in the colored quarters, it should boost business."[43] The skit, which ran between fifteen and thirty minutes and involved various costume changes, was always effective in getting people out of their houses and into the theater.[44]

Yet only a few weeks before *The Flying Ace* was released on September 1, 1926, Norman admitted that had he known the final cost, he would never have tackled such an ambitious mechanical picture; and he only hoped that he would be able to get his investment back.[45] Fortunately, the film opened strong, quickly becoming another "box office smasher." Even though *The Flying Ace* had cost "75% more than any colored picture so far released," Norman reported that he was "coming out on it" because it was "doing a S.R.O. [Standing Room Only] business."[46] In Norfolk, Virginia, the picture completed a three-day run in the big Palace Theatre to S.R.O. each day. "And on the first day," Norman wrote, "we ran to 12:30 AM and then had to turn away over 300 who couldn't get in the big 980 seat house." Within a month of its release, "this great picture has broken 4 house records" and already "proven to be the biggest money maker for the colored exhibitor this year, BAR NONE."[47] In one black theater in Austin, Texas, where the average business was $15, *The Flying Ace* grossed over $100 a night; it did similar box office over a five-day run at the Pike Theatre in Mobile, Alabama. In another theater in Beaumont, Texas, it grossed $213 on the first day it played, matching the gross on a multi-day booking of Micheaux's *The Spider's Web,* which had played at higher admission prices.[48] "Columbus, Ohio," Norman told one exhibitor, "has just reported big business on Flying Ace. Dayton finished a three day run last week to capacity (we know, because we played them percentage). Cleveland ran Ace 2 weeks. Cincinnati is repeating it."[49] Interest in the film—"the first one with colored flying and the biggest novelty of the year"—was so high that at times both Norman and his road man worked separate routes roadshowing it simultaneously throughout the South and the Midwest.[50] Moreover, demand for the picture continued for almost a decade, during which time, according to the Norman Studios' records, it grossed over $20,000.[51]

But perhaps the greatest testament to the novelty of *The Flying Ace* was not its box office numbers or its longevity but rather its success in showing blacks in roles that they should have had but in reality were denied. As Phyllis R. Klotman noted, *The Flying Ace* "required the audience's suspension of disbelief" to accept the leap from intrepid flying performer to heroic flying ace and to "buy the American screen dream of rising to the pinnacle."[52] Yet that notion of racial uplift—the promise of advancement through individual achievement—was central to the film because it was consistent with contemporary black ideology; and Norman was determined to give his audiences the role models that they craved but never saw in studio productions.

While Norman touted *The Flying Ace* as an action-packed thriller, some of that action, particularly the film's representation of criminal violence and drug use, raised censors' concerns.[53] The Pennsylvania State Board of Censors, for instance, demanded the elimination of the subtitle "Drugs come in such little vials. Probably Ethyl Chloride" (Reel 3); the elimination of the subtitle "Jed, when you sprayed that Ethyl Chloride on Mr. Kimball and Mr. Sawtelle here, you spilled some on your finger" (Reel 5); and the elimination of a "view of man using a drug contained in a vial to drug a man, his purpose being to rob him after he is unconscious" (Reel 5).[54] The State of New York, Education Department, Motion Picture Division, objected to a scene "where crook actually takes bag containing money from express office" (Reel 4). "The reason for the above elimination," the censor explained, "is that it will tend to 'Incite to crime.'"[55] And the City of Chicago approved the picture only after cuts were made relating to the apprehension of the thief.[56]

Just as Norman was preparing *The Flying Ace* for release, he received a letter from Oscar Micheaux, one of his chief rivals. Ostensibly, Micheaux was writing to urge Norman to contact the Franklin Theatre in Harlem, a few blocks from Micheaux's New York City office, which was interested in playing *Regeneration*; but in fact he was curious to learn more about Norman's latest feature. And he wanted to bring to Norman's attention a new competitor in the race film industry (although he never mentioned the recently formed Colored Players Film Corporation by name). "Some Jews," Micheaux noted, "have produced a couple of features, the first of which [*A Prince of His Race*, starring Shingzie Howard, with whom Norman had corresponded concerning the lead in *The Flying Ace*] appears to draw very well although mighty badly acted and poorly photographed"—though outside of Philadelphia, where the film company was located, the film was being turned down by "critical houses" for first-run bookings.[57] "We could help them a great deal," Micheaux observed, "but since they seem to know it all, and regard all of us who have endured through the years gone by as dubbs, and know nothing, I am letting them find out for themselves the things we have learned from experience." The Colored Players' second film, *Ten Nights in a Barroom*, which was "not as good as the first," would— he predicted—be even more of a disappointment, especially since the producers expected it to earn between $175,000 and $200,000 in profit. In closing, Micheaux invited Norman, when he was "up this way again," to use the Micheaux Film Corporation's office as his headquarters and to avail himself of any services his corporation could render.

Norman was quick to respond and to thank Micheaux for the tip. He was already familiar, he wrote, with the Colored Players to whom Micheaux had alluded: the company had succeeded only in bringing out "more pictures to hinder the progress of the colored picture." And he agreed with Micheaux that they had a revelation coming to them, since securing revenue to make a profit from a race film was becoming more of a problem every day, especially with the rising cost of production and accessories such as lithographed posters and other advertising paper. Improvement in the race picture situation, Norman stated, would never come from the theaters; it would have to start with the manufacturers. But the manufacturers lacked organization; in fact, they lacked even a working agreement that would help them stabilize prices and solve the distribution problem. As a result, the exhibitors had learned how to pit them against each other—much to the detriment of the filmmakers, who, by their reluctance to work together, had inadvertently contributed to their own difficulties.

Surprisingly, Norman directed some of his industry criticism at Micheaux personally: "You are a genius in producing pictures, but your genius has led you astray by producing pictures that you havent been able to intensively distribute, and you have had to rely on help that has taken advantage of you." He believed that the time, money, and effort that Micheaux had invested had borne very little "good fruit"; the only real solution to the distribution problem was a national franchise that organized the exhibitor, let him pay for the picture upon release, and allowed him to play it when he wanted. Reiterating his now-familiar argument that "A BOX OFFICE STAR WILL DO THE TRICK," Norman asserted that if both he and Micheaux had a black star with the drawing power of a white actress like Gloria Swanson, they could command the situation and make money for themselves and for the exhibitor. And by controlling the distribution, they could take on any independent picture of merit and show the producers how to make a profit. The field was big, he concluded, and with a working agreement and "a strict policy which could be changed in conference each year as the conditions change," Norman could work the South while Micheaux worked the North, and both of them could clean up.[58]

Ironically, Norman's proposal to Micheaux was strikingly similar to the proposal George Johnson had presented to Norman five years earlier; and Micheaux's response to the proposal was just as dismissive as Norman's to Johnson had been. But like Johnson before him (and like Clarence Brooks, who at one time had considered joining Norman's operation), Norman was ultimately correct about the impact and importance of an effective distribution system on the success of race films.

Distribution had long been the bane of Norman's existence in the industry. As he wrote to actor Harry Henderson, at least half of the revenues from his pictures were "absorbed by the difficult and expensive distribution," most of which had to be "done by personal persuasion."[59] In his earliest years, Norman traveled widely to develop and nurture the necessary contacts with theater managers and owners; he also relied on his brother and partner Bruce to handle much of the distribution through his road work. Consequently, the company had no need for an outside road man—though, as Bruce Norman's daughter Katherine Norman Hiett recalled, occasionally when the brothers were both on the road at the same time, they impressed their mother into service, to mail them extra heralds, posters, and promotional materials and to assist with other routine tasks related to the business.[60]

But after Bruce Norman quit the film business in 1923, Richard Norman was forced to seek outside assistance. Over the next few years, he employed a number of different distribution agents, beginning with M. C. Maxwell, the trained magician and popular performer whom Norman later tapped to play the lead in his film *Regeneration*. Despite his extensive experience in the industry, Maxwell found life on the road hard; and after he left to spend more time with his family and to pursue his own professional interests, Norman turned to other men, with mixed results.[61]

One of Norman's best agents was "Regan" (David Reid Regan). An energetic young man who was conscientious in his recordkeeping and careful in his accounts, Regan provided regular and detailed reports to Norman about business and about the "crooked stuff" that he encountered on the road, such as the movie house manager in New Orleans who tried to stiff him on the door by selling admissions in advance, slipping cash customers through the exits, and then extorting him for 50 percent of the cashier's shortage. ("With me checking the doorman, running from one door to another and keeping 'a set of books' on them," Regan wrote, "am satisfied that the[y only] beat us for about six or seven dollars [gross] on the engagement.")[62] Just as Bruce Norman had, Regan seemed able to handle the vagaries of the demanding road work. In a letter of June 1, 1927, he described some of the "grief" he was dealing with and how he negotiated problems as they arose:

> Had to detour via New Orleans to reach Baton Rouge and do the same to reach Lafayette. This was necessary as the trains are not crossing the river at Baton Rouge. Left there at 5:10 Monday morning, reached New Orleans a little after 8: o'clock and got out of there for Lafayette at 11:50. Took the first train out and was due in here [Lafayette] at 4:35. As the train came through about thirty miles of high water and had to run over a raised track for twenty-two miles, didn't get in here until 8:10 that night. Had already wired the Opelousas mgr., that I would arrive on the 7:20 bus from Lafayette Monday night. The bus left here at 6:00 PM, after I got in so late there was nothing to do but call off the engagement or hire a taxi for the trip. Called up the mgr., and found that he had already started his show by running a borrowed feature. He insisted that I come over any way and said that it would pay me. He had not given me up and had not collected the tickets. Therefore, got the taxi and got over in time to get the feature started about 9:45. Collected the tickets first 'though. Mgr., said a number had gone home, refusing to wait.

We grossed $33.50 at that. Our bit was $20.10 and as he only had $13.40 left, didn't have the heart to charge the poor fellow 40% of the ad. He had to pay something for the feature he borrowed and returned most of the ad., in good condition. Of course we didn't make anything, but we did avoid a "Blow-up" and made expenses, not so bad at that.[63]

Unfortunately, such complications were common; and Regan's letters to Norman provided an excellent picture of the difficulties that independent filmmakers faced, especially in the waning years of the silent race film industry. Competition for bookings at the dwindling number of race theaters was fierce, and managers used that competition to their advantage, to negotiate the lowest rental fees. In parts of Louisiana and Texas, for example, *The Flying Ace* was booked into theaters right after Micheaux's *Spider's Web*, but Micheaux "blowed up" the towns and "played the devil with business," leaving Norman with "a dirty deal . . . play[ing] soley for the houses benifit."[64] As Regan observed, since the theaters reduced ticket prices on the Norman film to increase attendance and thereby compensate for their losses on the Micheaux feature, "We are going to feel the effects of Mechaux's 'Blow-up' and the high admission these birds [exhibitors] are charging us for it."[65]

Another concern was aging and deteriorating equipment that race theaters could not afford to maintain or replace, especially as new sound technology was being introduced at mainstream houses. The poor projectors, with their sprockets "all shot through," and inexperienced and inept operators wreaked havoc on the film prints; and Regan, while en route, was forced either to make cutouts, patches, and other repairs or to leave the "bad places" and risk creating a fire hazard.[66] "Honestly," Regan wrote of his current tour, "I do not beleive that I have played over 6 houses out of the 31" that did not have sprocket problems.[67] In Memphis, "we had a big negro picnic and hay ride as opposition the first night and a light thunderstorm the last night. Don't see how either one of [us] can make any money playing to such rotten business. The print [of *Regeneration*] caught hell in both Muskogee and Memphis. . . . I worked on the print in Tulsa and Muskogee, had to." Although "the print caught hell again in Austin," Regan hoped that with very careful handling, it might survive the run.[68] That was doubly important, since the depreciation of the print was a cost both to Regan and to Norman.[69]

Unfortunately, in late August, 1927, Regan became ill with heart trouble and abscessed teeth and was unable to return to work for the foreseeable future.[70] As his replacement, Norman hired thirty-eight-year-old Sam Kontas from Waco, Texas, a former Fox Series employee who was knowledgeable about the business.[71] Norman offered Kontas two salary options: the first was a guarantee of $50 per month plus road expenses, with a bonus of 10 percent of the net profits from any route that he covered; the second (which Kontas accepted) was a proposition of one third of the net profits, with no salary guarantee, and road expenses to be paid from the gross revenue.[72] Norman assured Kontas that, either way, he would have a real opportunity to advance himself, especially since he was being assigned one of the finest routes.[73] And he added that "19 years, ago, I would almost have given my right arm for the chance you now have."[74]

At first, Kontas seemed both enthusiastic and reliable. On tour, he scheduled ballyhos to attract moviegoers to Norman's films, which were often in direct competition with Micheaux's. And he kept Norman apprised of developments in the towns where the pictures were showing— for example, the fights and police arrests in Durham, North Carolina, which virtually closed the theaters; the increasingly frequent practice of managers booking vaudeville acts at rambles, which reduced box office returns for the films; the sale of a truck and calliope in Memphis, which forced him to lose a big bally that he had planned; and the changing ownership of one of Norman's best theaters in Baton Rouge, which threatened future bookings.

But Norman was concerned that, apart from the "cream territory" where Kontas admittedly did splendid work, he was not bringing in much additional revenue. Norman also worried about the high travel expenses that Kontas was submitting for reimbursement and about the number of missing reports and overdue remittances: "A man wants to know what business he does every day and as quick as possible and also secure returns due him."[75]

Kontas replied to the queries about his expenses with some indignation. "I was living, and very well at that, before I started to work for you and I believe that I can do the same if I leave you." Then he blamed Norman for withholding critical information about the nature of his position.

"You never told me from the start, that I would work a few weeks and then lay off just as many, . . . I do not want you to think that I blame you. I am old enough to know my mistakes. It was my mistake to not have a clear understanding with you before I started and it was your business to keep it from me. Now I have to suffer the consequences. No one to blame but me."[76]

Apparently, Norman's initial concerns about Kontas's integrity were well-founded. Only a few weeks after his peevish letter, Kontas stopped communicating entirely with Norman and abruptly left his employ, still owing $127. Norman later learned that Kontas had gone to Tampa, Florida, where he used a contact he had made while working for the Norman Studios to convince one of Norman's friends to buy a road picture for $1,800; then he deserted the show in Macon, Georgia.[77]

Another of Norman's road men, "Chas." (Charles K. Ellis), proved far more reliable than Kontas. "A very fine young man" with whom it was easy for exhibitors to conduct business, Chas. began working for Norman in 1925, when he assumed both southern and northern routes for the distribution of *The Crimson Skull* and *Regeneration*.[78] He too experienced a number of the usual hardships on the road, including friction with exhibitors who refused to honor the terms of their contracts. He even suffered a severe auto accident in Cleveland that left him "shot up pretty badly" but joking that "maybe with Steve's ['Peg' Reynolds] good leg and mine there will be one of us" at their next engagement in Philadelphia.[79] Chas. continued to work periodically for Norman over the next few years; and almost two decades later, they partnered again briefly to form an entertainment company.

Not all of Norman's distribution, though, was handled by road men. Some was done through exchange agents who State-Righted his pictures for certain territories, paying an outright fee for the rights and then exploiting the films themselves, keeping all the profit. In a few cases, Norman signed successful multi-year contracts with distributors such as Albert A. Fish of Superior Art Motion Pictures of Philadelphia, Pennsylvania, and True Thompson of the True Film Company of Dallas, Texas. Such arrangements were financially beneficial to Norman and relieved him of much of the burden of bookings in those localities. But even those arrangements could be problematic, as Norman's relationship with Abraham Rosen illustrates.

Rosen, of the American Colored Film Exchange, had first approached Norman about distributing his films in the Mid-Atlantic territory (New York, New Jersey, Delaware, Maryland, Virginia, Washington, D.C.) in January 1922. By early March, Richard and Bruce Norman, then co-partners in the Norman Film Manufacturing Company, signed an exclusive agreement with him for the distribution of *The Love Bug, The Green-Eyed Monster, The Bull-Dogger,* and *The Crimson Skull.* For the rights, Rosen agreed to remit, in installments, payments that ranged from $500 (*The Love Bug*) to $3,500 (*The Crimson Skull*).[80]

Almost immediately, however, tensions arose. Rosen complained that he was not receiving his prints as promised, that cuts needed to be made for the theaters in his territory, that he was short of the paper advertising he was due, that he should not be held responsible for payment of censorship fees, that Steve Reynolds failed to provide the appropriate ballyho—even that Norman was not responding promptly enough to his letters of complaint. In an undated letter (ca. 1922) to his brother Bruce, Norman noted, "If Rosen gets impatient—tell him that the world was not made in a day and that we are moving heaven and earth to get his picture [*The Crimson Skull*] in shape for exploitation and to be patient."[81] In another letter, Norman warned Bruce not to mention anything to Rosen about the problems that he was experiencing with printers and with censors; otherwise, Rosen would stall and delay paying the second installment of $1,000. He added that "Rosen wants all he can get" and will keep pushing to renegotiate the terms of their agreement by withholding payment that is due. "[Do] not let Rosen bluff you," Norman advised. "Rosen may find fault with the picture—in order to make you come down—pay no attention to this. . . . Rosen wants this proposition, but he wants to make it pay for itself . . . Tell him to be patient and to come across."[82]

Even as Rosen prepared to sign an agreement with Norman for distribution rights to another one of his films, *Regeneration,* his complaints kept coming. After paying top prices for *The Crimson Skull* and putting in a year of hard work, Rosen alleged that he was "still $850 to the bad. . . . I paid you $3250.00 and $300.00 for print and $300.00 for advertising + $260 expense such as RR fares and printing matters total amount $4110.00." Rosen added that "its not your funeral but my own + I learned a great lesson." Rosen had started buying pictures from Norman's competitors Oscar Micheaux, Ben Strasser, and Reol Productions; and he claimed he was considering moving to good white Western pictures, which would be a better investment since he could easily double his money on them. Yet Rosen concluded his letter by stating that he was still very interested in handling Norman's films; he just expected an "adjustment" in payment to offset his costs and a renegotiation extending his agreement.[83]

The correspondence between Norman and Rosen continued in the same vein for years. In elaborately detailed letters, Rosen described how much money, labor, and expense he was losing (though, on the rare occasion, he admitted that the loss was not entirely Norman's fault: "Nothing against the picture but times are awful bad + lots of theatres are closing down and those that are open will not pay enough to cover expenses.")[84] More typically, however, Rosen contended that he was being ignored, slighted, even cheated. He complained that his agreements with Norman were costing rather than making him money, implied that he was getting better deals from Norman's fellow filmmakers, and issued new demands for lower pricing and additional services. Norman, in turn, hinted that if Rosen was actually doing such poor business, he might want to yield his contract to other distributors who were anxious to acquire Rosen's territory. But in the end, since Rosen was a dependable, if quarrelsome, distribution partner, Norman usually placated him by offering inducements that Rosen happily accepted. "You are dealing with White Men," Norman reminded Rosen in one rather impolitic note, "and will get a square deal and our heartiest co-operation."[85]

That situation changed in early 1927, after Norman wrote Rosen to apprise him of the fact that his distribution rights had expired. Since no new agreement had been negotiated, Norman warned Rosen to stop showing his pictures and to surrender all copies that he had in hand.[86] Rosen never responded. Norman later learned that Rosen suffered a serious accident on the first of January as he exited a street car in front of one of the Chicago theaters where he was playing a Norman film, and he had been hospitalized for almost three months. Only in the aftermath of Rosen's death, however, did Norman learn how egregiously Rosen had violated the terms of their longstanding agreement. Writing to Rosen's widow to reclaim the prints of his films, Norman noted that her husband's death

> was a great shock to us, also no less a shock was the information that he had shown one of our pictures, The Green Eyed Monster, here in the Western Theatre [in Chicago], just prior to his accident. Mr. Rosen's contract calls only for exhibition of our pictures for a period of 5 years, ending March, 7th., 1927, in the states of, New York, Pennsylvania, Maryland, New Jersey, Washington, D.C., Virginia and West Virginia. But he has shown our pictures in Ohio, Indiana, Michigan and Illinois. This revenue that he secured should be ours. And when we went to book these theatres, we found that he had forestalled us and we could not secure any booking or revenue out of the theatres on this account.[87]

The resolution to the situation proved every bit as thorny and complicated as the relationship with Rosen had been. Unable to reach Mrs. Rosen directly, Norman was forced to enlist the help of his friend William George, manager of the Carey Theatre near the Rosens' former home in Baltimore. After numerous attempts to find Mrs. Rosen at various addresses, George finally located her, but only after a chance remark to the candy salesman who supplied his theater. "She hasn't got over the shock of her husband's death," George reported. "But she realizes that she has got to do something to provide for her four children the oldest a girl and just 14."[88]

Norman responded somewhat dispassionately to George's description of Mrs. Rosen's "pitifull" situation: "I too, feel sorry for Mrs. Rosen's plight," adding

> if Mr. Rosen, hadn't been out of his territory with my films, he would be alive and she wouldn't be a widow to-day. Mr. Rosen has unfortunately, given me no end of trouble. He cleaned up with my pictures, and his greed led to his death. He in several cases used my pictures as a club over the exhibitors head to book some of Michaux's pictures. But it is no use to malign the dead. But I only want to prevent the living from doing me more harm.[89]

While Norman had a legal right to the profits Rosen had made showing the pictures in prohibited territory, his lawyer advised him that "the right may not be as valuable as the cost, and the trouble and expense of enforcing your remedy."[90] So Norman finally settled with Mrs. Rosen, who was relieved of all damages upon the return of the film prints.[91] But it would seem that Mr. Rosen, who had caused such frustration to Norman throughout their relationship, nonetheless succeeded in delivering a Parthian shot.

Even as Norman was producing his own pictures, he continued to seek out opportunities for commercial filmmaking projects similar to—though more technically sophisticated than—those he had made as a traveling filmmaker in the 1910s. In a letter to prospective clients, for example, he outlined his proposal for the best picture ever filmed on Northeast Florida, if not on all of Florida, a picture that would "carry conclusive and convincing facts to the prospective Settler which will cause him to invest and migrate to your property." The picture would run two reels and consist of 136 scenes or set-ups to be made in four counties and with eighty-four titles; photography would be clear and sharp, with professional tinting; and the best angles would be selected "to adequately show up each subject from a pictorial and educational standpoint." The price for the finished two-reel film, titled and ready for projection, would be $3,200.[92]

Norman was also in regular contact with a number of fraternal organizations about making motion pictures that would stimulate interest in their groups, secure new members, and educate old members about the benefits of brotherhood. In a letter to William R. Shirley, president of the Brotherhood of American Yeomen in Des Moines, Iowa, for example, he stated that he had produced several such pictures, most recently for the A.O.U.W. (Ancient Order of United Workmen) in Little Rock, Arkansas. And he described his plan

> to produce for the B.A.Y. a five or six reel motion picture; this length would be a fair program. Such picture to show the advantages of having a B.A.Y. Policy through a story full of heart interest, romance and thrills. With the proper story and punch, this picture would have a wide circulation in the theatres; this being necessary to reap the greatest benefit. If it were a flagrant advertisement, it would not command a ready showing in the majority of theatres. More intimate views of the activities of the Organization could be shown in an extra picture which could be run in conjunction with the main picture when shown in cities and towns where Homesteads were.

To generate even more interest in the picture, Norman suggested that B.A.Y. members be invited to submit their own scenarios, with a prize or other suitable reward to be given to the best ones. Members could then compete for a part in the cast, with "beauty and screen personality to be the final determining factor" in the assignment of the lead roles. Winners would not only earn the honor of appearing in the picture; they would also be financially compensated and given a trip to Norman's Florida studio, where most of the picture would be shot. As in Norman's earlier pictures, that footage would later be intercut with location scenes: "If it were a farm story, it would be better filmed in Iowa; if the action called for a City, Des Moines would be admirable." Given his years of experience handling both amateur and professional casts, Norman was sure that the pictures he proposed would compare favorably with "the regular professional program picture" but could be completed at a fraction of the cost. [93]

Norman also discussed the possibility of making a picture for an interested party in Cuba. Although details of the discussion are not specified in their correspondence, it seems that the party wanted a full-length feature to be completed within a very tight timeframe. Norman replied that given a week, he could produce nothing longer than a two-reeler—and even at that, to meet the deadline, everything would have to be prepared in advance and experienced talent would be required. But he felt that it would be a shame to make a special trip to Cuba and "not to make something really worth while." [94]

In addition to soliciting business through such proposals, Norman sought to augment his income by distributing films produced by other filmmakers. Such arrangements, however, usually yielded only a small profit, as his correspondence with Miami theater founder Sidney Meyer confirms. In October 1927 Meyer contacted Norman regarding a three-reel black-cast picture made in Miami more than five years earlier. That picture, *Fighting His Way Thru,* produced by D. A. Dorsey, was, according to Norman, a decent film with an amateur cast and good photography. Back in March 1923, in fact, Norman had negotiated with Dorsey about handling the picture, but Dorsey had an exaggerated idea as to its possibilities and they never closed any deal. Norman believed that if the picture were to be shown now, it would require retitling and other editing; and "it would cost as much to paper and photo this picture as a longer picture." Even after that, the exhibitor would have to contend with a dissatisfied audience because "since 1922, colored pictures have made tremendous strides."[95]

Nonetheless, at Meyer's insistence, Norman agreed to distribute *Fighting His Way Thru,* though not to incur the full cost of furnishing prints, retitling, advertising accessories, and distribution expenses. Noting that times were harder for race pictures than ever before—with theaters scattered over twenty-six states, some of which supported only a single theater; with high-fee state censorship required in seven states and additional city censorship in five of the largest cities; and with on-site advance screenings necessary before Chicago, Detroit, Cleveland, New York, Baltimore, and Washington exhibitors would place bookings—he concluded that "colored pictures," especially older and otherwise undistinguished ones like *Fighting His Way Thru,* were at a distinct disadvantage. Only by handling such pictures at minimal expense to himself and by distributing them along with his other race films—possibly as a double feature—could he foresee making any profit.[96]

Norman persisted in trying to forge new distribution agreements as well. One good collaboration was between Norman and Albert A. Fish of Superior Art Motion Pictures: for distribution in Florida of Fish's pictures *Smiling Hate* and *Steppin' High,* Norman received 25 percent of gross and 50 percent of all percentage bookings, with Norman bearing booking costs and transportation on percentage runs and Fish covering advertising costs.[97] To one potential partner, W. S. Scales, Norman wrote: "We have successfully distributed 'Smiling Hate' here in the South for the Superior Art Motion Picture Co.," and he suggested a similar proposition. "We can make you money provided you have the prints and advertising. You ship the film, we secure the bookings."[98] In later years, Norman even became the distributor for several of the films of Oscar Micheaux, at one time his biggest competitor and chief rival.

While the handling of films by other producers provided some necessary and useful revenue, Norman's primary focus was still on his own feature filmmaking. For his next picture, *Black Gold,* Norman decided to travel back to the Oklahoma territory—this time to Tatums, Oklahoma, another all-black town. According to a news story that Norman included in his advertising materials and in the pressbook for the picture, "Prominent colored leaders over the United States finally induced The Norman Studios, of Arlington, Florida, to make a series of True Stories of Living Colored Examples, showing their dramatic rise to leadership and wealth, against overwhelming odds." Such a series would "inspire ambition in members of the colored race to accomplish things achieved by their leaders."[99]

Black Gold was based on the life story of John Crisp, a black leaseholder around Tatums who, years earlier, had brought in three producing wells on his property. One well was particularly valuable: because it contained high levels of the mineral antiseptics good for treating rheumatism, a big chemical company offered Crisp a handsome sum for its output. And the Humble Company closed deals with him on the other wells, one of which "flows oil in such a pure state that it needs no refining for lubrication."[100]

Tatums, Norman explained in his pressbook, was founded thirty years earlier by L. B. Tatums, a black pioneer who settled among "savage Indians and founded a colored empire" that stands as a monument to his daring and courage. After heading west from his home in the mountains of Kentucky, Tatums reached a beautiful spot near the Arbuckle Mountains, made famous by Jesse James and the Dalton Brothers, which he named for himself. Now a United States marshal, Tatums felt lucky to see his town—with its post office, modern schools, and hospitable population—experience an oil boom that was bringing wealth and prosperity to the black ranchers. Therefore he welcomed Norman and the publicity that his film would bring; and he also agreed to appear in the film.

A "Thrilling Epic of the Oil Fields," *Black Gold* was a story of love, greed, and adventure. After oil is discovered on the Oklahoma Range near Tatums, the locals abandon their ranching and succumb to "black gold fever." One of the ranchers, Mart Ashton, owner of the Bar Circle Ranch, invests all of his money and even sacrifices his prize cattle to drill the first oil well on his property. The Ohio Company, however, brings in a well on an adjoining claim and forces Ashton to drill an offset well within thirty days or lose the permit to drill on his own ranch. But Peter Barkley, Ashton's driller, refuses to drill further until he is paid the $4,000 he is owed for work that he has already done. Barkley, it turns out, has been scheming with Walter Worder, the cashier at the Ranchman's National Bank, to secure Ashton's permit for themselves by causing a delay on the drilling job. Ashton manages to borrow the money, which in turn forces Barkley to keep drilling; but Worder and Barkley ensnare him in a plot and accuse him of robbing the local bank. Ace Brand, Ashton's foreman, knows that his employer is innocent. Alice Anderson, the bank president's daughter, is in love with Ace and tries everything within her power to help him prove Ashton's innocence. But with Ashton in jail, his well lies idle; and only seven days remain to bring it in. With the aid of Peg Reynolds, the one-legged cowhand on the Bar Circle, Ace and Alice exert "superhuman effort," even going without sleep for forty-eight hours and fighting off a band of crooks. Just as everything seems lost, they expose the conspiracy, exonerate Ashton, bring in the well, and find their own fortune and their future together.

For his new film, Norman again cast veteran Lawrence Criner and his wife, Kathryn Boyd, as the leads. This time, Criner, the title character in his previous picture *The Flying Ace*, played another "ace"—the hero Ace Brand—while Boyd, daughter of the stationmaster and Criner's love interest in *The Flying Ace*, assumed a similar part in *Black Gold*, as the daughter of the bank president and the object of Criner's affection. Anxious to find a strong actor to play opposite Criner, Norman contacted popular actor Alfred Norcom, whom he initially had in mind as the "'heavy' who is the Cashier of a Bank" ("Must dress nattily in some of the scenes")—but whom he cast instead as the conspiratorial oil driller Pete Barkley.[101] In his letter to Norcom, Norman regretted that he could not provide definite dates of service; but since a portion of the picture was being filmed in the oil fields, he had to wait until one of the wells was actually being drilled before determining the start date of his film.

Norman also contacted other professional actors, including P. D. Horn, whose stage experience he valued. Norman proposed to pay Horn $7.50 for each day that he worked plus $2.63 transportation fare. Like many of the other actors, Horn was responsible for bringing his own costume, which included a pair of high-laced boots that Norman advised he could get "cheap" at some army and navy store.[102] And, as always, many actors and aspiring actors wrote Norman directly to inquire about roles.[103] The final cast, as Norman noted on his press sheets, "came from as far South as Jacksonville, Fla., and as far North as Chicago. Indeed, an ambitious undertaking, with such a few theatres for revenue. The cast need no comment. They are leaders in their profession."

On the afternoon of July 13, 1927, the actors assembled at the Dunhooe Hotel, the only black hotel in the town of Davis, Oklahoma. From there, they were taken by bus to Tatums, which was about twenty-five miles away. (The fact that *Black Gold* was made in an "All-Colored City" might "not mean anything to you," Norman emphasized in correspondence with exhibitors, "but it means much to your colored patrons and ment much to our expense of transporting the entire cast to Oklahoma to get REAL REALISM—and novelty in a colored picture.")[104] The filming began on July 14 and was completed in a matter of weeks; and *Black Gold* was in release by the early fall.

In a very public "Confidential Letter" that he published in the promotional materials for the film, Norman promised his exhibitors that *Black Gold* would "Swell YOUR BANK ACCOUNT." Calling it a novel picture, "the first big Oil Picture with an all-colored cast," he assured them that

> The story can't be beat for thrills. It's real and staged among the proper atmosphere. Through proper connections, I was able to secure the whole-hearted co-operation of the Standard Oil Company, who were drilling several oil wells on the Tatum's property which were best to film, and through their assistance, Black Gold, is authentic from every drilling detail, and aside from it's thrills, is a true portrayal of the Romance of Oil towards which no oil man can point a finger of criticism.

Norman touted the film's action, which he claimed had never before been seen in a race picture. "The Hero doesn't do all the fighting—he just pulls three different ones—but did you ever see a one-legged man fight?" In addition to fighting, this same man, Steve "Peg" Reynolds, "does a marvelous feat of skill on the precipitous 100 foot long roof of the derrick house on one leg that I can confidently say has never been done by a one legged man before." (In that jump, Reynolds—whom Norman had dubbed "Ole Reliable"—injured himself and was under a doctor's care for the next two weeks.)[105] Perhaps most impressive were the scenes of the actual wells. "Have you ever seen a picture of a gas well on fire," Norman asked, "that the roar could be heard for 6 miles, the fire was so big? Well, I caught one just as she blew in and just after it had melted down the steel derrick and burned all the woodwork for a block around. It's in Black Gold—just one of the many thrills." He urged exhibitors to book the picture and watch the black gold flow into their bank accounts; and he signed his letter "Yours for Action."[106]

Like *The Flying Ace, Black Gold* broke records in many of the theaters in which it played, especially when Reynolds performed his usual ballyho or when popular actors Criner and Boyd—"two great negro players . . . at the top of their profession," both of them "a cut above the average colored performer"—appeared in person to enact a "strong 15 minute dramatic sketch each show."[107] Writing to his colleague Guy Shriner, Norman bragged that he had just returned from a six-week-long trip showing *Black Gold,* "and due to good exploitation, I hung up 5 records . . . Grossed nearly $1200. in two days at the big Hippodrome in Richmond."[108] In an earlier letter to Shriner, Norman had urged him to book soon, since he had no open dates for almost three months ahead.[109] At the Pike Theater in Mobile, Alabama, the picture earned more than $300 over two nights; and it had good showings in places such as the Dixie Theatre in Newport News, Virginia, the Lincoln Theatre in Charleston, South Carolina, the Rex Theatre in Winston-Salem, North Carolina, and the Gem Theatre in Kansas City, Missouri.[110] Moreover, in several cities Norman's gross surpassed that of *The Millionaire* and other Micheaux films, which were often played in the same theaters at higher admission prices. And even in movie houses such as the Forrest Theatre in Philadelphia, Pennsylvania, where the film did not make expenses because of "present conditions and weather being hot," the manager admitted that "the picture itself was a nice little picture."[111]

Even while *Black Gold* was still in production, Norman began planning new films. To one exhibitor, he wrote that his next picture would be a six-reel Western titled *Each to His Own,* which he had earlier described as having "A SMASHING THEME." To aspiring actress Dorothy Lee Jackson, however, he wrote that he would soon be casting for a different Western, *A Short-Skirted Outlaw,* which would "require a girl who can RIDE as well as act."[112] And to Alfred Norcom, who inquired about a role in Norman's next film, he replied that "certain developments materialized . . . [in] the acoustical field of pictures, and this has made me partly to decide to produce a series of pictures here [at the Norman Studios in Jacksonville] this summer along the advanced line." Yet he assured Norcom that he had not fully abandoned the idea of making another picture in Oklahoma over the summer.[113]

But, in fact, there would be no more Norman productions. With the advent of talkies and with Hollywood's growing interest in the black movie market, the landscape of the industry was shifting quickly. Norman was no longer simply in competition with other producers of black silent films; he was competing against the Hollywood studios and the promise of the new technology of sound film, which was already revolutionizing the industry. Most significant of all, in the advent of the Great Depression, black theaters—always Norman's primary and largest clientele—were closing, thus making distribution more problematic than ever.

Unlike most independent race producers, for whom the late 1920s sounded a death knell, Norman would continue to be engaged in the film business, albeit in different capacities, for the next two decades. But *Black Gold* proved to be his final feature film.

CHAPTER SEVEN

"It Takes a Darn Good One to Stick": Norman's Later Career

EVEN AS NORMAN was producing *The Flying Ace* and *Black Gold*, the industry was changing dramatically. In the peak years of early race cinema from the late 1910s to the mid-1920s, Norman and his fellow independents—Oscar Micheaux, the Johnson Brothers, Reol Productions—had constituted a kind of separate, or underground, cinema. Through their pioneering pictures, they attempted to reach the black audience that was virtually ignored by the major motion picture studios. Despite problems with small budgets and poor distribution channels, those independent race filmmakers were somehow able to release films that went beyond mere representation of blacks on the screen to depict blacks as a presence in American life and to highlight black achievement—from the ambition of pioneer Jean Baptiste in Micheaux's *The Homesteader* and the heroism of Shiftless Joe with the famous fighting Tenth Cavalry during the battle of Carrizal in Mexico in Lincoln's *Trooper of Troop K* to the wartime bravery of Captain William Stokes in Norman's *The Flying Ace*.[1]

The end of the 1920s, however, brought many changes. For black Americans in general, as film historian Thomas Cripps noted, the Great Depression proved a shattering experience that hit sooner and more severely than it did for whites. Migrations from the South into urban centers like Harlem and Chicago's South Side had already left many blacks only marginally employed and living in segregated areas that further removed them from white contact and culture. Even the Republican Party at Herbert Hoover's so-called "lily white" convention of 1928 cast blacks aside and gave rise to a kind of laissez-faire apathy in the face of economic decline that reinforced the racial discrimination, residential covenants, closed ballot boxes, and Jim Crow accommodations from the Wilson years almost a decade earlier.[2]

For Norman and his fellow race filmmakers, the changes were just as revolutionary. The number of black theaters continued to decline, as did the rental fees that the remaining theaters were able to pay; yet production costs continued to rise. Distribution became increasingly complicated, especially as independent filmmakers were forced to play their pictures on a percentage basis rather than on straight rental (that is, on speculation rather than on a guarantee of return) and to organize costly, tedious, and at times impractical roadshows in an attempt to recoup some of their investment. "Out of less than a hundred theatres," Norman had estimated in 1926, "we must get our production costs and a possible profit, with the difficult feature of an excessive distribution cost occasioned by these few theatres being scattered over some 21 states."[3]

Even more importantly, perhaps, the new technology of sound that had evolved in the 1920s marked both the end of the silent film era and the beginning of the modern Hollywood film industry. As a handful of established producers and distributors gained prominence and consolidated power, many independent filmmaking companies were forced to close. This was especially true of race producers, most of whom had struggled mightily to compete in the silent market and therefore had neither the resources nor the technical expertise to make the transition to talkies. Moreover, the major studios, stumbling over each other as they tried to exploit the new medium through the use of "Negro themes and motifs" and to tap the growing minority market, were so successful that their work instigated the turning away of black audiences—and, to a lesser extent, of the influential black press—from race movies and toward Hollywood features.[4] A different kind of pressure from Hollywood—Universal's demand that Noble Johnson resign his position and affiliation with the Lincoln Motion Picture

Company—had, in effect, caused the demise of that distinguished film company; and Reol Productions folded not long afterward, with founder Robert Levy attributing the closing to the fact that black patrons preferred to frequent white theaters and pictures over their own.[5] Only Oscar Micheaux made a successful transition—although by then, he too had filed for bankruptcy and had been forced to reorganize his company with new capital from white investors.

Nonetheless, initial hopes for blacks in sound films were high. Concurring with William Foster's earlier prediction for "rapid growth in this industry among Negroes" and "unquestionable ultimate success," Romeo L. Dougherty stated that the possibilities for blacks in performance as well as in production and distribution of talking pictures appeared to be unlimited.[6] James Weldon Johnson agreed. In 1929, he wrote to Foster: "I do not see how they are going to keep the Negro from achieving a permanent place in the movie world so long as they have talkies."[7] Robert Benchley went even further: it "may be that the talking movies must be participated in exclusively by Negroes," he observed, because of "a quality in the Negro voice, an ease in its delivery, and a sense of timing in reading the lines that makes it the ideal medium for the talking picture."[8]

For its landmark first synchronous sound and spoken film in 1927, Hollywood looked to an enduring, if antiquated, aspect of black and popular American culture. Warner Brothers' *The Jazz Singer* starred white singer Al Jolson as Jakie Rabinowitz, a cantor's son, who is torn between an assimilative desire to be part of America and a more melancholy pull toward the traditional song and religion of his fathers. Jakie ultimately chooses assimilation.[9] Transforming himself into "Jack Robin," he rejects the Orthodox Judaism of his parents, falls in love with a gentile girl named Mary Dale, and prepares for his big premiere on Broadway as a so-called Mammy singer who performs a vulgarized minstrel-type blackface act. But he gives up his opening night to return home and reconcile with his dying father. The film's final number, which occurs some time later, shows "Jack" on the Broadway stage performing "My Mammy" (Jolson's signature song), as Sara Rabinowitz gazes adoringly from the front row and Mary watches from the wings. Thus, Michael Rogin noted, Jakie succeeds in achieving it all: assimilation to a whiteness that includes access to the gentile woman and the continued adulation of his mother after his father's death.[10] The film itself, though, managed to eradicate the particularism of black history by emptying Jolson's "pathetic figure in blackface" of its iconic black suffering and investing it instead with the Jewish dilemma of integration and intermarriage.[11]

After the success of Warner Brothers' *The Jazz Singer,* other studios began looking to black imagery for the subject of some of their feature films. Within a year of the release of *The Jazz Singer,* both Fox and Metro-Goldwyn-Mayer had all-black-cast productions in the works.[12] Fox's *Hearts in Dixie* (1929) was a two-reel musical of plantation life that fully captured the familiar mythology of the Old South by rehashing many of the standard and stereotypical elements of earlier silent productions: Toms dutifully served their masters; contented slaves worked the fields; happy pickaninnies ran playfully about; and steamboats traveled down the river to the melodious strains of old Negro spirituals.[13] *Hallelujah!* (1929), the second and more memorable musical, was a modern-day morality tale about Zeke Johnson, a decent young black man who is tempted and seduced by pleasures of the flesh, especially by Chick, the flashy, lusty young woman who conspires with her gambler boyfriend Hot Shot to cheat him out of his earnings. But after atoning for his actions, Zeke returns to the embrace of his loving and forgiving family. Both films were innovative by Hollywood standards and raised the expectations of black moviegoers.[14] Nevertheless they harked back to many of the old black stereotypes and established the screen models that filmmakers would imitate for years to come.[15]

Even before the release of Hollywood's pioneering black musicals, Norman recognized the changes that were occurring in the race film industry. In a letter to Evans Sprott of the Bijou Amusement Company in Nashville, Tennessee, he wrote:

> We both might as well put our cards on the table and face facts—the price of colored pictures can't come down. Production costs are going up and also distribution costs. . . . Only the fellow who puts out the good picture and gives the Exhibitor service is going to survive. There are three outfits now fighting for survival and two of them are pretty well winded. Yours truly has god a few good friends who are trying to encourage me to stay in the game and make them money—so I still have my wind.

But that "wind" was not without its limits. As Norman was quick to point out, whereas other organizations existed by virtue of the fact that they sold stock or "promote[d] some angel" (typically a white investor) to fund their productions, his was the only company to make pictures on the proceeds coming out of the theaters. With so many smaller filmmakers already having gone on the rocks, he speculated that it was only a matter of time before "the two remaining outfits will go the same way." Yet, he insisted, he was committed to keeping his company from suffering the same fate.[16]

Norman's commitment alone, however, could not ensure his success. Once sound had become the rage among audiences who were fascinated by its novelty, exhibitors began pressing filmmakers for talking pictures.[17] Although Norman claimed that he was doing "as well as in boom times" with his silent films and that he was deliberately holding off on talkies until more theaters acquired sound capability, he knew that he lacked the resources and technology to produce true talking pictures.[18] But, ever the entrepreneur, he decided to move into the business of sound from another angle—by developing and marketing a nonsynchronous sound system that he called Camera-Phone. As he explained to a theater manager who had written him to inquire if his picture *Regeneration* was synchronized with sound-on-disc:

> Please be advised that the market is so restricted for an all-colored cast picture, that it would be an entirely unprofitable venture to add sound to this class of picture. Our only alternative is to furnish cue sheets to be used with non-synchronous equipment, a list of records to use, or to furnish the records along with the picture. This is serving excellently, and at a great saving to the Exhibitor. All colored theatres so far having sound, have non-sync equipment, and if you haven't added this feature, it would soon pay for itself. We are enclosing [a] folder of our non-sync equipment made by our Camera-Phone Company which makes talking picture equipment.[19]

In his promotional materials, Norman touted Camera-Phone as a small, portable talking picture unit that allowed exhibitors to move almost immediately from silents to talkies. "Our apparatus," he declared, "is instantly attached to ANY make of machine, and can be attached to either side of machine. This saves tearing out booth walls. Our machines also will play with the arc rectifiers or motor generators in the booth."

Moreover, the apparatus "does not pick up ther vibration or their electrical interference" and comes with "Dual-Amplification (two amplifiers) with double throw switches which assured UNFAILING OPERATION in event of tube burn-outs." Unlike similar systems that cost $5,500 and charged service fees of $40 a week or more, Camera-Phone sold for one half, had no service fee, and was purportedly "fool-proof."[20] Norman's price sheets showed that the equipment could be purchased as an entire system or by individual components, some of which were discounted because they had been used and refurbished.

Norman noted that Camera-Phone was a lifesaver for the small manufacturer and independent cameraman, for whom full truck equipment, which could run as high as $30,000, was "prohibitive." And it was also ideal for road men who needed reliable equipment that they could easily transport in an automobile or truck and quickly set up and later dismantle for an evening's show in a hall, theater, or church. Norman's extensive experience roadshowing his own films had taught him that road men were "too busy to be fussing with apparatus that must be nursed along and requires from 10 to 28 connections of a hay wire nature to get it into operation. These hit or miss methods mean a possible return of the patron's money."[21] Camera-Phone, Norman assured potential buyers, overcame those problems and offered tremendous possibilities in a "field [that] is Virgin—Unworked and full of profit for you if you have a Good Program." And he could supply all their needs.[22]

To friend and colleague Guy Shriner, Norman bragged that he had been successfully manufacturing the Camera-Phone since early 1928.[23] To another colleague, William George, he made an even bolder claim: that he had perfected his "Talking Picture Equipment," which was proving to be the best operating modest equipment on the market: "Has no waver line like the other machines and I am actually replacing some of the cheap systems with my turntable." If George had already installed sound equipment in his theater, Norman only hoped he "didn't get stung like some or many of the 'Boys.'"[24]

Norman was, in fact, a lifelong inventor and a skilled technician. In addition to maintaining and refurbishing much of the equipment in his own studio, he often repaired faulty equipment in those theaters with which he did business. In a letter of July 1929 to his former road man Regan, Norman stated that he had just come back from Tampa, where he rebuilt the Movie-Phone at the Rivoli Theatre in Ybor City. "It had completely broken down and refused to make a 'Sound,'" he wrote. "The thing had never talked plainly since its installation. Every shaft was running like a broken leg, pick-ups jumping grooves and the speakers sounding like a wail from the 'lost world.' It made me sick to look at the thing." But since the manager was a friend, Norman refurbished the Movie-Phone so that it no longer ruined records; and afterward it talked better than it ever had. Although "the 'boys' froth at the mouth down here when you say 'Sound,'" Norman added, he was moving forward aggressively with his own equipment and would have four new Camera-Phone models ready for the fall rush. "They will look, taste and smell" like the more costly systems, because "it seems that the Exhibitors want something that looks like a 'near kin' without paying the price."[25]

That was indeed the appeal of Norman's Camera-Phone: it was a relatively inexpensive way for theater owners and managers to introduce sound into their theaters, at a fraction of the cost of similar apparatus.[26] And for a short time, from 1928 until the very early 1930s, the equipment—purchased by theaters from Florida to California—turned a profit. But despite Norman's claims of having perfected his system, Camera-Phone had numerous flaws. Eunice Kirkland of Tri-County Amusement Company in Live Oak, Florida, who in late 1929 purchased complete equipment for a five-hundred-seat theater for $775—equipment that Norman alleged was quoted at $1,750 by his nearest competitor using similar accessories and by his highest competitor at over $10,000—reported that she had received many compliments from her patrons; but the pick-ups already needed adjusting to eliminate jumping of the grooves.[27] She also noted that she would not have installed the equipment when she did had she been aware of the fact that her machines would not hold up under the heavy load.[28] Those were not the only problems. A few months later, at the same theater, the amplifier that had worked properly on installation was malfunctioning and not shutting off.[29] And J. M. McKinney of the Princess Theatre in Cross City, Florida, had been having trouble all along: the fader was poor, the talking was low at changeover, the machines were operating too slowly, the pickups were not putting out properly, and the speaker failed to register high notes.[30]

Unfortunately, Norman was running out of money to keep investing in improvements to the system. Realizing that he needed the backing of an outside investor, he pressed several acquaintances for assistance. After one colleague, identified only as Walter, mentioned that he had a financier friend who might be interested in underwriting the product, a hopeful Norman provided the particulars. Camera-Phone, he wrote, "has proven highly satisfactory. Equipment is still operating over a period of as much as a year without one cents worth of repair or upkeep," something he noted that could not be said of any similar apparatus. Moreover, "not one single [system of Camera-Phone] equipment has been taken out of any theatre which is a remarkable record." The equipment, though, was being sold on terms, with Norman himself providing the financing; and while exhibitors were still clamoring to install sound to meet moviegoers' demands, he had reached the point where he had to turn down new orders because "the initial investment was rolling up too rapidly" and he was not in a position to expand.[31]

In a follow-up letter to Walter, Norman explained his proposition in greater detail. Getting a major investor with executive ability and vision to subsidize Camera-Phone would be beneficial in perfecting an organization to manufacture talking picture apparatus and in improving the marketing of the equipment, thus ensuring even more sales. Claiming that he had already declined quite a few opportunities to take on promoters "of the shoe string variety, all for themselves, and with absolutely no vision other than making a quick dollar for themselves," Norman believed that Walter, with his excellent connections, could find a backer with the appropriate talents and resources. And he mentioned a further incentive: incorporation and sale of stock would in turn open up several new positions in his company, including one that Walter himself could assume.

By way of collateral, Norman noted that the Camera-Phone Company and Norman Studios, which covered an entire block of ground and was composed of five buildings with water, light, and sewerage as well as power, "is owned and operated by myself, is a going concern and does not owe a dollar." With strong financial backing, Norman insisted that he could get a big return for himself and for his investors on sales of the Camera-Phone equipment. And perhaps more importantly, with additional new funding (which unfortunately he never secured), he felt he could convert his studio into a facility for the production of actual talking pictures.[32]

Not only was Camera-Phone less efficient than Norman claimed; its cost, while lower than other early sound systems, was simply too high for many of the small white theaters that had been deeply affected by the economic decline leading up to the Depression and for the handful of black theaters that were still in operation. Even some of the exhibitors who had contracted for or already purchased Norman's equipment were forced to default on it. S. A. Austin at Jacksonville's Strand Theatre, for example, was facing legal action by Norman, who insisted on settlement—either full payment or an immediate return of the entire purchase—"NOW."[33] Another creditor, Harry Simons of the Skydome Theatre in Miama, Florida, was in a similar bind. As he informed Norman, a beautiful theater had just opened nearby and was drawing all of his customers. While he was hopeful that things would improve once the novelty of the new theater wore off, he was currently unable to make payment on his Camera-Phone system contract. Yet a few months later, in the spring of 1931, the situation seemed no better. "I do not know every morning," Simons confessed, "whether I will be open that day or if the sheriff will take charge of the place for the landlord."[34] But he guaranteed Norman that he would never betray a friend in terms of payment, even though the equipment he had purchased from him was already obsolete and he needed to make a deal on sound-on-films in order to stay in business.[35] And in fact Simons was true to his word: he eventually reached an agreement with Norman to reduce the payment, which canceled the debt.

Exhibitors like Austin and Simons were not the only ones experiencing serious financial setbacks. Norman was increasingly in default of payments himself. Writing to J. C. Wertman in the credit department of the Multigraph Company, Cleveland, Ohio, in August 1932, Norman acknowledged that he had been billed for a payment of $8 plus $1.60 interest. "[I] assure you that you would have received it [the money owed] long ago but things have been at a standstill with me during July and August and this is why I asked [for] the refinancing of my contract." Norman promised that he would try to send a remittance soon but asked the company to exercise patience until the fall, when prospects were sure to open up for him.[36]

While the state of the economy—both Norman's and the nation's—and the technical problems with the system itself imperiled Norman's Camera-Phone Company, it was a new development in sound technology that ultimately spelled its doom. Sound had been introduced into motion pictures through Vitaphone, which Warner Brothers used in *The Jazz Singer*. A system of disc recording that was groundbreaking at the time, Vitaphone was impractical for large-scale motion picture production: the process, which required the steady hand of a projectionist to hit the correct groove in order to keep the voice and the picture in sync, made it prone to trouble; and the disc itself could not be edited. Clearly a better system—one that actually incorporated sound-on-film—had to be found. Fox Studios' Movietone soon followed: it provided a single system that merged sound and picture but required a gas-filled tube called an AEO light, which, when activated by an audio input, responded by producing sound-modulated light that could be photographed. But Movietone allowed only minimal editing, and the quality was poor. Another optical sound system, RCA Photophone, employed a galvanometer-type device in which a tiny mirror twisted and turned in response to sound waves and photographed those sound waves on film. As Edward Bernds, an early and pioneering Hollywood production sound man who worked with legendary directors from D. W. Griffith to Frank Capra, described: "This produced a negative, white-on-black, in which the profile of the sound resembled a mountain range with many peaks and valleys. Printed, the mountain range became black; the background white. Photophone could be edited and development and printing of the film was not critical."[37]

But it was the variable density sound system developed by Western Electric that proved far superior to the others. Even Regan, Norman's former road man, sang its praises. In a letter to Norman in 1929, Regan wrote, "I've been on Western Electric sound, uptown [in Atlanta] for five months. Have worked the other systems but have found none that can touch W. E. for reproduction and service."[38] Its sound image was recorded not as a black-and-white mountain range, but as a series of black, white, and gray bars of infinite complexity and accuracy. At the heart of the system was a brilliant invention called a light valve, by which a pair of ultralight metallic ribbons provided a slit through which a strong source of light was focused on the film as it passed through the recording machine and photographed the sound. Though cumbersome in some of its components, the Western Electric sound system quickly became the industry standard; in fact, it served well for many years, until film production switched to magnetic sound (that is, tape recording).[39]

As soon as it was introduced, Western Electric's sound-on-film system rendered the Camera-Phone's mechanical apparatus—which at one time seemed so revolutionary—obsolete. Norman, who had sunk most of his money into Camera-Phone, found himself in dire financial straits. As Captain Richard E. Norman recalled, his father was forced to declare bankruptcy and, although he continued to create new roles for himself in the industry, was never able to return to feature film production again.[40]

Notably, even after Camera-Phone's failure as a sound system in movie theaters, Norman tried to rebrand the product and to promote it as a "Voice and Band" unit that could be installed on trucks to advertise and sell various kinds of merchandise. In a letter to Jacksonville dentist Dr. E. A. Welters, for example, Norman wrote that he had noticed that Welters had brought his Dodge truck into the local machine shop "for the purpose of placing a large tooth-pow[d]er can on the top." While Norman agreed that this was an excellent advertising device, he suggested that it could be made even more effective by the installation of his "Giant Voice and Band" equipment. "In the case of your truck," Norman proposed, "the loud speaker could be mounted in the bottom of your tooth-powder can and the bottom of the can could be hinged so as to drop down when the apparatus was in use." Since the system left an indelible impression due to its unique delivery, it offered an unparalleled "live wire" bally: "You can ride it up in front of a Drug Store, snap a switch in your truck and instantly attract a crowd," or "you [can] operate a moving picture machine from it," thereby providing "educational pictures on oral hygiene."[41] Over the years, Norman pushed the sale of other audio equipment, too. Writing to a colleague he addressed as Friend King in the summer of 1933, for instance, Norman wondered about King's interest in seeing the dope on a new sound head from Mellaphone, which had a better amplifier with wide range recording. That equipment, he advised, could be secured at a payment of $10 a week.[42]

Filmmaking, however, remained Norman's primary interest. Although he had not produced a new race picture since 1928, Norman continued to seek out fresh ways to distribute and promote his older films. In September of 1929, for example, he began a correspondence with F. Bund Jr., the branch manager of the U.S. Army Motion Picture Service in Washington, D.C., who was interested in booking black-cast pictures that could be screened at the black theater at Fort Benning, Georgia.[43] Norman immediately contracted to play five of his feature films—*The Flying Ace, Black Gold, Regeneration, The Crimson Skull,* and *The Green-Eyed Monster*—on a rental basis, beginning November 1, 1929. The rental fee was $10 per picture, with transportation and advertising fees for posters to be paid by Bund.

That same year, Norman was contacted by J. Pitman Harmon Jr., the secretary to the board of directors of the Heroh Motion Picture Company of Liberia. Harmon's company was anxious to introduce "Negro Artists" into their shows in Liberia, and he requested a full list of prices for Norman's films, both "old and latest," as well as any available posters and advertising.[44]

The Liberian interest in American race films and performers likely originated in the Back-to-Africa Movement, which began in the nineteenth century but found its strongest voice in Marcus Garvey, an early-twentieth-century black nationalist who believed that black men and women needed to rediscover their race pride by returning to Africa and establishing a permanent homeland there. Through the United Negro Improvement Association, which he initially organized in 1914, and especially through the "Liberia program" that he launched around 1919–1920, Garvey—who had extensive plans for the implementation of improvements such as transportation and education—hoped to create an African base of operations for the thousands of American, South American, British, and Caribbean followers who had answered his call to black self-determination. But ultimately he was unable to persuade the Liberian government to provide the necessary land for settlement; and by the mid-1920s, opposition from Europeans with vested interests in the country effectively terminated the program. Garvey himself was arrested in 1923 and sentenced to jail (and eventually deported) for defrauding investors in his Black Star Line.[45] Nonetheless, his movement continued to inspire a number of blacks to migrate, on their own, to their ancestral land.

Norman welcomed the opportunity to explore the new Liberian market for his films. In response to Harmon's inquiry, he sent quotes on his "greatest successes," all of them "acclaimed by a million theatre-goers in North America" and "well known by every theatre owner." Those pictures—which included *Black Gold* (6 reels), *The Flying Ace* (6 reels), *Regeneration* (6 reels), *The Crimson Skull* (6 reels), *The Bull-Dogger* (5 reels), *The Green-Eyed Monster* (5 reels), *Spooks* (1 reel), and *A Natural Born Shooter* (1 reel)—were priced by running foot of film: ten cents per foot for the first print, eight cents per foot for the second print, and six cents for the third print (including waxing of the prints to safeguard them against projector damage). "In other words, in the case [of] Black Gold, the first print would cost you $584.00, Flying Ace, $520. etc." Norman also enclosed folders for his Camera-Phone talking picture equipment, which he suggested could be used to play Heroh's pictures as well.

All of his pictures, Norman boasted to Harmon, were

> full of Action, and each and every one of them is a Novel Colored Picture. Also there is no mimicry of the Colored man in the Feature Pictures. They are full of Ambition, Uplift, without preaching, and please both young and old. There is no similar type of picture made in this country by colored artists. They are either too high brow and unreal, or low brow and amateurish. We have enjoyed the greatest success of any in this type of picture as we have struck the type of story that has made a hit with all types of colored audiences which have made them a financial success.

He concluded that even on the fifth or sixth run in the same theaters, the pictures still drew capacity houses; and he assured Harmon that the pictures would meet with great approval in Liberia and "will live long useful and profitable runs."[46]

Although no deal with Harmon appears to have been struck, the Liberian interest in Norman's films continued. In 1932, the BER Motion Picture Company in Monrovia, Liberia, contacted Norman to inquire about rental or purchase prices for pictures that he had produced or was distributing. In reply, Norman offered the company some bargains, including used copies of *The Flying Ace* and *Black Gold* (at $100 each or $150 for the pair), with a full line of advertising available on both for a small additional cost, as well as a number of one- and two-reel comedies and "many fine white western pictures" that ranged from two to six reels in length. Norman noted that, if the company were interested in talking pictures, he could also provide quite a few fine subjects with talking and sound on the large sixteen-inch discs that could be run with his "Camera-Phone Talking Picture Equipment" (turntables, amplifier, speakers, sound effect records), which he would sell at sacrifice prices. The talking pictures included several white-cast Westerns; *Mawas*, a jungle thriller; and *Ingagi*, a "wild animal sensation, gorillas consorting with African natives." (African jungle or tribal films were becoming a popular Hollywood genre—an unfortunate metaphor for what many white filmmakers perceived as the primitivism of blacks.) Norman also reminded BER that he carried religious subjects.[47] Again, no deal was made.

A few years later, though, after the WER Company bought the BER operation, Managing Director S. Raymond Horace contacted Norman, noting that WER wanted to purchase "an All Coloured Cast of silent films, as many as possible." Since Liberia was "a Coloured Nation," Horace was sure that such pictures would meet with "high approbation from the entire populace." Horace especially wanted to acquire the thrilling adventure *The Flying Ace*.

Norman replied that *The Flying Ace* was indeed available, as were *Black Gold, The Crimson Skull,* and *Regeneration*—all pictures still in great demand because of their popular appeal. Prints of the films, with all rights for Liberia, were available for $75 each or $125 for two; and for an additional $50 each, Norman would include two motor-driven Zenith machines, rebuilt but in first-class shape, to provide sound. The films, Norman claimed, were still so profitable that "we have refused to sell any rights" to them in the United States; and he promised that they would be "steady money makers" for WER as well.[48]

The Liberian film companies were not Norman's only connection to Africa. In the fall of 1930, he and his colleague Ben Burbridge discussed the possibility of financing and filming a planned expedition to Africa. Norman urged Burbridge to pursue the creation of a corporation that would underwrite the project. There were, Norman believed, several advantages to such a corporation. Paramount among them was the fact that if its stockholders decided to make another picture, the organization would already be in place for immediate action. He also assured Burbridge that he was not "a novice in raising funds for a worthy purpose in which there is a fair certainty of profit for the investor."[49]

In addition to cultivating such foreign interests, Norman continued to try to muster business closer to home. One way was to lease his studio and equipment to other producers or potential filmmakers like R. J. Hersey, vice president of International Publishers in Wheeling, West Virginia, who had made inquiries about renting the facilities. International Publishers was planning to run two newspaper contests and to avail the winners of "the opportunity of entering into a motion picture career"; and Hersey sought a guarantee that Norman could handle all the arrangements that such a project would entail.[50]

Norman replied affirmatively and enthusiastically. His experience with those types of productions, he stated, was extensive: he had been directing pictures since 1912, and his efficiency was without equal. "I will state that I hold the record here for actual number of scenes shot in one day on action melodrama—142."[51] He noted, though, that if the production involved an all-amateur cast, it might "require that the Director turn his Studio into a Kindergarten for these aspirants, and a scenario requiring any great amount of ability or emotion, will be flat." But an action picture would no doubt "get over," especially if Norman were able to place one of his professionals in the cast and to write a suitable part for him.[52]

Putting his property in proper shape to accommodate the picture, however, would demand an outlay of about $4,800. Adding necessary improvements such as running water to the dressing rooms, sanitary accommodations, and a cistern—plus the expense of extra insurance—would bring the total rental cost of the studio to $5,400. But for that price, International Publishers would have exclusive use, for a period of one year, of the office, projection room, cutting room, drying room, darkroom, still room, and printing room; all machinery necessary for developing and processing the pictures; sets, lights, and generating equipment; and pool and grounds. The offer was a real bargain, Norman claimed, because at Pacific

Coast prices it would cost about $39,000 for the use of the smallest studio with similar facilities.[53]

International Publishers and the other filmmakers seeking rental facilities, though, wanted studios that were already set up to handle all-talking productions. Jimmie Burns, for example, of Jimmie Burns Productions in New York City, replied to a preliminary proposal from Norman with some disappointment upon learning of the studio's limitations: "Of course the fact that your plant is not equiped for talking pictures alters the situation somewhat."[54] A few years later, when Abraham Wax of Keamco Theatrical Enterprises contacted Norman about making a film "for colored patronage" that required four principals and a single location—a wooded area with a sawmill and a house—Norman assured him that there were many such locations available in the Jacksonville area. But as for the other requirements for making a sound picture, he could offer only "the latest type of Bell & Howell Sound camera with Movietone type of recording on film with cameraman and sound man—also truck for sound apparatus"—although he guaranteed excellent sound and photography.[55]

The failure of Camera-Phone also had other implications for Norman's career. In the fall of 1927, when he was still actively making race features, Norman had dismissed an inquiry from F. J. Hilburn in Chickasha, Oklahoma. "We do not rent our pictures for non-theatrical purposes," he wrote. "That is, for use in Churche's and Schools. We only do business with well established and responsible theatres."[56] In the aftermath of the collapse of his Camera-Phone business and bankruptcy and in the worsening years of the Depression, however, Norman recognized that the market for his pictures had radically changed.[57] With so many black theaters closing and with talkies garnering all the attention at the white movie houses, Norman realized that he needed to consider other outlets for distribution. Schools and churches became his new venue.

Writing to his old friend and former road man M. C. Maxwell, who was now in the picture business himself, Norman admitted: "I have only one good copy of each picture which I am road-showing myself." As a result, he had turned down several rentals, because it did not pay him to make additional copies to accommodate so few requests from exhibitors—especially since, with business so bad, the theater machines were in worse condition than before and quickly destroyed even brand new prints. "I am road-showing everything now, and like yourself, takeing a projector along and showing in Churches and Schools where there is no colored theatre. Many of the theatres have not been able to put in sound equipment or pay the high licenses and as a result are shut down, many for good."[58]

So, once again, as in his earliest years in the industry, Norman became essentially a one-person operation. He would contact local church or civic leaders as well as principals of black schools (whom he unfailingly addressed with the respectful title "Professor") by mail and offer them various entertainments or educational programs; and after lining up dates, he would take to the road on his own—although he was occasionally joined by Steve "Peg" Reynolds, who performed as part of certain shows (especially *Monster Walks, The Phantom, Gorilla Ship, Trails of Danger,* and a few slapstick talkie comedy shorts and cartoons).[59] Reynolds's appearances, which included a fifteen-minute skit on stage, always boosted business and drew crowds.[60]

In addition to showing his own films, Norman relied on a few staple pictures, which he screened alone or as part of a double feature. They included *Modern Minstrels,* an "All Talking, Singing, Dancing Extravaganza" that provided "fine clean entertainment [for both] white and colored schools"; *Silent Power,* whose religious theme appealed to church audiences; and two Superior Art Motion Picture productions that he had been distributing since the mid-1920s, *Smiling Hate,* a story of love and intrigue set in a gold mine and starring Harry Henderson, Josephine Talley, and Howard Agusta, and *Steppin' High,* a two-reel comedy.[61] (For theater exhibition only, Norman also offered the nine-reel picture *Her Unborn Child,* which he promised managers was "not the usual sex slop" but rather "a high class talkie of the stage play that ran one year on Broadway and can be played with no after regrets"—though not for children under sixteen, who would not understand it and therefore should not be admitted.)[62]

Norman's terms were fairly standard: the church or school would receive 25 percent of the gross receipts. But he often added an incentive, raising the school or church's share to one third of all receipts beyond $25 and 40 percent on all receipts beyond $40—and sometimes even as high as 50 percent on receipts over $50.[63] As Norman promised potential exhibitor Reverend Lee of Goulds, Florida, he would furnish entertainment, tickets, and lights. Lee's expense would be the use of his building and the services of his workers in selling advance tickets. As further motivation, "every worker selling a card of tickets is to receive a Free Admission." The entertainment itself would run two hours and include *The Fourth Alarm,* a white-cast "all-talking clean drama—no fighting—no drinking—no dancing—no shooting," a second all-talking "singing picture" featuring the Fordney Jubilee Singers performing spirituals such as "Swing Low, Sweet Chariot," and "an ending number for the children (comedy)."[64]

The routes that Norman established took him through Florida and into the neighboring states. "I have all I can take care of here in Florida," he wrote a potential client, "but I never lose the opportunity to spread out and develop other territory."[65] On one tour in the late summer and fall of 1932, for example, he played grade schools, high schools, and training schools in Belmont, Farmville, Greenville, Hickory, Kannapolis, Lincolnton, Salisbury, Statesville, and Zebulon, North Carolina, and then another string of schools, churches, seminaries, and AME (African Methodist Episcopal) chapels in Adel, Albany, Bainbridge, Camilla, Cordele, Fort Valley, Madison, McRae, Milledgeville, Sylvester, Thomasville, Tifton, Valdosta, Vidalia, Waycross, and Winder, Georgia. His "program of sound pictures" typically included a double or even a triple feature, with *The Flying Ace* or *Black Gold* (using nonsynchronous sound recordings) as the main billing and shorter films such as *School Day Frolics,* a light song-and-dance entertainment, or *Crazy Cat* rounding out the program—although at some of the churches he substituted the religious picture *As We Forgive* for *Frolics* and *Cat.* On a good night, Norman netted $30.49 (at the Colored School in Farmville); on a poor night, as little as $4.64 (at St. Paul AME in Vidalia and again at the Magnolia Grammar School in Valdosta). Most nights, the net was somewhere in between—still a meager return for a filmmaker whose pictures had grossed hundreds of dollars per night only a few years earlier.[66]

The road work was onerous and repetitive. On a route through Louisiana during the fall of the next year, Norman played mostly AME churches and religious halls in Crowley, Franklin, Jeanerette, Jennings, Lafayette, Morgan City, and New Iberia. His program included *The Flying Ace* and *As*

We Forgive; but his receipts were even more modest than on earlier road-shows. A spring tour through Florida's AME churches in Apalachicola, Blountstown, DeFuniak Springs, Monticello, and River Junction proved no more profitable, although it had the distinct advantage of keeping Norman a little closer to home.

It was around this time that Norman added a new element to some of his roadshows: in addition to his own pictures, he began screening a few of Oscar Micheaux's features. Micheaux had long been one of Norman's biggest competitors in the race film industry, and there was a fierce, if for the most part friendly, rivalry between the two men. Micheaux was the more formidable figure, in large part because he was the more prolific: he began film production in 1918 and ultimately made over forty films over the course of his three-decade-long career.

Throughout the 1920s, while Norman was still involved in race film production, exhibitors would routinely pit the two filmmakers against each other in an attempt to get reduced rental fees for their pictures. In booking *Regeneration*, for example, Molton Gray, manager of the Palace Theater in Ensley, Alabama, offered Norman $30, a sum considerably less than what Norman had originally quoted. But Gray countered that his theater had never paid more than $25 for a colored picture and, in fact, had just played a Micheaux feature that week at that price.[67] Sometimes Norman would lose bookings to Micheaux, as happened with C. A. Sappal, manager of the Central Theatre, Tampa, Florida, who could not accept an offer from Norman because he had already promised the date to Micheaux's *Deceit*, or again, with several exhibitors whom Norman was trying to line up for a planned route through Virginia.[68] As Norman wrote to D. Ireland Thomas: "The balance of the places I visited [in Virginia] were all booked up by a lot of Michaux pictures and of course didn't give me much encouragement."[69]

Naturally, when Norman bested Micheaux, he gloated a little, as any rival would. Writing to Albert A. Fish of Superior Art Motion Pictures (who had sworn to "have nothing to do with Micheaux or any thing connected to him"), Norman bragged that he had recently played the Koppin Theatre in Detroit, Michigan: "Secured $500. for a week's run on Regeneration. Transaction was okay. This information is strictly confidential. Michaux had been receiving $450. for his pictures for each one."[70] Later, when

Micheaux's *Millionaire* did not fare well in Florida, Norman was quick to advise William George that his *Black Gold* and *Flying Ace* had been doing fine.[71] And when Norman received a first-run showing in one of the largest movie houses in Washington, D.C., he immediately drew a comparison to Micheaux, who had not been able to book his pictures on a first run in Washington for two years.[72]

Yet even then the relationship between Norman and Micheaux was oddly symbiotic: since the two competed for business in the same limited market of race theaters, the success of Micheaux's pictures often depended upon—or adversely affected—the gross of Norman's.[73] For instance, in a letter chronicling the box office returns on one of his routes, Norman's road man Regan noted that "Mechaux's 'SPIDER WEB' is responcible for the poor business in Orange and here [in Hattiesburg, Mississippi]. Orange played 'SPIDER WEB' to very good business on the Monday just before I played on Thursday," leaving no opportunity for profit.[74] And, in turn, Norman was quick to take credit for the strong showing of some of Micheaux's pictures. As he claimed to M. C. Maxwell: "Michaux has been having some trouble financing his pictures, but he has just completed a vigorous booking campaign with good results, he says, because I had left the bars down with Regeneration and he followed behind it and had no trouble getting bookings."[75]

Both men, moreover, were keenly aware of each other's film projects. At times, during booking tours or roadshows, their paths would cross; but more often they kept abreast of new developments by way of reports from the exhibitors they shared.[76] In his only surviving letter to Norman, Micheaux mentioned, with deliberate casualness, that he had heard about Norman's latest film *The Flying Ace* and was anxious to learn more about it. Apparently Norman followed Micheaux's activities just as closely. In a letter to William George, he asked: "I understand Michaux has a new talkie? Wonder how he is making out with it?"[77] That new talkie turned out to be *The Exile* (1931), the first black-produced sound picture, now recognized as a milestone in American film history. A remake of Micheaux's first feature *The Homesteader* (1919), it chronicled the adventures of Jean Baptiste, a "decent colored man" of high moral values who tries to realize his ambition as a self-sufficient landowner on the South Dakota plains and to find love. And—like the features that Norman and the Johnson Brothers produced—it was a story of racial pride and uplift.

Yet Micheaux's successful transition from silent to sound pictures was no doubt a sensitive, even painful, issue for Norman, whose own lack of capital, compounded by the failure of his Camera-Phone company, prevented him from producing talking features, as he had once hoped. Nevertheless, by the early 1930s, mainly in Florida, Norman began distributing and roadshowing *The Exile* along with some of his own films; and ultimately he roadshowed other Micheaux pictures, including *The Girl From Chicago* (1931), a sound reworking of Micheaux's earlier silent picture *The Spider's Web*, about the unfortunate repercussions of gambling and policy-playing. Bookings for the Micheaux films came not only from small theaters but also from schools—a curious venue, perhaps, given the sensational nature of some of the films' themes and characters. But the films were such a draw that Norman was able to book them at a premium. Contracts show that Norman usually received a 60–40 or even 75–25 split with exhibitors rather than the usual 50–50 arrangement on the other pictures that he handled.

By 1936, Norman found an even more lucrative and exciting opportunity: distributing films featuring black fighter and knockout puncher Joe Louis. Born in 1914, Louis had demonstrated his exceptional skills as an amateur fighter and a Golden Gloves titleholder before turning professional in 1934. Over the next few years, he defeated six heavyweight champions, beginning with Primo Carnera; and in 1937, he beat "Cinderella Man" James J. Braddock to become the heavyweight champion himself, a title that, in an unprecedented tenure, he held until 1949. One of his best known fights, and his first loss as a professional, was in 1936 against the German champion Max Schmeling. But two years later, in a highly publicized rematch that was billed by the media as a battle between American Democracy and Nazism, Louis knocked out Schmeling in the first round. Louis later enlisted in the Army and served in a segregated unit. Although he made millions of dollars over the course of his long career, he gave much of his wealth away; and in his final years he was forced to return to the ring, first as a boxer and later as a wrestler, in order to pay off his debts. But at the height of his career, Louis—"The Brown Bomber"—was unparalleled;

a source of pride and inspiration, he became a hero to black Americans and a role model for black youth.

While boxing as a sport was never officially segregated, some white Americans of that era were reluctant to celebrate a black champion, especially in the wake of the often outrageous conduct of former champion Jack Johnson, whom they could not wait to see dethroned by a "Great White Hope." Accordingly, at first, white theaters would not run films of Louis's fights. But black audiences were eager to witness Louis's triumphs; and that provided distributors like Norman, who roadshowed the films at black theaters and in black schools, churches, and auditoriums, a singular chance to give those moviegoers what they wanted. As Norman explained to one exhibitor, U. P. Bronson in DeLand, Florida, "We have presented the Joe Louis films in the Schools with great success—as the white theatres would not run him due to his success as a Negro Fighter."[78]

One of the most popular Louis films was *Roar of the Crowd*. Norman described its appeal in a letter he wrote to his exhibitors:

ROAR OF THE CROWD with Joe Louis will make you money. In ROAR OF THE CROWD you see Joe Louis literally grow from the $50. a year fighter to the Colored Man who brought back the Million Dollar Gate to Fightdom. The transformation of this savior of Boxing Sport is startling. You see his mistakes and as time marches on you see him correct them, ever adding new laurels and prestige to his race. Only Joe Louis can pack a thrill a minute to Every Colored Man, Woman, and Child. The great weekly Negro Papers that have a wide circulation in your territory dare not publish an issue without news of Joe Louis. Books have been written about him, Liberty, Collier's and Saturday Evening Post circulating millions, all carry articles about him. He has appeared in as much footage of film as some of the best stars.

Norman underscored that "Louis Now Stands At The Door Of His Goal" to be the best fighter ever. And he urged exhibitors to satisfy the "Tremendous Undercurrent of Interest" in Louis while it was still at its height by booking this "great panorama" of Louis's ability.[79] The terms were the usual ones: Norman would furnish the whole show, including window cards and heralds, for 50 percent of the gross.

The Louis films, in fact, became a vital part of the complete show packages that Norman organized for road touring and from which his exhibitors could choose. From the late 1930s into the early 1940s, scores of high school principals, ministers, and black civic groups throughout the South booked *Roar of the Crowd* and other Joe Louis shows such as the all-fight combination of attractions that included the Louis–Pastor, Louis–Galento, Louis–Schmeling, and Louis–Farr fights.

Among the other complete shows that Norman promoted and exhorted as suitable for black or white audiences were *Crime Does Not Pay*, "the U.S. Government educational picture based on John Dillinger" (which also included a "western comedy and either Joe Louis–Galento or Louis–Pastor late fight"); *Explorers of the World*, an "educational thriller 2 hours long [along] with any Joe Louis fight and comedy"; and a two-hour entertainment "for young and old" that comprised *Happy Landing*, a story of the U.S. Coast Guard, *Main Street Follies*, a musical, a comedy to be determined, and the "Late Louis–Schmeling Fight in which Louis knocks him out."[80] Especially popular with audiences was Micheaux's *The Girl from Chicago*, which Norman billed as a semi-educational picture suitable for students because, despite its racy musical numbers, it had an all-colored cast and its story was based on the exposé of an urban Bolita [Numbers Game].[81] (A full night's entertainment sometimes included a rather bizarre combination of pictures such as "Mickey Mouse, Musical and Girl from Chicago.")[82] All were fine programs, Norman boasted, and all "have met with a great reception in the schools."[83]

As always, he extolled the quality and efficiency of his shows, writing, "We have two fireproof machines that give professional results comparable to the finest theatres. We furnish ample advertising, tickets and present the show at our expense. Your expense is about 20 cts., worth of electricity."[84] And he devised various promotional gimmicks to boost attendance, including free admissions to students or church members who sold large numbers of advance tickets to the shows.

Although Norman spent much of his time throughout the 1930s and into the early 1940s roadshowing films, he continued to employ his studio in Jacksonville for other commercial projects. No longer actively engaged in feature film production, he returned to industrial filmmaking, completing a series of promotional pieces for the Pure Oil Company; and he also shot some commercial advertising for local businesses. But he was not the only one in the family to use the facilities. For almost twenty years, until the 1950s, his wife Gloria operated a dance studio, originally on the second floor of the main production and film processing building and later—when the noise from the ballet, tapping, and acrobatics grew too distracting for Norman—in the nearby set building. The dance studio became a Jacksonville institution in its own right, with the flame-red-haired Gloria sometimes picking up and dropping off her students in a Hudson Terraplane automobile (one of the matched pair that the Normans owned) that had been converted into a mini-limousine outfitted with wooden benches.[85]

By the mid-1940s, Norman was no longer showing pictures on the road; but he found yet another way to keep his hand in the business of film distribution and exhibition. A lease signed in August 1945 by Norman, representing "Chas. K. Ellis [Norman's former road man] and R. E. Norman of Ace Amusements of Arlington, Florida," indicates that he contracted with the Trustees of the Odd Fellows for the use of their Odd Fellows Hall in Crescent City, Florida, as a "Moving Picture Theatre."[86] According to the agreement, Norman rented the ground floor of the hall "for at least two nights use each week or as many nights as the lessee shall need each week," while on the nights that he was not showing motion pictures, the Trustees reserved the right to use the hall for "Vaudeville, Prize Fights, Dances, Socials and other gatherings, provided no motion pictures are shown." For each night's rental, Norman paid a $1.75 fee.

By February 1946, Norman had taken out a State and County Occupational License to operate his own motion picture house—the Ace Theatre, in Apopka, Florida. That little theater, he wrote friends, kept him very busy. Over the next few years, he updated it by painting the building and installing a new concrete floor, new seats, and a new marquee—all improvements that helped business.[87] Norman soon acquired a second theater, the Famous Theatre (For Colored) in Winter Park, Florida. Although he tried to bring in as many black-oriented pictures as he could to the Famous—a sample order for film purchases in early 1952 included *Lazy Rhythms,* featuring the Mills Brothers, *Sepia Swing,* starring Cab Calloway, and *Harlem Syncopation,* with the Nat King Cole Trio—the majority of films that Norman screened were the typical popular Hollywood fare of the day. In January 1951, for example, the monthly program included a sports biography (fighter Joe Louis in *Spirit of Youth*), a jungle movie (*Tarzan and the Slave Girl*), a comedy (*Blondie's Anniversary*), an "outdoor adventure" (*Call of the Forest*), two mysteries (*A Dangerous Profession, Blonde for a Day*), and a host of Westerns (*Range Law, Return of the Badmen, Oklahoma Badlands, North from the Lone Star, Masked Raiders, Prairie Bad Men, The Big Steal, Outcasts of the Trail, Hands Across the Rockies, Song of Old Wyoming,* and *Hopalong Returns*). The schedule for May similarly mixed popular genre films, from literary adaptations (*The Grapes of Wrath*) to traditional Westerns (*Swamp Water, Denver Kid, Jesse James, North of the Border, Kiss of Death, Tucson Raiders*), from black musicals (*Harlem Follies, Stormy Weather*) to white screwball comedies (*His Gal Friday*).

A good evening at the Famous brought in $100 or more (including concession sales of popcorn and candy); a poor one, $20 or less. Black-interest pictures usually did strong business: *Harlem Follies,* for example, earned $118.02 at the box office alone (although, since the film was part of a roadshow, Norman had to split the net). *Stormy Weather,* featuring black star Lena Horne, earned $51.59; *Pinky,* a familiar "passing-for-white" story that starred Ethel Waters, netted $51.80. But action Westerns such as *Texas Panhandle* (which netted $59.14) often fared just as well.

To enhance business, as he had done with the ballyhos for the pictures he produced and distributed, Norman devised various ways to attract mov-iegoers to the theaters he managed. One popular promotional gimmick was a "FREE PASS—GOOD ANYTIME IF TAX PAID"; another was a "buddy ticket" that admitted a second admission free when accompanied by one paid adult admission. On special occasions, Norman would of-fer double features or show serials along with the title picture. And using another shrewd marketing technique, he would print and distribute flyers that moviegoers could post in their homes for easy reference. Those fly-ers not only advertised all of the programs for the month ahead but also exhorted patrons to "Attend the Church of Your Choice Every Sunday" or to "GO TO CHURCH . . . and thank God you are free to go to church." Apparently, the gimmicks and promotions were effective in generating interest and boosting attendance. After visiting Florida in the summer of 1951, one of Norman's relatives wrote to say that she was delighted by "the buisness increase" for Richard and by the fact that his theaters were "so profitable"—though, she added, "through family wide fame its no more than I expected."[88]

After a few years, just as they had done with the Ace Theatre, Norman and his wife refurbished both the interior and the exterior of the Famous. Adding "New" to the theater's name, they marked the occasion with a Grand Opening. Norman described the process in detail to his friend Woody. In addition to "working over" much of the movie equipment, including an amplifier that had gotten damp and was malfunctioning, and replacing the emergency lighting battery,

> Gloria and I spent about a month of extra time getting things back into shape [before the official reopening in October]. We had to go all over the seats—and the bottom of the seat stanchions where they fasten into the concrete floor were badly rusted—tightened all I could and she wire brushed them off [and] painted the bottom of the stanchion with rust coat paint to stop that. Hevent been able to get around to put new leather on seat bottoms of many that are torn. I painted the front white and took down the sign and painted it—as well as all the wood on the marquee. Also touched up the poster frames with red and light green paint.

The upshot was a strong opening night "on a Sunday—4 to 11 with a gross of $77. and $13. candy sales with a 4 hour show that would knock your eyes out. Double feature, shorts consisting of sport, 2 reel comedy, Serial and 6 acts of new vaudeville Colored on the screen." Afterward, Norman continued to run double programs, excellent shows about three-and-a-half hours long. But he expressed concern to Woody about some of the clientele, noting that "all the good negros got weaned away from the show while it was closed." To lure customers back to the theater, he initiated a family matinee from three to six on Saturday, at a reduced rate of 15¢ for adults and 9¢ for children, down from the usual 30–40¢ and 14–15¢ admissions, respectively.[89] And he also scheduled an exciting lineup of popular films that he thought would attract new customers as well.

By 1953, according to another letter that Norman wrote to Woody, he was still operating the Famous Theatre, but only on Saturdays (for matinees) and Sundays. "I changed Sunday price to a straight 35¢ for all—and the same bunch of noisy kids come anyway and pay the 35¢ which leaves them just that much less to eat up in Candy. Use to charge them 14¢ but that

35¢ has cut out the noise—they are scared I will up it to 50¢ Sat. Mat. They get in for 9[¢] and 15¢. My trouble now is getting the bunch to mix—as on Sundays only the roughnecks come and since I do not run on Mondays— the Church folks do not come." (Mondays were one of his show days at the Ace in Apopka: he could not afford to "kick it off" because "it is too good there and a sure thing.") Overall, however, attendance at both theaters had been affected by the recent flu epidemic in Florida, which forced authorities to close the schools in some of the counties and had cut movie business in half: people would not go to the show or send their children for fear that they would contract it.[90]

It is not clear how many more years Norman operated the theaters or what remaining ties, apart from his Norman Studios, he may have had to the film industry. But the final years of the 1950s were not easy ones for him: he grew increasingly ill and died, of cancer, in Jacksonville on November 7, 1960. His death brought to a close a remarkable but often underappreciated career.

Only lately have Norman's achievements begun to be recognized and celebrated. An entrepreneur and inventor of products from Passi-Kola to Camera-Phone sound equipment, a businessman who for more than two decades distributed largely black- but also white-cast films, an independent roving "home talent" filmmaker who established his own laboratory for developing his prints, a pioneering producer of high-quality feature-length race pictures that challenged longstanding racial stereotypes, the first and only race filmmaker to own his own studio—Richard E. Norman Jr. was an extraordinary and influential figure in the movie industry. The successes and the frustrations of his long and distinguished career offer a singular portrait of a fascinating era in American film history—and of a man who, alongside his better-known contemporaries Oscar Micheaux and Noble and George Johnson, helped to define early race filmmaking.

Afterword

IN 1976, a decade and a half after Richard E. Norman's death, his wife, Gloria Norman, auctioned off most of the contents of the former Norman Studios in Jacksonville, Florida, and sold the property to Hugh Smith and James E. Holland. Over the next few years, the five buildings on the premises went unused and fell into disrepair.

In 1996, the structure that had served as Norman's set building was purchased from Hugh Smith by the Circle of Faith Ministries, a small local church founded by Johnny Wells and Joseph I. McRoy Sr. The church restored the building, held regular services there, and, as the predominantly black congregation grew, expanded by the purchase of additional land.

In 2002, led by members of the civic organization Old Arlington, Inc., preservationists realized the historical value of the former studio property and convinced Jacksonville officials to purchase the remaining four buildings, which were acquired for $260,000. "We all knew the Norman studios were important," recalled Ann Burt, the former president of Old Arlington, Inc., who spearheaded the preservation effort. "The truth is the City of Jacksonville didn't know it."[1] Through Burt's intercession, the National Trust for Historic Preservation was apprised of, and soon endorsed, the restoration proposal. It deemed the Norman Studios—the only remaining silent film studio complex and thus a rare remnant of American cinema history—to be "of national significance."[2] A separate but related nonprofit group, the Norman Studios Silent Film Museum, was formed a few years later for the sole purpose of restoring and reopening the premises and preserving the Norman legacy.

In the decade since then, a massive resurrection has begun. External renovations and structural repairs to the four original studio buildings were completed in 2007, and the next phase of the project will involve a renovation of the interiors. Plans are also in place to purchase the fifth building from its owners, the Circle of Faith Ministries, which has now outgrown the facility. The hope is to develop a museum, film center, and production facility that will honor Norman's achievements and recognize the accomplishments of other early silent filmmakers who produced their movies during Florida's golden age of filmmaking.[3] "A whole new generation of young filmmakers stands to benefit from the efforts of the Norman Studios Silent Film Museum," Captain Richard E. Norman observed. "My father would be proud."[4]

The Museum's ambitious plans include workshops, field trips, film screenings, and even a proposal for a summer camp for at-risk youngsters, who would come on scholarship to learn about the film industry. As Devan Stuart, Chair of the Museum's Board of Directors, has noted, "If all goes as planned, it's going to be an epic comeback" for the studio.[5] Indeed, Richard E. Norman himself could not have scripted a better or more exciting ending.

APPENDIX 1

SHOOTING SCRIPT: *THE GREEN-EYED MONSTER*

THE ORIGINAL shooting script of the 1919 version of *The Green-Eyed Monster*—preserved in the Black Film Center/Archive at Indiana University in Bloomington, Indiana—had a double plot. The main plot featured the courtship of Helen Powers, daughter of Railroad Superintendent Bernard Powers, and Jack Manning, a young engineer who must win the great mail race in order to earn Helen's father's approval for their marriage. A secondary comic plot involved Quintus Weefalls and the two marriage-hungry women who seek his attention. The film was originally released in eight reels. But after audience response was confused and unenthusiastic, Norman cut the comic subplot and released the footage as a separate film, a short comedy he titled *The Love Bug*. Both the recut version of *The Green-Eyed Monster* (1920), edited down to five reels, and the two-reel *The Love Bug* (1920) proved to be popular with black filmgoers; and Norman continued to show and distribute both films for the next decade.

The script has been reproduced with the original wording, spelling, and punctuation (even when incorrect); inconsistencies in numbering of the scenes and variant spellings have also been preserved. Norman's annotations are indicated in italics. *Reproduced by permission of Captain Richard E. Norman and the Black Film Center/Archive, Indiana University, Bloomington, Indiana.*

MAIN TITLE
THE GREEN EYED MONSTER
Part 1
Produced by
Norman Film Mfg. Co.
Chicago.

SUB TITLE

This story occurs before the nation had assumed chaperonage over the arteries of travel and transportation, when railroads were on a competitive basis for the Government Fast Rail Contract.

SUB TITLE

E. N. Armstrong, financial banker of the rich and renowned, the proud and powerful, the famous and farflung M. N. & Q. Railroad,—[*played by*] *S. D. McGILL*

SCENE NO. 1

Armstrong is seated in his office before a flat topped desk looking over some plans.

SUB TITLE

Henry High, the traffic manager, who had outwitted rivals on other lines and caused the annual high peaks of freight and passenger carrying to grow higher,—[*played by*] *J. A. SIMMS*

SCENE NO. 2

High is standing before Armstrong's desk. He is explaining details of the plans on the desk and says,—

SUB TITLE

"Traffic has reached such magnitude that a double track is needed on our Chicago branch."

SUB TITLE

J. Frank Keeley, the advertising director, whose clever compositions had standardized its slogan and caused the road to be known everywhere,— [*played by*] *IRA P. DAVIS*

SCENE NO. 3

Keeley is introduced seated at Armstrong's desk. He is facing him and High is standing, Keeley says,—

SUB TITLE

"In spite of all my tall advertising assertions, the M. N. & Q. is losing prestige since we lost the government fast mail contract to the T. P. & W."

SCENE NO. 4

Close-up of High. He is speaking to Armstrong and Keeley, he says,—

SUB TITLE

"With double trackage to Chicago, we can regain the fast mail contract."

SCENE NO. 5

Close-up of Armstrong, he says,—

SUB TITLE

"I will place the plans in the hands of our contractor for immediate action."

SCENE NO. 6

Long shot of the three characters. Armstrong finishes making his statement. Fade.

SUB TITLE

Bernard Powers, Sup't of the M. N. & Q., whose loyalty and unflagging devotion in his unparaleled career of service and fidelity to duty has earned him the sobriquet of "Old Faithful"—[*played by*] *DR. R. L. BROWN JR.*

SCENE NO. 7

Powers in the railroad yards. Close-up of him reading a message—fade to railroad man standing besides him. He directs the disposal of the message.

SUB TITLE

Helen Powers, his daughter,—[*played by*] *LOUISE DUNBAR*

SCENE NO. 8

Helen is introduced coming out of the Power's home. She gets in auto and drives away.

SUB TITLE

James K. Hilton, a railroad contractor and very much smitten with Helen,— [*played by*] *BUDDY AUSTIN*

SCENE NO. 9

Hilton is pointing out details on some plans.

SUB TITLE

Planning the new double track system to Chicago.

SCENE NO. 10

Powers and Hilton are looking over the plans and locations for the new tracks.

SCENE NO. 11

Helen drives up to the railroad yards in her auto, sees her father and Hilton— exits.

SCENE NO. 12

Powers and Hilton looking over plans. Enter Helen full of vivacity. Hilton takes off his hat and greets her. Powers puts his arm around her and she asks what they are doing etc.

SUB TITLE

Jack Manning, crack engineer on the Cannon Ball Limited,—[*played by*] *EARL CUMBO*

SCENE NO. 13

Manning descends steps of engine cab with oil can in his hand—looks up, sees Powers, Helen and Hilton.

SCENE NO. 14

Powers, Helen and Hilton look Manning's way.

SCENE NO. 15

Manning doffs his hat to Powers.

SCENE NO. 16

Powers and Hilton take off their hats.

SCENE NO. 17

Manning puts on his hat and exits.

SCENE NO. 18

Close-up of Powers and Hilton. Hilton asks Powers who Manning is.

SUB TITLE

Who is he, Father? [*added to the TS. by hand*]

SUB TITLE

Quintus Weefalls—timid, clumsy at anything but handling the shovel on the Cannon Ball Limited,—[*played by*] *ROBERT STEWART*

SCENE NO. 19

Quintus is introduced filling the fire box of an engine with a shovel full of coal.

SCENE NO. 20

Manning oiling his engine.

SCENE NO. 21

Quintus descends steps of engine cab and exits.

SCENE NO. 22

Manning oiling engine. Enter Quintus. Manning halts him with a greeting and tells him—

"We are running low on sand. Take on a few buckets."

SCENE NO. 23

Quintus exits to follow out Mannings orders.

SCENE NO. 24

Powers, Hilton and Helen. Powers and Hilton interested in the plans. Helen is interested in everything but them.

SCENE NO. 25

Close-up of Helen. She looks slowly and covetly around at Manning.

SCENE NO. 26

Close-up of Manning oiling his engine—he looks slyly up and catches Helen looking at him.

SCENE NO. 27

Close-up of Helen—she snubbs Manning.

SCENE NO. 28

Manning is standing in foolish attitude with oil can in his hand unconsciously pouring oil in his other hand.

SCENE NO. 29

Close-up of oil can running down Mannings fingers.

SCENE NO. 30

Back to full view of Manning's figure. He realizes with a start what he is doing and wipes his hand on his overalls.

SCENE NO. 31

Helen, unknown to Manning is quietly amused at this incident.

SUB TITLE

Quintus has a strong back, but a timid heart when it comes to the fair sex.

SCENE NO. 32

Quintus is on top of engine boiler pouring sand in the sand done—he looks up and sees Helen.

SCENE NO. 33

Close-up of Helen to establish what Quintus is looking at.

SCENE NO. 34

Back to Quintus still pouring sand. He says—

SUB TITLE

"My! She sho am purty."

SCENE NO. 35

Back to scene of Quintus still pouring sand. Long shot showing Manning standing under sand dome still wiping oil from his hands—Quintus in his absent way pours the balance of the sand on Manning while looking at Helen. Manning splutters and berates Quintus—throwing his oil can at him—Quintus retreats in haste.

SCENE NO. 36

Back to Powers, Hilton and Helen. Powers and Hilton are unconscious of everything but the business in hand. Helen is amused at Manning. They exit, powers walking out with his arm round his daughter.

SCENE NO. 37

Exterior railroad offices. Enter Powers, Hilton and Helen. They pause at door. Powers tells Hilton—pointing at plans which Hilton puts in his pocket—

SUB TITLE

"Work must commence immediately and the track rushed through in time for the Mail Race."

SCENE NO. 38

Helen tells her father good-bye and exits with Hilton, Powers goes in railroad building.

SCENE NO. 39

Hilton and Helen enters her auto and drive off.

SCENE NO. 40

Hilton and Helen riding on shaded road.

SUB TITLE

Engine Trouble. [*written in by hand*]

SCENE NO. 41

Hilton and Helen riding on country looking road—the car slows down—stops—chauffeur tries to shift gears—gets out—and examines engine. Hilton gets out and asks if he can help—Helen gets out also. Chauffeur says—its a broken connection. Helen admires the scenery and trips off to gather some wild flowers—Hilton follows her.

SCENE NO. 42

Helen enters scene with flowers. Hilton enters and she puts flower in his button hole. They seat themselves on a fallen log.

SUB TITLE

The proposal.

SCENE NO. 43

Hilton proposes to Helen. She gets to her feet and he follows suit—she says—

SUB TITLE

"No Jim—I don't love you."

SCENE NO. 44

Hilton registers disappointment.

SCENE NO. 45

The chauffeur has just finished making repairs on the car. Enter Hilton and Helen and the car drives off—fade.

SUB TITLE

String Bean Oldfield was a "speed maniac" besides being an expert at "clickin' golf"—

SCENE NO. 46

String Bean dashes up to curb in cut down racer—takes off his goggles and gets out of car—enter cop—who says to String Bean—

SUB TITLE

"String Bean, the next time I see you streaking down "Dirty Six," I'll arrest you for speeding."

SCENE NO. 47

String Bean assured cop he will be good. Cop exits—and String Bean exits.

SCENE NO. 48

Delapidated building. Enter man leading goat—enter String Bean—who greets him—

SUB TITLE

"Cinnamon, you measley dog-robber, how is you?" [*SLIM JONES, written in by hand*]

SCENE NO. 49

Cinnamon while shaking hands with String Bean, says—

SUB TITLE

"Poo'ly in de flesh but my spirit's rollin' high."

SCENE NO. 50

String Bean says—

SUB TITLE

"How come?"

SCENE NO. 51

Cinnamon, pointing at the goat, says—

SUB TITLE

"Boy, ever since Ise at de other end of the rope what's round Lily's neck me an' Lady Luck's been married."

SCENE NO. 52

String Bean says—

SUB TITLE

"Sho' nuff! Dat goat brung you luck?"

SCENE NO. 53

Cinnamon says—

SUB TITLE

"I'se made mos' a million dollahs since I had dis mascot Lilly."

SCENE NO. 54

String bean says—

SUB TITLE

"How much you take to divorce yo'self from Lily an' marrify me to Lady Luck?"

SCENE NO. 55

Cinnamon says—

SUB TITLE

"Two dollahs am cheap fo' dis mascot."

SCENE NO. 56

String bean pays over the two dollars and exits with the goat—Cinnamon laughs and intimates that String Bean is stung.

SCENE NO. 57

String Bean meets Mustard Prophet, another cube artist, who asks him what he is doing with the goat, String Bean says—

SUB TITLE

"I'se marrified to Lady Luck wid dat mascot."

SCENE NO. 58

Mustard Prophet looks the goat over and laughs—and says—

SUB TITLE

"String Bean, I got some divorcin' dice. Does you crave action?"

SCENE NO. 59

String Bean reaches down in his sock and fishes up a pair of dice and says—

"Don't start sarcastin' me. Ah cleans you beggin' in fo' passes."

SCENE NO. 60

String Bean rattles his dice and looks around on a crowd of lazy onlookers and says—

SUB TITLE

"All ah says, does anybody crave a ride to the poo' house? Follow me." ["*Follow me*" *has been written in by hand.*]

SCENE NO. 61

The crowd signify that they are willing to take a ride, and String Bean says—

SUB TITLE

"Follow yo' shepherd an' prepar' to be shorn of yo' wool."

SCENE NO. 62

The crowd straggle after String Bean, who leads them behind a delaptdated building.

SCENE NO. 63

Close-up of String Bean talking to the goat, he says—

SUB TITLE

"Lily," "stan' by me! Ah aims to collect heavy wid dese li'l gallopers."

SCENE NO. 64

Close-up of Cinnamon—he says—

SUB TITLE

"Dat's the onluckiest goat what ever was. Here's whar I collect heavy."

SCENE NO. 65

String Bean fishes in his pocket for a dollar and tells them all to shower down their money—he makes a pass—says—

SUB TITLE

"Readin' class, read 'em. They says seven."

SCENE NO. 66

String Bean makes another pass—says—

SUB TITLE

"~~Read 'em an' weep.~~" "Whuf! Ah heads for seven, but Ah swerves to eight. Dice, Ah marks yo' duty."

SCENE NO. 67

Close-up of dice—they show eight.

SCENE NO. 68
Close-up of String Bean—says—

SUB TITLE
"Ise a eighter f'm Decatur."

SCENE NO. 69
String Bean collects—and says to other player—

SUB TITLE
"Hogface, shower down yo' money."

SCENE NO. 70
Hogface does—String Bean makes another pass—says—

SUB TITLE
"Whang—she reads eleven! Hogface, feel the knife."

SCENE NO. 71
String Bean makes a pass—another player—Cinamon says—

SUB TITLE
"Slow death."

SCENE NO. 72
String Bean caresses goat and makes pass—says—

SUB TITLE
"Nine Ah craves! Bones, git right! Come great deliverer!"

SCENE NO. 73
String Bean throws seven—Cinnamon says—

SUB TITLE
"String Bean, you is dead. Yo' tombstone reads seven. Hand me 'em bones."

SCENE NO. 74
Close-up view of goat eating money out of String Beans hat which is by his side and full of money.

SCENE NO. 75
Cinnamon makes a pass—says—

SUB TITLE
"Here's whar Ah starts! Reads five! Ah's alive! Wham!"

SCENE NO. 76
Cinnamon makes another pass—looks surprised—says—

SUB TITLE
"Reads seven! Ah views the remains!"

SCENE NO. 77

String Bean says—

SUB TITLE

"You sure slings painful bones, ~~but you pains yo'self. Han' dem babies to Pink Eye~~.

SCENE NO. 78

Pink Eye warms the bones for action—String Bean says—

SUB TITLE

"Lady Luck, at yo' feet, at yo' feet!"

SCENE NO. 79

String Bean looks around to caress his goat and sees goat with remains of a one dollar bill sticking out of his mouth—looks down and discovers that his money is gone. Gives cry of surprise which attracts the attention of the other players—he staggers to his feet—the players ask him where he is going—he says—

SUB TITLE

"Ah aims to give dis goat exercise to digest dat spondulix."

SCENE NO. 80

String Bean exits with goat.

SCENE NO. 81

String Bean ties goat to the back of his racer—gets in and starts away in the car—the crap players come in scene and laugh.

SCENE NO. 82

View of car down the road at swift speed with goat hitting the high spots.

SCENE NO. 83

Cop sees this and chases after him.

SCENE NO. 84

View of Helen and Hilton in automobile driving slowly down road.

SCENE NO. 85

Jack Manning is lighting cigarette and standing by lamp post on street corner.

SUB TITLE

"In the loom of destiny, woven by fate."

SCENE NO. 86

Helen and Hilton riding in car.

SCENE NO. 87

String Bean going madly down the road in his car, the string pops and the goat goes head-over-heels.

SCENE NO. 88

String Beans car rounds corner and runs head-on into the car in which Hilton and Helen is riding.

SCENE NO. 89

Manning sees collision and rushes from scene.

SCENE NO. 90

Helen's car is in flames. She is unconscious and Hilton is struggling to free her from the car—Manning rushes in and resecues her.

SCENE NO. 91

String Bean was none the less worse off for the accident. He is gracefully draped over a fence—dazed—when the cop comes in and jerks him to his feet—String bean bats his eyes and says—

SUB TITLE

"Whar is I?"

SCENE NO. 92

String Bean still dazed—his hand gropes around and comes in contact with the cop's star—he starts and comes out of his daze—says—

SUB TITLE

"Wuz hard luck a dewdrop, I mus' be a lake."

SCENE NO. 93

Cop drags String Bean from scene.

SCENE NO. 94

Helen is placed on a cot in an ambulance by Manning.

SCENE NO. 95

Close-up of Helen on cot. She has fainted. She regains consciousness and recognizes her resecuer—Manning.

SCENE NO. 96

Close-up of Hilton registering anger and jealousy.

SCENE NO. 97

The cot is placed in the ambulance and Manning gets in with it—the ambulance drives off.

SCENE NO. 98

Hilton slams his battered hat on his head and walks disgustedly away—fade.

SCENE NO. 99

Fade in view of satan—action fade out.

SUB TITLE

Skeeter Butts, proprietor of the "Shin Bone Eating House." Among the colored folks he is Sir Oracle. He was matrimonial adjuster in courtship, marriage, and divorce; ~~he was confidential adviser at baptisms and funerals;~~ his expert advice was sought in all matters, ~~pertaining to lodge and church and social functions,~~—[*played by*] *BILLY MILLS*

SCENE NO. 100

Skeeter is seated outside the Shin Bone Eating House reading a paper upside down.

SUB TITLE

Gizzard Buster, a New Orleans brunet barely able to eat several times a day when he was not playing a guitar.

SCENE NO. 101

Gizzard Buster is playing his guitar and singing.

SCENE NO. 102

Enter Quintus Weefalls. He greets Skeeter and sets down—getting confidential with Skeeter—says—

SUB TITLE

"Skeeter, I wants to mahry and sottle down."

SCENE NO. 103

Skeeter looks surprised and then says—

SUB TITLE

"Dis is whar you gits exputt advices. I done courted 'bout a millyum womens my own self, an' I knows all de funny curves dey tries on."

SCENE NO. 104

Quintus asks him—

SUB TITLE

"Does yo' know of a hard workin' black gal wid teeth like milk an' dahk eyes wid blue in 'em what aims to marrify?"

SCENE NO. 105

Skeeter thinks a minute—says—

SUB TITLE

"I knows of two soch womens hard to chose betwix."

SCENE NO. 106

Quintus says in alarm—

SUB TITLE

"Ah aint goin' to commit bigatry."

SCENE NO. 107

Skeeter thinks a minute—scratches his head and says—

SUB TITLE

"You writes a letter to both of 'em an' puts in you hat an' draws one out an' sends it."

SCENE NO. 108

Quintus agrees to this—Gizzard Buster is sent for paper and ink—Quintus gets down on the bench and looks up to Skeeter for inspiration—Skeeter thinks a minute and dictates the following letter—

LETTER

Mis Cuspidora Lee

23 Hucklebury stret City

de rose am red and de vilet am blue

sugar am sweet an so am you.

      Ah sees you by de Shoo Fly Chuch under

      de chinabury tre Satiddy nite.

           yos for matrimoney,

              Quintus Weefalls.

SCENE NO. 109

The letter is finished after much thought and a duplicate and addressed to Mrs. Margerine Scrubb. They are put in Quintuses' hat and he draws one from the hat held over his head—upon inspection it proves to be for Mrs. Scrubb.

SCENE NO. 110

Close-up of letter addressed to Mrs. Scrubb.

SCENE NO. 111

Skeeter is holding both letters—he says—

SUB TITLE

"Ah ~~posts~~ sends dis one!"

SCENE NO. 112

Skeeter exits with letters—Quintus turns to Gizzard Buster and says—

"Boy, distribute some melody; my feet feels triflin.'"

SCENE NO. 113

Gizzard gets busy with his guitar—and sings—

SUB TITLE

"Jada, Jada, Jada, Jada Alyce Lee."

SCENE NO. 114

Quintus dancing says—

SUB TITLE

"Vinegar juice, jazz my yo trailin' feets."

SCENE NO. 115

Quintus still dancing.

SUB TITLE

With a practical joke in mind, Skeeter mails sends both of the letters.

SCENE NO. 116

Mail box. Enter Skeeter—he looks at both letters which are stamped— laughs—mails them—exits.

SCENE NO. 117

Quintus is still dancing—enter Skeeter—he gets the fever—says—

SUB TITLE

"Rub me back of de ears! They's wild blood in my veins."

SCENE NO. 118

Quintus and Skeeter trying to outdance each other—fade.

SUB TITLE

Miss Cuspidora Lee, an old maid not at all adverse to matrimony. ["*LIGHT-FOOT*" *has been written in by hand, in connection with the subtitle or with the previous scene.*]

SCENE NO. 119

Miss Cuspidora Lee is seen in front of her cottage—Mail man comes along and hands her letter—she opens and reads—

SCENE NO. 120

Close-up of letter—

SCENE NO. 120 [*The misnumbering appears in the original script*]

Cuspidora becomes excited—says—

SUB TITLE

"Oh! Lawdy mussy! A man at las'!"

SCENE NO. 121

She begins to tidy up—and bustles into house.

SUB TITLE

Mrs. Margerine Scrubb had already outlived her second husband and was looking for a third. [*"Maud" is written over the name "Margerine," indicating that the role is being played by Maud Johnson.*]

SCENE NO. 122

Margerine is in the yard vigorously operating on the wash board with some clothes—enter Mail man and hands her letter—she opens it—reads—

SCENE NO. 123

Close-up of letter to her—

SCENE NO. 124

Margerine gets excited says—

SUB TITLE

"Come great deliverer! He am my man."

SCENE NO. 125

She dances around and in her excitement falls into the steaming washboiler.

SUB TITLE

With the passing days, Helen is convalescent. Jack has been a regular caller since the accident which threw them so strangely togeather.

SCENE NO. 126

Fade in—Helen is seated in reclining chair on porch with robe over her. Jack is talking to her.

SCENE NO. 127

Hilton coming down walk of Powers home. He stops sees Helen and Jack. Flash scene of Helen and Jack talking.

SCENE NO. 128

Back to Hilton, he registers jealousy—fade.

SUB TITLE

Work is being feverishly pushed forward on the M. N. & Q.'s new double track to Chicago.

SCENE NO. 129

Fade in—men are seen building the tracks.

SCENE NO. 130

Hilton in a surveyors suit is assisting in laying out a survey. Men are staking the right-of-way. Hilton exits after giving some orders.

SCENE NO. 131

Flash scene of men working on tracks.

SUB TITLE

Jealousy.

SCENE NO. 132

Hilton is standing by cowcatcher of engine with cigarette in his hand—he is looking intently at nearby engine where—

SCENE NO. 133

Jack Manning is oiling up his engine.

SCENE NO. 134

Back to scene 132. Hilton registers determination—flicks cigarette out of hand exits.

SCENE NO. 135

Back to scene 133. Enter Hilton. Manning looks up and sees him—greets him—but Hilton refuses to shake hands with him, Manning asks him what is the matter—Hilton says—

SUB TITLE

"The next time I catch you lamping around Helen I'll trim your lights."

SCENE NO. 136

Manning takes off hat—throws down his gloves and says—

SUB TITLE

"If you are going to do any trimming, start now."

SCENE NO. 137

Hilton does—and there is a fast and furious fight.

SCENE NO. 138

Powers is in the railroad yards giving some directions to railroad men.

SCENE NO. 139

Hilton and Manning fighting. Manning grabs Hilton around the waist and throws him—they roll on the ground fighting.

SCENE NO. 140

Powers still talking to railroad men—he exits.

SCENE NO. 141

Hilton and Manning fighting. They roll over. Hilton sees a big lump of coal—edges over to it and just as he gets it and is about to brain Manning with it—manning sees him and wrentches it out of his hand.

SCENE NO. 142

Powers approaching engine—he hears commotion stops—

SCENE NO. 143

Manning knocks Hilton down.

SCENE NO. 144

Powers sees Hilton and Manning fighting—he exits to separate them.

SCENE NO. 145

Close-up of Hilton coming to on the ground he staggers slowly to his feet—and makes a rush for Manning.

SCENE NO. 146

Long shot of scene. Powers rushes in and seperates Hilton and Manning—lectures them for fighting and takes Hilton out.

SCENE NO. 147

Hilton and Powers going down track, he turns and says to Manning—

SUB TITLE

"I'll get you yet!"

SCENE NO. 148

Manning tells him to come back and get more.

SCENE NO. 149

Satan laughs at the hatred that has been stirred up.

SUB TITLE

Saturday night arrives at last. Miss Cuspidora Lee and Mrs. Margerine Scrubb are all aquiver over their romance.

SCENE NO. 150

Cuspidora comes out of her house—dressed in her best—she says—

SUB TITLE

"Lawd a mussy! I hopes he's a big hansom man."

SCENE NO. 151

She caresses her letter—and exits.

SCENE NO. 152

Margerine comes out of her house all excitement—she almost falls down the steps—and says—

"My heart am quiverin wuf excitement fo' dat meetin'."

SCENE NO. 153
Margerine exits.

SUB TITLE
Skeeter decides to see the fun.

SCENE NO. 154
Skeeter exits from the Shin Bone Eating House in a new white suit.

SUB TITLE
Mr. Quintus Weefalls had on his "Sunday Best."

SCENE NO. 155
Quintus exits from his house in all his glory—carrying a walking cane and everything.

SUB TITLE
~~They arrive early.~~

SCENE NO. 156
Cuspidora is seated on a bench under a chinaberry tree. The Shoo Fly Church is seen in the background. She is very fidgety. Enter Margerine—who glares at her—sits down on the opposite end of the bench—they both pretend not to notice each other—finally Margerine loses patience looks over at Cuspidora and says—

SUB TITLE
"How come you here womans?"

SCENE NO. 157
Cuspidora says—

SUB TITLE
"I'se got appointments wif my financee."

SCENE NO. 158
Margerine gets suspicious and says—

SUB TITLE
"How come?"

SCENE NO. 159
Cuspidora naively shows her the letter—Margerine reads it and gets excited, shows Cuspidora her letter. Cuspidora says—

SUB TITLE
"That nigger man is up to some foolishness."

SCENE NO. 160

Margerine reaching down in her sock pulls out a wicked looking razor—feels its saw tooth edge—says—

SUB TITLE

"Ah aint gwine stan' fo' no fumadiddles frum no nigger man."

SCENE NO. 161

Margerine whets her new razor on her shoe and looks around for Quintus with an eye that bodes no good.

SCENE NO. 162

Cuspidora pulls out a wicked looking revolver—says—

SUB TITLE

"Mr. Weefalls, de weepin' willows am ~~goin'~~ gwine to weep over yo' grave."

SCENE NO. 163

About this time Quintus pokes his head around the side of the Church and sees much waving of the gun and stropping of the razor—he resorts to flight—

SCENE NO. 164

Cuspidora and Margerine see him and pursue—

SCENE NO. 165

Quintus trips on a fallen limb and Cuspidora and Margerine pounce on him and drag him to his feet—he is shaking with the ague—Cuspidora says—

SUB TITLE

"Did you written dis here epistle, ~~nigger man~~?"

SCENE NO. 166

Quintus looks from one to the other—speech failing him.

SCENE NO. 167

Margerine says—brandishing her letter—

SUB TITLE

"An' dis one too?"

SCENE NO. 168

Quintus stutters out—

SUB TITLE

"Yes'm. How come?"

SCENE NO. 169

Margerine flashes her razor and says—

SUB TITLE

"Ah teach yo' how to triflicate wif a poo' widow's affectations."

SCENE NO. 170

Cuspidora flashing her revolver—says—

SUB TITLE

"Ma heart am injured an' demands justis. ~~You am a dead nigger man.~~"

SCENE NO. 171

Quintus'es eyes are wide with horror—he looks over towards the grave yard and sees something white jumping up and down.

SCENE NO. 172

Skeeter in his white suit jumping up and down in the grave yard and laughing and slapping his legs at the predicament that Quintus is in.

SCENE NO. 173

Quintus points at apparition in grave yard and says in horror—

SUB TITLE

"Lawdy! Look at de hant!"

SCENE NO. 174

Cuspidora and Margerine look at grave yard and see apparition. Cuspidora discharges her revolver at it and they all scatter in opposite directions.

SCENE NO. 175

Close-up of Skeeter in grave yard. Pistol bullet hits him in the seat—he exits in haste too.

SCENE NO. 176

Cuspidora and Margerine making tracks down a dusty road. They are raising plenty of dust.

SCENE NO. 177

Skeeter comes steaming down a forked road and Quintus down the other angle of the road—they come to the fork and collide and roll in the dust. They get on their hands and knees and glare at each other—then get to their feet— finally Quintus gets his breath and says—

SUB TITLE

"Here I is in de wuss mess I'm ever got into."

SCENE NO. 178

Skeeter tells him he is sorry and that—

SUB TITLE

"What you needs is experience in cotin'."

SCENE NO. 179

Quintus agrees with Skeeter and asks—

SUB TITLE

"How is I gwine to git it?"

SCENE NO. 180

Skeeter thinks a minute—says—

SUB TITLE

"Ah knows a smart actress gal what can give you lessons in cotin'."

SCENE NO. 181

Quintus tells him that he don't want to get mixed up with any actress gal—but finally Skeeter overcomes his objections and they exit.

SUB TITLE

Dazzle Zeanor was a woman who met all the exactions of Ethiopian beauty. She possessed the wisdom which comes from many varied experiencies as an actress, dancer and singer.

SCENE NO. 182

Dazzle is standing in a tiny flower garden picking flowers when Skeeter comes along with Quintus in tow and hails her. He introduces Quintus and explains things to her—Skeeter discreetly withdraws and leaves them alone. Dazzle asks him—

SUB TITLE

"How much money you got?"

SCENE NO. 183

Quintus reluctantly produces two dollars—and she appropriates it—and leads them away.

SCENE NO. 184

Bench in garden. Enter Dazzle and Quintus—she bids him be seated and she sits down too. She moves over towards him—and he inches away she says—

SUB TITLE

"Put yo' ahms around me and kis' mah rubin lips."

SCENE NO. 185

Dazzle inches over towards him and puts out her lips—Quintus inches away very embarrased—she makes a grab for him—and Quintus falls off the seat.

SUB TITLE

In spite of Hilton's threats, Jack has pressed his suit at every opportunity.

SCENE NO. 186

Helen is feeding the gold fish in a tiny fountain on the Powers lawn. Jack is bending over her. They exit.

SCENE NO. 187

Flower garden. They come along the path and Helen picks a flower and puts it in Jack's button hole—They exit.

SCENE NO. 188

Rustic seat with flower setting. Enter Jack and Helen they sit down and talk.

SCENE NO. 189

Entrance to Power's home. Hilton enters scene to visit Helen—stops—hears voices—Flash of Jack and Helen talking.

SCENE NO. 190

Hilton recognizes Helens voice and exits to investigate.

SUB TITLE

The old, old story.

SCENE NO. 191

Jack proposes to Helen—says—

SUB TITLE

"Helen—you know how long I have loved you—now I want your decision."

SCENE NO. 192

Helen bashfully turns her head away from him and thinks over his proposal.

SCENE NO. 193

Hilton parts bushes and sees Jack and Helen.

SCENE NO. 194

Helen makes her answer yes—and Jack takes her in his arms.

SUB TITLE

A disappointed suitor.

SCENE NO. 195

Hilton registers disappointment.

SCENE NO. 196

Satan registers.

SCENE NO. 197

Hilton parts the bushes again.

SCENE NO. 198

Jack is putting diamond ring on Helen's finger—she kisses the ring and Jack kisses her.

SCENE NO. 199

Hilton registers jealousy.

SCENE NO. 200

Jack and Helen are walking on lawn—they stop and Helen pointing—says—

SUB TITLE

"Now you must get fathers consent to our marriage."

SCENE NO. 201

Jack looks towards where she is pointing—

SCENE NO. 202

Flash scene of Powers in chair reading paper.

SCENE NO. 203

Back to Jack and Helen. Jack takes fright and starts to sneak—Helen grabs him and leads him away.

SCENE NO. 204

Hilton still registering hate—slowly backs out of bushes which close after him—fade.

SCENE NO. 205

Fade in—Powers, Helen and Jack are standing. Jack has his hat on. Powers has his arm around his daughter—he turns to Jack who is very nervous and after looking him over says—

SUB TITLE

"Something seems to be on your mind, young man. What is it?"

SCENE NO. 206

Jack thinks a minute—looks up at his hat—says Oh! and takes off his hat—saying—

SUB TITLE

"Fine day!! Fine day!!"

SCENE NO. 207

Powers agrees with him and asks him what he can do for him—Helen urges Jack on—and he blurts out his story—Powers putting his arm around his daughter says—

SUB TITLE

"What! Marry my daughter! Why you couldn't support her in her accustomed luxury."

SCENE NO. 208

Close-up of Jack. He tells Powers that he don't make a fortune—but that Helen has talked it all over and they will get along allright.

SCENE NO. 209

Close-up of Powers and Helen. Powers is obdurate—and will not give his consent. Helen coaxes and nestles her head on his shoulder—finally he relents and turning his head looks down at her—she says—

SUB TITLE

"But, father—I love him."

SCENE NO. 210

Powers smiles and gives in.

SCENE NO. 211

Powers, Helen and Jack. Powers takes his arm from around Helen and thinks things over—finally he gets an idea from the paper he has been holding in his hand—says—spreading the paper open—read this—they do—

SCENE NO. 212

Close-up of article in paper telling about the coming mail race etc.

SCENE NO. 213

Back to Scene No. 212. Powers says—

SUB TITLE

"Your engine will pull the mail special. If you win the mail race I will appoint you my assistant, then you can marry Helen."

SCENE NO. 214

Jack shakes him by the hand etc. Powers puts his arm around his daughter etc.—fade.

SCENE NO. 215

Fade in—view of freight train running.

SUB TITLE

"Weary Willie," A Dusky Knight of the road. [*The name "Weary Willie" has been written in by hand.*]

SCENE NO. 216

Happy, a tramp slowly opens the door of a box car and peers out—he props himself up in the door and sings—

SUB TITLE

"Ah kin ride a freight train,
Ah don't pay no fare;
Ah kin ride a steamboat mos' anywhere.
'At's de reason Ise as happy as a bee—
Ah don't bother work and work don't bother me."

SCENE NO. 217

Tramp gets out of box car and feels in pocket and brings out flask—it is empty—he turns it up—says—

SUB TITLE

"Mah las' dram of koonyak is gon'."

SCENE NO. 218

Tramp throws flask down—it hits his foot—he yells and limps down tracks.

SCENE NO. 219

Quintus is filling his engine with water at the water tower.

SCENE NO. 220

Tramp sees him—and says—

SUB TITLE

"Ise powerful thirsty."

SCENE NO. 221

Tramp exits.

SCENE NO. 222

Tramp enters scene with tin can holds it up for Quintus to fill—Quintus turns the water spout over to him and lets the water go—drenching him all over—Quintus laughs and the tramp does a flop in a water puddle.

SUB TITLE

Coming events cast their shadow.

SCENE NO. 223

Jack is oiling his engine. Enter Quintus and is given some directions.

SUB TITLE

Fifteen miles away.
      Lone Point.

SCENE NO. 224

Section gang is working on tracks. Enter Hilton who talks to the foreman and inspects the tracks—he exits.

SUB TITLE

Silver Reed, the train despatcher at Lone Point.

SCENE NO. 225

Silver Reed is standing outside a small railroad station talking to a railroad man—railroad man exits and Reed takes a newspaper from his pocket and starts to read it.

SCENE NO. 226

Happy the tramp comes shuffling down the tracks.

SCENE NO. 227

Reed still reading the paper. Enter Hilton who greets him—Reed asks—

SUB TITLE

"How is the double trackage?"

SCENE NO. 228

Hilton tells him—

SUB TITLE

"We have just laid the last rail."

SCENE NO. 229

Hilton asks Reed for news—Reed tells him—

SUB TITLE

"Manning is going to run the mail special—"

SCENE NO. 230

Hilton looks surprised and asks where he got the information—Reed shows him an article in the paper—Hilton reads—

NEWSPAPER

Close-up of article.

SCENE NO. 231

When Hilton looks up from paper—Reed says—

SUB TITLE

"—and if he wins the race, he is to marry the Superintendent's daughter."

SCENE NO. 232

Close-up of Hilton registering hate.

SCENE NO. 233

Reed tells him not to take it so hard and exits—Hilton crushes the paper in his rage and exits.

SCENE NO. 234

Flash of tramp making a stew over a small fire besides the railroad tracks.

SUB TITLE

The seed of hate, already sown, takes root.

SCENE NO. 235

Box car. Hilton enters scene. Rests his arm against box car and, crushes paper and let it fall—looks up intently, studying—fade in scene of Jack and Helen kissing just after the ring is placed on her finger—fade away vision—Hilton registers emotion—turns head—fade to—

SCENE NO. 236
Fast passenger train speeding down tracks.

SUB TITLE
No. 76 Northbound and 83 Southbound trains due to pass on the double track before the mail race starts.

SCENE NO. 237
Passenger train going in opposite direction to No. 236.

SCENE NO. 238
Fade in view of Hilton—he is thinking deeply—he turns his head and sees—

SCENE NO. 239
Fade in—view of railroad switch—fade out.

SUB TITLE
Temptation.

SCENE NO. 240
Fade in—view of Hilton—register—fade out.

SCENE NO. 241
Satan tempts Hilton to throw the switch and wreck the north and southbound trains to tie up the tracks and prevent Manning from winning the race.

SCENE NO. 242
Fade in—Hilton says—

SUB TITLE
"I'll prevent Manning winning that race at any cost."

SCENE NO. 243
Hilton exits.

SUB TITLE
The Wrecker.

SCENE NO. 244
Railroad switch. Enter Hilton who stealthily throws it—he exits.

SCENE NO. 245
Satan registers—and fades into side of box car.

SCENE NO. 246
Trains 76 and 83 speeding to their doom.

SCENE NO. 247

Fade in—Powers, Helen and Manning are standing besides steps of engine cab—Powers says to Manning—

SUB TITLE

"Trains 76 and 83 are reported on time and the tracks should be clear for the mail race."

SCENE NO. 248

Manning tells him that his engine is in good shape for the run—fade.

SCENE NO. 249

Trains 76 and 83 speeding to their doom.

SCENE NO. 250

Train 76 strikes the open switch and runs on 83's track.

SCENE NO. 251

Trains 76 and 83 collide in a fearful wreck.

SCENE NO. 252

Hilton sees the catastrophe he has wrought and dashes down a railroad bank in horror.

SUB TITLE

Toll of the green eyed monster.

SCENE NO. 253

View of the tangled and burning wreckage.

SCENE NO. 254

The Mail Special. The time for its departure has arrived. Powers tells Manning good-bye and he tells Helen good-bye—and in rushes messenger with telegram—

TELEGRAM

Trains 76 and 83 wrecked. Hold mail special. [*signed*] Redding.

SCENE NO. 255

Manning says he will run down to the wreck. Powers orders him to stay there and exits.

SCENE NO. 256

Clearing the wreckage. The Wrecker is despatched etc.

SCENE NO. 257

Manning waits for orders at his engine. Enter Powers with telegram. Manning reads—

TELEGRAM
Tracks clear. Mail special may proceed to Chicago. [*signed*] Redding.

SCENE NO. 258
Manning jumps into the cab and the Mail Special is off.

SCENE NO. 259
Mail special speeding on the main line.

SCENE NO. 260
The Mail Special passes the wreck.

SUB TITLE
90 miles an hour.

SCENE NO. 261
The Mail Special speeding away into the distance.

SUB TITLE
Investigating the cause of the wreck.

SCENE NO. 262
A railroad detective and Policeman examine a switch—detective says—

SUB TITLE
"Whoever tampered with this switch, caused the wreck."

SCENE NO. 263
They look around and exit.

SCENE NO. 264
Pile of railroad ties. Tramp asleep behind them. Enter Detective and Policeman. Tramp awakes and sees them and starts to run—they collar him and shake him—exit with him.

SCENE NO. 265
The fatal switch. Enter Detective, Patrolam and tramp, Detective says—pointing at switch—

SUB TITLE
"Have you been tampering with this switch?"

SCENE NO. 266
Tramp says—[*A handwritten note indicates placement of "title at cut" before Scene No. 266.*]

SUB TITLE
"~~No suh! Ah didn't do it.~~"

SCENE NO. 267
Patrolman shakes tramp and says—

"What do you know about the wreck?"

SCENE NO. 268
Tramp says—

SUB TITLE
"Ah was makin' my Mulligan on de fire when Ah sees a man sneaking up to dat switch easy like—"

SCENE NO. 269
Tramp making stew in a tin can over the fire—he looks up—sees—

SCENE NO. 270
Hilton throwing switch—fade.

SCENE NO. 271
Fade in—of tramp still talking—he says—

SUB TITLE
"Den dose trains go—Bam!"

SCENE NO. 272
Collision of 76 and 83.

SUB TITLE
"An' Ah fades from dere."

SCENE NO. 273
Tramp registers horror at catastrophe and beats it at break neck speed through woods—fade.

SCENE NO. 274
Fade in—Tramp still talking. Detective and Patrolman lead him away for evidence.

SUB TITLE
Arrested for his crime. [*written in by hand*]

SCENE NO. 275
Hilton talking to friend on street corner. Enter Detective, Patrolman and Tramp—Tramp points him out. Detective places Hilton under arrest—Hilton makes a pass at Tramp who shrinks back from him—they exit.

SCENE NO. 276
Hilton and Detective walking down street. Patrolman and Tramp following. Hilton breaks from Detective's grasp and dashes down street. Patrolman and Detective follow. The tramp takes a sneak in the opposite direction.

SCENE NO. 277

Hilton runs in doorway, draws pistol and fires at Detective—

SCENE NO. 278

Detective seeks shelter in a doorway and fires at Hilton.

SCENE NO. 279

Hilton is forced to run for it—Detective pursues him.

SCENE NO. 280

Hilton in open running—he turns fires his pistol—

SCENE NO. 281

Bullet is seen hitting Tramp—it sets him afire—he dashes madly up the road.

SCENE NO. 282

Patrolman fires at Hilton.

SCENE NO. 283

Hilton's gun is shot out of his hand. Patrolman and Detective run in and capture him and lead him away—

SCENE NO. 284

Tramp dashes to edge of pond—jumps in to put fire out—fade—

SCENE NO. 285

The Powers Home. Helen has just driven up in her car. Powers enters scene and gives her a telegram—she reads.

TELEGRAM

Manning wins mail race. Mail contract ours. [*signed*] Dixon.

SCENE NO. 286

Helen throws her arms around her father in ecstacy and kisses him for the good news.

SUB TITLE

~~A week or two later.~~

SCENE NO. 287

Helen is picking flowers in the garden.

SCENE NO. 288

Jack sees her.

SCENE NO. 289

She sees Jack and runs to hide.

SCENE NO. 290

Jack dashes after her.

SCENE NO. 291

Big tree. ~~She~~ Helen, dashes behind the tree—Jack tries to catch her as she dodges him around the tree—finally he catches her and clasps her in his arms—fade.

SUB TITLE

After all, hate is sometimes next door to love.

SCENE NO. 292

Mrs. Margerine Scrubb in her best dress, parasol and all—is leaving her home.

SUB TITLE

A widow's wiles.

SCENE NO. 293

Quintus Weefalls coming down the street. Margerine enters the scene and drops her handkerchief. Quintus picks it up and hands it to her with a bow. They chat and Quintus walks down the street with her.

SCENE NO. 294

Miss Cuspidora Lee is coming down the street. She meets Margerine and Quintus and drops her handkerchief—Quintus picks it up and hands it to her with a bow—they chat and Margerine gets mad and says to Cuspidora—

SUB TITLE

"Ah seen you flirtin' wif my man."

SCENE NO. 295

Cuspidora says to Margerine—

SUB TITLE

"He am my little Quintus."

SCENE NO. 296

Cuspidora and Margerine get in an argument as to which one Quintus belongs to. Each one grabbing him away from the other one—finally they get into a fight and Quintus takes a sneak and leaves them to fight it out.

SUB TITLE

When it comes to winning women, Dazzle Zeanors teachings had borne fruit with Quintus.

SCENE NO. 297

Bench in Dazzle's yard. She is seated on it with Quintus and Quintus is telling her his experience. Dazzle edges over towards him and says—

SUB TITLE

"Don' you go chasin' after those two no account womens."

SCENE NO. 298

Quintus says—

SUB TITLE

"What's I gwine to do when deys hot after me?"

SCENE NO. 299

Dazzle taking him by the hand, says—

SUB TITLE

"Ah'l fix dat, cause dis is leap year and I want's you fo' myself."

SCENE NO. 300

Quintus snuggles over to her and says—

SUB TITLE

"Does you really mean dat, Dazzle, honey?"

SCENE NO. 301

Dazzle crosses her heart and lays her head on Quintus breast—says—

SUB TITLE

"Hones' an' true! Crost my heart an' hope to bust!"

SCENE NO. 302

Quintus hugs her and says—

SUB TITLE

"Put yo' rubin lips on mine and cement de bargin'!"

SCENE NO. 303

They kiss—fade out.

SUB TITLE

Dazzle's scheme to put an end to the matrimonial intentions of Cuspidora and Margerine.

SCENE NO. 304

Quintus in the back end of a black looking covered wagon with "Pest House" written on it. She is smearing big dobs of white on Quintus face.

SCENE NO. 305

A sad and comical procession down the street. Quintus is in the covered wagon drawn by a near dead bony old horse—Quintus is rolling his eyes and twisting his head in the back of the wagon and a motely procession is followering in the rear made up of Dazzle, a preacher and others.

SCENE NO. 306

The procession passes Margerines house—she sees it—Quintus jumps up and down like a monkey and gives an awful yell and groan—Margerine yells—

SUB TITLE

"Small poxes! An' I bets Ah gots it!"

SCENE NO. 307

Margerine throws her apron over her head and bolts in her house.

SCENE NO. 308

The procession passes Cuspidoras house and the same performance takes place.

SUB TITLE

Instead of a Funeral—there's a wedding at the Pest House Plantation. [*The location has been written in by hand.*]

SCENE NO. 309

The procession draws up to a shaded dell and stops under a big moss covered tree—Quintus gets out and a marriage is performed by the preacher between him and Dazzle.

SUB TITLE

The new assistant superintendent receives his reward.

SCENE NO. 310

Fade in—Marriage ceremony being performed over Jack and Helen—fade out.

SCENE NO. 311

Fade in view of Hilton behind the bars.

SCENE NO. 312

Fade in view of wedding procession down runner—little flower girls are strewing flowers etc.

SCENE NO. 313

As Jack and Helen get in waiting limousine—they are showered with rice and drive away.

SCENE NO. 314

Powers and other wedding guests get in another car and are driven away.

SCENE NO. 315

Back end of Helen's car in motion. Jack and Helen start to kiss—she sees father's car following and stops him from kissing her—he—looks surprised and seeing them following—he pulls down the shades—fade.

THE END.

CHARACTERIZATIONS.

1. E.N. Armstrong. A railroad president.
2. Henry High. The traffic manager.
3. J. Frank Keeley. The advertising director.
4. Bernard Powers. Railroad superintendent.
5. Helen Powers. His daughter.
6. Jack Manning. Railroad engineer.
7. Jim Hilton. Railroad contractor.
8. Quintus Weefalls. Railroad fireman.
9. String Bean Oldfield. Speed Maniac.
10. Cinnamon. Gambler.
11. Mustard Prophet. Gambler.
12. Hogface. Gambler.
13. Pink Eye. Gambler.
14. Skeeter Butts. Proprietor of the Shin Bone Eatin House.
15. Gizzard Buster. Musically inclined.
16. Miss Cuspidora Lee. An old maid.
17. Mrs. Margerine Scrubb. A widow.
18. Dazzle Zeanor. An actress.
19. Weary Willie. A tramp.
20. Silver Reed. Train despatcher.
21. Detective.
22. Patrolman.
23. Minister.
Section Gang.
Surveying outfit.
Wedding outfit.
Railroad Messenger, Chauffeur.

LOCATIONS AND SETS.

Elegantly furnished office.
Beautiful Home.
Flower Garden with rustic seat.
Fountain.
Park.
Railroad yards.
Exterior railroad offices.
Several shaded roads.
Woody scene with fallen log.
Rear of delapidated building.

Exterior of unpretentious restaurant with bench on side.
Mail Box.
Cuspidora Lee's cottage.
Margerine Scrubbs cottage.
Dazzle Zeanor's cottage.
Ginny Babe Chew's Boarding House.
Church.
Graveyard.

PROPS.

Railroad engine.
Touring Car.
Limousine.
Racing automobile.
Ambulance with cot.

Black covered wagon.
Surveying outfit.
Railroad Plans.
Oil can.
2 suits Overalls.

1 pair working gloves.
2 Bandanna Handkerchiefs.
2 Trainmens caps.
Stage money.
Goat.
Dice.
Guitar.
2 letters, pen and ink.
Slightly worn derby hat.
Surveyors suit.
Wash tub, clother, wash board,
   wash boiler.

Smoke pots.
6 twenty shot roman candles.
2 thirty eight pistols.
38 blanks.
Big razor.
Newspaper.
Wedding ring, and Diamond
   ring.
Empty whiskey bottle.
Flowers, runner, rice.

THE COMPLETE script of *The Bull-Dogger* (1922) was long thought to exist only in fragmentary form, the two extant portions being the opening scene—a two-page fragment—of the shooting script (Autry Library, Autry National Center; 98.154.2) and a draft of the scenario (Autry Library, Autry National Center; 98.154.1), both now in the collections of the Autry National Center in Los Angeles, California. That fragment and scenario are reproduced below. In April 2013, however, a typescript described by the seller as the "original script of *The Bull-Dogger*" was offered for sale in an online e-Bay auction and purchased by an unknown buyer.

As the scenario confirms, *The Bull-Dogger* was an action-packed "Round-Up" Western that showcased the rodeo skills of Bill Pickett and other black cowboy "Champions of the World." The surviving script fragment established the film's rather slight frame tale—a romance between Pickett's daughter Anita (played by Anita Bush) and Tom Stone, the cattle boss on the Millmans' Bar L Ranch, where Pickett is foreman. The fragment also introduced the supporting character of Sleepy Steve (played by Norman's favorite actor, Steve Reynolds), a one-legged cowboy at the Bar L who participates with Pickett in the rodeo events that are clearly the focus of the film.

At one point, Norman had planned a second round-up picture incorporating the extra riding and roping footage he had already shot. The script that he prepared for that picture (tentatively titled "Bill Pickett in *A Round-Up Star*") borrowed heavily from the scenario and titles of *The Bull-Dogger*, particularly the bulldogging and other popular stunt scenes. It also utilized the same locations, including the Bar L Ranch, the round-up contests at the Miller Brothers Ranch and at Okmulgee, and the town of Boley. But *A Round-Up Star* was never produced or completed. Instead Norman turned his attention to another Western feature, *The Crimson Skull*, which used the leading actors from *The Bull-Dogger* (filmed the same month). Reproduced below with original wording, spelling, and punctuation preserved (even when incorrect), the script fragment and the scenario of *The Bull-Dogger* were extensively annotated by Norman to indicate reel and roll numbers, timings, cuts, and changes. *Reproduced by permission of Captain Richard E. Norman and the Autry National Center, Los Angeles, California.*

Bill Pickett and Anita Bush
In
"THE BULLDOGGER"

———

Produced By
Norman Film Manufacturing Co.
Jacksonville, Fla.

TITLE.

The Broad acres of the great Millman Bros., Ranch, stretch their 150,000 acres over the Oklahoma Prairie.

SCENE NO. 1.

Fade in Panorama of the Ranch. Fade out.

TITLE.

"Here lives Joe and Zack Millman, owners of the Milliam Bros. Ranch."

SCENE NO. 2.

Panorama of Ranch Headquarters and Residence.

TITLE.

"But, eighteen miles away on the Millman Bros., Bar L. section, lives Bill Pickett, their trusted Foreman of The Bar L."

SCENE NO. 3.

Introduction of Pickett in some typical pastime.

TITLE.

Explaining a brief history of Pickett and his exploits. Stating the fact that he is the first cowboy to bulldogg a steer by biting it in the mouth and explaining how he lost most of his upper front teeth.

SCENES NO. 4-5-6.

Three typical scenes of Pickett using six-gun, rope spinning etc.

TITLE.

Anita Pickett, his motherless daughter.

SCENE NO. 7.

Anita comes out of the house, dressed in a homey costume as if she had been cooking. Is greeted by her father—who puts his arm around her and says—

TITLE.

"The Boss has sent for me to take part in the Bulldogging contests for the big Rodeo."

SCENE NO. 8.

Anita says—

TITLE.

"How lovely!" "But Dad! do be careful! Some day one of those dreadful Bulls might kill you.

SCENE NO. 9.

Pickett assures her that there is no danger.

TITLE.

Tom Stone, Cattle Boss on the Bar L. Secretely in his heart, he cherishes a great love for Anita.

SCENE NO. 10.

Tom Stone is unsaddling his horse.

SCENE NO. 11.

Pickett calls to him.

SCENE NO. 12.

Stone exits, after letting his horse into corral.

SCENE NO. 13.

Enter Stone—and Pickett tells him—

TITLE.

"I am leaving to take part in the Rodeo. See that no harm comes to Anita, and take good care of the Bar L."

SCENE NO. 14.

Stone says—

TITLE.

"Boss! It will be as quiet as a grave yard around here while you're gone."

SCENE NO. 15.

They talk over business of the Ranch.

TITLE.

"Sleepy Steve," a happy, go-lucky cowboy on the Bar L who lost his leg in the Fall Round-Up.

SCENE NO. 16.

Steve is seated on a box by the bunk-house singing—playing as if his crutch is a musical instrument.

VERSE.

"I don't bother work, work don't bother me;
I'se fo' times happy as a bumblebee.
Eats when I kin git it, sleeps mos' all th' time;
I don't give a dog-gone if the sun don't neveh shine.

SCENE NO. 17.

Steve is still singing, when enter a cow-boy leading saddeled horse—and says to Steve—

TITLE.

"Stow your horn, and take the Boss's horse to him.

SCENE NO. 18.

Steve takes the horse and hobbles away with it.

SCENE NO. 19.

Anita, Pickett and Stone are talking, enter Steve with horse and gives it to Pickett, he bids them good-bye and mounts. Anita waves him good-bye.

SCENE NO. 20.

Pickett on the road—fade.

TITLE.

"The Great Millman's Bros., Rodeo is in progress and cowboys and champions from all over the country are gathered to compete for the big prizes for skill and daring.

SCENE NO. 21.

Fade-in of enclosure with Rodeo in progress. Scenes of Bucking, Fancy Riding, bulldogging.

SCENE NO. 22.

Bill Pickett is entered in the contest and bulldoggs a steer.

TITLE.

"While back at the Bar L——"

SCENE NO. 23.

Anita and Tom Stone are seated on a fallen tree talking—their horses are tethered near,by. Tom is very nervous—he finally says in a bashful way—

TITLE.

"Anita! There is something I want to s-s-say to you."

SCENE NO. 24.

Close up of Anita—she says—

TITLE.

"Go on Tom! What is it."

SCENE NO. 25.

Tom is very nervous—says—

TITLE.

"Anita will you—will you—"

SCENE NO. 26.

Anita knows it is a proposal and says to encourage him—

TITLE.

"Yes Tom! Go on."

SCENE NO. 27.

Tom stutters and fidgets and says—

TITLE.

"Will you—will you go riding with me again to-morrow."

SCENE NO. 28.

Anita shows her disappointment—and says—

TITLE.

"Certainly Tom! Maybe the fresh air will be good for your nerve."

SCENE NO. 29.

Tom is fidgeting with his horse's bridle—fade.

[*end of opening script fragment*]

[*beginning of scenario*]

FEATURING

Champions of the World.
Pitted against each other in tests of daring and skill.

The Spirit of the West still lives. And the many fertile acres of its' vast rolling prairie have been tilled; great herds still range on its' virgin soil.

The Cowboy, Romantic Figure of History, is the same cowboy of the past. He still takes pride in his prowess with the six-gun and the lariat. And at the various Rodeos, he displays his skill in competition with others.

Unique in Cowboy History stands Bill Pickett: a native of Texas. He is a negro who has achieved the distinction of being one of the best trained ropers, riders and Wild West performers in America.

Bill Pickett is the Father of "Bulldogging." He is the man who invented the stunt of jumping from a fast galloping horse on a wild steer's neck and throwing him with his bare hands.

He is the first man to "throw the bull" with his teeth.

Bill lost most of his upper front teeth when he was kicked in the mouth by a horse in the Bull Ring in Mexico City on the memoriable occasion when he outstunted the Mexican bull fighters. He went them one better at bull fighting and his record still stands after 15 years.

Though 56 years old, Pickett had been "Bulldogging" for 38 years and is still the undisputed World's Champion of this sport, which he invented.

It is a very dangerous sport and many have been killed at it. Pickett knows no fear and has had many miraculous escapes, the scars of which he will bear to his grave.

Pickett is a regular He-man. His hands are almost as strong as those of a gorilla. It takes more than hot air to "throw the bull" and dust his back.

When Pickett is not touring the Country in exhibitions, you will find him at the Bar L Ranch, of which he is Foreman.

A Prize Beauty.
Puzzle; which is the Beauty?

Bill's Favorite Meat, "Bully Beef."

Mexican Wild Steers.

If it was not feeding time, they would be chasing Bill over the fence.

It is almost impossible to catch a wild steer unless you are on a horse.

Bill lands one that he has tamed.

"Dusting his back."

"Looks easy, but be sure your steer's tame."

Champions from all sections of the West are gathered to compete at the rodeo.

They say our grandfathers' crossed the Prairie.

Calf Roping for a $2000.00 Prize.

It takes a good roper to catch and tye the little yearlings. They are fleet of foot and sometimes shake off the rope.

Riley Burgess leads the field in calf roping. Roping, throwing and tying his calf in 23 1/5 seconds.

Chester Byars of Oklahoma City, Worlds' Champion Trick and Fancy Roper gives an exhibition of his skill.

Chester Byars spinning two ropes at one time.

Johnny Judd of Los Angeles, shows he can handle the rope deftly.

Steer roping for a $1000.00 Prize.

Ben Johnson of Butte, Montana, wins first place in the day's events. Roping and tying a steer in 37 seconds.

Bronk riding for a $1000.00 purse.

Crazy Snake throws Henry Ashby of El Reno, Okla.

Guy Schultz of Bliss, Okla., on Scar Back.

Accidents happen to the best of riders.

"Red Ward" of Ness City, Kansas is thrown while riding "Crazy Snake" and killed.

Soapy Williams riding "Sorrel Top."

Shorty Cox rides "B. C. Brownie."

Riding Tarazon.

When Maud Tarr, Champion Cowgirl, known as "Big Mother," rides a Bronk, he knows that he has found his master.

Trim little Ruth Roach, Cowgirl from Texas, rides "Calamity Jane."

Lloyd Saunders on "Creeping Moses."

Rose Smith, Cowgirl from Los Angeles rides "Influenza."

~~Bill Pickett saddles the Outlaw "Omaha."~~

~~Guy Schultz riding "Omaha."~~

~~A livery stable owner sold this horse four times and had it returned each time. He says "the boys" can't ride him.~~

~~The trouble was, he never sold him to a cowboy.~~

Clarence Schultz roping 2-3-4-5 horses.

You aren't a good "puncher" unless you can spin the old "maguey."

Pete Haddon, (colored) of Pawhuska, shows 'em how to do it.

Eddie Schultz spins a few.

Looks easy, so when you are home borrow the wife's clothes line and try it.

Try this over your cigar.

Steer riding.

Bill rides a wild mexican steer.

The steer only "shimmies" a little as he knows that he has found his master.

Ed. Schultz Bulldogging a steer.

"Bill shows him how to do it—"

"—and throws him with his teeth."

Fred Atkinson of Tucumcari, New Mexico, throws his steer in 27 seconds.

Emmett Schultz loses time in the catch, but makes a lucky throw. Time 41 seconds.

~~Bill Pickett makes the best time of the day. A quick throw in 24 seconds.~~

"Little Willie" the Cowboy Gob, goes hunting.

Maverick Race.

In the olden days when a steer was found on the Range without any brand, he was turned loose and given a start and was the property of the first cowboy who roped him.

Princess Winona, Worlds Champion Lady Crack Rifle Shot.

Her trick pony "Rabbit" performs.

"Silver Dan" High School Cow-Pony.

Goat Roping.

Fred Beason ropes a goat in 16 2/5 seconds.

~~Floyd Gale of Foraker, ropes a steer in 24 seconds, winning first place.~~

Charlie Smith, Colored Cowboy of Ft. Worth, Texas.

Charlie "laps his strings" on a long-horn in 37 seconds flat.

Cowboy Surprise Package Race.

"Little Willie" gets the cowgirl outfit.

Charlie Smith ropes and tyes a steer in 28 seconds.

Bill Pickett makes a quick catch.

Using the "stop watch" on Pickett. He throws the steer in 18 seconds; winning First Prize Money.

Harnessing a wild mexican steer.

"Little Willie" takes a fast ride.

Wild Horse Race.

Fred Atkinson bulldoggs a steer from a speeding automobile.

Charlie Smith Roping.

Rein Stone loses his steer.

Floyd Gale Roping.

Saddleing "Dynamite."

Buck Nelson, Colored Puncher, rides "Dynamite."

Shorty Kelso on "Funeral Wagon."

Tommy Scarett on "Sorrel Top."

Lee Robinson on "Flying Cat."

Nate Williams, Colored Puncher on the Bar L. saddleing "Weeping Widow."

Nate Williams riding "Weeping Widow."

Charley Johnson on "Easy Money."

John Henry on "Wild Jack."

Joe Alvarado on "Kangaroo."

Oklahoma Curley on "Henry Ford."

Ruth Roach riding "Rocking Cradle."

Ruth Roach riding "Kaiser Pete."

Bud Ross loses his steer.

A tough customer.

Buck Nelson, Colored Puncher from Tucumcari, New Mexico, fights a wild Mexican steer.

The steer is not considered down until he is lying flat on his side, all feet out and head straight.

After an eight minute fight, Buck throws him.

Buck Lucas "Bulldogging."

Roy Mayes "Bulldogging."

Soapy Williams "Bulldogging."

Roy Quick "Bulldogging."

Fred Atkinson of Tucumcari, New Mexico, "Bulldogging."

Boley Oklahoma, the All-Colored City near the Bar L Ranch.

Pickett gives an exhibition of his skill and drags a steer with his teeth.

The Last Chance Saloon.

Wild Bill takes his liquor "straight."

Clarence, the town dude, has a thirst also.

"A glass of buttermilk, sir!"

"No, no! Buttermilk! BUTTERMILK!"

"That's the stuff that makes a man out of you!"

"Some manic man!"

"Watch the Dude dance!"

"~~You rude thing~~!"

The "Gunpowder Shimmie."

"Wow! Mother wants me!"

Steve Reynolds, Colored Puncher on the Bar L Ranch.

"I bet "Old Peg" can dance!"

"Shake your boots, and shake 'em fast!"

A Holy Jumper.

"Bill, we've got a steer on our ranch that you can't touch!"

"The steer doesn't live that I can't throw."

"Bill, this fellow will kill you before you can touch him!"

"I wager you that I can go in the pen on foot and throw him in less than a minute!"

"I'll take your wager, and ship your poor carcass to your widow!"

A feat of daring and skill. Facing an enraged Mexican steer on foot and throwing him with his teeth. Note: Bill nearly lost his life in this encounter, when the steer got him down and almost gored him.

Lem Nelson, owner of the Bar L Ranch.

"Bill, your request for leave to take part in the Okmulgee Round-Up Contest is granted. I will have Lawrence Chenault do your work while you are absent.

Part Two Will Follow.
Part Three Will Follow.
Part Four Will Follow.
Part Five Will Follow.
[end of scenario]

NORMAN'S BLACK-CAST WESTERN *The Crimson Skull*
(1922) was a feature-length mystery/thriller in which the villainous Skull
and his Terrors wreak havoc on the citizens of the small town of Boley,
Oklahoma, until Bob Calem, the film's hero, joins the gang and exposes
them. For his bravery, he earns a big reward from the Law and Order
League and wins the hand of the woman he loves. The twenty-one-page,
384-scene script, reproduced below, appears to be the original shooting
script. It contains various annotations in Norman's hand, including the
note "MADE" at the bottom of every script page and check marks next to
each scene confirming that it was shot. But Norman's correspondence with
his brother Bruce and with other colleagues—as well as the promotional
materials for the film—suggest that, before releasing the picture, Norman reworked the role of the sheriff (recasting real-life Boley Sheriff John
Owens as the sheriff and Bill Pickett, whose "bull-dogging" stunts were
spectacular but whose acting was weak, as one of the deputies instead) and
reshaped the part of the villain.

The script (Autry Library, Autry National Center; 98.154.8) has been reproduced with the original wording, spelling, and punctuation (even when
incorrect); inconsistencies in numbering of the scenes and variant spellings

have also been preserved. ("The Skull," for example, appears in the text alternatively as "the 'Skull,'" "Skull," "the skull," or "skull.") *Reproduced by permission of Captain Richard E. Norman and the Autry National Center, Los Angeles, California.*

THE CRIMSON SKULL

Produced by
Norman Film Mfg. Company
Jacksonville, Fla.

TITLE NO. 1.

In the production of this Picture, the Producers gratefully acknowledge the co-operation of the authorities and colored citizens of the fast growing All-Colored City of Boley, Oklahoma.

TITLE NO. 2.

Snuggling itself on the Great Oklahoma Prairie, is the Peace-loving little City of Boley.

SCENE NO. 1.

Fade in and out of City.

TITLE NO. 3.

Of late, it's Peace has been disturbed by a band of outlaws; and hardly a day goes by without news of some fresh ~~deprivation~~ outrage.

SCENE NO. 2.

Scene of "The Crimson Skull" and his band of outlaws. "The Skull" is dressed in a skeleton costume and his band have one piece jumpers on with hoods showing nothing but their eyes. They dash up road and come to fork and ride up this into the underbrush.

TITLE.

The Sheriff and his deputies are hot on their trail.

SCENE NO. 3.

Sheriff and deputies dash up to fork of road—argue and go strait up trail.

TITLE.

"The Skull" so called from his make-up, had with his band of "Hooded Terrors" sown mortal fear into the hearts of the less intrepid of the countryside.

SCENE NO. 4.

Close-up of "the skull"—he is talking with hooded followers—says—

TITLE.

"Terrors"! I guess we have eluded the law, and if we can reach the State Line, we are safe for another raid."

SCENE NO. 5.

They ride away.

SCENE NO. 6.

Sheriff and his deputies galloping down road—they draw rein—look around—argue and retrace their trail.

SCENE NO. 7.

"The Skull" and his gang galloping down road.

TITLE.

Bill Pickett, before he purchased the Crown C Ranch, was known as one of the best riders, ropers and "bulldoggers" in the Southwest.

SCENE NO. 8.

Pickett has just finished tightening cinch on horse—looks up towards daughter—

TITLE.

Anita Pickett, his motherless daughter. Anita Pickett—

SCENE NO. 9.

Anita is feeding her pony sugar and pats it—looks up towards father as he mounts—then she mounts and they ride away.

TITLE.

The Sheriff picks up the last trail.

SCENE NO. 10.

Sheriff and posse dash up—stop—Sheriff says—

TITLE.

"Boys, they are making for the Texas line, and if they reach it, they will be out of our jurisdiction." ["Cut" has been written in by hand.]

SCENE NO. 11.

Sheriff and posse dash away.

SCENE NO. 12.

Skull and his gang down road.

SCENE NO. 13.

Sheriff and his posse in pursuit.

SCENE NO. 14.

Skull and gang down road.

SCENE NO. 15.

Sheriff fires at them.

SCENE NO. 16.

Skull and gang fire in return.

SCENE NO. 17.

Sheriff and posse firing as they gallop.

SCENE NO. 18.

Skull and gang also firing in return.

TITLE.

"Hard Pressed. "The Skull" decided to make a stand and shoot it out."

SCENE NO. 19.

Skull and gang come to sheltered retreat and dismount—shelter theirselves and fire.

SCENE NO. 20.

Sheriff and posse dash up and scatter for shelter. Fire at gang.

SCENE NO. 21.

Skull and gang firing.

SCENE NO. 22.

Sheriff and posse firing.

SCENE NO. 23.

Anita and Bill riding down road.

SCENE NO. 24.

Skull and gang firing.

SCENE NO. 25.

Sheriff and posse firing.

SCENE NO. 26.

One of hooded terrors firing.

SCENE NO. 27.

Sheriff raises up and shoots at him.

SCENE NO. 28.

Terror shoots at sheriff.

SCENE NO. 29.

Sheriffs hat is shot off. [*"Black thread" has been written in by hand.*]

SCENE NO. 30.
Skull shoots.

SCENE NO. 31.
One of the posse clasps hand to arm—he is shot.

SCENE NO. 32.
Sheriff crawls over to two of the deputues—says

TITLE.
"Make every shot tell, Boys. We are running low on ammunition."

SCENE NO. 33.
Boys assure him they will—one of them fires—

SCENE NO. 34.
Hooded terror is wounded.

SCENE NO. 35.
Skull sees this—says—

TITLE.
"We must rush them before help arrives."

SCENE NO. 36.
Terrors start creeping towards Sheriff, stop. Skull says—

TITLE.
"Half of you approach from the rear and take them by surprise." [*A handwritten note, "one title," suggests that the previous title and this one should be combined.*]

SCENE NO. 37.
The party split and creep away.

SCENE NO. 38.
Five of the gang creeping past camera.

SCENE NO. 39.
Skull and remainder sheltered—Skull says—

TITLE.
"Keep up firing to cover the rear attack."

SCENE NO. 40.
The gang fire a couple of times.

SCENE NO. 41.
Sheriff and posse firing. Sheriff is wounded.

SCENE NO. 42.
Gang creeping towards Sheriff and posse.

SCENE NO. 43.

View of Sheriff and posse from rear. Terrors creep towards them—suddenly rise and hold them up at point of gun. One cowpuncher knocks gun out of terrors hand and fights with him.

SCENE NO. 44.

Skull and gang rush forward.

SCENE NO. 45.

Skull and gang arrive and help other members bind up sheriff and posse. Fight is stopped between cowpuncher and Terror. They are bound and gagged, and tied to trees.

SCENE NO. 46.

Close-up of Skull and Sheriff. He is binding Sheriff to tree—steps back.

SCENE NO. 47.

Terrors form semi-circle around Skull and fold arms across breast. Skull steps forward and says—

TITLE.

"Sheriff! Let this be a lesson to you. I will spare your life this time. But if you cross my path again—you shall suffer the verdict of the "Crimson Skull."

SCENE NO. 48.

Close-up of Sheriff. He is all-in and too exhausted to make reply.

SCENE NO. 49.

Skull and his gang take the wounded Terror and mount and gallop away.

SCENE NO. 50.

Pickett and Anita riding down road.

SCENE NO. 51.

Sheriff and posse trying to loosen bonds. One member loosens his gag.

SCENE NO. 52.

Skull and gang riding away from camera.

TITLE.

On the way to Boley for their Mail, They discover the Sheriff's plight and his badly shot up posse. ["*Cut*" *has been written in by hand*.]

SCENE NO. 53.

Anita and Bill riding down road.

SCENE NO. 54.

Close-up of member of posse—he shouts—

TITLE.

"Help!"

SCENE NO. 55.

Shouting help again.

SCENE NO. 56.

Anita and Bill stop. Hear call—locate direction and gallop to resecue.

SCENE NO. 57.

Sheriff and posse tied to trees. Anita and Bill release them. Sheriff is badly wounded and Anita assists in binding up his wounds—Anita says—

TITLE.

"Boys we must get the Sheriff to a Doctor quick."

SCENE NO. 58.

The Boys assist her get him on a horse—fade.

TITLE.

Zack Lucas, an old time cattleman and owner of the Bar X Ranch—

SCENE NO. 59.

Lucas is standing by his horse talking.

TITLE.

Bob Calem, Foreman of the Bar X.—

SCENE NO. 60.

Bob is talking to Lucas.

TITLE.

Zack Lucas had one failing, his love for his wastrel son. Buck Lucas—

SCENE NO. 61.

Buck Lucas around side of stable. He takes a drink from flask. Looks cautiously around. ["Flask" has been written in by hand, indicating the necessary prop.]

SCENE NO. 62.

Zack and Bob talking—Zack says—

TITLE.

"Have the Boys cut out the fattest beeves in the morning for shipment. I am afraid our herd is getting a temptation for the Rustlers." [Note: beeves are adult bulls, steers, or cows, usually raised for their meat.]

SCENE NO. 63.

Buck hears this—shows that he has formulated a quick plan.

SCENE NO. 64.

Zack gets on his horse and rides away. Bob leads his horse away.

SCENE NO. 65.

Buck Lucas sneaks away. Fade.

TITLE.

"And so that night "The Skull" and his "Terrors" Rustle the Bar X Herd."

SCENE NO. 66.

Close-up of the skull—he is looking towards herd.

SCENE NO. 67.

Terrors driving herd away.

SCENE NO. 68.

Close-up of the skull—fade.

TITLE.

With the coming of the dawn, Bob Calem has bad news to report.

SCENE NO. 69.

Zack is coming out of the house—Bob dashes up on horse—dismounting he says—

TITLE.

"Rustlers have driven off most of the Herd, again."

SCENE NO. 70.

Zack is very much worked up over this—says—

TITLE.

"This is the last straw. If the Sheriff don't get "The Skull" and his outfit, he is out of a job."

SCENE NO. 71.

As above—fade.

TITLE.

"After a two weeks rest in the Hospital—the Sheriff decided it was the first peace he had since his election."

SCENE NO. 72.

Sheriff is talking to angry men—Zack Lucas is among them—Zack says—

TITLE.

[*"Title about cattle" has been written in by hand.*] "Something has got to be done—and done quick."

SCENE NO. 73.

Sheriff unpins star—and hands it to Zack—says—

TITLE.

"Men I won't need this any longer. I will turn it over to you until next election. I resign."

SCENE NO. 74.

Men and Sheriff talk heatedly—Sheriff walks away—

SCENE NO. 75.

Zack says to men—

TITLE.

"Men ain't there a man in this County for this job who isn't a cold-footed, chicken-hearted heap of Four-flush?"

SCENE NO. 76.

One of the men—says—

TITLE.

"Yes, there is one man, if you can get him to take the job."

SCENE NO. 77.

Zack says, who is he?—man says—

TITLE.

"Bill Pickett. He totes more spine and less blubber, and hasn't got a yellow streak down his back."

SCENE NO. 78.

The men discuss this idea and exit. Fade.

TITLE.

["*Owens at corral—Pickett*" *written in by hand*.] Branding a Maverick. Instead of roping him, Bill "Bulldoggs" him.

SCENE NO. 79.

Pickett throws steer.

TITLE.

He is the man who invented "Bulldogging" and tho 64 years old, he is still the undisputed World's Champion of the sport he invented.

SCENE NO. 80.

Pickett throwing steer with his teeth.

SCENE NO. 81.

Cowboy brands it.

TITLE.

A delegation call on Bill Pickett to wish him the hard job of Sheriff of Okemah County.

SCENE NO. 82.

Zack and party ride up to corral and dismount.

SCENE NO. 83.

Pickett lets up steer and seeing party, exits.

SCENE NO. 84.

Pickett greets party and shake hands with them.

SCENE NO. 85.

One of the party who suggested Pickett says to Bill—

TITLE.

"Bill! Joe Goshwiler has kicked over the Sheriff's job and we reckon you are a likely successor?"

SCENE NO. 86.

Pickett talks to them—finally says—

TITLE.

"There is only one way I will take the job—and that is to run things my own way."

SCENE NO. 87.

Spokesman says to Bill—

TITLE.

"We are with you Bill, and the blessings of the community if you clean up "The Skull" and his gang."

SCENE NO. 88.

They shake hands with him and pin star on him. ~~Fade.~~

SCENE NO. 89.

[*"Skull Pickett & Terrors"* has been written in by hand.] Buck Lucas rides up to corral and dismounts—he is under the influence of liquor. Bob Calem rides up—Buck greets him—Buck takes out flask—offers Bob drink—and as he extends flask—

SCENE NO. 90.

Close-up of Flask—showing queerly designed ring on Bucks hand. [*"Flask" has been written in by hand, indicating the necessary prop.*]

SCENE NO. 91.

Bob notes this—but refuses drink—says to him—

TITLE.

"Buck! Better cut the booze. It will be your ruin some day." [*Written in by hand: "Buck, your snake emblem ring reminds me [of] the snake concealed in that bottle. Booze will be etc."*]

SCENE NO. 92.

Buck says to Bob—

TITLE.

"Preachin' Hey! Thought you was Foreman of this outfit, not "Sky Pilot."

SCENE NO. 93.

Bob dissents—Buck says—

TITLE.

"Well, when I need a nurse, I will notify you."

SCENE NO. 94.

Buck takes drink—Bob exits.

SCENE NO. 95.

Bob taking saddle from his horse.

SCENE NO. 96.

Buck starts to take saddle from his horse and hurts it—horse rears—he kisks at it and jerks at bridle cutting its mouth—horse rears and plunges.

SCENE NO. 97.

Bob looks up and sees this.

SCENE NO. 98.

Horse rearing and plunging and Buck abusing it.

SCENE NO. 99.

Bob exits on run.

SCENE NO. 100.

Buck abusing his horse—Bob rushes up and says—

TITLE.

"Quit abusing that critter—you beast!"

SCENE NO. 101.

Buck says—

TITLE.

"Guess it's my nag. And what's it your business?"

SCENE NO. 102.

Bob says—

TITLE.

"I will make it my business if you don't stop!"

SCENE NO. 103.

Buck jerks horse and it rears—Bob jerks reins out of his drunken hands and strikes him—he falls, Bob drops horses reins as Buck staggers to his feet and fights with Bob—Bob knocks him down again.

SCENE NO. 104.

Zack Lucas coming from Barn—hears scuffle—

SCENE NO. 105.

Bob and Buck fighting—

SCENE NO. 106.

Zack locates sound and leaves to investigate—

SCENE NO. 107.

Buck is just struggling to his feet—Zack comes in and says—

TITLE.

"What is the trouble?"

SCENE NO. 108.

Buck says—pointing to Bob—

TITLE.

"He was abusing my horse!"

SCENE NO. 109.

Bob is amazed at this false charge. Zack becomes angry—says to Bob—

TITLE.

"Unsaddle that horse, and come to the house for your time. You are fired!"

SCENE NO. 110.

Zack exits. Buck and Bob glare at each other. Bob exits with horse. Buck takes drink and stumbles away.

SCENE NO. 111.

Bob unsaddling Buck's horse. Notices black cloth hanging out saddle bag. Investigates—sees Black hood of "Terrors".

SCENE NO. 112.

Close-up of hood—showing eye holes.

SCENE NO. 113.

Buck registers suspicion—looks towards Buck's retreating figure.

SCENE NO. 114.

Buck going towards house.

SCENE NO. 115.

Bob replaces the hood in saddle bag and hangs up saddle. Fade.

TITLE.

Bob had loved Anita ever since she was a little girl, but had never felt that his fortunes were great enough to ask her to marry him.

SCENE NO. 116.

Bob and Anita are setting on a fallen tree talking. Their horses are nearby. Bob says—

TITLE.

"—and when I interfered with him abusing his horse, the low down scoundrel accused me of the trick, and his father believed it."

SCENE NO. 117.

Anita tells him that he did right—they talk and mount their horses.

SCENE NO. 118.

Anita and Bob riding down road.

SCENE NO. 119.

Pickett rides and tethers his horse at corral. Anita and Bob ride up. Pickett greets them and says to Bob.

TITLE.

"I hear you are pretty busy over at the Bar X!"

SCENE NO. 120.

Bob says to him—

TITLE.

"The Bar X have dispensed with my services because I would not stand for Buck Lucas abusing his horse."

SCENE NO. 121.

Pickett says—

TITLE.

"Any onery galoot who will abuse his nag ain't worth living."

SCENE NO. 122.

They talk—finally Pickett says—

TITLE.

"Bob, since I have had the Sheriff's job wished on me, there is a job open on my Ranch as Foreman, if you will take it."

SCENE NO. 123.

Bob looks at Anita and sees pleading look in her eyes.

SCENE NO. 124.

Close-up of Anita—she registers.

SCENE NO. 125.

Bob studies—says—

TITLE.

"I will take it on one condition and that is that you let me help you round up "The Skull" and his gang."

SCENE NO. 126.

Pickett says—

TITLE.

"That's the man Bob! And I will be right glad to have your help."

SCENE NO. 127.

Bob and Bill shake hands. [*"Pickett is cut" was written in by hand and then excised.*]

SCENE NO. 128.

Anita smiles.

SCENE NO. 129.

Bob and Pickett talk—plan—fade.

TITLE.

Steve Reynolds, a happy, go-lucky cowboy on the Bar. L. He lost his leg punching cattle.

SCENE NO. 130.

Steve is setting down near bunk house—singing and playing as if on his crutch—

VERSE.

"I don't bother work, work don't bother me;
I'se fo' times happy as a bumblebee."

SCENE NO. 131.

Steve still singing.

SCENE NO. 132.

Bob walks over to where Steve is singing—says to Steve—

TITLE.

"And so work don't bother you? Well, you have it cut out for you. Every "puncher" on this Ranch is deputized to help catch "The Skull" and his gang."

SCENE NO. 133.

Steve gets up—says—

TITLE.

"'Scuse me! Did you say the "Skull and his Gang"?

SCENE NO. 134.

Bob tells him "yes"—Steve says—

TITLE.

"I resigns while I has one good leg. I don't chase no bony spooks."

SCENE NO. 135.

Steve does a right about face and ambles away—Bob calls him back—he comes back—Bob shows him card saying—

CLOSE UP OF CARD.

$5000.00 REWARD
Dead or Alive
This sum will be paid to the
person or persons apprehending
"The Skull" and his Gang known
as "The Terrors."
The Law and Order League,
Zack Lucas, Pres.

SCENE NO. 136.

Steve looks at the reward card again—rubs his eyes—looks again—draws himself up and says—

TITLE.

"Ise done spent the money already!"

SCENE NO. 137.

Steve takes out his big gun—examines it—puts it back in holster—does a right about face and hobbles off. Bob laughs and exits. [*"Gloves" has been written in by hand, probably indicating the necessary prop.*]

TITLE.

The "Pawnee Kid" lived somewhere in the hills, by methods that everybody suspected, but nobody had been able to verify. The Pawnee Kid—

SCENE NO. 138.

Pawnee Kid dashes up on horse—looks down on City—a notice tacked on post nearby catches his eye—he goes over to it—reads—

SCENE NO. 139.

Close-up of Reward sign for "The Skull."

SCENE NO. 140.

The Kid laughs—tears it up and throws pieces in bushes, gallops on.

TITLE.

Boley was very proud of its new Electric Light Plant and bright new lights studded its streets.

SCENE NO. 141.

View of Electric plant.

SCENE NO. 142.

The Pawnee Kid dashing up Main street—he has his gun out and is shooting at the electric lights—

SCENE NO. 143.

Close-up of electric lights breaking.

SCENE NO. 144.

Pawnee Kid shooting again.

SCENE NO. 145.

Close-up of saloon—fade into—

SCENE NO. 146.

Joe the barkeeper is behind bar polishing glasses. Boys are lined up drinking—Joe listens—

SCENE NO. 147.

Pawnee Kid shooting lights on street.

SCENE NO. 148.

Close-up of Joe in saloon—says—

TITLE.

"That's the Pawnee Kid! Know his yell! Hope the fool decides to throw away his cash in some other place! Glass is getting too expensive!"

SCENE NO. 149.

One of the Boys says to Joe—

TITLE.

"Tell it to 'im. Tell it to 'im, why don't cha?"

SCENE NO. 150.

Joe says—

TITLE.

"Got a wife and two kids. Besides, I ain't figurin' on leavin' my dust to no undertaker!"

SCENE NO. 151.

The boys laugh.

SCENE NO. 152.

Exterior Saloon—Pawnee Kid dashes up and dismounts. Goes into saloon.

SCENE NO. 153.

Close-up swinging doors—the Kid opens them suddenly—stands framed in them and says—

TITLE.

"Hello, folks!" ["Cut" written in by hand.]

SCENE NO. 154.

The boys look sober—start to edge from bar—

SCENE NO. 155.

The Kid smiles—says—as he releases door and steps inside—

TITLE.

"Didn't see no brass band waitin' to usher me in with glad music, so had to put on a celebration myself!"

SCENE NO. 156.

Boys stare at him with cold respect. Kid says—

TITLE.

"Hope I didn't spoil none of them purty new lamps, boys, but human natur' wasn't rigged to resist such temptation!" ["Cut" written in by hand.]

SCENE NO. 157.

Strides over to bar—says—

TITLE.

"How's the old acid, Cemetery? Got anything with a kick?"

SCENE NO. 158.

Joe silently pours him a drink and takes his money. Kid drinks it.

SCENE NO. 159.

Exterior Saloon. Pickett is just tying his horse at hitching rack—unlimbers his gun—strides into saloon.

SCENE NO. 160.

Kid at bar still drinking. Pickett steps up and rests his arm on bar—studies Kid. Kid looks up and says—

TITLE.

"Hello Puncher! Think you'll know me the next time you see me? Have a drink?

SCENE NO. 161.

Bill looks him steadily in the eye and says—

TITLE.

"Yes, I'll know you the next time I see you, and I don't want a drink."

SCENE NO. 162.

Kid says—

TITLE.

"Sociable as a flock o' tombstones! And what might be your business?"

SCENE NO. 163.

Pickett says—

TITLE.

"Ord'narily, I run the Circle C Ranch. But just now I am actin' in the capacity of Sheriff for the growing and prosperous town of Boley."

SCENE NO. 164.

Pickett pushes aside his bandana and discloses star—Kid sees it—says—

TITLE.

"So you're the new all-wool, fourteen karat Sheriff I been hearin' about."

SCENE NO. 165.

Pickett nods his head and says—

TITLE.

"Them was purty nice little lamps you shot up!"

SCENE NO. 166.

The kid says—

TITLE.

"Shucks, Sheriff, what's a few hundred bucks to the growing and influential town o' Boley? Keeps it from stagnatin' when I throw a little lead around, generous like!"

SCENE NO. 167.

Pickett says—

TITLE.

"Some one has given you a heap of wrong information as to the perticular status of this here metropolis." [*"Cut" written in by hand.*]

SCENE NO. 168.

Kid looks interested.

SCENE NO. 169.

Pickett says—

TITLE.

"This town is workin' towards law and order. And disrespectfully invites you to shut the door from the outside, and stay out."

SCENE NO. 170.

Kid leers at Pickett says—

TITLE.

"Who in hell's a goin' to keep me out?"

SCENE NO. 171.

Pickett says—

TITLE.

"I been figurin' on doing that little job myself."

SCENE NO. 172.

Kid says—

TITLE.

"Maybe, you been figurin' on comin' out to call on me?"

SCENE NO. 173.

Pickett says—

TITLE.

"I been figurin' on that, too."

SCENE NO. 174.

Kid says—fingering gun—

TITLE.

"When you come, you better figur' out beforehand if you got enough dust to pay the funeral expenses."

SCENE NO. 175.

Sheriff and the Kid—Kid is still saying the above.

SCENE NO. 176.

Exterior saloon—two rough cowpunchers enter saloon.

SCENE NO. 177.

Steve rides up and goes into saloon.

SCENE NO. 178.

Interior Saloon. Two rough characters sit at table.

SCENE NO. 179.

Close-up of Kid—he sees two charcters—

SCENE NO. 180.

Close-up of characters—one has hand on table—

SCENE NO. 181.

Close-up of his hand—makes sign by crossing first and second finger a couple of times.

SCENE NO. 182.

Close-up of the Kid—he does the same.

SCENE NO. 183.

Steve rides up to Bar, and looks around.

SCENE NO. 184.

Close-up of Pickett and the Kid looking calmly at each other—Kid says—

TITLE.

"Well, got t' be goin'. Got to pay a visit to Buckboard to-night. No spirit o' hospitality here, nohow! An' now Sheriff, so's you won't forget me, I bid you a fond ajoo—thusly."

SCENE NO. 185.

Kid takes off gauntlet—and slaps Sheriff across mouth—their hands flash to their guns—fire at about the same time—Pickett shoots gun out of Kids hand.

SCENE NO. 186.

Close-up of two rough cowboys—they jump to feet and put hands on guns—Steve draws his gun and tells [them] to put up their hands—they comply.

SCENE NO. 187.

The Kid has his hands above his head—Pickett with his gun on him—Kid edges over towards Pickett and suddenly kicks his gun out of his hand—they grapple—break and fight.

SCENE NO. 188.

Scenes of other cowboys—Steve etc. looking on.

SCENE NO. 189.

Kid and Pickett fighting—he finally gets him by neck and twists it back like he Bulldoggs a steer—Kid gives up in great agony. And while he is fingering his throat—Pickett regains his gun—and helping him up—exits with him from Saloon. Steve still holding gun on toughs who menace him—backs from saloon.

SCENE NO. 190.

Exterior saloon. Pickett and Kid come out—then Steve.

SCENE NO. 191.

Interior Saloon—crooks exit.

SCENE NO. 192.

Exterior Saloon. Crooks come out and look down street at retreating figures of Steve, Kid and Pickett—talk and exit.

SCENE NO. 193.

The Boley Jail. Pickett and Kid arrive, also Steve. Kid is locked in jail and Pickett tells Steve—

TITLE.

"Guard this hombre, as I am afraid his friends may try to help him escape."

SCENE NO. 194.

Steve is left on guard.

SCENE NO. 195.

Two crooks looking at jail—they exit after talking.

SCENE NO. 196.

Steve walking up and down before jail. Fade.

TITLE.

"And so that night, Sheriff Pickett's prediction came true."

SCENE NO. 197.

The ten terrors dash up street and halt.

SCENE NO. 198.

Steve is sitting on box in front of Jail. He is very sleepy and nods.

SCENE NO. 199.

Terrors dismounting horses—leave them with one of the members—and taking out guns sneak away.

SCENE NO. 200.

Steve nodding on box—hears noise.

SCENE NO. 201.

Terrors sneaking along side of building.

SCENE NO. 202.

Steve gets suspicious and taking out his gun—goes along side of building—stops—Terror comes up behind and holds him up. They bind him and gag him and leave him in front of Jail.

SCENE NO. 203.

Door of Jail is being opened and the Kid comes out.

SCENE NO. 204.

Kid with terrors getting on horse, gallop away.

SCENE NO. 205.

Steve bound and gagged, tried to burst his bonds—is unsuccessful.

TITLE.

"With the coming of midnight, Sheriff Pickett brings Bob to relieve Steve of his vigil."

SCENE NO. 206.

Pickett and Bob come to front of jail—see Steve bound and door open—hastily release steve and Steve tells them the news—says—

TITLE.

"Yes suh! There wuz about 500 of 'em. They all jumped on me and run away with the "Pawnee Kid.""

SCENE NO. 207.

Bill says—to Steve—

TITLE.

"Was "The Skull" with them?"

SCENE NO. 208.

Steve says—

TITLE.

"No suh! They was all "Terrors.""

SCENE NO. 209.

Bill nods his head and says—

TITLE.

"I thought so!"

SCENE NO. 210.

Bill closes the door of the Jail—they talk exit. Fade.

TITLE.

With the dawn of another day, Bob discloses his plans for the capture of "The Skull" and his gang.

SCENE NO. 211.

Bob and Pickett are standing by their horses—Bob looks all around to see if they are alone—satisfied he says—

TITLE.

"I have a plan to get "the skull" and his gang!"

SCENE NO. 212.

Pickett says, "What is it?" Bob says—

TITLE.

"Join "The Skull's" gang!"

SCENE NO. 213.

Bill says in surprise—

TITLE.

"Join his Gang?"

SCENE NO. 214.

Bob says—

TITLE.

"Yes! And when I am on the inside and know their plans, we can capture them by surprise.

SCENE NO. 215.

Bill tells him that he thinks it can't be done, Bob says—

TITLE.

"Here's my plan. The Bar X Ranch Pay Roll will be heavy Saturday. Get Zack Lucas in the Last Chance Saloon and—"

SCENE NO. 216.

They talk—fade.

SCENE NO. 217.

Exterior Bank. Fade in—Zack Lucas comes out—Bill comes up and greets him—tells him that he wants to speak to him in private—they walk off.

SCENE NO. 218.

Secluded spot. Zack and Pickett enter—look around—Pickett talks to him earnestly—Zack says—

TITLE.

"Bill, I don't have much faith in the plan. But I am with you just the same."

SCENE NO. 219.

They exit.

SCENE NO. 220.

Exterior Last Chance Saloon. They enter after Bill stopping and inviting Zack to have drink.

SCENE NO. 221.

Interior Saloon. Zack and Bill sit at table and give order.

SCENE NO. 222.

Two crooks drinking at nearby table—they look up.

SCENE NO. 223.

Zack and Bill take drink—Bill looks around and sees backs of two crooks—

SCENE NO. 224.

Back view of two crooks.

TITLE.

Laying the bait.

SCENE NO. 225.

Bill says—

TITLE.

"I hear your pay roll will be big Saturday."

SCENE NO. 226.

Close-up of crooks—they look at each other.

SCENE NO. 227.

Zack says—

TITLE.

"Yes! I have extra harvest hands to pay as well as my "punchers."

SCENE NO. 228.

Bill says—

TITLE.

"Better let me send a guard along with your Pay Roll."

SCENE NO. 229.

Zack says—

TITLE.

"Thanks Bill, but I will not need one. I will get the pay roll and if any hombre trys to hi-jack me, he will feel the bite of my old .45!"

SCENE NO. 230.

Zack taps his gun as he says this.

SCENE NO. 231.

Close-up of crooks—they look at each other—one crosses his first finger over the second one and the other does the same.

SCENE NO. 232.

Bill lights a cigar.

SCENE NO. 233.

Crooks get up—toss dollar on table and exit.

SCENE NO. 234.
Exterior Saloon—they exit.

SCENE NO. 235.
Interior—Zack and Bill get up—exit.

SCENE NO. 236.
Close-up of swinging doors—they slowly open and Bill looks out at Zack—
~~Bill says~~

SCENE NO. 237.
Crooks riding off.

SCENE NO. 238.
Zack and Bill in doorway—Bill says—

TITLE.
"I think suckers are biting to-day."

SCENE NO. 239.
Zack tells him that he thinks he is mistaken. Fade.

SCENE NO. 240.
Fade in—Anita and Bob are seated on fallen tree—she says to him—

TITLE.
"Bob! Dad has told me all about your foolish plan to join "The Skull's Gang."
I just know you will get killed."

SCENE NO. 241.
Bob thinks a minute—says—

TITLE.
"It is the only way I see to help your father capture them."

SCENE NO. 242.
Anita says—

TITLE.
"But Bob, you will promise to be careful, very careful, for my sake?"

SCENE NO. 243.
Bob looks at her tenderly—says—

TITLE.
"Little woman, I didn't think you cared so much!"

SCENE NO. 244.
Bob takes her in his arms—and she places her head on his breast—then he
kisses her—Fade.

TITLE.

The Decoy.

SCENE NO. 245.

Exterior Bank. Zack comes out with big sack apparently filled with money, puts it in carriage and drives off.

SCENE NO. 246.

Wooded scene. Bob is just getting off his horse. Takes out bandana handkerchief and ties around his face.

TITLE.

Figuring that the band of "The Skull" would swallow "the bait" and try to hold up Lucas at Willow Bend—Bob plans to beat them to it and in plain sight of them.

SCENE NO. 247.

Bob still adjusting his bandana. Takes out pistol and exits.

SCENE NO. 248.

Lucas driving down trail.

TITLE.

At Willow Bend.

[*No Scene 249 in the typescript.*]

SCENE NO. 250.

The skull and his gand are waiting in the thicket along the Bend.

SCENE NO. 251.

Lucas coming down trail—Bob steps out and holds him up—takes sack and makes him drive off—but while he is doing this—

SCENE NO. 252.

Skull and outlaws—Skull says—

TITLE.

"Curses! Some hombre has beat us to it!"

SCENE NO. 253.

Lucas driving madly off—Bob threatens him then exits to thicket.

SCENE NO. 254.

Skull and his gang exit on horseback.

SCENE NO. 255.

Bob makes bluff as if trying to get on horse—Gang dash up and stick him up—he drops sack—and throws up his hands—one of the gang takes sack—

SCENE NO. 256.

Member of gang starts to untie sack—

SCENE NO. 257.

Close-up of Bob with hands over head—looking at Terror untying sack—

SCENE NO. 258.

Close-up of sack being untied—and queer ring on hand—

SCENE NO. 259.

Bob still looking at his hand—Terror unties sack and dumps out sand and paper—rubbish—

SCENE NO. 260.

Skull says—

TITLE.

"Curses! We have been cheated."

SCENE NO. 261.

Bob says—

TITLE.

"We", is right, partner!"

SCENE NO. 262.

Skull says—

TITLE.

"Who are you?"

SCENE NO. 263.

Bob says—

TITLE.

"Bird of a Feather!"

SCENE NO. 264.

Skull takes a step forward and snatches off Bob's bandana—

SCENE NO. 265.

Close-up of ringed Terror—he starts back in surprise.

SCENE NO. 266.

Bob says to Skull—

TITLE.

"I know of easy pickings that will pay you to let me flock with you."

SCENE NO. 267.

Skull says—

TITLE.

"If you can prove this—we will spare your life."

SCENE NO. 268.

Gang get on horses—Bob gets on his horse while member of gang holds pistol on him—they ride away. Fade.

TITLE.

A week passes and no news of Bob. Anita and her father become anxious for his safety.

SCENE NO. 269.

At corral. The Boys are on horseback. Anita and her father is talking—Anita says—

TITLE.

"Father do make a good search for Bob. I fear he has met with foul play?"

SCENE NO. 270.

~~Pickett~~ Nelson [*written in by hand*] assures her he will and he mounts. Party ride off. Close-up of Anita looking after them—registers. Steve is in the party.

SCENE NO. 271.

Party riding down trail.

SCENE NO. 272.

Party come to divided trails—and split—part going one way and part the other.

SCENE NO. 273.

Steve with small party of searchers—lags behind—and turning behind tree—dismounts and—[*"unbuckles gun—hangs on saddle" written in by hand*].

SCENE NO. 274.

Steve takes out flask and takes drink.

SCENE NO. 275.

Close-up of the Skull looking through the bushes.

SCENE NO. 276.

Steve just finishing drink—looks up and sees the Skull.

SCENE NO. 277.

Clos-up of of the Skull.

SCENE NO. 278.

Steve rubs his eyes and looks again.

SCENE NO. 279.

Full view of the skull.

SCENE NO. 280.

Steve rubs his eyes again, looks at bottle—says—

TITLE.

"The Boss told me to let this Koonyak alone."

SCENE NO. 281.

Steve looks at the skull—starts to reach out his hand to touch him and see if he is real—draws it back—finally gets courage and touches him—draws back like he has been burnt—backs off—skull advances a little—Steve whirls around and starts to walk away—turns around—skull takes a step forward—Steve starts away again—turns around to look at Skull and sees him coming towards him and he flees. Skull exits to horse.

SCENE NO. 282.

Skull getting on horse—exit.

SCENE NO. 283.

Steve doing a zigzag on foot through the woods.

SCENE NO. 284.

Skull galloping past camera.

SCENE NO. 285.

Steve climbs tree and gets out on limb with his crutch—Skull gallops under him and Steve makes a swing at him with his crutch and misses—Steve falls out of tree.

SCENE NO. 286.

Skull gallops past camera.

SCENE NO. 287.

Steve fleeing across field. Skull has out lariat and swinging it trys to rope Steve—Steve throws himself flat and he misses—starts to run towards camera and Skull ropes him.

SCENE NO. 288.

Pickett and party in woods. Pickett finds Bandana handkerchief with holes in it—says—

TITLE.

"Boys, this belongs to Bob—but it don't tell us anything."

SCENE NO. 289.

Bill still talking—they get on horses.

SCENE NO. 290.

Skull on horseback—he is leading Steve at end of rope.

TITLE.

"The Skull's Rendezvous" [*"On Bobs entrance"* *has been written in by hand.*]

SCENE NO. 291.

Exterior shack screened by bushes—The Skull leads Steve blindfolded into door.

SCENE NO. 292.

Interior Shack. Steve is placed in chair and bound to it by two of the terrors. Skull says—

TITLE.

"We will get the Sheriff next and he will suffer the same fate you are goin' to."

SCENE NO. 293.

Close-up steve—he says—

TITLE.

"If the Boss ever gets you, he will make yore bones rattle."

SCENE NO. 294.

Skull talks to terrors—exit. Leaves terror on guard with Steve.

[*No Scene No. 295 in typescript.*]

SCENE NO. 296.

Pickett and his party ride up to his Ranch. Pickett dismounts and his party go to corral. Anita rushes out and says to him—"Have you found Bob? Bill says—

TITLE.

"We have scoured the County and cant locate Bob. Steve has disappeared too."

SCENE NO. 297.

Anita registers disappointment. Fade.

TITLE.

Gaining the confidence of "The Skull," Bob is admitted to his band of "Terrors."

SCENE NO. 298.

Interior Scene of shack. Altar with two burning torches. The Crimson Skull is swung between the torches. Bob with bared head is before the altar. Skeleton is administering oath to him. Terrors have on hoods and have arms crossed over breast—Skull with upraised hands—says—

TITLE.

"By the blood of the "Crimson Skull" I now pronounce you a member of the "Terror's Empire.""

SCENE NO. 299.

Bob puts on hood—fade.

TITLE.

Trouble in spirit, Anita decides to make a lone search for Bob.

SCENE NO. 300.

Anita getting on her horse rides away.

SCENE NO. 301.

Anita riding down road. She comes to fork and chooses road Steve took.

SCENE NO. 302.

Anita discovers Steves horse—sees tracks and follows them—leading Steve's horse.

TITLE.

Bob baits a trap for a surprise capture of the Skull and his gang.

SCENE NO. 303

Skull and gang in deep woods—Bob is talking—says—

TITLE.

"The Boley Bank is a mighty fat proposition and easy pickings."

SCENE NO. 304.

Bob still talking.

SCENE NO. 305.

Anita with horses—stops hears voices.

SCENE NO. 306.

Bob and terrors talking.

SCENE NO. 307.

Anita parts bushes and looks at them.

SCENE NO. 308.

Bob is talking—says—

TITLE.

"The Bank is fat with Ranchmen's money from the sale of the Fall Round-Up."

SCENE NO. 309.

Close-up of Anita—she is amazed.

SCENE NO. 310.

Bob is still talking—says—

TITLE.

"A daylight raid would be a success. Everyone looks for us after nightfall. Let us move boldly shortly after noon Monday when no one will be on guard?"

SCENE NO. 311.

The skull says—

TITLE.

"Terrors! It looks like a good plan. All those in favor, vote with the sign."

SCENE NO. 312.

Terrors cross their hands over breast.

SCENE NO. 313.

Anita starts to leave—trips and falls.

SCENE NO. 314.

Terrors hear commotion—Skull says—

TITLE.

"Someone has overheard our plans. Catch them."

SCENE NO. 315.

Terrors spring on their horses and gallop away.

SCENE NO. 316.

Anita galloping away.

SCENE NO. 317.

Skull and gang after her.

SCENE NO. 318.

Anita down road.

SCENE NO. 319.

Gang after her.

SCENE NO. 320.

Bob getting on his horse—First takes off outfit.

TITLE.

"Having other plans—Bob does not join in the chase."

SCENE NO. 321.

Bob galloping away.

SCENE NO. 322.

Anita comes to bobwire fence—her horse vaults over this. Gang come to fence and are forced to detour. Skull out distances his gang. [*"Bob Wire" has been written in by hand, indicating the necessary prop.*]

SCENE NO. 323.

Anita down trail—Skull is gaining on her.

Anita goes across field—Skull uncoils his lariat and ropes her. Terrors dash up and bind her. Exit with her.

TITLE.

Having sent word to Pickett, Bob meets him in secret.

SCENE NO. 325.

Pickett dashes up to wooded thicket—whistles.

SCENE NO. 326.

Bob hears this and whistles in return.

SCENE NO. 327.

Pickett exits.

SCENE NO. 328.

Pickett joins Bob—they talk—first shake hands.

SCENE NO. 328A [*written in by hand*].

Ext. hut. Anita is taken in it. Bind eyes. [*The entire scene has been added by hand.*]

SCENE NO. 329.

Interior hut. Anita is placed in same room with Steve. [*Next to the name Steve, "bind eyes" has been written in by hand.*] He is surprised to see her—and so is she. Steve says—

TITLE.

"Where is Bob?"

SCENE NO. 330.

Anita enjoins silence with her finger to her lip—fearing that Steve will give him away.

SCENE NO. 331.

Pickett and Bob talking. Bob says—

TITLE.

"Have all good shots placed in the Bank and in nearby buildings and out of sight. When the Gang starts to go in the Bank—I will stampede their horses and it will be an easy capture."

SCENE NO. 332.

Bill tells him that this is a good idea. Bob leaves him.

SCENE NO. 333.

Anita and Steve trying to release themselves—are unsuccessful.

SCENE NO. 334.

Terror goes into shack.

SCENE NO. 335.

Interior. Terror sees Anita and Steve—is surprised—looks around and going up to Anita—places his hands to lips to enjoin silence.

SCENE NO. 336.

Close-up of Bob and Anita. After looking all around—he lifts up his hood and reveals his self. Anita stifles an exclimation. Bob releases her. They embrace.

SCENE NO. 337.

The Terrors ride up and dismount outside shack.

SCENE NO. 337 [*The misnumbering appears in the original script*].

Bob releasing Steve.

SCENE NO. 338.

One of Terrors is smoking—close up of his hand as he holds cigarette—it shows queer ring.

SCENE NO. 339.

Anita and Bob are talking in whispers—He says—

TITLE.

"You will find two horses hitched outside. Now is the time for you and Steve to escape."

SCENE NO. 340.

Anita and Steve exit.

SCENE NO. 341.

Anita and Steve exit from building on run.

SCENE NO. 342.

Two terrors look up—

SCENE NO. 343.

Anita and Steve unhitching horses.

SCENE NO. 344.

Terrors shout at them and exit to capture them.

SCENE NO. 345.

Steve and Anita on horses. Terror seizes Steves bridle and the other one seizes Anitas. Steve hits Terror on head—he falls and he hits the other one and knocks him out—they dash away. Terrors get up and shake fists at them.

SCENE NO. 346.

Steve and Anita dashing down trail.

SCENE NO. 347.

Bob framed in doorway of shack.

SCENE NO. 348.

Skull and members of gang arrive at shack. Two terrors dash up and say—

TITLE.

"The prisoners have escaped!"

SCENE NO. 349.

Skull and gang go in shack.

SCENE NO. 350.

Interior shack—they see empty chairs. Skull says—

TITLE.

"Who aided them to escape?"

SCENE NO. 351.

Queer ringed terror says—pointing at Bob—

TITLE.

"I believe your new "brainless wonder" did the trick."

SCENE NO. 352.

Skull says—

TITLE.

"Bind him up Terrors!" ["Cut" has been written in by hand.]

SCENE NO. 353.

They bind up Bob to center post in shack. [Written in by hand immediately after the first word: "grab him" and "cut" followed by "enter to trial room."]

TITLE.

The Trial.

SCENE NO. 354.

Bob is bound to post at one side of room. The terrors are grouped in a semi-circle around the skull—he says—

TITLE.

"Did anyone see him release the prisoners?"

SCENE NO. 355.

Terrors shake heads. Skull says—

TITLE.

"As many as think him guilty—vote by the usual sign."

SCENE NO. 356.

One half of the terrors cross hands over breast. Skull says—

TITLE.

"Since it is a tie vote, the judgement of the "Crimson Skull" shall decree if you are guilty and shall die the death of a traitor."

SCENE NO. 357.

Close-up of Bob—he shows his tense feeling.

TITLE.

The test of the "Crimson Skull."

SCENE NO. 358.

A grim skull is suspended over a table with white cloth on it. A burning torch is placed under it. Skull pointing to it says to Bob—

TITLE.

"Each drop of melted blood shall spell your guilt or innocence. If their number is uneven, you die."

SCENE NO. 359.

Skull moves to table and bends over it—so do the terrors. Terror with queer ring has hand in view.

SCENE NO. 360.

Close-up of skull with blood dropping from jaws.

SCENE NO. 361.

Close-up of cloth being spattered with the blood.

SCENE NO. 362.

Close-up of Bob—he is breathing hard from the nervous strain.

SCENE NO. 363.

View of table and jury around it—Skull is counting.

SCENE NO. 364.

Close-up of Bob breathing hard.

SCENE NO. 365.

Skull is counting drops—says—

TITLE.

"Fifty-three, fifty-four, fifty-five—fifty-five—"

SCENE NO. 366.

Skulls finger is poised in air—no more drops appear.

SCENE NO. 367.

Close-up of Bob. He strains forward, breathing hard—closes eyes—looks again—

SCENE NO. 368.

One more drop falls—Skull says—

TITLE.

"Fifty-six, the even number. You are saved. Your trial by the test of the bloody skull decrees that you are innocent."

SCENE NO. 368 [*The misnumbering appears in the original script*].

Bob says—

TITLE.

"Thank God!"

SCENE NO. 369.

They release Bob.

SCENE NO. 370.

Anita and Steve dash up to her home. Pickett comes out to meet them—they talk—Anita says—

TITLE.

"—and Bob says that if I escape—to tell you to change the surprise for Tuesday instead of Monday."

SCENE NO. 371.

They talk.

SCENE NO. 372.

Bob talking to Skull—says—

TITLE.

"The prisoners escape will make no difference in our plans. We can make the raid on Tuesday when vigilence is relaxed by us not showing up on Monday."

SCENE NO. 373.

Skull nods his head—fade.

TITLE.

The Fateful day [*written in by hand*]. At noon Tuesday, armed men were seen to secrete themselves near the Boley Bank.

SCENE NO. 374.

Men going into buildings. Pickett and Zack secret themselves on top of porch across street. They have rifles.

SCENE NO. 374-A.

Skull and his gang leaving the rendezvous. Ride away.

SCENE NO. 375.

Skull and gang dashing down trail.

SCENE NO. 375 [*The misnumbering appears in the original script*].

They dash up main street of Boley and stop at Bank. Go in—leave Bob with horses. When they get in Bank—Bob stampeded horses. They run out of Bank and shoot. Bob has torn off his robe, and shoots at them. Citizens fire—some of the Gang drop.

SCENE NO. 376.

Pickett and Zack firing.

SCENE NO. 377.

Gang firing. one lone member is seperated from rest. He is about to fire at Bob—

TITLE.

The hand of Fate.

SCENE NO. 378.

Zack fires at lone outlaw—

SCENE NO. 378 [*The misnumbering appears in the original script*].

Outlaw drops dead. Close-up of ring on his finger.

[*Written in by hand: "Insert scene of Steve capturing outlaw," followed by a title that reads: "Ah! Ha! That bad Mexican Guy."*]

SCENE NO. 379.

The skull is shot and balance of band surrounded.

SCENE NO. 380.

Close-up of Skull—pickett removes his mask—and sees the "Pawnee Kid."

SCENE NO. 381.

Close-up of lone bandit—Zack and party remove mask—see Zack's son. Zack says—"My God! My own son," and weeps on his breast. The boys take off their hats. Fade.

TITLE.

With the dawn of the New Day.

SCENE NO. 382.

Anita and Bob are on horseback. Their horses are drinking. He looks around and drawing her to him—kisses her. They ride off.

SCENE NO. 382 [*The misnumbering appears in the original script*].

The corral—they ride up to it. Pickett comes over to them with big bundle of money in hand—says—

TITLE.

"Bob! "The Law & Order League" instruct me to give you the reward offered for "The Skull's capture. It was due to your plans that the Gang was broken up."

SCENE NO. 383.

Bob says—

TITLE.

"It will make a nice wedding present, if you will give your consent to our marriage."

SCENE NO. 384.

Bill looks at both of them—Anita looks shyly down—Bill takes her hand and Bob's and places them in each other, Bob places her arm around her—Fade.

THE END.

NOTES

FOREWORD

1. See W. Fitzhugh Brundage's essay, "Working in the 'Kingdom of Culture,' African Americans and American Popular Culture, 1890–1930,"in W. Fitzhugh Brundage, ed., *Beyond Blackface* (Chapel Hill: University of North Carolina Press, 2011), pp. 1–42.

2. See Matthew Bernstein with Dana F. White, "'Scratching Around' in a 'Fit of Insanity': The Norman Film Manufacturing Company and the Race Film Business," *Griffithiana*, 62/63 (1998): 81.

3. Marc Ferro, *Cinema and History* (Detroit, MI: Wayne State University Press, 1988), pp. 151–152.

4. For relations between Norman and Oscar Micheaux, see Gloria J. Gibson-Hudson's account, "The Norman Film Manufacturing Company," *Black Film Review*, 7, no. 4 (1993):16–21.

5. Jacqueline Najuma Stewart, *Migrating to the Movies: Cinema and Black Urban Modernity* (Berkeley: University of California Press, 2005).

6. See Michael T. Martin and David Wall, "The Politics of Cine-Memory: Signifying Slavery in the History Film," in Robert A. Rosenstone and Constantin Parvulescu, eds., *A Companion to the Historical Film* (New York: John Wiley & Sons, 2013), pp. 448–450.

INTRODUCTION

1. André Gaudreault, *American Cinema 1890–1909* (New Brunswick: Rutgers University Press, 2009), p. 10.

2. See Langston Hughes, Milton Meltzer, and C. Eric Lincoln, *A Pictorial History of Blackamericans*, 5th rev. ed. (New York: Crown Publishers, 1983); Paul Johnson, *A History of the American People* (New York: HarperCollins, 1997); and James R. Grossman, *A Chance to Make Good: African Americans, 1900–1929* (Oxford: Oxford University Press, 1997).

3. Amy Louise Wood, *Lynching and Spectacle: Witnessing Racial Violence in America, 1890–1940* (Chapel Hill: University of North Carolina Press, 2009), p. 2. See also Stewart E. Tolnay and E. M. Beck, *A Festival of Violence: An Analysis of Southern Lynchings, 1882–1930* (Urbana: University of Illinois Press, 1995).

4. James Oliver Horton and Lois E. Horton, *Hard Road to Freedom: The Story of African America* (New Brunswick: Rutgers University Press, 2001), p. 199. See also Richard Wormser, *The Rise and Fall of Jim Crow* (New York: St. Martin's Press, 2003), and C. Vann Woodward, *The Strange Career of Jim Crow* (New York: Oxford University Press, 2002).

5. Robert Whitaker, *On the Laps of Gods: The Red Summer of 1919 and the Struggle for Justice That Remade a Nation* (New York: Crown, 2008), p. 41.

6. See Chad L. Williams, *Torchbearers of Democracy: African American Soldiers in the World War I Era* (Chapel Hill: University of North Carolina Press, 2010).

7. See Isabel Wilkerson, *The Warmth of Other Suns: The Epic Story of America's Great Migration* (New York: Random House, 2010); Mark Whalan, *The Great War and the Culture of the New Negro* (Gainesville: University Press of Florida, 2008); Alferdteen Harrison, ed., *Black Exodus: The Great Migration from the American South* (Jackson: University Press of Mississippi, 1991); and James Grossman, *Land of Hope: Chicago, Black Southerners and the Great Migration* (Chicago: University of Chicago Press, 1989).

8. See Cameron McWhirter, *Red Summer: The Summer of 1919 and the Awakening of Black America* (New York: Holt, 2011); Jan Voogd, *Race Riots & Resistance: The Red Summer of 1919* (New York: Peter Lang, 2008); and William M. Tuttle Jr., *Race Riot: Chicago in the Red Summer of 1919*, 2nd edition (New York: Atheneum, 1996).

9. Robert Jackson, "The Celluloid War before *The Birth*: Race and History in Early American Film," p. 29, in Deborah E. Barker and Kathryn McPhee, eds., *American Cinema and the Southern Imaginary* (Athens: University of Geor-

gia Press, 2011). See also Lucy Fischer, ed., *American Cinema of the 1920s: Themes and Variations* (New Brunswick: Rutgers University Press, 2009).

10. In some of his films, in fact, Ernest Morrison (Sunshine Sammy) was credited simply as "Sambo" or "Little Sambo."

11. Butters, BMSS, 9; Leab, FSS, 11; and Wood, *Lynching and Spectacle*, 138.

12. Donald Bogle, *Bright Boulevards, Bold Dreams: The Story of Black Hollywood* (New York: One World Books, 2005), p. 181.

13. Stewart, MM, 28, writes that theater managers justified segregating blacks because white moviegoers complained of their "offensive odor," thus extending "stereotypes about Black uncleanliness and undesirability into places of leisure to exclude or discriminate not only against members of the Black working class but against African American theatergoers as a whole."

14. Bogle, *Bright Boulevards*, 162, 191, notes that, as late as the 1940s, the celebrated dancers Fayard and Harold Nicholas were turned away from the commissary at Fox Studios while the extras on the films in which they starred were admitted "just 'cause their faces are white."

15. Snead, WSBI, 107–108.

16. Leab, FSS, 8.

1. RACE MATTERS

1. Johnson, OR, Tape Two, July 28, 1967, called Foster the "Dean of Negro Motion Pictures" and also discussed other contemporary filmmakers, including Micheaux and Levy.

2. Blacks, especially black writers, also understood the importance of racial uplift in fiction. See, for example, Gene Andrew Jarrett, *Representing the Race: A New Political History of African American Literature* (New York: New York University Press, 2011). Moreover, as Patricia A. Turner, in *Ceramic Uncles & Celluloid Mammies: Black Images & Their Influences on Culture* (Charlottesville: University of Virginia Press, 1994), observed, even more dangerous than blatant caricatures were "the subtle distortions that have emerged and continue to dominate all genres of popular culture."

3. Johnson, OR, Tape Four, October 17, 1967.

4. Bowser and Spence, WHH, 14. In his foreword, Thulani Davis writes that race films indeed validated blacks' self-perceptions and counterbalanced notions of inferiority within the black communities. Davis quotes the authors, who conclude that "by bringing Black voices and visibility to popular culture, by portraying identities more diverse and more complex than had previously

been expressed in mainstream commercial culture, by declaring their own identity, they [black race filmmakers] were writing their world into existence" (xiv). Jane Gaines, FD, 17, similarly observed that "the race pioneers carved something significant out of nothing—race movies were an audacious invention that helped to make an audience that most white entrepreneurs did not see, that helped to imagine a separate community into existence."

5. Gaines, FD, 13.

6. Gaines, FD, 270.

7. Qtd. in Regester, "African-American Press," 44.

8. Stewart, MM, xiv, 3–4.

9. Cited in Stewart, MM, 282.

10. Qtd. in Sampson, BBW, 178.

11. These estimates, cited in Gaines, FD, 105, and elsewhere, originally appeared in Norman's letters (in the Lilly Library and the Black Film Center/ Archive, Indiana University).

12. Stewart, MM, 189.

13. Johnson, OR, Tape Four, October 10, 1967.

14. Stewart, MM, 189, 191.

15. For more on these and other important black productions, see Karen Sotiropoulos, *Staging Race: Black Performers in Turn of the Century America* (Cambridge: Harvard University Press, 2006).

16. Qtd. in Sampson, BBW, 174–175.

17. Qtd. in Bowser and Spence, WHH, 97.

18. Sampson, BBW, 3.

19. Qtd. in Cripps, SFB, 221.

20. Stewart, MM, 7. The position of Pullman porter—that is, as a porter on the Pullman overnight sleeping cars on the American railroads—was considered to be one of the best jobs that black Americans could hold in the late nineteenth and early twentieth centuries. The position was not particularly high-paying, and many of the porters' responsibilities were menial. But Pullman porters traveled throughout the country, and their positions were usually secure. (At one time, in fact, the Pullman Company was the largest employer of black men.) They eventually unionized; and the Brotherhood of Sleeping Car Porters went on to become one of the most important social and political organizations of the twentieth century.

21. Johnson, OR, Tape Two, July 28, 1967.

22. Reid, RBF, p. 8.

23. Ibid, p. 9.

24. Mark A. Reid, "Early Black Independent Filmmakers," *Black Film Review* 12.4 (1988): 22, cited in Butters, BMSS, 93.

25. Baldwin, CNN, 119. Baldwin called Foster's comedies "uplift comedies ... within the uplift comedy genre."

26. See, for example, the pioneering studies FSS and TCMMB. See also more recent studies, such as Susan Courtney, *Hollywood Fantasies of Miscegenation: Spectacular Narratives of Gender and Race, 1903–1967* (Princeton: Princeton University Press, 2005).

27. Cripps, "Making," 44, and SFB, 71–72.

28. Cripps, "Making," 45–46.

29. Bogle, TCMMB, 103.

30. Cripps, "Making," 48–49.

31. Qtd. in Sampson, BBW, 208–209.

32. Johnson, OR, Tape Two, July 28, 1967.

33. As cited in Johnson, OR, Tape Two, July 28, 1967.

34. In late 1918, Emmett J. Scott, who was then Army Assistant Secretary for Negro Affairs, met with George Johnson of the Lincoln Motion Picture Company. As a result of the meeting, Johnson was able to purchase a copy of a war film of black troops in action in France during World War I. As Sampson, BBW, 140–141, writes, "The film was distributed by the Lincoln Motion Picture Company to black theaters all over the United States." In his recollections, George Johnson described his interactions with Scott.

35. Butters, BMSS, 110–111.

36. Johnson, OR, Tape Two, July 28, 1967.

37. Gaines, FD, 107.

38. Bowser and Spence, WHH, 110.

39. Cited in Stewart, MM, 204.

40. Stewart, MM, 207.

41. Gaines, FD, 109.

42. Johnson, OR, Tape Two, July 28, 1967.

43. Bowser and Spence, WHH, 90. According to George Johnson (OR, Tape Two, July 28, 1967), in a letter to Lincoln, Robert R. Moton and Emmett J. Scott (then principal and secretary, respectively, at the Tuskegee Institute) concurred, adding that "Your Lincoln Motion Picture Company is entitled to the gratitude of the Negro people everywhere for the effort being made to give Negroes places of distinction in [the] moving picture industry."

44. Johnson, OR, Tape Two, July 28, 1967.

45. Sampson, BBW, 132.

46. Butters, BMSS, 116.

47. Bowser and Spence, WHH, 90.

48. Gaines, FD, 102.

49. Gaines, FD, 99.

50. Johnson, OR, Tape Two, July 28, 1967.

51. Paula J. Massood, "African American Stardom Inside and Outside of Hollywood: Ernest Morrison, Noble Johnson, Evelyn Preer, and Lincoln Perry," in Patrice Petro, ed., *Idols of Modernity: Movie Stars of the 1920s* (New Brunswick: Rutgers University Press, 2010), p. 231.

52. Sampson, BBW, 138, 140.

53. Stewart, MM, 209.

54. Johnson, OR, Tape Two, August 9, 1967.

55. Qtd. in Jane Gaines, "In-and-Out-of-Race: A Story of Noble Johnson," *Women & Performance* 15.1 (2005), p. 37.

56. Gaines, FD, 103. Johnson (OR, Tape Seven, February 28, 1968) clearly recognized, early on, the importance of keeping records on black actors and films, black film reviews and articles, black journals and newspapers, and black new releases: "To me that is history."

57. Massood, in Petro, p. 230. Reportedly, according to George Johnson, in his later years Noble Johnson increasingly downplayed his own racial heritage and even, by some accounts, tried to conceal it entirely, just as his oldest brother Virgel had.

58. Gaines, FD, 125, 117; Johnson, OR, Tape Two, July 28, 1967.

59. Johnson, OR, Tape Two, July 28, 1967.

60. Gaines, FD, 118–119. Davarian L. Baldwin (CNN, 144) offers another perspective on their failure to come to terms. He writes that "the Johnson brothers felt that the central romance between the black homesteader and a white neighbor would not encourage 'support from white houses.' For Micheaux, it was precisely 'the litho reading SHALL THE RACES INTERMARRY' that would entice the public." (In the film, the homesteader ultimately learns that the white neighbor is actually a woman of his own race.)

61. Gaines, FD, 121.

62. Gaines, FD, 125, Johnson, OR, Tape Two, July 28, 1967.

63. Daniel J. Leab, "A Pale Black Imitation: All-Colored Films, 1930–1960," *Journal of Popular Film* 4.1 (1975): 4, as cited in Butters, BMSS, 123.

64. For a fuller discussion of Micheaux's films, see also Pearl Bowser, Jane Gaines, and Charles Musser, *Oscar Micheaux and His Circle* (Bloomington: Indiana University Press, 2001); J. Ronald Green, *Straight Lick: The Cinema of*

Oscar Micheaux (Bloomington: Indiana University Press, 2000) and *With a Crooked Stick: The Films of Oscar Micheaux* (Bloomington: Indiana University Press, 2004); Patrick McGilligan, *Oscar Micheaux: The Great and Only* (New York: HarperCollins, 2008); Earl James Young Jr., ed. by Beverly J. Robinson, *The Life and Work of Oscar Micheaux: Pioneer Black Author and Filmmaker, 1884–1951* (San Francisco: KMT Publications, 2003); and Barbara Tepa Lupack, *Literary Adaptations in Black American Cinema*, rev. ed. (Rochester: University of Rochester Press, 2010).

65. Bowser and Spence, WHH, 40.

66. Chester J. Fontenot Jr., "Oscar Micheaux, Black Novelist and Film Maker," in Virginia Faulkner and Frederick C. Luebke, *Vision and Refuge: Essays on the Literature of the Great Plains* (Lincoln: University of Nebraska Press, 1982), p. 122. According to Richard Gehr, "One-Man Show," *American Film* (May 1991): 36, for almost thirty years, Micheaux would "shoot a film in the spring and summer, edit it in the fall, then travel with a driver throughout the Northeast, South and East, where he would show stills of his stars to ghetto theater owners."

67. Bogle, TCMMB, 115.

68. Butters, BMSS, 124.

69. Gehr, "One-Man Show," 36.

70. Sampson, BBW, 487. According to Gary Null, in *Black Hollywood: The Negro in Motion Pictures* (New York: The Citadel Press, 1975), p. 11, Micheaux's "exploitationary gimmick[s]" included posters with "large photos of rape scenes and semi-nude figures."

71. The extent to which Micheaux relied on white sponsorship is not absolutely clear. Gehr, Regester, Cripps, Reid, and Bowser and Spence—among others—discuss Micheaux's bankruptcy and subsequent partnerships.

72. "The first thing to be considered in the production of a photo-play," Micheaux wrote (as quoted in Everett, RTG, 134), "is the story. Unfortunately, in so far as the race efforts along this line have been concerned, this appears to have been regarded as a negligible part."

73. Qtd. in Sampson, BBW, 279.

74. Pines, BF, 33.

75. Cripps, SFB, 177.

76. Johnson, OR, Tape Four, October 17, 1967.

77. Sampson, BBW, 5, 7.

78. Sampson, BBW, 207, 240–241, 266.

79. In Chicago, where *Ebony* was based, the black press was highly critical of its pictures. The *Chicago Defender* found them to be low, degrading comedies.

Tony Langston, the *Defender's* theater editor, characterized them as "what is commonly called crap" and advised members of the race to save their money and their self-respect by avoiding the productions (BBW, 207).

80. Qtd. in Sampson, BBW, 213–214.

81. Bogle, TCMMB, 105, 107.

82. Johnson, OR, Tape Four, October 10, 1967.

83. Bowser and Spence, WHH, 102.

84. Johnson, OR, Tape Four, October 17, 1967.

85. Qtd. in Sampson, BBW, 215, 174–175.

86. Cripps, BFG, 29.

87. Cripps, "Race Movies," 47.

88. Jane Gaines, "*The Scar of Shame:* Skin Color and Caste in Black Silent Melodrama," p. 69, in Valerie Smith, ed., *Representing Blackness: Issues in Film and Video* (New Brunswick: Rutgers University Press, 1997).

89. Cripps, "'Race Movies,'" 56.

90. Sampson, BBW, 218.

91. See, for example, *Chicago's New Negroes*, especially chapters 3 and 4, in which Baldwin discusses "the economic success for 'race' films and the possible creation of a viable race market," which depended on the black mass audience.

92. Sampson, BBW, 9.

93. Bowser and Spence, WHH, 210.

94. Regester, "African-American Press," 41–42.

95. Regester, "African-American Press," 49.

96. Bogle, TCMMB, 107.

97. Qtd. in Sampson, BBW, 169.

98. The term "separate cinema" was popularized by John Kisch, founder and director of the Separate Cinema Archive (an invaluable educational resource for preserving black film culture) and co-author (with Edward Mapp) of *A Separate Cinema: Fifty Years of Black Cast Posters* (Noonday Press/Farrar, Straus and Giroux, 1992).

2. "HAVE YOU TALENT?"

The title of the chapter is a reference to "Have You Talent?," the promotional booklet that Norman developed and distributed to potential clients. The booklet explained how potential photoplayers could make their screen debuts in one of Norman's pictures.

1. I am grateful to Mrs. Katherine Norman Hiett, family historian and daughter of Kenneth Bruce Norman Sr. (Richard E. Norman's brother and one-

time business partner), for providing much of the family history that appears here.

2. Richard E. Norman Sr. (Norman's father) to REN, June 21, 1915, and Passi-Kola advertising cards (BFC-20).

3. Passi-Kola advertising cards (BFC-20).

4. Captain Richard E. Norman (Norman's son), interview May 23, 1978, qtd. in Nelson, FAMPI, Vol. 2, 433.

5. Passi-Kola advertising cards (BFC-20).

6. Correspondence from REN Sr. to REN, from Little River, Florida, July 26, 1912 (LL-1). The elder Norman wrote: "I thought best to make it a different color from Coca Cola."

7. REN Sr. to REN, July 26, 1912 (LL-1).

8. REN's handwritten notes (BFC-20).

9. REN Sr. to REN, April 22, 1915 (LL-1).

10. The Des Moines Brewing Company to REN, June 1, 1915 (LL-1).

11. REN Sr. to REN, June 21, 1915 (BFC-20).

12. The two ventures—the development of Passi-Kola and the manufacture of feature, industrial advertising, and special films—overlapped, as confirmed by undated handwritten documents [ca. 1915] in BFC-20.

13. See, for example, Bean, FH.

14. Gloria J. Gibson-Hudson, in her essay "The Norman Film Manufacturing Company," *Black Film Review* 7.4 (1993): 16, states that Norman studied "motion pictures as a college student in Tampa." There is no evidence, however, to corroborate Gibson-Hudson's claim.

15. Captain Richard E. Norman, interview May 23, 1978, qtd. in Nelson, FAMPI, Vol. 2, 433.

16. REN to Wm. R Shirley, President, Brotherhood of American Yeomen, in Des Moines, Iowa, August 9, 1926 (LL-1). Norman continued to make advertising films, even after achieving success with his race films. A letter of April 30, 1926, to "Messers Brangyn & Clark" of Jacksonville, Florida, for instance, concerns a script that Norman wrote "showing the moving picture possibilities of your Colonization Development" (LL-1). A particularly interesting early advertising film, according to Mrs. Katherine Norman Hiett, was one that Richard and Bruce Norman produced for "Hav-a-Tampa Cigars." In a letter to Barbara Tepa Lupack (November 2011), Mrs. Hiett wrote that the film was a "short made during WWI using stop frame photography," with German puppets—"one dressed as soldier and one as sailor"—in uniforms sewn by Bruce Norman's wife Annie R. Norman. But, as Mrs. Hiett noted, "Result very 'jerky' film."

17. Contract with Chas. G. Bakcsy, June 28, 1922 (BFC-20). Norman agreed "to complete finished motion picture containing 1400 feet of film depicting field meet and Fourth of July celebration."

18. Blank contract forms used by the Capital City Film Manufacturing Company and the Superior Film Manufacturing Company of Des Moines, Iowa (LL-4).

19. According to undated literature in Norman's files, home talent moving pictures, the "very latest stunt," have "become quite popular all over the country" (LL-4).

20. Captain Richard E. Norman, interview May 23, 1978, cited in Nelson, FAMPI, Vol. 2, 433–434.

21. Proof in *Photoplay Magazine* (LL-4).

22. "Have You Talent?" (BFC-10).

23. Promotional herald for *The Wrecker* (LL-4).

24. Undated, in Norman's scrapbooks (LL-4).

25. Bernstein and White, "Scratching," 93.

26. Captain Richard E. Norman, interview May 23, 1978, qtd. in Nelson, FAMPI, Vol. 2, 433.

27. Undated, in Norman's scrapbooks (LL-4).

28. Undated, in Norman's scrapbooks (LL-4). During filming of *The Wrecker* in Kankakee, for example, the local paper announced, "Miss Mary Wheeler Seriously Injured in Automobile Collision," before revealing that Miss Wheeler was only acting out the collision scene in Norman's railroad drama (Undated, in Norman's scrapbook [LL-4]).

29. W. M. Savage, December 17, 1915, in "Talent" (BFC-10).

30. W. F. Tilford, January 16, 1916, in "Talent" (BFC-10).

31. Undated review, in Norman's scrapbook (LL-4).

32. John G. Frederick, January 25, 1916, in "Talent" (BFC-10).

33. D. H. Bestor, May 26, 1916, in "Talent" (BFC-10).

34. W. F. Tilford, January 26, 1916, in "Talent" (BFC-10).

35. A. W. Barth, February 26, 1916, in "Talent" (BFC-10).

36. Chas. H. Carey, July 13, 1916, and Frank McCarthy, July 18, 1916, in "Talent" (BFC-10).

37. J. B. Price, November 24, 1915, in "Talent" (BFC-10).

38. *The Theatre Bulletin of Oklahoma City, Okla.*, December 6, 1919 (LL-4). *The Wrecker* was occasionally filmed under the titles *The Man at the Throttle* or *The Green-Eyed Monster*. These alternative—and likely early—titles appear in promotional materials preserved among Norman's papers in the Lilly Library. From the plot summary, cast of characters, and still photographs, it is clear that

the films advertised on these materials are in fact versions of *The Wrecker* and not separate or distinct productions.

39. As outlined by Norman in "Money Making Motion Picture Proposition," his promotional material for *Sleepy Sam*. (A fragment of one local version of *Sleepy Sam* survives; both the Library of Congress and the Black Film Center/Archive have a copy.)

40. Promotional herald for *Sleepy Sam* (LL-5 and BFC-10).

41. Klotman, "Planes," 168.

42. Bean, FH, 110.

43. Undated review of *Sleepy Sam*, in Norman's scrapbooks (LL-4).

44. Bernstein and White, "Scratching," 119, suggest that *Pro Patria* was apparently Norman's "own version of the controversial 1916 World War I Hearst propaganda serial *Patria*, with members of an acting troupe at the University of Illinois." But they do not elaborate on this connection.

45. Promotional herald for *Pro Patria* (LL-4).

46. Promotional herald for *Pro Patria* (LL-4).

47. "F. L.," *Illini*, No. 44 (no date), in "Talent" (BFC-10).

48. "The Critic," *Illini*, No. 42 (no date), in "Talent" (BFC-10).

49. The starring role was, improbably, as the baby.

50. Lyn Lazarus, "I'll Make You a Star, He Told Her," [Jacksonville] *Times-Union and Journal*, November 30, 1975, H-7.

51. All references are to—and all quotations are from—an original shooting script of *Buried Alive: Historical Indian Production of John Stink, Osage Indian Outcast* (Autry Library, Autry National Center; 98.154.5), a short film in sixty-nine scenes. I am grateful to Marva R. Felchlin, Director, Autry Library and Archives, at the Autry Institute, for her generous assistance in affording me access to this script and to other scripts in the Autry's collections, as noted below. My thanks as well to Marilyn Kim, Rights and Reproductions Coordinator, Autry National Center, for assisting me with permissions.

52. All references are to—and all quotations are from—an original shooting script of *Real Facts About the North Field Minnesota Robbery, or The Younger Brother in Minnesota* (Autry Library, Autry National Center; 98.154.6), a short film in twenty-six scenes. Once again, I am grateful to Marva R. Felchlin for her assistance.

53. All references are to—and all quotations are from—an original shooting script of *Bell Starr, A Female Desperado* (Autry Library, Autry National Center; 98.154.4), a short film in eighty scenes. My thanks yet again to Marva R. Felchlin.

54. Undated, in Norman's scrapbooks (LL-4).

55. Henry Starr promotional materials (BFC-27).

56. *A Debtor to the Law*, IMDB (Internet Movie Database, imdb.com) "Trivia."

57. For instance, in a letter to Norman (September 15, 1923 [BFC-9]), Alfred N. Sack wrote that he was very glad "to note from your stationery that you are now handling such a big line of attractions."

58. M. K. Fink letter to REN, January 27, 1922 (LL-1).

59. REN letter to M. K. Fink, January 30, 1922 (LL-1). Scout Younger is referenced in a letter that Norman wrote on August 21, 1921, to Joe Miller, owner/manager of the 101 Ranch in Bliss, Oklahoma: "The writer never had the pleasure of meeting you, tho I had quite a correspondence with you about 9 years ago in regard to taking over the technical work of the motion picture plant on 'The 101.' My friend Scout Younger was the one who made the recommendation" (BFC-9). Norman's Younger films include *Real Facts About the North Field Minnesota Robbery, or The Younger Brother in Minnesota*; Cole Younger also makes an appearance in Norman's Belle Starr picture.

60. REN to M. R. Lubin, January 10, 1923 (LL-1).

61. M. R. Lubin to REN, January 31, 1923 (LL-1).

62. All suggested promotions are from the pressbook for *A Debtor to the Law* (BFC-18).

63. These and other materials concerning *A Debtor to the Law*, including correspondence, paper orders, newspaper promotions, exploitation stunts, quality of prints, and production of title cards, are among the Lilly Library's holdings at Indiana University.

3. "NOT A WHITE MAN IN THE CAST"

"Not a White Man in the Cast" refers to a claim that Norman made in advertising he developed for *The Green-Eyed Monster*, in which he touted the fact that his race films were all black-cast. He repeated the phrase in promotions for his later pictures as well.

1. Lyn Lazarus, "I'll Make You a Star, He Told Her," [Jacksonville] *Times-Union and Journal*, November 30, 1975, H-7. Lazarus referred to Jacksonville as the "mecca of modern filmmaking," a phrase that was later adopted by other journalists and critics.

2. Nelson, FAMPI, Vol. 1, 96–97.

3. *The Florida Times Union* (May 6, 1914), cited in Nelson, FAMPI, Vol. 1, 162.

4. Nelson, FAMPI, Vol. 1, 133.

5. Terry Ramsaye, *A Million and One Nights: A History of the Motion Picture* (New York: Simon and Schuster, 1926), cited in Nelson, FAMPI, Vol. 1, 162.

6. FH, 48–49. Gene Gauntier, "Blazing the Trail," *Women's Home Companion* (November 1928), qtd. in FH, wrote, "For the motion picture industry [Kalem's] venture was almost epoch-making, establishing as it did new artistic standards, particularly in atmosphere, and inaugurating the custom of traveling far and wide in search of effective and authentic backgrounds."

7. "Motograph Film Company Opens Studio at Dixieland," *Florida Times Union* (February 18, 1910), and Wesley W. Stout, "When They Made MOVIES in Jacksonville," *Orlando Sentinel* (April 21, 1963), as cited in Nelson, FAMPI, Vol. 1, 147–148. Nelson notes that Motograph's secretary, Elmer Walters, "'after half a day's motoring about the city and surrounding country . . . was so agreeably impressed with the scenic advantages' that he enthused to local reporters: 'This is the ideal spot for us. No use going any further. My! But this country is made on purpose for my business. Nothing like it anywhere I've ever been and right here we, us and company camp. . . . we'll sure turn out a few films around this man's burg that will create a sensation with the "picter" men of this blooming hemisphere.'"

8. For more on Hardy, see Nelson, FAMPI, Vol. 2, 539, and Bean, FH, 70. See also John McCabe, *Babe: The Life of Oliver Hardy* (London: Robson Books, 2004), and Simon Louvish, *Stan and Ollie: The Roots of Comedy* (London: Faber & Faber, 2001).

9. Bean, FH, 68. According to Nelson, FAMPI, Vol. 1, 165–166, Thanhouser chose to film many of the company's films in Jacksonville rather than in California for several reasons. One was "the city's 'accessibility to the great Eastern centers.' Another was 'the climate and the fact that pictures can be made out-of-doors the year around, together with the metropolitan advantages of having properties and supplies at hand with little expense.'" Yet another was "the location of other studios in the city" and the "skilled people." Some of the pictures filmed in Jacksonville by Thanhouser include *The Hidden Valley* (1916), *Carriage of Death* (1915), *The Evil Woman* (1916), *Oval Diamond* (1916), *The Nymph* (1916), *Perkins' Peace Party* (1916), and *The Water Devil* (1916). Gaumont's Jacksonville films include *The Idol of the Stage* (1915), *According to the Law* (1916), *The Drifter* (1916), *I Accuse* (1916), *The Isle of Love* (1916), and *Pipe Dream* (1916). Vitagraph's *The Ordeal of Elizabeth* (1916) was also filmed in the city.

10. According to the official website of the Norman Studios Silent Film Museum, the "complex began as part of a planned cigar factory and later became

Eagle Film City. After the company filed bankruptcy, the property became the home and workplace of filmmaker and inventor Richard E. Norman."

11. According to Mrs. Katherine Norman Hiett, her father Bruce Norman initially entered the film business through his association with Jacksonville native Henry Klutho, and he later served as a photographer and cameraman for Klutho Studios before partnering with his brother Richard in the Norman Film Manufacturing Company (Letter to Barbara Tepa Lupack [November 2011]).

12. Bean, FH, 49, 2–3. Bean notes that "The first Jacksonville studio, in fact, predates the first Hollywood studio by three years."

13. H. G. Till to REN, February 23, 1921 (LL-1).

14. REN to M. Barney, March 20, 1922 (LL-1).

15. Captain Richard E. Norman, interview, Hollywood, Florida, May 23, 1978, qtd. in Nelson, FAMPI, Vol. 2, 434.

16. Klotman, "Planes," 168.

17. The advertising for *The Love Bug*, in fact, referenced the earlier film. For example, the ads noted that "The Cast Also Includes Robert Stewart (the man with the shovel in the Green Eyed Monster)."

18. REN to Albert Fish, June 6, 1925 (LL-1). Norman made a similar observation in a letter to Allen Jenkins, August 24, 1929 (BFC-6). He wrote: "This picture was originally designed to be released in 8 reels, but as it contained two stories in the one and one a comedy showing ambitionless characters in contrast with the ambitious story, we found that the negros did not like the comedy part, so we released the picture in 5 reels and cut the comedy out. This in no way hurt thr melodrama, but made it an instant success."

19. REN to Auditorium Theatre, Atlanta, Georgia, January 28, 1922 (LL-3).

20. Press materials for *The Green-Eyed Monster* (BFC-10).

21. City of Chicago Censor's Report, June 14, 1921 (LL-1).

22. Norman typically compiled footage that he used or reused in later productions. The scene of the train wreck, for example, was first used in versions of his home talent picture *The Wrecker*. But for the black-cast feature-length *The Green-Eyed Monster*, Norman likely contracted for some additional new material. At the Lilly Library, a contract dated April 29, 1920, notes that "the Norman Film Manufacturing Co. of Chicago, Illinois," with offices at No. 1614 Laura Street, Jacksonville, Florida, "has requested use of an engine on the Mayport Branch of the Florida East Coast Railway Company . . . in connection with the taking of certain moving pictures by certain agents and emploes of said Norman Film Manufacturing Co. on May 4th, 1920."

23. True Thompson to REN, May 24, 1922 (LL-1).

24. George P. Johnson to Gordon Boney of Kinston, North Carolina, December 30, 1927, as cited in Bernstein and White, "Scratching," 93.

25. REN to Majestic Theatre, Waco, Texas, October 25, 1921 (BFC-5).

26. The letters and testimonials from Wax, Kennedy, Murray, and Silberman appear in the press materials for *The Green-Eyed Monster* (BFC-10).

27. F. C. Dillon to REN, September 18, 1921 (LL-3).

28. Paul E. Thompson to REN, May 24, 1922 (LL-1).

29. The letters and testimonials from the Pike Theatre and Barraco appear in the press materials for *The Green-Eyed Monster* (BFC-10).

30. REN to Bruce Norman, March 28, 1921 (LL-1).

31. S. H. Henderson to REN, March 15, 1921 (LL-3).

32. Klotman, "Planes," 161.

33. Cited in Sampson, BBW, 311.

34. REN to E. A. Jacobson, August 6, 1921 (BFC-6).

35. REN to Bruce Norman, September 2, 1922 (LL-1).

36. Letter from manager, Grand Opera House, Meridian, Michigan, to REN, July 20, 1923 (BFC-1).

37. Davarian L. Baldwin, CNN, 119, used the term "uplift comedy genre" to describe Foster's short films. "Uplift comedies," Baldwin wrote, combined sensational entertainment with moral instruction and "offered reform-oriented lessons of sobriety, thrift and honesty through comedy." The term "uplift comedy" also applies to Norman's *The Love Bug*.

4. "TAKING TWO HIDES FROM THE OX"

The title comes from a letter from Richard E. Norman to his brother Bruce Norman (December 25, 1922), in which he confirmed that their company did not have to pay tax on those bookings done on percentage (rather than on straight rental) because "you can't take two hides from the ox." Yet by simultaneously utilizing the same cast in his race pictures, Norman did in effect take two hides from the same ox.

1. Bernstein and White, "Scratching," 93.

2. See Paul C. Spehr, "1890–1895: Movies and the Kinetoscope," in André Gaudreault, *American Cinema 1890–1909*, p. 38.

3. *The Bull's Eye*, which starred Eddie Polo and Vivian Reed, also featured Noble Johnson as Sweeney Bodin.

4. Norman was not the only early race filmmaker to be interested in the Western. Another was the Bookertee Investment Company of Los Angeles,

founded by Sidney P. Dones, who starred in the company's only production, a Western titled *The $10,000 Trail* (1921).

5. The federal government had opened up the Oklahoma territory for settlement in 1889: land would be available for anyone willing to settle there. Promising prosperity and respite from the violence of lynching, promoters such as John Mercer Langston attracted large numbers of black settlers to the territory. Ultimately, over thirty black towns were established. When Oklahoma was admitted to statehood in 1907, however, it entered the Union as a segregated state. See, for example, Jim Haskins, *The Geography of Hope: Black Exodus from the South After Reconstruction* (Brookfield, CT: Twenty-First Century Books, 1999).

6. Baldwin, CNN, 141–142, notes: "For Micheaux, the western frontier was a 'mythic space of moral drama and the site of opportunities seemingly free of the restrictive and discriminatory laws and social arraignments of the rural South and the urban metropolis.'" Baldwin adds that "Micheaux sought to reform social vice and immorality by explicitly exhibiting the downfall of his characters as they struggled directly within dangerous urban settings and amid behavioral temptations."

7. REN to Bruce Norman [hereafter cited as BN], August 19, 1921 (LL-1).

8. Letter from Mrs. Katherine Norman Hiett to Barbara Tepa Lupack (November 2011). Mrs. Hiett added that, at one point, all three Norman brothers—Richard, Bruce, and Earl—had hoped to make a feature film together. But Earl's unfortunate death by drowning prevented them from fulfilling that original plan.

9. Pressbook for *The Bull-Dogger* (BFC-18).

10. REN to John Owens, August 15, 1921 (BFC-9). Norman not only offered a part in the film to Owens; he wrote that he could "also use the other Sheriff that works with you." The reference to the "civic picture" appeared in the press sheet for the completed film.

11. REN to BN, August 19, 1921 (LL-1).

12. In his correspondence and promotional materials, Norman gave varying accounts of Pickett's age (usually between 54 and 64).

13. REN to BN, September 7, 1921 (LL-1).

14. REN to BN, August 19, 1921 (LL-1), as cited in Bernstein and White, p. 21.

15. "Articles of Agreement" between the Norman Film Manufacturing Company of Jacksonville, Florida, and the Rainbow Division Veterans, Oklahoma Chapter, Oklahoma City, Oklahoma, dated August 20, 1921 (LL-1).

16. REN to BN, September 7, 1921 (LL-1). At the Wellington Round-Up, Norman hoped to have "a good Round-Up that we can put under the head of

'Bill Pickett' in [a short film entitled] 'A Rodeo Star.' And with a western front
—it will make some easy money."

17. REN to BN, August 19, 1921 (LL-1).

18. REN to BN, September 7, 1921 (LL-1).

19. REN to BN, August 5, 1921 (LL-1), as cited in Bernstein and White,
"Scratching," 21.

20. REN to BN, August 31, 1921 (LL-1). At this time, Norman was still hoping to "secure enough of this Rodeo stuff—to make a 3 reel 'Cowboy Contest
Film' and use the [extra] scenes of Bill Pickett in it."

21. REN to BN, September 21, 1921 (LL-1).

22. The proof copy of the ad in the *Chicago Defender*, for which Norman paid
$9.80, is in the Lilly Library. Norman refers to both ads in a letter to BN, Sep-
tember 7, 1921 (LL-1).

23. REN to BN, September 21, 1921 (LL-1).

24. *In Dahomey*, the story of a group of African Americans who find gold,
travel to Africa, and become rulers of Dahomey, was based on the book by Jesse
Shipp, with lyrics by poet Paul Laurence Dunbar and music by Will Marion
Cook. It opened in February 1903 at the New York Theater and then enjoyed a
four-year tour, first in England and later in the United States. For more infor-
mation, see William Marion Cook, Paul Laurence Dunbar, and Jesse A. Shipp,
In Dahomey: A Negro Musical Comedy (Google Books); Thomas L. Riis, ed., *The
Music and Scripts of "In Dahomey"* (Madison, WI: Music of the United States of
America 5, A-R Editions, 1996); Marva Griffin Carter, *Swing Along* (New York:
Oxford University Press, 2008); and Thomas L. Riis, *Just Before Jazz: American
Musical Theatre in New York, 1890–1915* (London: Smithsonian Institution Press,
1989). See also John Graziano, "In Dahomey," in *Black Theatre: USA* (New
York: The Free Press, 1996).

25. Anita Bush to REN, July 12, 1921 (LL-1).

26. Anita Bush to REN, July 24, 1921 (LL-1).

27. REN to Anita Bush, July 20, 1921 (LL-1).

28. Anita Bush to REN, July 24, 1921 (LL-1). Bush makes the same claim
about being a "drawing card" in a later letter, of September 11, 1921 (BCF-9):
"My reputation is easily worth that. As I am known in nearly every home in the
country. Also white Vaudeville and Burlesque. As you will see how I am billed
in white Burlesque. As my name is a drawing card in both."

29. Anita Bush to REN, July 30, 1921 (LL-1).

30. REN to Anita Bush, August 31, 1921 (LL-1).

31. REN to BN, August 31, 1921 (LL-1).

32. REN to Anita Bush, September 7, 1921, and September 25, 1921 (LL-1).

33. REN to BN, August 31, 1921 (LL-1).

34. George Johnson, OR, Tape Four, October 17, 1967.

35. REN to Anita Bush, September 26, 1921 (Box 1).

36. REN to Anita Bush, September 23, 1921 (LL-1).

37. REN to Lawrence Chenault, September 26, 1921 (LL-1).

38. REN to BN, August 30, 1921 (LL-1).

39. REN to BN, August 31, 1921 (LL-1). In a later letter to BN, September 7, 1921 (LL-1), Norman noted: "I wrote Kansas City about costumes and they want $135. rental for two weeks for the chaps and $525. deposit, and as luck would have it, I stumbled on to a salesman in Okmulgee who was traveling for the Tennison Wholesale Saddelery Co. of Dallas and offered to sell me all the stuff I needed for $104. I get 9 pairs of chaps, 16 holsters, 12 pairs spurs, 12 belts, 12 pairs cuffs. So I get the stuff at wholesale and for less than the rental. We can use it on the front of the show."

40. REN to BN, August 31, 1921 (LL-1).

41. In that same letter (August 31, 1921 [LL-1]), Norman added "also as to how the bunch works if we don't get too tired working with them and they don't wear me out after I get through with the first film."

42. REN to BN, August 31, 1921 (LL-1).

43. REN to BN, September 7, 1921 (LL-1).

44. REN to BN, September 21, 1921 (LL-1).

45. REN to BN, September 21, 1921 (LL-1). Norman ultimately cast Owens in the part originally intended for Pickett.

46. A copy of a script entitled *A Round-Up Star*, featuring Bill Pickett and other rodeo stars (both black and white), survives; but there is no evidence that the picture was ever completed.

47. REN to BN, September 21, 1921 (LL-1). In that letter, he also noted that "'The Crimson Skull' has more action and less acting than 'The Bulldogger.'"

48. REN to Joe Miller, October 7, 1921 (BFC-9).

49. REN to BN, August 19, 1921 (LL-1).

50. Pressbook for *The Crimson Skull* (BFC-18).

51. Although *The Bull-Dogger* was released in five reels, there were, apparently, shorter versions as well. The Kansas censor, for instance, notes that *The Bull Doggers* [*sic*] was a three-reeler.

52. Herald/promotional material for *The Bull-Dogger* (BFC-12).

53. BFC-12. According to the ads, there was "a great line of advertising on this feature" available for sale, including "2 styles one sheet (one with 15 cuts on

it), selling for 5¢ each. 5 color 3 sheets. Window cards. Tack cards selling for 2¢ each. 2 styles slides, 20¢ and 35¢ each. Photos at 75¢ and $1.50 a set. Heralds at $2.50 and $4.00 a thousand."

54. Herald for *The Bull-Dogger* (BFC-12).

55. In a letter to A. Rosen, February 20, 1922 (LL-1), Norman wrote: "Anita Bush also appears in THE BULL-DOGGER and rides an outlaw horse." George Davis, in "Black Motion Pictures: The Past," *New York Amsterdam News*, September 18, 1971, D-13, writes about Bush's recollections of her time with Norman in Boley: "She admits that there was very little memorable about Crimson Skull or the other Western she starred in in Boley."

56. Pressbook for *The Crimson Skull* (BFC-18).

57. As Norman noted in the pressbook (BFC-18): Boley is "a real colored city" and "a thriving municipality, owning its own electric light plant and modern water works. It contains two modern cotton gins and the only Colored First National Bank in the United States. The population is All-Colored, from the Station Agent to the United States Deputy Sheriffs who police the City."

58. Summary of the film is taken from the press sheet for *The Crimson Skull* (BFC-18).

59. Title card, from an original early shooting script of *The Crimson Skull* (Autry Institute, Autry National Center; 98.154.8). I am grateful to Marva R. Felchlin, Director, Autry Library and Archives, at the Autry Institute, for her generous assistance in affording me access to this script and to other scripts in the Autry's collections.

60. The anecdote was related by Mrs. Katherine Norman Hiett, in correspondence with Barbara Tepa Lupack.

61. Pressbook for *The Crimson Skull* (BFC-18).

62. In a letter of August 21, 1921 (LL-1), before filming began, Norman wrote Anita Bush regarding Chenault: "You would do me a favor to hand him this letter, suggesting that he put on Mexican make-up with mustache of the higher class Mexican. In this case representing a Mexican Ranch owner . . . I may be able to use Mr. Chanault in the part of a Mexican Heavy, and a straight lead."

63. REN to Shingzie Howard, March 15, 1926 (LL-1).

64. Press sheet for *The Crimson Skull* (BFC-18).

65. REN to BN, November 29, 1921 (LL-1). Norman also noted that while he was staying up "until 2 AM" to assemble the negatives, he was working with a local photographer to plan and print one-sheets, inserts, and other paper for the films.

66. REN to BN, September 21, 1921 (LL-1).

67. REN to BN, December 15, 1921 (LL-1).

68. REN to BN, December 15, 1921 (LL-1).

69. REN to BN, December 25, 1921 (LL-1). The curios, he added, would also be useful "on . . . any Jesse James show too." Norman had already sent Bruce a box of items—three guns, a Moki Indian idol, a breechcloth, a scabbard, and a knife ("eagles claw"). The box also included a chief's necklace ("too valuable" to display, "heavy and cant be fastened in a case") and a buckskin shirt ("not to be used [because] it completes an Indian costume I have").

70. REN to True Thompson, April 21, 1922 (LL-1).

71. Pressbook for *The Crimson Skull* (BFC-18).

72. In a letter to the Auditorium Theatre, Atlanta, Georgia, January 28, 1922 (LL-3), Norman wrote: "We furnish the above pictures [*The Bull-Dogger, The Green-Eyed Monster,* and *The Love Bug*] and our big Western lobby of guns, chaps, western curios, and animals and all advertising, percentage fifty-fifty." He added: "We have found by putting out our lobby on the first day and playing the Green Eyed Monster that day and following the next day with The Bull-Dogger and Love Bug we get them in on both attractions."

73. Undated letter from REN to "Mr. Hill" [probably James Hill]. The cost for the ballyho described in the letter was $75 a week, which was sometimes split between two theaters. (That salary is confirmed by one of the receipts that Reynolds submitted to Norman, dated May 27, 1927 [LL-3].)

74. After F. C. Holden, booking agent for the Southern Amusement Company, received the "dodger covering the Bull Dodger," he inquired about the price for a three-day run—two days in Vicksburg, Mississippi (Princess Theatre), and one day in Monroe, Louisiana (Dreamland Theatre). In his letter of November 28, 1921 (LL-10) to Norman, he noted that, "owing to the prices we have had to pay," he had virtually stopped showing race pictures. "We have been unable to make anything out of it."

75. As per an undated promotional mailing to exhibitors and theater managers.

76. REN letter to Roland Single, manager of the Community Theatre, Pine Bluff, Arkansas, November 11, 1924 (LL-2). Norman wrote: "Our pictures hold box office records over all other colored pictures." The pictures please "[the colored man] 100%, bring you the largest returns, and each succeeding picture will gross larger returns."

77. REN to A. Rosen, February 20, 1922 (LL-1).

78. REN to O. E. Belles, November 22, 1922 (LL-1).

79. REN to James Hill, November 22, 1922 (LL-3).

80. Undated letter from REN to exhibitors. Norman repeated these numbers in a letter to A. Rosen, April 9, 1923 (LL-1).

81. REN to James Hill, November 22, 1922 (LL-3).

82. As per Norman's letters to M. Barney, Petersburg, Virginia (March 25, 1922), Pike Theatre, in Mobile, Alabama (February 20, 1922), and Mrs. H. E. Cutherbert at the Midway Theatre, Daytona, Florida (January 13, 1923) (LL-2). In a letter to H. E. Hall, manager of the Lyric Theater in Louisville, Kentucky, January 10, 1927, Norman noted that he had just learned that "the Crimson Skull was yet a first run picture in Louisville" (LL-3).

83. REN to C. B. King, June 23, 1925 (BFC-1).

84. REN to A. Rosen, February 20, 1922 (LL-1).

85. Among the Micheaux films that drew censors' attention were *The Home-steader, Within Our Gates, The Brute, The Symbol of the Unconquered, Deceit, The Gunsaulus Mystery, The Dungeon, The Virgin of the Seminole, Birthright, Body and Soul, The House Behind the Cedars, A Son of Satan, The Spider's Web,* and *The Millionaire.*

86. As per the bill to Norman, dated September 9, 1922, from Maude Gandy, "For Handling *The Bull Doggers* 3 Reels [and] *The Crimson Skull* 6 Reels," for a total "Paid Kansas" of $21.00. Norman references the Kansas City censoring office in his letter of September 7, 1922 (LL-1), to Bruce Norman.

87. Snow's censor report of March 22, 1922. (The picture was submitted under an alternate title: *A Rodeo Star.*) The censorship report for *The Crimson Skull* (Parts 1–6), however, shows "Eliminations. None." The report is dated September 28, 1922. No. 1995. "Vernon M. Riegel, Director. Class: Drama. Feet: 6000. Fee: $6.00. Manufacturer: Norman Film Mfg. Co." (LL-1).

88. REN to BN, March 27, 1922 (LL-1). Norman added, "Those Censors must be crazy and I cant see why they should make such cuts. Never-the-less that does not change things and maybe it is a good thing that you found that Bull-dogging scenes would not pass."

89. Pennsylvania State Board of Censors, April 6, 1922 (LL-1).

90. REN to BN, March 27, 1922 (LL-1).

91. REN to BN, March 31, 1922 (LL-1).

92. REN to A. Rosen, April 9, 1923 (LL-1). Norman wrote "no doubt you can get this picture bye now." In a letter to REN, April 14, 1923 (LL-1), Rosen replied: "I tried hard enough several times to get the Crimson Skull through the Pa State Board of Censors with no results but maby in a year or two I may be able to change the name and ask for a new censorship as I can not expect any results from same now."

93. George Johnson, OR, Tape Four, October 10, 1967.

94. George Johnson to REN, March 1, 1922 (LL-1).

95. George Johnson to REN, March 1, 1922 (LL-1).

96. REN to Lincoln Motion Picture Company, March 20, 1922 (LL-1).

97. Nelson, FAMPI, Vol. 2, 729. Nelson also notes: "This state rights practice became a common method for independent distribution, particularly after the major studios obtained control of large chains of theatres."

98. REN to A. Rosen, February 14, 1922 (LL-1). Norman wrote: "'The Crimson Skull' has been produced, but will not be released until April 1st. World Rights will be sold on this picture on the $20,000. basis. $10,000. cash will handle this picture. And on that basis you can figure out your territory. If you want a real proposition, 'The Crimson Skull' is the greatest buy in the field today and at the above figure."

99. REN to True Thompson, April 21, 1922 (LL-1).

100. The contract between Norman and Thompson was dated June 7, 1922 (LL-1). Thompson, however, did not consider *The Crimson Skull* to be Norman's best work. In a letter to REN (May 24, 1922 [LL-1]), Thompson wrote: "The quality of your film is very good," with "Steve Reynolds part being especially good." However, "'THE CRIMSON SKULL' is not the equal of 'THE GREEN EYED MONSTER', very few—if any colored pictures are—for we believe that you have made the best colored picture yet in 'THE GREEN EYED MONSTER.'"

101. REN to Paul E. Thompson, November 14, 1922 (LL-1). True Thompson, in his letter to REN of November 17, 1922, noted: "We used the [skull] costume you spoke of for the Dallas engagement [of *The Crimson Skull*] and had some paper mache skulls which we also used and sent them to the cities in which we played."

102. See, for example, the letter from True E. Thompson to REN of April 9, 1923 (BFC-9), in which Thompson outlines Sack's "desire to take the picture [*The Crimson Skull*] off our hands for Texas and Oklahoma." In reply to Thompson, in a letter of April 12, 1923 (BFC-9), Norman also suggests that Sack might be interested in *The Green-Eyed Monster:* "Mr. Sack can also handle The Green Eyed Monster in this territory with advantage to himself. . . . And if he is interested, we will make him an attractive proposition."

103. REN to M. Barney, March 25, 1922 (LL-1). Norman wrote, "When you see the picture and talk with Mr. B. Norman, my brother, he will convince you of this [opportunity to 'clean-up']." In a March 27, 1922 (LL-1) letter to Bruce, he writes, "I have been corresponding with Mr. Barney of Petersburg and trying to interest him in North and South Carolina, Georgia and Florida on 'The Crimson Skull.' I will hear from his this week if he will go to Baltimore and you can show him the film at the same time you show Rosen. Price it at $3000 and

give him a print at that—if it is not a deal—come down to $2500 and he pays for a print. We could take as low as $2000 and must have 60% down" (LL-1).

104. REN to A. Rosen, February 3, 1922 (LL-1). Within a few years, however, the preponderance of Norman's bookings would be on a percentage basis.

105. Bernstein and White, "Scratching," 103. They reference a letter from REN to BN (December 2, 1921).

106. REN to BN, July 25, 1922 (LL-1).

107. REN to BN, August 29, 1922 (LL-1).

108. REN to BN, September 2, 1922 (LL-1).

109. REN to BN, September 7, 1922 (LL-1).

110. REN to BN, September 10, 1922 (LL-1).

111. REN to BN, September 15, 1922 (LL-1).

112. REN to BN, September 27, 1922 (LL-1).

113. REN to BN, September 27, 1922 (LL-1).

114. REN to BN, September 22, 1922 (LL-1).

115. REN to BN, September 27, 1922 (LL-1).

116. REN to BN, September 10, 1922 (LL-1).

117. REN to A. Schustek, January 5, 1923 (LL-1).

118. According to Mrs. Katherine Norman Hiett (in a letter to Barbara Tepa Lupack [November 2011]), after 1923, her father Bruce Norman owned several businesses in Florida: a drugstore at Broad and Bay Streets in Jacksonville; Norman's Candy Company, also in Jacksonville; and Norman's Fish Camp on Lochloosa, in Hawthorne, Florida (where he died, on February 25, 1970). Mrs. Hiett added that "he never returned to filmmaking."

119. E. L. Cummings to REN, May 25, 1923 (BFC-9). Norman contacted Maxwell on May 11, 1923 (BFC-9), to say that "Mr. Cummings . . . is high in his praise of you and we have the same confidence in your ability as he has." In the same letter, Norman offered Maxwell a position "both in an acting and distributing capacity in the near future." J. A. Jackson concurred with Cummings's judgment: in *Billboard,* Jackson described Maxwell as a "bear" who focused much of his activity on "the selling end of the film game" (qtd. in Sampson, BBW, 329).

120. REN to Alfred N. Sack, October 1, 1923 (BFC-9); Alfred N. Sack to REN, October 5, 1923 (BFC-9).

121. M. C. Maxwell to REN, November 8, 1923 (LL-3).

122. M. C. Maxwell to REN, November 10, 1923 (LL-2).

123. M. C. Maxwell to REN, November 13, 1923 (LL-2). In a letter a few days later (November 17, 1923 [LL-2]), he noted: "I got a letter from my wife that she has had the doctor twice, and I haven't sent he any money since I left there, I

was sure that I would had a settlement here, my expense is such that what little I had and the $10.00 I taken up at Columbus is about gone, I can't get by to save me on less than $15.00 a week for expense, (personal) and it would cost a white man that for three days, as you are getting the cost of paper, I think it only fair that I should get my expense, as I don't get any of my cost or wear and tear on my clothing, I tore the only pair of pants I had on this trip on side of an old car and had to have them fixed, my laundry and pressing is all expensive when you have so little to go on, please let me have a report on what's coming to me as soon as possible."

124. In a letter to Norman, June 22, 1927 (BFC-9), Norman's agent Regan observed: "Saw Maxwell in Beaumont. He has his magic show down there. Said tell you where he was and that he was open for a proposition, in case you could use him in the new picture. Don't think you want him though, he may be a good magician but as an actor think he's all wet." As late as August 23, 1930, Maxwell was in contact with Norman, writing that he had played North and South Carolina and was "thinking of trying Florida"—and suggesting that he was open to further acting work with Norman (BFC-9).

125. REN to K. Lee Williams, December 12, 1922 (LL-1).

126. REN wrote to K. Lee Williams, February 3, 1923 (LL-1): "Regret that you have no extra copy of the Buffalo Bill Picture that is not working. . . . Business is fair with us, due to the fact that the only money the negro shows make is when they run a negro picture. Have everything booked and one road show out playing percentage. And will have another out next month."

127. K. Lee Williams to REN, November 29, 1922 (LL-1).

128. REN to Better Film Company, January 4, 1923 (LL-1). The same letter was sent to numerous other companies.

129. Chas. Marks to REN, April 5, 1923 (LL-1).

130. Chas. Marks to REN, April 5, 1923 (LL-1).

131. REN to Clarence Brooks, May 17, 1923 (LL-1).

132. REN to John T. Glynn, March 30, 1924 (LL-1).

133. John T. Glynn to REN, April 3, 1924 (LL-1).

134. REN to John T. Glynn, April 16, 1924 (LL-1).

5. "A RISKY EXPERIMENT"

The title is taken from letters that Norman wrote to Clarence Brooks, Abraham Rosen, and others, in which he described the fifteen-part serial he was proposing as "a risky experiment."

1. Leab, FSS, 1.

2. The original Rastus series was produced by Lubin. But the Rastus character was such an audience favorite that other companies also produced Rastus shorts—for example, Lubin's *Rastus Knew It Wasn't* (1914); Pathé's *Rastus' Riotous Ride* (1914); *A Barnyard Mix-Up* (1915); and *Rastus' Rabid Rabbit Hunt* (1915). The Rastus type also appears in numerous other early shorts and films, including *Darktown Duel* (1912), *Darktown Wooing* (1914), *The Elite Ball* (1913), and the cartoon *A Hot Time in Punkville* (1915). Another typical "coon" figure similar to Rastus was the "Sambo" character, who appeared in several series and also in numerous films, including *The Haunted Bachelor* (1912), in which a rich bachelor strikes his black valet Sambo and believes that he has killed him; but Sambo revives and frightens his employer, who thinks he has seen a ghost. The antics attract the attention of the police, and the pair ends up in the station house. And in *Darktown Wooing* (1914), Sambo almost loses his girlfriend Verbena to his rival Rastus; on the day of Rastus's wedding, however, Sambo steals a suit, which Rastus in turn steals from him. With the aid of the clothing dealer and a policeman, Sambo gets Rastus arrested and is reunited with Verbena. And, of course, there was also the *Little Black Sambo* book by Helen Bannerman, now considered a racist classic, and the popular cartoon film based on it (Ub Iwerks, 1935).

3. Chicken-snatching was a common plot device in early comic shorts. As Leab, FSS, 14, writes, "A 1910 advertisement for *C-H-I-C-K-E-N Spells Chicken*, an Essanay production, began 'Ah love mah wattah melon but Oh, You-OO Chicken.' The black man, usually dubbed Rastus in the title or in advertising blurbs, generally was shown in these movies to be childlike, foolishly pretentious, shiftless (except where gambling or chickens were concerned), clumsy and vulgar." Some films even managed to incorporate several stereotypes simultaneously into the plot. *The Ranch Chicken* (1911), for example, combined chicken-stealing with the fear of ghosts.

4. Cited in Sampson, BBW, 422. In reviews, the Cabin Kids were usually referred to as "clever little pickaninnies," "the pickaninny outfit," or a similar racially derogatory term.

5. The announcement appeared, under "Coming! Norman Attractions," in the pressbook for *Regeneration* (BFC-18).

6. Advance flyer for *Zircon* (BFC-18).

7. Although the actual costs cannot be confirmed, in correspondence with his brother Bruce during the preproduction and production of the two Western films, Norman wrote that he hoped to keep within a budget of $3,000.

8. Fontenot, "Oscar Micheaux, Black Novelist and Film Maker," 122.

9. Bernstein and White, in "Scratching," cite Norman's "untitled budget" (LL-4).

10. Agreement signed by W. S. Scott, manager, Dunbar Theatre, May 25, 1923 (LL-3).

11. Agreement dated June 4, 1923 (LL-3).

12. REN to John Mills, June 13, 1923, and to J. A. Long, May 19, 1923 (LL-5).

13. REN to Elk Theatre Company, June 13, 1923 (LL-4), replying to Elk's earlier inquiry. The representative of the Elk Theatre Company replied, on July 18, 1923, inquiring about an even lower price: "I have the Negro show here closed at the present time and will not open it till the First of September but I would like to run this serial and start it some time in September if you can make me a price on it at $7.50 an episode" (Elk to REN, July 18, 1923 [LL-4]).

14. REN to Exhibitors, May 18, 1923 (LL-1). Sometimes, however, theater managers wrote back to Norman with ridiculously low quotes. J. F. Mann, of Mart, Texas, for example, quoted Norman a rental fee of $2 per serial episode. In a letter of June 13, 1923 (BFC-5), Norman replied: "Don't expect to get a colored serial at $2. an episode. It can't be done." He noted that "a colored serial will do more business than a white serial" and advised Mann to "think this over."

15. REN to P. A. Engler, May 18, 1923 (LL-1).

16. P. A. Engler to REN, May 19, 1923 (LL-1).

17. E. Wilson, from the True Film Company, to REN, May 21, 1923 (LL-1). Wilson notes that he has received the circular, which states that "you are now ready for engagements," and asks to be advised of terms for handling the subject.

18. REN to A. Rosen, April 9, 1923, and May 14, 1923. Norman reiterated his comment about risk in a letter to Clarence Brooks, June 12, 1923, in which he wrote: "The making of a 15 reel serial is a risky experiment" (LL-1).

19. W. L. Sanders to REN, February 29, 1924 (LL-1).

20. REN to D. O. Chisohm, June 13, 1923 (LL-1).

21. William Redfearn to REN, May 14, 1923, and REN reply (to "Redfern") (LL-1).

22. REN to E. Wilson, June 13, 1923 (LL-1).

23. D. Ireland Thomas to REN, June 18, 1923 (BFC-9).

24. D. Ireland Thomas to REN, May 1, 1923 (LL-1).

25. REN to Clarence Brooks, May 4, 1923 (LL-1).

26. Clarence Brooks to REN, May 12, 1923 (LL-1).

27. In a letter to Norman of June 26, 1923, Brooks noted that, if Norman wanted Thompson to appear in his picture, Brooks needed to give her the dates

of filming. "Miss Thompson," he wrote, "is planning a trip to New York in September to be a Brides-Maid for Mme. [C. J.] Walker's niece and it is imperative that it be known whether you would want her services before or after that time" (LL-1).

28. REN to Clarence Brooks, May 17, 1923 (LL-1). Norman added: "And another picture we have in mind, 'The Soul Robber,' a prison picture with the Electric Chair[,] will be a knock-out and have wonderful exploitation possibilities."

29. Clarence Brooks to REN, May 30, 1923 (LL-1).

30. While Norman was corresponding with Brooks, he was also keeping Thomas apprised of their negotiations. In a letter of June 18, 1923 (BFC-9), to Thomas, Norman wrote: "Brooks has written me a lengthy letter in which he has stated that he is in love with California and would not like to consider a permanent connection in Florida, but would like to lead in the serial with a guarantee of three months work. He is no doubt the man for this serial and we will no doubt be able to get togeather with him."

31. Notably, that figure would be a male hero, since—according to Brooks's "Outline"—"it is hardly possible for a woman to hold the position because of insistent public demands of fights—foot races—thrills etc." Emphasis, Brooks continued, needed to be placed on the prestige and popularity of the actors, the quality of the picture (to prevent the use of other "inferior productions, even at smaller rentals"), and the lowest production expenses to ensure the largest profit for the business. Of course, in the "Outline" of the Lincoln proposal, the "star" in question was Clarence Brooks. The report concludes: "It is to be positively understood that this program of procedure is not offered because of any personal ambitions of Mr. Brooks, but is offered because it is sincerely believed that it is the wisest and most profitable course to pursue for the Lincoln Corporation."

32. REN to Clarence Brooks, June 12, 1923 (LL-1).

33. In the same letter in which he announced Brooks's casting, Norman also noted that "Steve ['Peg' Reynolds] is in it, and the villian is played by Arthur English, former head-liner on Keith Vaudeville and the only colored man capable of playing a real character part." But, in fact, neither Brooks nor Albert English had been definitely cast.

34. Clarence Brooks to REN, June 26, 1923 (LL-1).

35. Norman elaborated: otherwise, "he will realize that he is financing the serial and will never do anything but shoot you a lot of 'Bull' and kid you along."

36. REN to Clarence Brooks, July 18, 1923 (LL-1).

37. It is possible that Norman felt Brooks was not really interested in a collaboration. As Norman wrote Thomas (July 4, 1923 [BFC-9]), "We had offered him a proposition for permanent employment. Now in his letter received today, he does not state his position one way or the other, but reading between the lines, it looks like he would like to come East and if he finds things agreeable, that he will make a permanent connection. This is business policy, and we are too conscientious to ask him to give up his home, friends and his present interests in California, when we ourselves can't predict what the market for colored pictures will develop into."

38. In a letter to REN, June 26, 1923 (LL-1), Brooks expressed his concern over the use of his name in conjunction with the project before an agreement between them was reached; and he noted that he feared that Norman might consider his statement antagonistic.

39. REN to J. Albert English, May 4, 1923 (LL-1).

40. J. Albert English to REN, May 6, 1923 (LL-1).

41. REN to J. Albert English, May 10, 1923 (LL-1).

42. See, for example, REN letter to E. Wilson, June 13, 1923 (LL-1), in which Norman also announced that "Clarence Brooks is the hero. Steve [Reynolds] is in it."

43. S. T. Whitney to REN, July 18, 1923 (LL-1).

44. Edward G. Tatum to REN, July 24, 1923 (LL-1).

45. Hazel Perry to REN, September 4, 1923 (BFC-9). Perry described herself as follows: "My hair is dark brown, eyes brown, color fair, hair waist long, bright eyes, weigh 150 high 5 feet & 5 inches."

46. REN to Hazel Perry, September 4, 1923 (BFC-9), and REN to M. C. Maxwell, September 11, 1923 (BFC-9). "I received photos from Mazel [*sic*] Perry of Winston Salem," Norman wrote, "and regret to state that she is unsuited for the part. . . . She would do for a cabaret scene, but not for leading lady of REGENERATION."

47. REN to D. Ireland Thomas, June 18, 1923 (BFC-9).

48. REN to N. F. Garner, January 23, 1922 (LL-1). One of the distributors whom Norman queried was H. E. Sudduth, manager of the film department of the Queen Feature Service. Sudduth replied, "We do not have a five or six reel feature showing undersea life, mermaids or a feature along the lines of the Jules Verne stories." But he sent a list of films the company had for sale. Bruce Norman queried Western Feature Films of Chicago, Illinois, and received a similar response. Jawitz Pictures Corporation in New York (January 23, 1922) offered

Norman their eight-reel *20,000 Leagues Under the Sea* for purchase at what they considered the "very satisfactory" price of $175. The Economy Film Company in Philadelphia (undated letter [actually January 22, 1922]) replied that they had just sold their copy of Annette Kellerman's *Sea Pictures* and had "no films at the present time of the 'Jules Verne' order" but would try to secure the popular *Neptune's Daughter* for his use. Standard Film Company, of San Francisco, responded to Bruce Norman that while they had no Verne pictures in stock, they would investigate "secur[ing] same." (All letters are in the Lilly Library.)

49. N. F. Garner, in a letter of January 27, 1922, replied to Norman that he was willing to sell his mermaid for $20. "I would not sell it but I am thinking about going out of business." Norman (January 31, 1922) replied to accept the price. He added: "If you have any other curios, we would be glad to receive price on them also." He also contacted other sources, including the Texas Snake Farm in Brownville, to inquire about the purchase of "stuffed animals or snakes" in conjunction with his sea picture. (The letters are in the Lilly Library.)

50. J. A. Jackson, Review of *Regeneration, Billboard*, November 17, 1923, qtd. in Sampson, BBW, 329.

51. The summary is based on the description of the film as it appeared on one of Norman's heralds for the film (BFC-10).

52. REN to Irma Boardman, September 11, 1923 (BFC-9); undated letter from REN to Earline Jackson (BFC-9). But in a letter of September 4, 1923 (LL-1), Norman wrote to Abraham Rosen that "we have started on this picture" and that "Earline Jackson is the leading lady." In that same letter, he also noted that "Steve Reynolds has just returned from New York on the steamer Comanche and I have brought M. C. Maxwell from Winston Salem, N. C. . . . and Jack Austin, villain of Green Eyed Monster[,] is the Villain and also Dr. R. L. Brown and several members of old Green Eyed Monster talent." In a letter of August 7, 1923 (BFC-9) to W. S. Scales, owner and manager of the Lafayette Theatre, Winston-Salem, North Carolina (who had written on behalf of actor Bobbie Smart), REN wrote, "We could afford to give Bobbie Smart $50. for his services. We feel at this figure that he should be able to pay his expenses. Our expenses are mounting up so high in this picture due to bring a cast from New York that we must keep down expenses if we are going to realize a profit through the small distribution of a Colored Picture." The need for Smart's services, he noted, would depend on the weather and on "our ability to shift locations [from the studio to the beach, for the island scenes]."

53. REN to M. C. Maxwell, September 4, 1923 (BFC-9).

54. REN to M. C. Maxwell, September 14, 1923 (BFC-9).

55. REN to M. C. Maxwell, August 23, 1923 (BFC-9).

56. REN to M. C. Maxwell, August 23, 1923 (BFC-9).

57. Edna Morton to REN, August 26, 1923 (BFC-9). In another letter to Norman (July 19, 1923 [BFC-9]), Morton noted that she had "portrayed characters from a child of 12 yrs. to an old lady."

58. REN to Edna Morton, August 7, 1923 (BFC-9).

59. REN to M. C. Maxwell, August 29, 1923 (BFC-9).

60. REN to M. C. Maxwell, August 29, 1923 (BFC-9).

61. REN to M. C. Maxwell, September 4, 1923 (BFC-9).

62. REN to A. Rosen, September 4, 1923 (LL-1).

63. M. C. Maxwell to REN, September 2, 1923 (BFC-9). Maxwell had written: "I hope you will have success in getting the leading lady, I am doing all in my power to locate one, I have gone to some expense." In that letter alone, he noted that he had just contacted several "girls" and encouraged them to write Norman directly detailing their experience and enclosing pictures. In subsequent letters, Maxwell suggested other possible actresses, including Mozel Perry and his sister-in-law Irma Boardman (Maxwell to REN, September 8, 1923 [BFC-9]).

64. REN to M. C. Maxwell, August 29, 1923 (BFC-9). In another letter (July 3, 1923 [BFC-9]), Norman wrote to Maxwell: "I have you in view as lead in this picture as it is a sea story, requiring a man of a mature physique."

65. REN to M. C. Maxwell, July 17, 1923 (BFC-9). When the illness of one of the other cast members caused production to be delayed, Maxwell wrote Norman, noting that he had been forced to cancel plans "made at a sacrifice, to be at your service Aug. 6" and also to "lose time" since he could not make definite plans for other work in the interim. Therefore, he asked Norman for additional compensation. "When I accepted your propersition it was with the understanding that we would begin work the first of August, which would have been during the dull season. After losing so much time, I could not accept the position [of lead actor] at this time for less than $50.00 a week and transportation, with the understanding I start no later than Sept. 3, 1923" (August 16, 1923 [BFC-9]).

66. REN to A. Rosen, September 4, 1923 (LL-1).

67. REN to Edna Morton, July 24, 1923 (BFC-9); REN to M. C. Maxwell, July 17, 1923 (BFC-9); REN to W. S. Scales, August 7, 1923 (BFC-9).

68. REN to M. C. Maxwell, July 17, 1923 (BFC-9).

69. REN to A. Rosen, September 4, 1923 (LL-1); M. C. Maxwell to REN, August 27, 1923 (BFC-9); REN to M. C. Maxwell, August 29, 1923 (BFC-9).

70. In the letter to Rosen, written on September 4, 1923 (LL-1), Norman stated that he had already "started on this picture," which (at that time) starred

Earline Jackson as the leading lady and Jack Austin (the villain from *The Green-Eyed Monster*) as the villain, in addition to M. C. Maxwell, Steve Reynolds, and Dr. R. L. Brown. Of course, Jackson was soon replaced by Stella Mayo and Austin by Albert English. Norman's explanation of his rising costs may also have been a tactic to get more money from Rosen for distribution rights in his territory.

71. Bean, FH, 116.

72. REN to J. H. MacShane, February 22, 1924 (LL-3).

73. REN to J. H. King Jr., February 14, 1924 (BFC-1).

74. REN to Guy Shriner, February 13, 1924 (BFC-9).

75. "I will boost it all I can," Maxwell promised in a letter to Norman (August 21, 1924 [BFC-9]). Although he had been out of town for a few days, he assured Norman that he would "remain here [in Greenville, South Carolina] untill the picture plays." Maxwell made appearances both formally and informally. In letters to the Pekin Theatre (October 23, 1923 [LL-2]) and the Valdosta Theatre (October 10, 1923 [LL-3]), for example, Norman offered Maxwell's services in promoting the picture (sole appearance at the Pekin, dual appearance with Reynolds at the Valdosta). In a letter to Norman (July 13, 1924 [BFC-9]), Maxwell wrote that he had left New Orleans because it was too hot for his family, especially his baby, and therefore missed several performances of the picture in that town. But he was currently in Greenville, South Carolina, where "Mr. Wilson" of the Liberty Theatre was interested in showing the picture, even though business was "dull." Wilson "would like to play it while I am here." In a separate letter (Wilson to REN, July 28, 1924 [BFC-4]), from Robert Wilson of the Liberty Theatre, Greenville, South Carolina, Maxwell's hometown, Wilson wrote that "Mays Maxwell is here and will be here for about six weeks and of course he is talking the picture up, and I would like to suggest that if you have any way of having some cards doped to the effect that a Greenville boy is in this picture it might boost it some, in other words work the local boy stunt as much as you can." Leo G. Garner, manager of the Columbia Theatre in Bristol, Tennessee, who was about to feature the Mayo Magicians in his theater, suggested a similar marketing gimmick: in a letter to Norman of March 19, 1924 (BFC-4), he wrote: "Incidentally, this is Stella Mayo's home-town, and I think if you intend sending 'Regeneration' out on the road that we could get some money here with it."

76. Press sheet for *Regeneration* (BFC-18).

77. REN to Paul Zerilla, March 27, 1924 (LL-4).

78. REN to Guy Shriner, February 13, 1924 (BFC-9).

79. REN to Paul Zerilla, March 15, 1924 (LL-4).

80. REN to Geo. T. Chester, April 21, 1924 (LL-1).

81. REN to W. S. Scales, July 25, 1924 (BFC-2).

82. REN to Chas. A. Somma, August 16, 1926 (LL-5).

83. REN to Ralph Goldberg, May 19, 1924 (BFC-2).

84. REN to Paul Zerilla, October 25, 1926 (BFC-4).

85. M. C. Maxwell to REN, June 3, 1924 [BFC-9]). Apropos of the Lyric Theatre, Norman wrote to R. D. Goldberg (May 2, 1924 [BFC-2]), that *Regeneration* "played to 5279 paid admissions at top price of 40¢ admission at Lyric Theatre, New Orleans, yesterday."

86. REN to Guy Shriner, February 20, 1924 (BFC-2). Norman repeated the fact that all copies of *Regeneration* were "booked solid" through June in a letter to Geo. T. Chester, April 21, 1924 (LL-1).

87. REN to Thos. Armistead, in Laurel, Mississippi, January 26, 1925 (BFC-1).

88. REN to Robert Wilson, August 18, 1924 (BFC-4).

89. REN to M. C. Maxwell, July 7, 1924 (BFC-9).

90. REN to M. C. Maxwell, July 7, 1924 (BFC-9).

91. REN to M. C. Maxwell, July 19, 1924 (BFC-9); REN to W. S. Scales, July 25, 1924 (BFC-2).

92. REN to "Mr. Brecker," Plaza Theatre, October 8, 1924 (LL-5). Norman wrote that he showed theater manager Mr. Scheiffman "box office reports of our percentage" to support the claims of record attendance, "for after all, it is the box office angle that interests the theatre manager most."

93. REN to Thomas James, November 27, 1924 (BFC-9).

94. REN to A. Mendel, June 19, 1925 (BFC-5).

95. REN to Guy Shriner, February 13, 1924 (BFC-9).

96. REN to Paul Zerilla, February 27, 1924 (LL-5).

97. The Virginia State Board of Censors License, issue date September 15, 1924. Total amount paid: $10.00 (LL-1).

98. Pennsylvania State Board of Censors Certificate of Censorship, approval with eliminations, September 23, 1924. Total amount paid: $10.00 (LL-1).

99. The Motion Picture Commission of the State of New York License, issued "with elim." on November 8, 1924. Total amount paid: $15.00 (LL-1).

100. With respect to *A Colored Sherlock Holmes*: in a letter to M. C. Maxwell of August 29, 1924 (BFC-9), Norman promised Maxwell that "if REGENERATION goes over, we will follow that with A COLORED SHERLOCK HOLMES using all appliances for the mechanical detection of crime and you with your

magical training should be a good lead for this picture." Yet, while *Regeneration* did indeed "go over," *A Colored Sherlock Holmes* was never made. Norman's idea of using a professional magician in the role of the great detective was, however, a clever one.

101. REN to M. C. Maxwell, July 19, 1924 (BFC-9).

102. REN to M. C. Maxwell, August 29, 1923 (BFC-9).

103. REN to A. Schustek, January 5, 1923 (LL-1). Norman wrote: "When I talked with you last September, I was considering opening up a factory here … [But] the party who was going to put up a special building, a Mr. Klutho of the Klutho Moving Picture Studios, has been waiting until he made about $25,000 worth of additions to his studio to go further with me in erecting a building adjoining his studio. And he has been holding off making these additions because the usual influx of Northern companies have not materialized this year." Ultimately, Klutho never made the additions; in fact, faced with major losses, he was forced to sell the studio to Berg Productions. But that venture proved to be short-lived; and the studio closed permanently in 1922.

104. Richard Alan Nelson writes, mistakenly, that the sale occurred in 1922; and Shawn C. Bean (FH, 115) repeats the error. Bean claims that Norman and his brother shopped around in 1922 for a facility "that could accommodate their growing operation" and that the "most appealing was the old Eagle Studios." But the contracts for the purchase of the Eagle Studios (like Norman's own letters) indicate that it was not in 1922 but in the following year (1923–1924) that Norman acquired and closed on the property.

105. Bean, FH, 115.

106. Nelson, FAMPI, Vol. 2, 438.

107. REN to Clarence Brooks, July 18, 1923 (LL-1).

6. "YOU KNOW WE HAVE THE GOODS"

The title comes from a letter (March 15, 1924) that Norman wrote in response to Paul Zerilla, of Memphis, Tennessee, who had offered an "insultingly" low price for one of Norman's pictures. Norman replied, "You know as well as anyone that Moving Pictures can't be made to sell like a can of tomatoes nor like a piece of cheese when they are all wool and a yard wide." Asserting that his pictures "smash records," Norman reminded Zerilla "you know we have the goods."

1. That studio was officially purchased on October 26, 1924. Norman's lawyer, Frank E. Jennings, wrote to Norman, "The motion picture property was sold the first Monday in October by the Court and bought in your name for

$3250." The parties on the other side, he indicated, would prefer "the mortgage notes made separately instead of all in one note as we had signed before" (LL-1). But Norman apparently occupied the premises for at least a year prior to the actual purchase.

2. REN to C. W. Kramer, February 21, 1925 (LL-1).

3. REN to Albert A. Fish, March 7, 1925 (LL-1).

4. Promotional materials for the Afro-American Film Producers (BFC-9).

5. Promotional materials for the Afro-American Film Producers (BFC-9).

6. REN to Captain E. C. McVey, May 20, 1924 (BFC-9).

7. Captain Edison C. McVey to REN, June 3, 1924 (BFC-9).

8. REN to Captain E. C. McVey, May 20, 1924 (BFC-9).

9. Captain E. C. McVey to REN, July 7, 1924 (BFC-9).

10. REN to Captain E. C. McVey, July 19, 1924 (BFC-9).

11. Captain E. C. McVey to REN, August 6, 1924 (BFC-9).

12. REN to Captain E. C. McVey, October 7, 1924 (BFC-9). In that same letter, Norman suggested that perhaps McVey's story "Coming From the Clouds" might be made "instead" of or "in addition to the one I have." But he noted that the title would have to be changed, "as a picture of that name has already been released with a white cast."

13. REN to Captain E. C. McVey, August 23, 1924 (BFC-9). Norman did express interest in hearing more about the flight, but at a later time.

14. REN to Captain E. C. McVey, August 23, 1924 (BFC-9).

15. Captain E. C. McVey to REN, October 15, 1924 (BFC-9).

16. REN to Captain E. C. McVey, October 25, 1924 (BFC-9).

17. REN to E. B. Dudley, June 30, 1925 (LL-5).

18. Sampson, BBW, 185, writes that *Shadow and Sunshine* was based on "an original story by Jesse Shipp, then the dean of black stage directors and producers." The film, however, "was never completed and this was due in part to the lack of cooperation by the star, Bessie Coleman. Miss Coleman was brought to New York at the expense of the company but later abruptly changed her mind and left the city without giving notice to the director." But according to Doris L. Rich in *Queen Bess: Daredevil Aviator* (Washington, D.C.: Smithsonian Institution Press, 1993), Coleman's intentions were far more admirable. In the first scene, she was supposed to appear as a racial caricature, wearing tattered clothing and carrying a pack; by walking off the set, Coleman was making a statement of principle. "Opportunist though she was about her career, she was never an opportunist about race. She had no intention of perpetuating the derogatory image most whites had of most blacks." There are other similar stories. Once,

for example, she reportedly refused to perform in an airshow in her hometown of Waxahachie, Texas, because white and black audiences were forced to enter through separate admission gates. Before she performed, she insisted that both audiences be allowed to use the same gate. Unfortunately, it was a small victory, because once the spectators were inside, they split into their own designated— and segregated—sections.

19. D. Ireland Thomas to REN, January 15, 1926 (LL-1).

20. REN to D. Ireland Thomas, January 19, 1926 (LL-1).

21. REN to D. Ireland Thomas, January 19, 1926 (LL-1).

22. Bessie Coleman to REN, February 3, 1926 (LL-1), and February 23, 1926 (LL-1). Coleman wrote: "as any intelegent colored person know that I am the worlds first col Flyer, man or woman." Norman, in a letter to Coleman (February 8, 1926 [LL-1]), agreed that "properly acted and full of action with you in the leading role, [the picture] would be a good drawing card in the colored theatres."

23. Coleman was flying with her manager, William Wills. It was he who was actually in the pilot's seat at the time of the tragic accident. Coleman reportedly was unbelted because she was looking over the cockpit sill to examine possible landing sights for a parachute stunt that she planned to perform. Since she was not wearing a belt, as the plane dove and spun, she was thrown to her death. Wills managed to pull out of the dive and momentarily regain control of the plane; but he too was killed when the plane plummeted and caught fire. It was later determined that a loose wrench had jammed the plane's instruments. For more on Bessie Coleman, see Doris L. Rich, *Queen Bess: Daredevil Aviator*; see also Elizabeth Hadley Freydberg, *Bessie Coleman: The Brownskin Lady Bird* (New York: Garland, 1994) and Dominick Pisano and Von Hardesty, *Black Wings: The American Black in Aviation* (Washington, D. C.: Smithsonian Institution Press, 1984).

24. REN to Shingzie Howard, June 16, 1926 (LL-1).

25. Shingzie Howard to REN, January 25, 1926 (LL-1).

26. REN to Shingzie Howard, February 1, 1926 (LL-1).

27. Shingzie Howard to REN, February 17, 1926 (LL-1).

28. Butters, BMSS, 193, suggests that Norman's films, which he called "standard action-adventure fare," always starred "a light-skinned man who was respected and reputable and who faced a formidable challenge. . . . Also included in the Norman standard was the dark-skinned villain, conforming to the color-coded assessment of African-American character traits." According to Butters's argument, the light-skinned Bishop would have been appropriate for the hero but not the villain role.

29. Norman wrote Henderson on April 15, 1926 (BFC-9), noting that Shing-zie Howard had given him his address "in connection for the cast of our next picture we will produce. We watched your work in Smiling Hate and was favorably impressed with it, and might be able to use you as one of the leads in 'The Flying Ace.'" He added that "the present market for colored pictures will not justify high salarys." Henderson replied quickly and graciously. In his letter to Norman of April 23, 1926 (BFC-9), he wrote: "I regret to state that it is impossible for me to consider the same [a position] as at the present time I am under contract to the Colored Players Film Corporation for one year and a half from date, and am right in the middle of a production." He thanked Norman for the offer and assured him that if he were "at liberty," he would have been glad to accept.

30. REN to Shingzie Howard, March 15, 1926 (LL-1). In his letter, Norman observed that "We have spent the last three weeks on props for it [The Flying Ace]."

31. Among those actors and actresses were R. Martello (undated/ca. March 15, 1925 [LL-1]), to whom Norman wrote: "This year, we will make 'The Black Ace' and have you in mind as a possible member of the cast. If you were here, we would be glad to give you a try out in The Dehorners, the picture we will make next month." Still other actors contacted Norman directly. For instance, in a letter of March 4, 1925 (LL-1), Ben C. Haynes, who was featured in a Pathé serial as "a pal to the leading man," inquired about possibilities for himself and his "friend lady." He noted that he could "ride a bucking broncho drive automobile fight lasso a rope quick with a gun also my fist." He added that "What you want is ambition and courage and we have all that. I can ride a horse when its running go under neat her stomach with both legs under so any thing just say you will try us and if I don't do this what I say you owe me nothing what more do you want a fellow to say." And Anna M. Dumas (in a letter of August 26, 1926) wrote: "I want to be in the moving pictures. I am a girl of 20 yrs—5 ft-4 ins with brown skin. Very attractive. I weigh 116 lbs. Can sing and dance. Am very apt to learn anything. Have long hair. . . . I have a good education."

32. REN to Albert Fish, January 16, 1926 (LL-1).

33. Albert A. Fish to REN, January 27, 1926 (LL-1). Fish wrote: "To-day I found a company has been formed, for colored productions. They are at present equiping a studio and are already shooting exteriors. . . . On this account I presume the cast are tied up and did not come around to see me. I understand [Harry] Henderson (the lead) is tied up for two years. How the others are tied I don't know, will probably learn later." Norman replied to Fish (February 1, 1926 [LL-1]) that he had just received a letter from actress Shingzie Howard. "She advised me that she was working for a newly formed corporation in Phil., com-

posed of a number of wealthy jews who planned to make a series of 6 pictures and already were engaged in production of the first, 'A Prince of His Race.'"

34. Contract between J. Lawrence Criner and R. E. Norman, dated June 24, 1926 (BFC-9).

35. REN to W. L. Sanders, August 6, 1926 (LL-3). Norman wrote almost identical letters to other exhibitors, including W. C. Kennedy, August 24, 1926 (BFC-4).

36. REN to S. Berry, September 21, 1927 (LL-3). Similarly, Norman wrote W. D. Cooper on May 24, 1927 (LL-1): "With all eyes turned on aviation, due to Captain Lindberg's tiumps over the Atlantic, the colored people are also enthused over conquests of the air. And their own airplane picture The Flying Ace is breaking box office records in spite of a drop in the regular business on white pictures."

37. Promotional material for The Flying Ace (BFC-18).

38. Klotman, "Planes," 161, 164. Regarding black participation in the Armed Services, Klotman cites Charles E. Francis, The Tuskegee Airmen (Boston: Branden, 1988).

39. "Articles of Agreement," between the Norman Film Manufacturing Company and the "Owners of the Development known as Christenia," unsigned (LL-1).

40. Klotman, in "Planes," 316, suggests that the footage of the Mayport Station may, in fact, have been shot six years earlier, when Norman was filming the railroad action for The Green-Eyed Monster, at which time he had contracted with the Florida East Coast Company to shoot at its Mayport Branch.

41. Captain Richard E. Norman, interview by Wendy Chamber, July 10, 2010, cited on Chamber's website, "Black Gold: The Norman Film Manufacturing Company."

42. REN to J. V. Ritchey, August 27, 1926 (LL-1). Norman added, "The local negro theatre owner here, Mr. Seligman has made the same criticism of these posters, and from past experience, I know the balance of the exhibitors will do the same."

43. REN to Douglas Theatre, April 19, 1926 (LL-3).

44. Undated letter from REN to "Mr. Hill" (LL-3). The cost of Reynolds's bally was $75, half of which Norman was willing to cover himself. "I will meet you half way and stand the balance," he wrote Hill, "and I feel that we will not miss it."

45. REN to Oscar Micheaux, August 9, 1926 (LL-1).

46. REN to H. A. Wasserman, October 12, 1926 (BFC-21).

47. REN to H. A. Wasserman, October 9, 1926 (BFC-21).

48. Regan to REN, June 5, 1927 (BFC-9).

49. REN to Earl (Tex) Spencer, June 23, 1927 (BFC-3).

50. REN to Geo. C. Jackson, May 11, 1927 (BFC-3). In a letter (December 19, 1928 [BFC-2]) to Cale K. Burgess in Raleigh, North Carolina, he mentions lining up a "route solid from Jacksonville, Fla., up through South Carolina and into North Carolina."

51. Klotman, "Planes," 163.

52. Klotman, "Planes," 167.

53. The picture occasionally was passed without eliminations, as in the case of the State of Ohio's Board of Censors, June 13, 1927. Fee for 6 reels: $6.00 (LL-1).

54. Pennsylvania State Board of Censors, Approval with Eliminations, six-reel *Flying Ace*, May 3, 1928 (LL-1).

55. State of New York, Education Department, Motion Picture Division, May 7, 1928. Fee paid: $3.00 per reel (LL-1).

56. City of Chicago, approved with cuts, May 23, 1927, *The Flying Ace* in 6 reels. Fee: $18.00 (LL-1).

57. Oscar Micheaux to REN, August 7, 1926 (LL-1). Micheaux suggested that the poor photography was "due to the use of some Cooper-Hewitt banks alternating current which flicker alternately through all the interiors and refuse to permit a fade-out with any degree of smoothness at all."

58. REN to Oscar Micheaux, August 9, 1926 (LL-1).

59. REN to Harry Henderson, April 15, 1926 (BFC-9), and to Chas. A. Somma, August 16, 1926 (LL-4).

60. Undated material [ca. November 2011] sent by Mrs. Katherine Norman Hiett to Barbara Tepa Lupack.

61. Norman received several inquiries for work, including one from S. L. Lockett in Atlanta, Georgia, to whom Norman replied in a letter of December 31, 1925 (BFC-9): "If your application had reached me at any other time, I would have snapped up the opportunity immediately to acquire your services, but coming at a dull time and also at a time when I haven't completed new pictures, it left only the old ones to play and after looking over possible runs, I became convinced that it would not pay either of us." But he hoped that if Lockett were "foot loose" at a later time, they could "get togeather on a proposition we can both make money at." Another inquiry (December 12, 1925 [LL-1]) came from W. R. Arnold of First National Pictures, Incorporated. "I am ready to take up the work, whatever you assign to me, wherever you are or can, use me. As I told

you. I am looking for *advantages,"* he wrote. "I know the road like a book, having been on it at oft times, since the season of 1903, in which time I handled advance and publicity work for some of the very best road shows on tour, motion pictures, included."

62. Regan to REN, April 3, 1927 (LL-2).

63. Regan to REN, June 1, 1927 (LL-3).

64. Regan to REN, June 5, 1927 (BFC-9).

65. Regan to REN, June 1, 1927 (LL-3).

66. In a letter of June 7, 1927 (BFC-9), Regan wrote Norman that "No doubt, our views about cutting out bad places and making repairs, differ. Whenever I beleive that a bad place will go through with-out a possibility of causing damage, I leave it in just as long as possible. Of course, that increases the fire hazard but at that I still think it better, under low amperage, to leave them in rather than have a patch at every foot."

67. Regan to REN, June 7, 1927 (BFC-9).

68. Regan to REN, June 18, 1927 (BFC-9).

69. Regan to REN, July 1, 1927 (BFC-9).

70. Norman did, however, promise Regan that when he was ready to return, there would still be routes available for him to assume. Ultimately Regan did not return to work for Norman, but the two men remained in contact and on good terms for many more years. Regan, in fact, invited the Normans to his wedding to Mary Frances Colson in College Park, Georgia, on August 3, 1929.

71. Bernstein and White, "Scratching," 107, write that, at the time he was hired by Norman, Kontas was a "theater owner, film salesman and projectionist."

72. REN to Sam Kontas, August 26, 1927 (LL-1). Norman noted: "We can discuss this further in a personal interview. Both propositions have their good points, and I want you to realize that I am offering you a real inducement to work for us both."

73. Norman originally anticipated that Kontas's first route would take him through Texas, Louisiana, Alabama, and Georgia; the next trip, beginning in mid-November, would be "up the Atlantic seabord or into Ohio." But in a letter of September 10, 1927 (LL-1), Norman advised him that because of slow contracts, he was changing the route. It would now begin in Texas and move north through Oklahoma and possibly Alabama or Mississippi. Nonetheless, Norman emphasized that the new route, one of the "finest," would allow Kontas to make big money for both himself and Norman.

74. REN to Sam Kontas, September 20, 1927 (LL-Box 1).

75. REN to Sam Kontas, January 28, 1928 (LL-1).

76. Sam Kontas to REN, January 30, 1928 (LL-1).

77. As per Norman's response (February 18, 1929) to a query about Kontas's whereabouts.

78. Charles P. McClane to REN, November 13, 1925 (LL-1). Other exhibitors had similarly good things to say about Chas. Albert A. Fish, for example, in a letter to Norman of December 1, 1925, wrote: "I saw you[r] man Ellis when he was in Philadelphia last, fine chap."

79. Chas. [Charles K. Ellis] to REN, September 22, 1925 (BFC-9).

80. As per letters and "Agreement in Duplicate" between Norman and Abraham Rosen (LL-1).

81. REN to Bruce Norman, undated [ca. 1922] (LL-1).

82. REN to Bruce Norman, March 31, 1922 (LL-1).

83. A. Rosen to REN, April 4, 1923 (LL-1).

84. A. Rosen to REN, June 15, 1922 (LL-1).

85. REN to A. Rosen, April 13, 1922 (LL-1).

86. REN to A. Rosen, March 14, 1927 (LL-1).

87. REN to Mrs. Abraham Rosen, April 6, 1927 (LL-1).

88. William George to REN, May 14, 1927 (LL-1).

89. REN to William George, May 26, 1927 (LL-1).

90. Frank E. Jennings to REN, June 3, 1927 (LL-1).

91. Norman laid out settlement terms in his letter of April 6, 1927 (LL-1) to Mrs. Rosen. "Under the unfortunate circumstances of your husbands death," he wrote, "we are willing to overlook the fact of him renting these pictures outside his territory, provided all prints of these pictures are returned to us in the next 10 days by Express to our Arlington, Florida, office. Mr. Rosen had two prints of Green Eyed Monster, 5 reels each, one print of Bull-Dogger, 5 reels, one print of Crimson Skull, 6 reels, and one print Love Bug, 2 reels. These prints were to be surrendered to us with all rights on March 7th., as per his contracts, which you can refer to. We are willing to reimburse you for a return of any new advertising you may have on these pictures that we sold Mr. Rosen. In regard to these prints, there can be no reimbursement on them, because they are worn out, and we merely want to destroy them to prevent any further trouble."

92. REN to "Messers Brangyn & Clark," April 30, 1926 (LL-1). In that letter, Norman outlined "the historical, civic and industrial, sporting and agricultural phases" of the project. He noted further: "I will produce this picture in two reels of motion pictures, good clear and sharp photography, selecting the best

angles to adequately show up each subject from a pictorial and educational standpoint, coloring such subjects green, blues and browns with pink, yellow and orange tints and some scenes black and white, furnishing you the two reels titled and ready for projection for the sum of $3200.00."

93. REN to Wm. R. Shirley, August 9, 1926 (LL-1). Norman wrote that "By way of making the most satisfactory and most interesting contest, all of the successful canidates could be given a trip to Florida, and appear in the picture, tho some would be used in only the big scenes calling for a number of extras." Norman, himself a member of the Brotherhood, signed his letter "Fraternally yours."

94. REN to Justo Gonzalez, July 27, 1926 (LL-1).

95. REN to Sidney Meyer, October 14, 1927 (LL-1). Norman added that possibly, if run at the regular admission with a double program, the film would get by.

96. REN to Sidney Meyer, October 19, 1927 (LL-1).

97. REN to Albert A. Fish, April 6, 1925 (LL-1). Norman wrote: "It is going to take some hard work on our part to put over these pictures to good profit to you at this time, and we expect your co-operation." He added: "To give you an idea as to how we exploit our product in near-by territory, we are just now sending out Regeneration in this State with M. C. Maxwell, the leading man and star of the picture, to make a personal appearence and boost the attraction. We have always done everything possible to assist the exhibitor and have been fairly successful in making him money and gaining his confidence."

98. REN to W. S. Scales, December 1, 1925 (BFC-2).

99. Pressbook for *Black Gold* (BFC-18).

100. Pressbook for *Black Gold* (BFC-18).

101. REN to Alfred Norcom, June 18, 1927 (LL-1). In a letter of June 14, 1927 (LL-1), Norcom had replied to Norman's initial letter. "Very glad to hear from you," Norcom wrote. "Of course, the salary part is O.K. if I can do straight time and realize anything. But I'm sure I will have character all through the picture. And I'm sure I will get more billing matter than before. So everything is O.K."

102. REN to P. D. Horn, July 7, 1927 (LL-1).

103. In a letter (July 17, 1928 [LL-1]) to beauty contest winner and aspiring actress Dorothy Lee Jackson, for instance, Norman thanked her for writing and sending photos, which he promised to keep on file in the event that he could use her "type" in an upcoming production. Jackson had written Norman on July 9, 1928 (LL-1), asking for work. She included a photograph of herself and noted that she had a good wardrobe as well as her own ideas for stories.

104. REN to "Mr. Schafer," June 17, 1928 (LL-4).

105. REN to Paul Zerilla, February 27, 1924 (LL-4).

106. Pressbook for *Black Gold* (BFC-18).

107. REN to H. E. Hall, September 26, 1926 (LL-3). In the same letter, Norman wrote, "They make a pleasing personal appearence." Kathryn, he added, was the former wife of Irving Miller and headed the "'Running Wild' show"; her father was "one of the most famous negros of to-day."

108. REN to Guy Shriner, July 7, 1930 (BFC-2).

109. REN to Guy Shriner, May 6, 1928 (BFC-2).

110. At the Rex, in fact, *Black Gold* grossed $146.72 on its first night.

111. Charles Hirsh to REN, June 25, 1930 (BFC-9).

112. REN to Dorothy Lee Jackson, July 17, 1928 (LL-1).

113. REN to Alfred Norcom, June 25, 1928 (BFC-9).

7. "IT TAKES A DARN GOOD ONE TO STICK"

The title comes from a letter (June 2, 1925) from Albert A. Fish, President of Superior Art Motion Pictures, who wrote to Norman about the many obstacles in the race film industry: "So as I often said 'This colored picture business will always show what a man is made of.' It takes a darn good one to stick."

1. Cripps, BFG, 23–24.

2. Cripps, SFB, 150–151, 263, 43.

3. REN to Pekin Theatre, August 26, 1926 (LL-2).

4. Cripps, BFG, 30.

5. Sampson, BBW, 215.

6. Qtd. in Sampson, BBW, 10–11.

7. Cripps, SFB, 218.

8. Robert Benchley, "*Hearts in Dixie* (The First Real Talking Picture)," in Lindsay Patterson, ed., *Black Films and Film-Makers: A Comprehensive Anthology from Stereotype to Superhero* (New York: Dodd, Mead, 1975), 84–85.

9. Williams, PRC, 141–142. Williams cites Michael Rogin's argument that blackface was a means of whitewashing the assimilated Jew. Since Jewishness disappeared behind the mask of blackface, posing as black ultimately became a way of passing as white.

10. Williams, PRC, 154. The film is ultimately a critique of "the reduction of Jewish-American history to a family melodrama . . . in which the generalized woes of slaves speak for the woes of Jews." For Rogin, anti-Semitism is "the film's structuring absence, while blackface performance, reaching back to the origins of American mass entertainment in minstrelsy, disguises this absence through the substitute pathos of mammy songs."

11. Williams, PRC, 158.

12. According to Jim Pines, BF, 22, Hollywood's interest derived neither from liberal nor humanist tendencies; rather it reflected a newly acquired recognition of the viability of exploiting blacks on the sound movie screen and in the movie houses. But unlike the intense and genuine fascination with black folk drama that was occurring concurrently in literature, in films "Negro themes" remained an awkward concern and enjoyed at best modest though cautious commercial consideration, largely due to the stage popularity of vernacular entertainments, including the blackface masquerades of Jolson that blacks found so pernicious.

13. So convincing to white audiences were these sentimentalized images that even the reviewer for *The New York Times* (February 28, 1929) praised the film for cleverly capturing "the spirit of the Southern negro." The black press sought to find recuperative elements in the film. In an essay entitled "Folk Values in a New Medium," Sterling A. Brown, a professor at Howard University, and Alain Locke, a founding father of the Harlem Renaissance literary movement, praised "the first all-Negro talkie" for expressing the "vibrancy of the race" through acting and singing. Although they agreed that "the usual types are there—the Daddy, [the] Uncle, the Mammy, and the inevitable pickaninnies"—Brown and Locke suggested that "in this group they are real flesh and blood Negroes evoking a spontaneous and human interest"; and they concluded that although "the story is sketchy," *Hearts in Dixie* is nevertheless "the truest pictorialization of Negro life to date" (Sterling A. Brown, "Insight, Courage, and Craftsmanship," *Opportunity* 18 [1940]: 185–186; rpt. in Keneth Kinnamon, ed., *Critical Essays on Richard Wright's Native Son* [New York: Twayne, 1997], 26–27).

14. Nonetheless, black moviegoers took umbrage both at the resistance of certain Southern exhibitors to show all-black pictures and at the inherently racist way that MGM marketed the film, premiering it simultaneously at the Lafayette, a black theater, for black audiences, and at the downtown Astor. See Everett, RG, 175–177.

15. Sammy Davis Jr.'s portrayal of Sportin' Life in *Porgy and Bess*, for instance, clearly derived from William Fountaine's flashy, derby-sporting crapshooter Hot Shot; and the sensuous Carmen (Dorothy Dandridge) in Otto Preminger's *Carmen Jones* and the sexy Georgia Brown (Lena Horne) in *Cabin in the Sky* were patterned upon Nina Mae McKinney's brassy, hip-swiveling, and whorish Chick.

16. REN to Evans Sprott, October 17, 1927 (BFC-4).

17. As early as 1928, even some of the larger "colored theatres" had already installed sound. As Norman wrote to Allen Jenkins at the Strand Theatre in Roanoke, Virginia (October 24, 1928 [BFC-21]), "there are 4 large colored the-

atres which have sound installed that we know of at the present time and all are doing a big business. However, the net profits are not much because of the cost of the equipment and rentals." The changes were rapid. As M. C. Maxwell wrote Norman (August 23, 1930 [BFC-9]) from Greenville, South Carolina, in 1930: "Talkies are at Liberty here . . . Asheville, N.C. has talkies also a new house at Charlotte, N.C."

18. REN to Guy Shriner, July 7, 1930 (BFC-2).

19. REN to B. Engleberg, October 7, 1929 (LL-1), replying to Engleberg's inquiry. Similarly, Norman later wrote to B. E. Hall that "in regard to colored attractions for your theatre, we beg to advise that we have only silent prints. However, we have some discs which will furnish musical background" (May 28, 1931 [LL-1]).

20. REN to W. S. Scott, March 9, 1928 (LL-3).

21. REN to Walter, September 1, 1930 (LL-1). But, Norman reiterated, such a plan would require financing.

22. Promotional materials for Camera-Phone (BFC-8).

23. REN to Guy Shriner, July 7, 1930 (BFC-2).

24. REN to William George, November 15, 1929 (BFC-1).

25. REN to Regan, July 29, 1929 (LL-1).

26. REN to W. S. Scott, March 9, 1928 (LL-3).

27. In a letter to Eunice Kirkland, October 24, 1929 (LL-1), Norman had estimated his competitors' prices for comparable equipment.

28. Eunice Kirkland to REN, February 6, 1930 (LL-1).

29. Fred L. Freeman to REN, December 11, 1930 (LL-1).

30. J. M. McKinney, May 25, 1931 (LL-1). The problems with the fader are discussed in a letter from REN to McKinney, October 21, 1930 (LL-1).

31. REN to Walter, September 1, 1930 (LL-1).

32. REN to Walter, September 8, 1930 (LL-1).

33. REN to S. A. Austin, September 19, 1931 (LL-1).

34. Harry Simons to REN, April 24, 1931 (LL-1).

35. Harry Simons to REN, July 22, 1931 (LL-1).

36. REN to J. C. Wertman, August 15, 1932 (LL-1).

37. Excerpt from Edward Bernds's *Mr. B. Goes to Hollywood*, Scarecrow Press, as cited in "The State of the Art—1928—Part 1: Motion Picture Sound Recording In Its Infancy," on the "FilmSound.org" website. Accessed January 1, 2013.

38. Regan to REN, June 22, 1929 (LL-1).

39. As Edward Bernds recalled: "The man who invented the light-valve may have been a genius, but the engineers who designed the other Western Electric

equipment were decidedly not. Everything they provided for us was oversized and overweight. . . .. It was inevitable that the microphone Western Electric provided for us would also be heavy. Officially, it was called a condenser-transmitter-amplifier, CTA for short. The nature of a CTA required that an amplifier be a part of the device; this added to bulk and weight, so that the CTA weighed about eight pounds; and naturally, it was encased in bronze. The result was that this electronic heavyweight, which should have been light, agile and capable of quick movement, proved difficult to move. It was even, because of its size, difficult to conceal in the benighted days when we concealed microphones in flower arrangements and behind curtains."

40. Captain Richard E. Norman, interview, May 23, 1978, qtd. in Nelson, FAMPI, Vol. 2, 440.

41. REN to E. A. Welters, October 31, 1929 (LL-1).

42. REN to Friend King [possibly J. H. King of the Pike Theatre in Mobile, Alabama], June 5, 1933 (BFC-1).

43. F. Bund Jr. to REN, September 7, 1929 (BFC-1).

44. J. Pitman Harmon Jr., September 16, 1929 (LL-1).

45. The Black Star Line was a steamship company that was funded by sales of stock to members of the United Negro Improvement Association. The sale of shares was, Garvey claimed, a way of investing in the race and of ensuring employment and transportation in the Back-to-Africa movement of self-determination that he envisioned.

46. REN to J. Pitman Harmon Jr., October 23, 1929 (LL-1).

47. REN to BER Motion Picture Company, Attention of H. Nathan Eastman, May 6, 1932 (LL-1).

48. REN to S. Raymond Horace, WER Motion Picture Company, December 22, 1935 (BFC-9).

49. REN to Ben Burbridge, September 25, 1930 (LL-1).

50. R. J. Hersey to REN, October 3, 1929 (LL-1).

51. REN to D. J. Moore, International Publishers, Inc., October 3, 1929 (LL-1).

52. REN to International Publishers, Inc., Attention of R. J. Hersey, October 15, 1929 (LL-1). In an earlier letter, in response to D. J. Moore, also of International Publishers (October 5, 1929 [LL-1]), Norman had noted: "Just from the meagre information I have, I gather that your contestants will probably [be] photoplay aspirants with little or no experience. If this is the case, I might state that I have a varied and wide experience in handleing this kind of talent when I was operating out of Chicago a few years ago. I enclose some evidence of this."

53. REN to Elliot W. Butts, August 16, 1929 (LL-1).

54. Jimmie Burns to REN, May 28, 1930 (LL-1). "However," Burns added in his letter, "we may be able to work out a plan whereby the necessary equipment could be installed." But there is no contract or other documentation to suggest an arrangement was reached.

55. REN to Abraham Wax, February 11, 1933 (LL-1), replying to Wax's letter of February 6, 1933 (LL-1).

56. REN to F. J. Hilburn, November 18, 1927 (BFC-9).

57. Norman's former road man Regan, in a letter to Norman (June 22, 1929 [LL-1]), commented on some of the difficulties of that changing market: "All houses using sound have to have two men on duty at all times. The overhead for small houses is pretty tough, with such high film rentals for the 'Talkies', don't see how they make it."

58. REN to M. C. Maxwell, March 4, 1931 (BFC-8).

59. In his letter to Principal David C. Forrest, November 6, 1933 (LL-2), Norman wrote, "We gave a successful moving picture entertainment with One Legged Steve in your auditorium January 16th," and could offer another entertainment at this time.

60. REN to Frank, January 16, 1936 (LL-3).

61. REN to Principal David C. Forrest, November 6, 1933 (LL-2).

62. REN to H. J. Thornstadt, April 11, 1935 (LL-2). The plot of the film can be deduced from the title as well as from one of the lobby cards in the Black Film Center/Archive: "Oh, Doctor, how could such a thing happen to my little girl? How could it?" "A boy and girl fell in love, Mrs. Kennedy—forgetting everything else."

63. See, for example, REN to Professor Bragg, March 21, 1940 (LL-2), in which Norman explains his "one universal basis to all."

64. REN to Reverend Lee, March 4, 1934 (LL-2).

65. REN to Professor Patten, September 17, 1940 (BFC-8).

66. As per correspondence and contracts (BFC-7).

67. Molton H. Gray to REN, June 15, 1928 (LL-2).

68. C. A. Sappal to REN, April 8, 1925 (LL-3).

69. REN to D. Ireland Thomas, November 3, 1928 (BFC-9).

70. Albert A. Fish to REN, May 4, 1925 (LL-1). Others shared Fish's view of Micheaux. Allen Jenkins, for example, in a letter of October 16, 1928 (BFC-21), wrote Norman: "Am through with Micheaux stuff and look to you to afford us dates in the future."

71. REN to William George, December 21, 1927 (BFC-1).

72. REN to Thomas James, November 27, 1924 (BFC-9).

73. The films also served as a kind of gauge. In a letter to his brother Bruce (September 7, 1922 [LL-1]), for example, Norman wrote that he had driven to Gary, Indiana "and might as well have not gone there." After all, "They had tried a couple of Michauxs films to attract negros and they did not go over." So it was no surprise to Norman that he was having trouble booking his own films.

74. Regan to REN, June 5, 1927 (BFC-9).

75. REN to M. C. Maxwell, July 7, 1924 (BFC-9).

76. For example, Norman noted in a letter to his brother Bruce (September 15, 1922 [LL-1]) that business in Omaha was poor. "Met Michauxs brother [Swan Micheaux] there—he was playing The Dungeon on percent and not doing much."

77. REN to William George, June 18, 1931 (BFC-1).

78. REN to U. P. Bronson, February 11, 1936 (LL-2).

79. REN to Clyde R. Pierce, April 28, 1937 (LL-3).

80. REN to Professor Scrivens, March 14, 1940 (LL-2), and to the principal of the Union Academy, Tarpon Springs, Florida, October 18, 1939 (LL-3). Norman offered the same program to numerous exhibitors; see, for example, REN to the principal of the Elba Colored School, October 29, 1939 (LL-2).

81. REN to Professor D. A. Smith, October 30, 1939 (LL-2).

82. REN to Professor Fields, November 4, 1939 (BFC-8).

83. REN to principal, Hutto High School, Bainbridge, Florida, October 27, 1939 (LL-3).

84. REN to principal, Colored School, Greenville, Alabama, October 18, 1939 (BFC-8).

85. As per the Norman Studios Silent Film Museum website.

86. Lease Contract (dated August 10, 1945) between the Trustees of the Odd Fellows Hall of Crescent City, Florida, and Chas. K. Ellis and R. E. Norman of Ace Amusements (LL-1).

87. REN to Ruby [David] and Russ [Carrier], August 15, 1951 (LL-1).

88. Mary Anne Bruce Bell, undated (ca. June 1951 [LL-1]).

89. REN to Woody, October 30, 1952 (LL-1).

90. REN to Woody, January 27, 1953 (LL-1).

AFTERWORD

1. Bean, FH, 152.

2. Interview with Ann Burt, August 5, 2006, qtd. in Bean, FH, 152.

3. According to Devan Stuart, Chair of the Board of Directors of the Norman Studios Silent Film Museum, the "at-risk kids ... [would] come here on

scholarship and we'd teach them about the film industry. The kids would also be responsible for making a film, with each of them handling a different responsibility. The final product would be for the kids, but it's something to show at fund-raising galas as well" (Interview with Devan Stuart, June 26, 2006, qtd. in Bean, FH, 157).

4. Devan Stuart, "Norman Studios Readies for a Comeback," available at About.Com.Jacksonville [updated May 23, 2008]. Accessed January 2, 2013.

5. Devan Stuart, "Norman Studios Readies for a Comeback."

INDEX

References numbers in italics refer to illustrations.

BARBARA TEPA LUPACK has written extensively on American literature, film, and culture. Former Fulbright Professor of American Literature in Poland and in France and professor of English at St. John's University, Wayne State College, and SUNY, she is author of numerous critical studies, including *Literary Adaptations in Black American Cinema: From Micheaux to Morrison; Adapting the Arthurian Legends for Children; Critical Essays on Jerzy Kosinski; Insanity in Contemporary American Fiction; Take Two: Adapting the Contemporary American Novel to Film;* and *Nineteenth-Century Women at the Movies;* and, with Alan Lupack, *Illustrating Camelot, Arthurian Literature by Women,* and the award-winning *King Arthur in America.* She is also author of the children's picturebook *King Arthur's Crown* and the young adult novel *The Girl's King Arthur.* Her most recent book, with the late Mrs. Kiki Kosinski, is *Oral Pleasure: Kosinski as Storyteller,* a collection of Jerzy Kosinski's previously unpublished lectures and interviews.

CPSIA information can be obtained at www.ICGtesting.com
Printed in the USA
LVOW12*1434141113

361177LV00011BB/978/P